Please renew/return items by last date
shown. Please call the number below:

Renewals and enquiries: 0300 123 4049

Textphone for hearing or
speech impaired users: 0300 123 4041

About the Author

Arlene Okerlund is Professor of English at San José State University in California. She first encountered Elizabeth Wydeville, the mother of the two princes murdered in the Tower of London, in Shakespeare's *Richard III*. When she discovered that this queen's notoriety as a low-born, calculating, greedy and arrogant woman originated in slander spread by enemies, Professor Okerlund determined to expose the lies and to restore this Queen's reputation.

England's Forgotten Queens

edited by ALISON WEIR

Series Editor

Alison Weir has published eleven books: *Britain's Royal Families*, *The Six Wives of Henry VIII*, *The Princes in the Tower*, *Children of England*, *Elizabeth the Queen*, *Eleanor of Aquitaine*, *Henry VIII: King & Court*, *Mary Queen of Scots & the Murder of Lord Darnley*, *Lancaster & York: The War of the Roses*, *Innocent Traitor: A Novel of Lady Jane Grey* and *Isabella, She-Wolf of France, Queen of England*. She is at present researching for a book on Katherine Swynford and John of Gaunt. Alison Weir's chief areas of specialism are the Tudor and medieval monarchies. She has researched every English queen from Matilda of Flanders, wife of William the Conqueror, to Elizabeth I, and is committed to promoting the studies of these important women, many of whom have been unjustly sidelined by historians.

Published

Arlene Okerlund, *Elizabeth: England's Slandered Queen*
Michael Hicks, *Anne Neville: Queen of Richard III*

Commissioned

Patricia Dark, *Matilda, England's Warrior Queen*

Further titles are in preparation

ELIZABETH
ENGLAND'S SLANDERED QUEEN

ARLENE OKERLUND

TEMPUS

This book is dedicated to

Cynthia P. Soyster, the student and friend who first provoked
my passion for Elizabeth Wydeville.

Elizabeth Van Beek, a teacher who inspires students to study
and love history.

Linda Okerlund, my daughter whose wit and
achievements keep me humble.

Cover illustration:
Elizabeth Wydeville, by permission of the President
and Fellows of Queens' College, Cambridge.

This edition first published 2006

Tempus Publishing Limited
The Mill, Brimscombe Port,
Stroud, Gloucestershire, GL5 2QG
www.tempus-publishing.com

British Library Cataloguing in Publication Data.
A catalogue record for this book is available from the British Library.

ISBN 0 7524 3807 7

Typesetting and origination by Tempus Publishing Limited
Printed in Great Britain

Contents

Genealogical tables

Charts

Acknowledgements

Any student of historical biography stands shakily on the shoulders of preceding scribes and scholars. When writing about the fifteenth century, one discovers that truth is particularly tenuous. Most of the original documents are partisan in nature, reflecting both the bias of the writer and the opinions and prejudices of the informants. A modern biographer must piece together conflicting versions of the same event, provide coherence where information is missing, and develop a perspective guided by a sense of historical and psychological plausibility.

All authors are dependent on other scholars who have spent long, dusty hours deciphering the faded squiggles of documents handwritten centuries ago in idiosyncratic styles. Only after these source materials have been edited and published do they become available for analysis and synthesis by others. Thus, every scholar listed in the bibliography contributed to this work, but I must offer special gratitude to Anne Sutton and Livia Visser-Fuchs for their meticulously researched articles about Elizabeth Wydeville. Since much of their research was published by the Richard III Society, the members of that organisation deserve special appreciation for promoting 'in every possible way' research and scholarship about the fifteenth century.

Above all, this book could not have been written without the assistance of librarians. Most especially, I am indebted to the interlibrary loan staff at San José State University, who produced fifteenth-century texts and facsimiles otherwise unavailable in this future-focused Valley of Silicon: Cathy Perez, Kara Fox, Shirley Miguel and Elena Seto. Special thanks also go to Stephen Groth and Judy Strebel in Special Collections; Judy

Reynolds, English and Foreign Languages Librarian; and Florie Berger, Adjunct Librarian.

Librarians at the Huntington Library in San Marino also offered ready and efficient assistance: Susi Krasnoo, Mary Robertson, Steve Tabor and Mona Shulman.

I particularly thank everyone in the United Kingdom who warmly welcomed my research efforts and provided a sense of local history. Once again, my list of indebtedness begins with librarians and curators: Christine Reynolds, Assistant Keeper of the Muniments, Westminster Abbey; Christina Mackwell and Clare Brown, Lambeth Palace Library; C. Salles, Library Assistant, Stony Stratford Library; all superintendants and assistants – too many to list – in the Manuscript and Reading Rooms of the British Library.

A special place in my heart is reserved for all history-loving Brits – found in every cranny of the UK, but especially: the Duke of Grafton for permission to publish 'The Queen's Oak'; Lord Charles FitzRoy, who facilitated the acquisition of photographs from Grafton Regis; Sue Blake, local historian, and Peter Blake, keykeeper of St Mary the Virgin's Church at Grafton Regis, for inviting me into their living room to discuss history over tea; David and Rosemary Marks of Potterspury, who drew a map and provided directions to Queen's Oak Farm and the famous tree under which Elizabeth Wydeville changed history; Jill Waldram and Alison Coates, heritage wardens at Groby, who opened their homes and their books about the Greys of Groby; Juliet and Michael Wilson, church-wardens at Fotheringhay, and their two dogs (one an overnight guest), who led me up into the tower above the bells of St Mary and All Saints and down into the vault below the church floor, all the while narrating the history of Fotheringhay; Robin Walker, assistant bursar, Queens' College, University of Cambridge, who guided me through the Old Court that Elizabeth Wydeville visited; and Peter Monk, curator, Ashby-de-la-Zouch Museum, whose boundless enthusiasm for the history of the Hastings family is infectious.

Back at home, colleagues helped translate medieval texts: Sebastian Cassarino (Italian); Marianina Olcott (Latin); Danielle Trudeau (French); and Bonita Cox (Latin and French). Jean Shiota in Academic Technology provided essential computer assistance when my own technological expertise faltered. Other colleagues read the first inchoate manuscript and provided invaluable suggestions for improvements: Cynthia Soyster, Helen Kuhn, Judy Reynolds, Susan Shillinglaw, and Bonita Cox.

Without publishers, of course, history would never be transmitted from one generation to the next. Tempus Publishing and Jonathan Reeve assure that British history continues to thrive with twenty-first-century vigour. In selecting Alison Weir as general editor of their series of books about medieval queens, Tempus Publishing is adding a significant new dimension to historical research. Had I been offered my choice of historians to evaluate my manuscript, I would have chosen Alison Weir, whose books I have read and admired for years. I have benefited greatly from her graciousness in encouraging other authors, her acuity in correcting errors, and her generosity in providing dates and facts that augmented my own research.

Historical knowledge depends on the collective efforts of those who treasure the past as a way of comprehending the present. A great tradition of scribes, scholars, curators, librarians, writers, editors and publishers has made this biography possible.

England in the fifteenth century.

Foreword

Elizabeth Wydeville is one of the most fascinating and enigmatic figures in English history. She became the wife of Edward IV, and was the first English Queen whose marriage was made for love – or possibly lust – rather than for reasons of state, a circumstance that caused great scandal. She was also the grandmother of Henry VIII, and – more poignantly – the mother of the two princes in the Tower, Edward V and Richard, Duke of York, who were imprisoned in that fortress by their uncle, Richard III, and were never seen again.

Elizabeth Wydeville was one of the great beauties of her age, and by the clever use of her charms she ensnared its greatest womaniser, Edward IV. She lived through one of the most turbulent periods in English history. Yet her character is an enigma. Was she the scheming adventuress portrayed by contemporary writers, or is the truth rather different? It is possible that she has been grossly maligned by chroniclers and historians alike.

In this comprehensive and brilliantly detailed new biography, Arlene Okerlund presents a fresh and thought-provoking assessment of Elizabeth Wydeville. Her findings may prove controversial, but they will not fail to stimulate and engross the reader, nor to engage the emotions. For, as the author points out, Elizabeth's story is constantly marked by tragedy and loss. Arlene Okerlund unfurls this sad pageant with vivid clarity, re-evaluating every aspect of Elizabeth Wydeville's life and triumphantly crafting a three-dimensional portrait of a remarkable and much-misunderstood woman.

Alison Weir

The purest treasure mortal times afford
Is spotless reputation; that away,
Men are but gilded loam, or painted clay.

William Shakespeare, *Richard II* (1.1.177-79)

CHAPTER ONE

The Widow and the King

The newly widowed Lady Elizabeth Grey, *née* Wydeville, watched Edward IV, King of England, ride through the woods in the midst of his courtiers. Tall, handsome and already a bit hedonistic at the age of nineteen, Edward IV was celebrating his victories during the bloody and brutal Wars of the Roses. Loving the hunt, he had come to Whittlewood Forest in Northamptonshire for a holiday after his decisive victory at the battle of Towton. The royal hunting preserve near Stony Stratford lay close by the Grafton manor of Elizabeth's father, Richard Wydeville, Lord Rivers.

Recent battles had been particularly bloody in these wars between cousins. The Lancastrian troops of King Henry VI and his wife Margaret of Anjou had killed Edward's father, Richard, Duke of York on 30 December 1460, and spiked his head on a pole above Micklegate Bar in York to warn other rebels of the fate of traitors. The paper crown placed atop the Duke's head to taunt his royal aspirations did little to deter his eldest son, Edward, Earl of March from taking up his father's cause, commanding the Yorkist banner, and continuing the fight against the House of Lancaster.

The year 1461 brought more bloodshed, with battles seesawing across the English countryside. Edward's Yorkist victory at Mortimer's Cross on the border of Wales on 2 February was followed by a Lancastrian triumph at St Albans, just north of London, on 17 February. But when the Lancastrians failed to take control of London itself, Edward marched into the city where his charismatic vigour and the people's hatred of Margaret's marauding army allowed him to declare himself king on 4 March. Then he marched his army north to Towton, where the bloodiest battle ever fought on English soil ended in a Yorkist victory on 29 March. As Henry VI and Queen Margaret fled to Scotland, King Edward IV headed to London to celebrate.

How ironic that this newly proclaimed Yorkist King would stop to hunt at his royal preserve near the Wydeville home of Grafton manor. The Wydevilles were staunch Lancastrians, prominent and intimate members of the courts of both Henry V and Henry VI. Lady Elizabeth's grandfather had been 'Esquire of the body' to Henry V, and her father, Richard, had been knighted by Henry VI in 1426. Created Baron and Lord de Rivers in 1448, his service in fighting the Yorkist rebels had contributed significantly to Lancastrian success – until the bloody battle of Towton.

Elizabeth's mother, Jacquetta, had first married John, Duke of Bedford, and brother of Henry V. After Bedford's death, Jacquetta married Sir Richard Wydeville, but she retained her title as Duchess of Bedford and her status as the first lady of England until the marriage of Henry VI. When Henry VI contracted to marry Margaret of Anjou, the Wydevilles were sent to France to help escort the fifteen-year-old bride to England. Thus began a long friendship between Jacquetta and Queen Margaret. Jacquetta, the daughter of Luxembourg nobility, and Margaret of Anjou shared continental ties that bound them together in this new and different land of the Angles. No wonder that Jacquetta's firstborn, a daughter named Elizabeth, entered service with Queen Margaret and married into another prominent and landed Lancastrian family, the Greys of Groby.

On 17 February, however, Elizabeth's husband, Sir John Grey, was killed at the battle of St Albans, while leading the Lancastrian cavalry as its captain. Elizabeth, at the age of twenty-four, found herself a widow with two small sons, Thomas, aged six, and Richard, five. Even worse, the lands given by her husband as part of their marriage contract were in legal dispute, depriving her of income. She had moved from her husband's large estate at Groby to return to the warmth of the home where she grew up at Grafton.

Even here, her situation was perilous. Despite the bucolic peace of Grafton manor and the emotional support offered by her large, close-knit family, a word from the new monarch could attaint both the Wydevilles and the Greys. In May 1461, the King had issued a commission to confiscate all the possessions of Richard Wydeville.[1] Given the ferocity of the recent fighting, forgiveness seemed unlikely. The widow's future under the new Yorkist King could not have looked more bleak.

But Elizabeth was not without assets. Her beauty, her charm and her cultured background placed her among the most fortunate of women.

Besides, she was smart. When she heard that King Edward IV was hunting nearby, she devised a meeting where she might, in time-honoured tradition, request a boon of the King, a judgement that would restore her dower lands.

Elizabeth knew well the propensities of the nineteen-year old King, since their families had shared political and military ventures for decades. Her father, Sir Richard Wydeville, and Richard, Duke of York were knighted by Henry VI at the same ceremony in 1426. Sir Richard Wydeville had joined the Duke of York's French retinue at Pontoise in July 1441, just months before Edward was born at Rouen on 28 April 1442.[2] Mary Clive speculates that Jacquetta might even have been in the Duchess of York's room when Edward IV was born.[3]

The small world of English nobility placed the two families in close proximity, especially when the Duke of York served as Protector during Henry VI's bouts of insanity. In February 1454, York brought his twelve-year-old son and heir to the Parliament at Reading to learn about politics first hand. The adolescent Edward, then Earl of March, surely observed more than political ceremony at the various court affairs. Among the Queen's attendants, the sophisticated Elizabeth, an 'older woman' with the *savoir faire* of a seventeen-year-old beauty, must have ignited Edward with all the passion typical of adolescent boys.

At Grafton, Elizabeth was on home territory. The Wydeville manor lay within a mile of Whittlewood Forest where the King was hunting. Having grown up here, Elizabeth knew the course that the hunters would take, the fields where the deer would be chased for the kill, the grassy spots ideal for picnics. Choosing a large oak tree, she stationed herself and her two small sons beneath it and waited. Hard in pursuit of prey, Edward saw the beautiful young mother with her children, pulled his horse up short, and marvelled at the bucolic tableau.

Thomas More describes the encounter of Edward and Elizabeth:

This poor lady made humble suit unto the King that she might be restored unto such small lands as her late husband had given her in jointure. Whom when the King beheld and heard her speak, as she was both fair and of a good favour, moderate of stature, well made and very wise, he not only pitied her, but also waxed enamoured on her. And taking her afterward secretly aside, began to enter in talking more familiarly.[4]

But Elizabeth knew well the ways of men, as More takes great delight in recounting:

> Whose appetite when she perceived, she virtuously denied him. But yet did she so wisely and with so good manner, and words so well set, that she rather kindled his desire than quenched it. And finally after many a meeting, much wooing, and many great promises, she well espied the king's affection toward her so greatly increased, that she durst somewhat the more boldly say her mind…And in conclusion, she showed him plainly that as she knew herself too simple to be his wife, so thought she herself too good to be his concubine.[5]

Some critics dismiss More's tribute to Elizabeth's virtue as nothing more than Tudor propaganda, since some of his information came from John Morton, who served Henry VII (Elizabeth's son-in-law) as Archbishop of Canterbury and as Chancellor. More himself was in service to Henry VIII when he wrote *The History of King Richard the Third*. Yet decidedly non-Tudor sources tell similar stories about the encounter and Elizabeth's virtuous actions.

Antonio Cornazzano, a minor Italian poet, romanticised Edward's courtship of Elizabeth in 'La Regina d'ingliterra', a poem written sometime between 1466 and 1468 and published as a chapter in *De mulieribus admirandis*. While the poem contains many errors of fact, its dramatic homage to the widow's virtue indicates that her fame had spread to northern Italy soon after her marriage to the King. In Cornazzano's poem, Edward attempts to seduce Elizabeth, who had appeared at his court as a reserved, shy, retiring lady. Her modesty only inflamed the King, of course, who ordered her father to force his daughter to submit. Her father begs her to acquiesce to the King's pleasure, but she refuses – causing her father and his sons to be banished from the kingdom. Her mother, who also begs her to comply with the King's demands, is frustrated to the point of saying that she wishes her daughter had died at the moment of birth.

With her mother in tears, Elizabeth regrets the anguish and distress she has caused her family and finally agrees to be presented to the King. But she stands before the King not as a 'meretrice' (prostitute), but as an 'immaculata una phenice' (a pure, perfect, rare human being). She kneels before him and begs 'una gratia' (a gift from his Grace). The affable King tells her that he would give her the tallest mountain or make Antarctica navigable or pull out Hercules' columns, and swears that he means what he says.

At that point, the lady presents the King with a knife she had hidden under her dress and says:

> I implore you, my dear Lord, to take my life: this is the 'gratia' that I want from you, because, since I will lose what makes a woman live in glory, I want my soul to leave my body... Think, my Lord, King of Justice! Your vain pleasures will soon be over, but I'll remain in eternal filth and squalor... To be your wife would be asking too much. Let me then live and die on my terms and may God save you in a peaceful Kingdom.

The King, amazed at the lady's words and actions, becomes still and silent like a statue. He leaves the knife in her hands, takes a gold ring from his finger, lifts his eyes to heaven and says: 'God, you be my witness that this woman is my wedded wife.'[6]

If Cornazzano's idealised romance contains more fiction than fact, the story of the dagger was repeated almost twenty years later when Dominic Mancini, an Italian visiting England in 1482–3 to gather information for Angelo Cato, advisor to Louis XI of France, recorded a similar version in his official report:

> ...when the king first fell in love with her beauty of person and charm of manner, he could not corrupt her virtue by gifts or menaces. The story runs that when Edward placed a dagger at her throat, to make her submit to his passion, she remained unperturbed and determined to die rather than live unchastely with the king. Whereupon Edward coveted her much the more, and he judged the lady worthy to be a royal spouse, who could not be overcome in her constancy even by an infatuated king.[7]

Adding to the Queen's mystique, a contemporary chronicle compiled sometime between 1468 and 1482 commends Lady Elizabeth for her wisdom and beauty:

> ...King Edward being a lusty prince attempted the stability and constant modesty of divers ladies and gentlewomen, and when he could not perceive none of such constant womanhood, wisdom and beauty, as was Dame Elizabeth, widow of Sir John Grey of Groby late defunct, he then with a little company came unto the Manor of Grafton, beside Stony Stratford, whereat Sir Richard

Wydeville, Earl of Rivers, and Dame Jacqueline, Duchess-dowager of Bedford, were then dwelling; and after resorting at divers times, seeing the constant and stable mind of the said Dame Elizabeth, early in a morning the said King Edward wedded the foresaid Dame Elizabeth there on the first day of May in the beginning of his third year...[8]

Thomas More, therefore, was reporting a story that was generally current in England and throughout Europe. He further writes that Edward, who 'had not been wont elsewhere to be so stiffly said 'nay,' so much esteemed her countenance and chastity that he set her virtue in the stead of possession and riches. And thus taking counsel of his desire, determined in all possible haste to marry her.'[9]

Thus begins the modern reputation of Elizabeth, Queen Consort to Edward IV of England, as a 'calculating, ambitious, devious, greedy, ruthless and arrogant' woman (to quote Alison Weir's *The Wars of the Roses*).[10] In describing the marriage of Edward IV and Elizabeth, Anne Crawford, editor of *Letters of the Queens of England*, more subtly demeans the Queen: 'She was several years older than her royal husband and was generally believed to have demanded marriage as the price for her virtue.'[11]

'What price virtue?', one may well ask. Because Elizabeth refused to sell her virtue to please a King, history (or more accurately, historians) has maligned the woman mercilessly. To the majority of historians and novelists today, Elizabeth is a conniving, grasping, overreaching female, who was manipulative at best, greedy and ruthless at worst. Scholars who, on the basis of irrefutable facts, have applauded Elizabeth's benevolence, piety and lifelong loyalty to husband, children and siblings seem to have whispered their words into the wind. Perhaps even worse, to the general public she is an unknown woman.

The slander began immediately when the marriage was announced. Enemies attacked Elizabeth as unfit for a King who could choose his bride from the daughters of European royalty. Critics sneered the word *parvenu* in her direction. A whispering campaign accused both Elizabeth and her mother, Jacquetta, of witchcraft and sorcery in seducing Edward. Why else would a King, the handsomest man in England, marry a widow five years older than himself?

These attitudes have infiltrated the historical record. Charles Ross, Edward IV's biographer, accuses Edward of showing 'excessive favour to the queen and her highly unpopular Woodville relatives' ('Woodville' is a modernised spelling of the family name) and describes the Wydevilles as 'a greedy and grasping family'.[12] Michael Stroud identifies Elizabeth as 'a social-climbing widow of the lower nobility'.[13] Alison Weir succinctly summarises: 'In his choice of wife, King Edward was "governed by lust"'.[14] Hardly. Edward IV easily and frequently satisfied his lust elsewhere. He bragged about his illegitimate children before his marriage and about his mistresses afterwards. It was not lust, but love, that compelled Edward to marry Elizabeth, a love that persisted through nineteen years of trauma and tragedies that would have destroyed less devoted relationships – and lesser women.

The biographies of this remarkable woman vary in their objectivity and understanding of her life. Agnes Strickland's *Lives of the Queens of England* blames Elizabeth for many of Edward's problems as King:

> ...over his mind Elizabeth, from first to last, certainly held potent sway, – an influence most dangerous in the hands of a woman who possessed more cunning than firmness, more skill in concocting a diplomatic intrigue than power to form a rational resolve. She was ever successful in carrying her own purposes, but she had seldom a wise or good end in view; the advancement of her own relatives, and the depreciation of her husband's friends and family, were her chief objects. Elizabeth gained her own way with her husband by an assumption of the deepest humility; her words were soft and caressing, her glances timid.[15]

Not until 1937 did Katharine Davies provide a more balanced and less hostile judgment of Elizabeth in *The First Queen Elizabeth*. In the next year, however, David MacGibbon's better-known biography repeated spurious tales that subtly demeaned the Queen, in *Elizabeth Woodville: Her Life and Times* (1938).

Subsequent articles should have set the record straight. A.R. Myers in 1957 proved that Elizabeth was a careful manager of money who spent less on her household and personal needs that any predecessor Queen of the previous century. J.R. Lander in 1963 cleared Elizabeth of charges that she sought prestige and money for her family through inappropriate marriages for her siblings (see chapter 7 below: 'Marriages Made in Court'). Anne Sutton and Livia Visser-Fuchs, in 1995, verified Elizabeth

Wydeville's piety and culture in 'A "Most Benevolent Queen"', just one of several meticulously researched articles that refute past slanders.

Still, defamatory attacks rage on. Most egregiously, *The Book of Shadows*, a deservedly obscure novel published in 1996, sets its fictional stage with this demeaning and inaccurate 'Author's Note': 'The Woodvilles, as a group, were robber barons of the first order: brilliant, brave, charismatic and totally ruthless'.[16] The novel depicts Queen Elizabeth as a vain, hard, harsh woman actively involved in black sorcery. Edward is a hot-blooded fool besotted with love. A fictional commissioner of the King describes the Queen: 'She's a very dangerous woman. No injury, no slight, no threat is ever forgotten.'[17] Though historical fictions traditionally sensationalise their subjects, this characterisation is a particularly cheap shot.

Bertram Fields in *Royal Blood* (1998) defames 'the ambitious and greedy Woodvilles'[18] and condemns their social 'overreaching'[19] by studiously ignoring their stature and service in both Lancastrian and Yorkist courts. Cornazzano's contemporary poem, for instance, compliments the Wydevilles by comparing them to the wealthy and influential Borromei who served the Sforzas of Milan. Fields also repeats the speculation that Elizabeth might have plotted to kill Richard III, an accusation first promulgated by Richard himself, but the source of this charge is not mentioned. More subtly but no less demeaning, Fields refers to Edward V and Prince Richard as 'the Woodville princes' – as if their father had no part in their begetting or nurturing.[20]

More recently, Geoffrey Richardson's *The Popinjays* (published in 2000) characterises the Wydevilles as vain, pretentious, empty people. Richardson takes his title from Bulwer-Lytton's characterisations in his fictional *The Last of the Barons,* a paean of praise to Earl Warwick – the very man who hated and executed Elizabeth's father and brother, Warwick's personal *bête noire*. As with too many of his predecessors, Richardson relies on fiction and fabrications to build his case.

Countering such inaccuracies, David Baldwin's biography, *Elizabeth Woodville: Mother of the Princes in the Tower* (2002), begins by objectively examining the evidence, but concludes with unsubstantiated speculations about Elizabeth's opposition to Henry VII. Baldwin believes that Elizabeth supported the son of Clarence, a man she loathed, and Robert Stillington, the bishop whose testimony invalidated her marriage and bastardised ten of her twelve children. Such highly improbable speculations distort the final seven years of the Queen Dowager's life during the reign of Henry Tudor, her son-in-law, and Elizabeth of York, her daughter.

Telling the true story of Elizabeth Wydeville is important not merely to disprove the slanders and retrieve her from obscurity, but to explore how history happens. Her story provides essential insights into the historical process and the creation of reputation. It reveals that errors, if repeated often enough, become facts. It shows that writers, even if they may desire to tell truth, always and necessarily present information from a limited perspective. If we study history to avoid repeating it, the story of Elizabeth Wydeville embodies a quintessential warning about the power of propaganda to pervert truth.

As one small example, a letter written on 16 August 1469 to Galeazzo Maria Sforza, Duke of Milan helped establish Elizabeth's reputation: 'The king here took to wife a widow of this island of quite low birth'. The letter's Italian author, Luchino Dallaghiexia, accuses the Queen of exerting herself 'to aggrandize her relations, to wit, her father, mother, brothers and sisters'. This letter perpetuates the lies about Elizabeth's social status and the myth of her rapacious advancement of family. No one seems to notice that Dallaghiexia was a supporter of Warwick, the man who had just executed Lord Rivers and Sir John Wydeville four days earlier, even though Dallaghiexia commends 'the Earl of Warwick, who has always been great and deservedly so'.[21] In 1469, Warwick, a sworn enemy of the Queen and rebel against Edward IV, was spreading lies to promote his own quest for the throne. While the Italian correspondent should not be blamed for disseminating the propaganda of Warwick at the height of the Earl's power, subsequent historians must be chastised for not considering the letter's source, context and perspective.

Because such testimony has too often been accepted at face value, the negative reputation of Elizabeth Wydeville and her family grew. Lies, gossip and character assassination by enemies, both personal and political, slandered this woman who lived during one of the most troubled and violent eras of human history. In fifteenth-century England, this woman fought for family and life with intelligence and persistence against men who used swords, power and propaganda to annihilate their enemies. Her victories were few; her losses eternal.

Most famously, of course, Elizabeth Wydeville was the mother of the two princes who disappeared from the Tower of London during the reign of Richard III. Everyone knows about the two princes. Hardly anyone knows that they had a mother. Yet this mother desperately tried to save her sons from the grasp of ambitious men. The tragedy of the two princes was but one of many. Elizabeth's few years of glory and grandeur as Queen Consort to Edward IV were framed by profound suffering and personal tragedy:

1461	The death of her first husband, Sir John Grey, killed at the second battle of St Albans. Her dowry property was challenged by her mother-in-law.
1469	The beheading of her much-loved father, Earl Rivers, and her brother, Sir John Wydeville; murders ordered by Richard Neville, the Earl of Warwick (Edward IV's cousin) and by George, Duke of Clarence (Edward IV's brother).
1470	The exile of Edward IV, leaving Elizabeth alone in London, eight months pregnant and the sole custodian of their three daughters Elizabeth, Mary and Cecily (ages four, three and one).
1470	The birth of their first son and future King, Edward V, while Elizabeth was in sanctuary at Westminster Abbey.
1483	The untimely death of Edward IV at the age of forty on 9 April.
1483	The execution on 25 June of her cultured and scholarly brother, Anthony Wydeville, Earl Rivers, and her son, Sir Richard Grey (murders ordered by Richard III).
1483	The disappearance of her two sons, King Edward V and Prince Richard of York, from the Tower of London. They were last seen in late summer, and Elizabeth never knew their fate with any certainty.
1484	A parliamentary decree in January declaring her nineteen-year marriage to Edward IV to be adulterous and their ten children illegitimate.
1464, 1469, 1483	Repeated accusations of witchcraft and sorcery against her mother and herself, charges that had sent earlier royal women to imprisonment and exile.

1492   Death at the age of fifty-five while living in Bermondsey Abbey with so few worldly possessions that her will mentions only 'such small stuff and goodes that I have' for distribution to her family and debtors.

Elizabeth Wydeville was a survivor who ultimately found her own peace in a hostile world. Her contributions to posterity are enormous. Her grandson, Henry VIII, and her great-granddaughter, Queen Elizabeth I, are among the most famous and important of English rulers. Both of these famous monarchs inherited much of their spirit, intelligence and gutsy fortitude from the first English Queen to bear the name 'Elizabeth'. She was also the ancestor of Mary, Queen of Scots and of Lady Jane Grey. In fact, Elizabeth Wydeville's blood runs in the veins of every subsequent English monarch, even until today.

Elizabeth Wydeville's story deserves a fresh look and a reconsideration of the facts that have fallen into the cracks of history. Perhaps, after all, truth can be the daughter of time.

CHAPTER TWO

Edward's Decision to Marry Lady Elizabeth

No one knows exactly when Elizabeth and Edward IV first met. The encounter in Whittlewood Forest near Grafton manor, described by Edward Hall in his *Chronicle* of 1548, is dated 'during the time that the Earl of Warwick was in France concluding a marriage for King Edward':

> The King being on hunt in the forest of Wychwood beside Stony Stratford, came for his recreation to the manor of Grafton, where the Duchess of Bedford sojourned, then wife to Sir Richard Wydeville, Lord Rivers, on whom then was attending a daughter of hers, called Dame Elizabeth Grey, widow of Sir John Grey, Knight, slain at the last battle of St. Albans, by the power of King Edward. This widow having a suit to the King, either to be restored by him to some thing taken from her, or requiring him of pity, to have some augmentation to her living, found such grace in the King's eyes that he not only favoured her suit, but much more fantasied her person...[1]

Agnes Strickland's *Lives of the Queens of England* placed their meeting under an oak tree:

> Elizabeth waylaid Edward IV in the forest of Whittlebury, a royal chase, when he was hunting in the neighbourhood of her mother's dower-castle at Grafton. There she waited for him under a noble tree still known in the local traditions of Northamptonshire by the name of the Queen's Oak. Under the shelter of its branches the fair widow addressed the young monarch, holding her fatherless boys by the hands, and when Edward paused to listen to her, she threw herself at his feet and pleaded earnestly for the restoration of Bradgate, the inheritance

of her children. Her downcast looks and mournful beauty not only gained her suit, but the heart of the conqueror.

The Queen's Oak, which was the scene of more than one interview between the beautiful Elizabeth and the enamoured Edward, stands in the direct track of communication between Grafton Castle and Whittlebury forest.[2]

Despite several errors in Strickland's account (Grafton was not Jacquetta's dower-castle, but the ancestral home of the Wydevilles), the meeting beneath the oak tree rings true. The legend still lives today. A public footpath between Potterspury and Grafton Regis leads to the charred ruins of an oak tree on a farm whose gatepost sign proudly reads 'Queen's Oak Farm'. Sue Blake, an historian who lives in the village of Grafton Regis, dismisses the claim that the tree stump remaining after five centuries and innumerable lightning strikes is the same tree that stood tall in 1461, but she finds the meeting of the couple under a tree in the royal forest to be quite credible. Oral history sometimes preserves details lost in the written documents.

But surely, this meeting would not have been the first between Elizabeth and Edward. The prominence of the Wydevilles in Henry VI's court and the long association of Sir Richard Wydeville with the Duke of York during the French campaigns would have assured that their children met much earlier. The families of Lancaster and York, after all, were on the same side until 1455, attending the same court functions and spending time together in France. Even after the first battle of St Albans, the Duke of York remained superficially loyal to Henry until his 1459 rebellion at Ludford Bridge. The encounter by the oak tree must have renewed a long-standing acquaintance.

The written records provide tantalising facts. At the battle of Towton on 29 March 1461, Richard Wydeville, Lord Rivers led a Lancastrian force of 6,000–7,000 Welshmen who drove Edward's troops back about eleven miles. Elizabeth's brother Anthony, Lord Scales, was another Lancastrian leader prominent enough to be listed incorrectly among the dead by William Paston[3] and in five separate dispatches sent to continental courts, including one to Francesco Sforza, Duke of Milan.[4] Despite their efforts at Towton, the Lancastrians suffered a disastrous defeat, after which Lord Rivers accompanied King Henry, Queen Margaret and Prince Edward in retreat to Newcastle.[5]

Edward IV immediately began confiscating Lancastrian property. As prominent supporters of Henry VI, both Rivers and Scales were high on his list. On 14 May 1461, a commission was issued to 'Robert Ingleton, escheator in the counties of Northampton and Rutland, to take into the king's hand all the possessions late of... Richard Wydevyll, knight', one of twenty individuals whose property was seized.[6]

Edward IV may well have remembered an earlier encounter with the Wydevilles. In January 1460, Lord Rivers and his eldest son, Anthony, were at Sandwich organising Lancastrian troops and ships to attack Calais, then under control of Warwick's Yorkist faction. In a surprise raid, Warwick's troops, led by Sir John Dynham, sailed from Calais and attacked Sandwich between 4 a.m and 5 a.m.[7] Fabyan's *Chronicle* reports:

> [Dynham] took the Lord Rivers in his bed and won the town, and took the Lord Scales, son unto the said Lord Rivers with other rich preys, and after took of the King's navy what ships them liked and after returned unto Calais.[8]

Gregory's *Chronicle* adds that Jacquetta, Duchess of Bedford, was captured with her husband.[9] The prisoners were transported to Calais and turned over to the three rebel leaders: Warwick, Lord Salisbury (Warwick's father), and the seventeen-year-old Edward, Earl of March.

William Paston's letter of 28 January 1460 describes how Warwick, Salisbury and March taunted the Wydevilles for their low-class origins:

> My lord Rivers was brought to Calais and before the lords with eight score torches. And there my Lord of Salisbury reheted [scolded] him, calling him knave's son, that he should be so rude to call him [Salisbury] and these other lords traitors, for they shall be found the king's true liegemen when he [Rivers] should be found a traitor.
>
> And my Lord of Warwick reheted him and said that his father was but a squire and brought up with King Henry the Fifth, and sithen himself made by marriage, and also made lord, and that it was not his part to have such language of lords being of the king's blood.
>
> And my Lord of March reheted him in like wise. And Sir Anthony was reheted for his language of all three lords in like wise.[10]

These *ad hominem* slurs by political bullies may mark the beginning of the slander that has so discredited the Wydeville name. Ironically, Paston's letter failed to note that the titles of both Warwick and Salisbury were also gained by right of their wives, a point John Rous took care to emphasize in *The Rous Roll*: 'Dame Anne Beauchamp, a noble lady of the blood Royal… by true inheritance Countess of Warwick, which good lady had in her days great tribulation for her lord's sake, Sir Richard Neville,… *by her title* Earl of Warwick…'.[11]

If Salisbury and Warwick proudly traced their royal blood back to John of Gaunt, they conveniently overlooked the fact that their maternal ancestor Katherine Swynford had been the family governess who bore Gaunt's children illegitimately before the Duke was free to marry their mother, and that the Beaufort family name came from Gaunt's minor castle in Champagne. Further, the men of the Neville family had traditionally gained their titles through marriages to better-endowed heiresses. This would not be the last time, however, that the pot would call the kettle black.

Neither did Paston note that the language for which his detractors scolded Anthony reflected an erudition that put those of 'the king's blood' to shame. Anthony – whose translation of *The Dictes or Sayengis of the Philosophres* would become the first book published in England by Caxton – possessed an eloquence that even at this early age was apparently resented by his tormentors. His eloquence angered these men of 'the king's blood', whose slurs stuck and were repeated by enemies and historians alike until a bully's slander turned into 'truth' for those who knew only part of the story.

No surprise, then, that Wydeville property was confiscated by a victorious Edward IV. A letter to Francesco Sforza, dated 31 July 1461, reports the imprisonment of both men:

> I have no news from here except that the Earl of Warwick has taken Monsig. de Ruvera [Rivers] and his son [Anthony] and sent them to the king who had them imprisoned in the Tower. Thus they say that every day favours the Earl of Warwick, who seems to me to be everything in this kingdom, and as if anything lacked, he has made a brother of his, the Archbishop, Lord Chancellor of England.[12]

This news was old, however, since a Writ of Privy Seal on 12 June had already pardoned Lord Rivers of all offences and trespasses, an order recorded in the Patent Rolls on 12 July 1461: 'General pardon to Richard

Wydevill, knight, of Ryvers of all offences committed by him, and grant
that he may hold and enjoy his possessions and offices.'[13] On 23 July 1461,
the King ordered 'The like to Antony Wydeville, knight, of Scales.'[14]

The timing is interesting. Six weeks after Towton, the King confiscated
Wydeville property, but less than a month later he pardoned Lord Rivers
and within two months restored all his property. On 10 December 1461,
Edward IV confirmed that Jacquetta would continue to receive her dowry,
granting 'to Richard Wydewyll, lord Ryvers, and Jaquetta, duchess of
Bedford, his wife, for the life of the latter of the dower assigned to her on
the death of John, late duke of Bedford, her husband'. The list enumer-
ates almost 200 properties, providing to the Duchess 'a third part' of their
profits or a designated rent. The grant also restores to Lord Rivers the land
and buildings in Calais 'granted to Richard his father and Joan, wife of
the latter, both deceased, by letters patent dated 22 April, 9 Henry VI, for
a term of 90 years'. The southern boundary of the property, 'a little lane
on the side of the prince's lodging', indicates that Wydeville contiguity to
the court was geographical as well as political and personal.[15]

On 12 December 1461, a 'Grant for life to Richard Wydevill, lord of
Ryvers' restored him to

> the office of chief rider of the King's forest of Saucy, in the county of
> Northampton, with all trees and profits, viz. dry trees, dead trees, trees blown
> down, old hedges or coppice-hedges, boughs fallen without date, chattels, waifs,
> strays, pannage of swine, 'derefall wode', 'draenes', brushwood and brambles,
> perquisites of courts, swainmote and other issues within the forest, from the
> time when he had the same by letters patent of Henry VI.[16]

Although Edward IV pardoned some Lancastrians as he unified the nobility and won over his enemies, the pardons and restoration of property to
Lord Rivers and the Duchess of Bedford seem extraordinary, especially
in the context of their personal history (see Timeline p.274).

What could have happened to change Edward's mind about the
Wydevilles? By July 1461, the chiding at Calais and the fighting at Towton
had been forgiven by both sides. The Yorkist King had pardoned Rivers
and Scales for a lifetime of Lancastrian loyalty. In turn, Lord Rivers, the
Duchess of Bedford and Lord Scales became solid Yorkists, an allegiance
that remained unwavering until their deaths in service to Edward IV

(unlike Warwick, whose allegiances shifted with the sand dunes of power). In May 1462, Anthony, Lord Scales, and his wife Elizabeth received a grant of the manor 'called le Syche' and other lands in South Lynn.[17] By December 1462, his friendship with Edward IV was firm enough for Anthony to join the siege at Alnwick Castle near the Scottish border.

The part played by Lady Elizabeth Grey, *née* Wydeville, in securing the King's pardons and restoring the family lands may not pertain at all. Or it may explain everything. All we know is that Edward departed Towton for Durham on 5 April 1461, 'the feast of Easter accomplished'. After 'setting all things in good order in the North', he travelled southwards, reaching his manor of Sheen (in Richmond) on 1 June.[18] The records indicate a two-day stopover at Stony Stratford, when an encounter under the oak tree may have changed history.

Not until two years later does Lady Elizabeth Grey re-enter history. On 26 May 1463, the property dispute over the land granted as part of her marriage dowry was settled in her favour.[19] One year later, on 1 May 1464, King Edward IV and Lady Elizabeth exchanged vows and consummated their marriage in utmost secrecy. Thomas More claims that Edward's courtship involved 'many a meeting, much wooing, and many great promises', a claim corroborated by Caspar Weinreich's *Chronicle* of 1464: 'The king fell in love with [a mere knight's] wife when he dined with her frequently'.[20] Clandestine the courtship clearly was, but its duration we do not know. The secrecy, however, indicates that Edward well understood the powerful obstacles, both political and personal, that stood in the way of marrying the woman he loved.

Perhaps the most formidable obstacle was Edward's mother, the powerful Duchess of York. Like most mothers, Cecily Neville believed that her son could do better in choosing a wife. The young, handsome, charming King of England could take his pick of the European matrimonial market, where a plethora of princesses would bring dowries and political power to the nation. Thomas More eloquently summarises the mother's distress, imagining her thoughts and words in the manner typical of historians of his era:

> The Duchess of York, his mother, was so sore moved therewith that she dissuaded the marriage as much as she possibly might, alleging that it was his honour, profit, and surety also, to marry in a noble progeny out of his realm, whereupon depended great strength to his estate by the affinity and great

possibility of increase of his possessions... And she said also that it was not princely to marry his own subject, no great occasion leading thereunto, no possessions, or other commodities...[21]

Edward, who clearly had learned logic at his mother's knee (or from the flow of More's pen) responded with idealistic conviction:

Marriage being a spiritual thing, ought rather to be made for the respect of God where his Grace inclines the parties to love together, as he trusted it was in his, than for the regard of any temporal advantage. Yet nonetheless, [it] seemed that this marriage, even worldly considered, was not unprofitable. For he reckoned the amity of no earthly nation so necessary for him, as the friendship of his own. Which he thought likely to bear him so much the more hearty favour in that he disdained not to marry with one of his own land. And yet if outward alliance were thought so requisite, he would find the means to enter thereinto much better by other of his kin, where all the parties could be contented, than to marry himself [to one] whom he should happily never love, and for the possibility of more possessions... For small pleasure taketh a man of all that ever he hath beside, if he be wived against his appetite.[22]

The Duchess did not retreat. She reminded her son that Warwick was negotiating a marriage with Lady Bona of Savoy, sister-in-law of Louis XI of France. To marry someone else would not only alienate the French, but would embarrass the cousin whose power and money had won the crown for Edward. But Edward had an answer for that argument:

And I am sure that my cousin of Warwick neither loves me so little to grudge at that I love, nor is so unreasonable to look that I should in choice of a wife rather be ruled by his eye than by mine own, as though I were a ward that were bound to marry by the appointment of a guardian. I would not be a king with that condition to forbear my own liberty in choice of my own marriage.[23]

Those words would haunt Edward's future. Warwick, whose alienation began when Edward married Elizabeth, would indeed turn against the King, whose throne had been won with the help of Warwick's sword. Though not immediately, they would become enemies until Warwick's death on the battlefield at Barnet, fighting against Edward's army.

Edward understood the larger consequences of his decision. The issue was one of control. Would he, as King, make his own decisions or must he defer to others? In resisting the Duchess of York, Edward's enumeration of Elizabeth's advantages over other women revealed a wit that would charm anyone but a mother:

> That she is a widow and hath already children, by God's Blessed Lady, I am a bachelor and have some too, and so each of us hath a proof that neither of us is like to be barren. And therefore, madam, I pray you be content. I trust in God she shall bring forth a young prince that shall please you.[24]

The Duchess was not amused. These words, too, would return to haunt Edward's family after his death. The question of a prior commitment to marry, an oath that would invalidate any subsequent marriage, was apparently of sufficient concern for the bishops of the Church to investigate. More names the lady in question as Dame Elisabeth Lucy, but years later the *Titulus Regius* of Richard III would claim a prior contract with Dame Eleanor Butler. According to More:

> Dame Elisabeth Lucy was sent for. And albeit that she was by the King's mother and many other put in good comfort to affirm that she was ensured unto the King, yet when she was solemnly sworn to say the truth, she confessed that they were never ensured. Howbeit she said his Grace spoke so loving words unto her that she verily hoped he would have married her. And that if it had not been for such kind words, she would never have showed such kindness to him to let him so kindly get her with child. This examination solemnly taken, when it was clearly perceived that there was no impediment, the King with great feast and honourable solemnity married Dame Elisabeth Grey...[25]

If Edward's decision was ill-advised – a questionable supposition, given the nineteen harmonious and loving years that he and Elizabeth shared – it was not made hastily. Neither was Edward naïve about the benefits of a politically advantageous marriage. For years, negotiations had been ongoing in search of an appropriate wife for the Yorkist King. In the autumn of 1461, an embassy from England had approached Philip of Burgundy about a marriage with his niece, Catherine of Bourbon. Philip rejected that match, perhaps because Henry VI and his son Edward were still alive and Burgundy was unsure that Edward IV's throne was sufficiently secure. Mary of Gueldres, mother of King James II of Scotland, had earlier been proposed by Warwick as a possible consort, but she was much older than Edward, making the production of children uncertain. That liaison was also complicated by Scotland's ongoing collaborations with France, and the marriage negotiations soon ended.

Isabella of Castile was offered by her half-brother, Henry the Impotent, in February 1464, an alliance rejected by Edward himself. Since Edward married Elizabeth on 1 May 1464, his reason for declining the thirteen-year-old Isabella may be obvious. Nevertheless, Isabella apparently harboured resentment about her rejection for years, telling the ambassador of Richard III that she was 'turned in her heart from England in time past, for the unkindness the which she took against the king last deceased, whom God pardon, for his refusing of her, and taking to his wife a widow of England'.[26]

Against both political and maternal forces, Edward IV chose Lady Elizabeth Grey – a stunning act of independence that defied his mother, his chief military commander, and the King's Council. That he was aware of the consternation his decision would cause is best indicated by the secrecy maintained even after the marriage. The chronicler Fabyan records the event:

In most secret manner upon the first day of May, King Edward spoused Elizabeth, late the wife of Sir John Grey, Knight... which spousals were solemnised early in the morning at a town named Grafton near unto Stony Stratford. At which marriage was no persons present, but the spouse, the spousess, the Duchess of Bedford her mother, the priest, two gentlewomen, and a young man to help the priest sing. After which spousals ended, he went to bed, and so tarried there upon, two or three hours, and after departed & rode again to Stony Stratford, and came in manner as though he had been on hunting, and there went to bed again.

And within a day or two after, he sent to Grafton to the Lord Rivers, father unto his wife, showing to him that he would come and lodge with him a certain season, where he was received with all honour, and so tarried there by the space of four days. In which season, she nightly to his bed was brought, in so secret manner that almost none but her mother was of counsel. And so this marriage was a season kept secret after, til needly it must be discovered and disclosed.[27]

Edward may have been secretive, but he was no fool carried away by adolescent infatuation. The King knew well that the sword of political marriage could cut both ways. Most recently, the union of Margaret of Anjou and Henry VI had produced more chaos than national advantage. If that sad situation may be blamed on the husband's insanity and general ineptitude, other infamous royal examples revealed that marriage for financial and political gains could be personally infelicitous, most notably the unions of Henry II to Eleanor of Aquitaine and Edward II to Isabella of France.

Beyond Elizabeth herself, Edward may have been seduced by the life he witnessed at Grafton manor. The Wydevilles were a happy, loving family who cared deeply for each other, a sharp contrast to the malevolent rivalries within the family of York. While Edward's brothers were still too young to indulge in the sibling treacheries that would ultimately annihilate the family, the King must have felt deeply the differences between the two homes. The Wydeville sons would never have slandered their mother as an adulteress – as both Clarence and Gloucester subsequently pronounced their mother – in their quests after power.

Neither had Edward's childhood been particularly joyful. He and his brother Edmond, Earl of Rutland had been sent to Ludlow Castle at an early age for their education, and while no place was more beautiful and bustling than medieval Ludlow, Edward's experience there was not always pleasant. 'On Saturday in Easter week' 1454, the twelve-year-old Edward and eleven-year-old Rutland sent a letter to their father thanking him for 'our green gowns now late sent unto us to our great comfort' and asking that 'we might have some fine bonnets sent on to us by the next sure messenger, for necessity so requires'. But the letter went on to plead:

> Over this, right noble lord and father, please it your highness to wit that we have charged your servant, William Smith, bearer of these, for to declare unto your noblesse certain things in our behalf, namely, concerning and touching the odious rule and demeaning of Richard Crofte and his brother. Wherefore we beseech your gracious lordship, and full noble fatherhood, to hear him in exposition of the same, and to his relation to give full faith and credence.[28]

The boys' complaint about 'odious rule and demeaning' may represent nothing more than schoolboy whining, but Edward's subsequent adolescent years grew progressively worse. He had just turned thirteen when his father challenged Henry VI at the first battle at St Albans on 22 May 1455. While the Duke of York negotiated a deal to serve as 'Protector and Defender of the Realm' during the insanity of Henry VI, he chafed at his limited power and openly rebelled in 1459. The disastrous rout of York at Ludford Bridge on 12 October 1459 caused him to flee to Ireland while Warwick, Salisbury and Edward, then seventeen, fled to Calais.

The year of 1460 saw more political skirmishes, war, and personal tragedy. The Yorkists won a battle at Northampton in July, but the year ended with their defeat on 30 December at Wakefield, the beheading of Edward's father – his head spiked on a pole over Micklegate Bar – and the killing of his younger brother Rutland. That brother, who had shared Edward's love for his green gown and request for a fine bonnet just six years earlier, was dead at the age of seventeen, thanks to his father's ambition. At eighteen, Edward succeeded his father as head of the Yorkist clan.

Grafton manor offered a bucolic retreat from this brutal existence. Edward could hunt in the nearby royal preserve or saunter through the open fields surrounding Grafton village. From the London road, he could ride down either of two lanes lined with farmers' cottages to the Wydeville manor house and the Norman church of St Mary the Virgin. Inside the peaceful, quiet country church, the tomb of Elizabeth's ancestor Sir John Wydeville displayed a lifesize engraving of the man who had built the church tower with its five bells early in the fifteenth century.

A hermitage established in the twelfth century lay just a short distance away. The hermitage had flourished during the fourteenth century, with the Wydevilles appointing its masters. After the Black Death, however, the hermitage declined and became part of the Wydeville estate. With a cloister, chapel, dovecote and malt kiln, it was renovated during the fifteenth century. Excavations in 1964–5 discovered tiles decorated with the shields of the Wydevilles and the House of York, leading to speculations that Edward and Elizabeth were married in the hermitage. But the church of St Mary the Virgin, just steps away from the manor house, also offered a close and convenient site for a wedding. In the absence of records, the site of the ceremony remains unknown.

With thirteen children in the Wydeville family (two others died as infants), the manor house was the busy centre of ploughing, planting and harvesting – rural activities that dominated the life of the landed gentry. But Grafton manor was different. Jacquetta, its highly cultured matriarch, had grown up in Luxembourg and Burgundy, where classical learning and humanism were fast moving the medieval world towards the Renaissance. She transferred her culture and her love of books and knowledge to her children.

During Jacquetta's youth in Luxembourg, Flemish painters were flourishing, classical authors were being translated into French, and French writers were developing a new literature. Women of the nobility added reading and writing to the traditional female skills of music, dancing, embroidery and riding. When Christine de Pizan, whose Italian father served the French King as physician and astrologer, was left a destitute widow in 1389, she supported herself by writing. Jacquetta owned an exquisite illuminated manuscript of the *Oeuores poètiques de Christine de Pison*. Her neatly handwritten name, 'Jaquete', on the flyleaf of MS Harley 4431 in the British Library provides a rare instance of contact with this fascinating woman.

The Wydeville children shared Jacquetta's love of culture and the arts. The eldest son, Anthony, became the most erudite humanist of fifteenth-century England, his education derived in part from the *Oeuores poètiques de Christine de Pison*. His name, too, appears on the flyleaf of the manuscript, a proud hand-lettered 'ARIVIERES' that may record a gift from mother to son. Years later, Anthony would translate *The Morale Proverbes of Christyne* into English, an early text to be published by Caxton in England. A younger son, Lionel, became Bishop of Salisbury and Chancellor of Oxford University.

Lord Rivers shared his wife's love of books, and commemorated his daughter's coronation as Queen Consort by purchasing a copy of *The Romance of Alexander* in 1466 and inscribing on folio 274r:

Cest liure est a monseigno' richart de Wideuielle seigneur de riuieres vng dez compaignons de la tres-noble ordre de la jartiere & le dist seigneur acetast le dist liure lan de grace mille cccclxvj le premier jor de lan a landres & le V⁰ an de la coronacion de tres-victorieux roy eduard quart de che non & le second de la coronacion de tres-vertueuze royne Elyzabeth lendemain du jo' de sainct more. [This book belongs to Lord Richard de Wydeville, Lord Rivers, one of the companions of the very noble order of the Garter, and this Lord bought this book in the year of grace 1466, the first day of the year, in London, and the fifth year of the coronation of the very victorious King Edward, the for·

of this name, and the second of the coronation of the very virtuous Queen Elizabeth, the day after Saint Maure's day.][29]

The entire family loved books. A signature, 'E Wydevyll', appears at the back of an early-fourteenth-century illuminated manuscript of the Arthurian romances, *Romance of the Saint Graal* (Royal MS 14 E.iii). This autograph on folio 162 may indicate that Elizabeth owned the manuscript before her marriage to Sir John Grey. That the text was a family treasure is indicated by other names on the flyleaves: 'Elysabeth, the kyngys dowther' and 'Cecyl the kyngys dowther', children of Edward IV and Elizabeth. Another inscription on the same folio states, 'Thys boke is myne dame Alyanor Haute' – one of Elizabeth's cousins through the marriage of her aunt Joan Wydeville to William Haute. A fourth name, 'Jane Grey', may connect the manuscript to Elizabeth's sister Eleanor, sometimes called Joan, who married Anthony Grey of Ruthin, but it is tempting to speculate that the manuscript ultimately ended up in the hands of Elizabeth Wydeville's great-great-granddaughter, Lady Jane Grey. Ownership of the manuscript is uncertain, however, and the 'E Wydevyll' signature might belong to Elizabeth's brother Edward. Equally, the order of ownership is impossible to determine from the signatures, but collectively, the inscriptions certainly indicate that reading was a family affair and that books passed lovingly from one family member to another.

Perhaps most significantly, Elizabeth's affectionate family treated each other with playfulness and gentle humour. Anthony describes how he was asked to represent England in a tournament with the champion of Burgundy during Easter week of 1465. Just before Elizabeth's coronation, the court was in residence at Sheen Palace, where Anthony was making the traditional greeting to the Queen:

And as I spoke unto her Highness kneeling, my cap out of my head, as my duty was, I wote not by what adventure nor how it happened, but all the ladies of her court came about me; and I took no heed than that they of their grace had tied about my thigh a collar of gold garnished with precious stones, and was made of a letter [the letter was an 'S', meaning *Souvenance* or remembrance] the which, for to say the truth, when I perceived, was more nigh my heart than my knee... And then they all drew each of them in to their place. And I, all abashed of this adventure, rose up for to go thank them of their rich and honorable present.[30]

While the ladies were playfully tying the gold necklace around his knee, someone else placed in Anthony's hat 'a letter written on fine parchment, sealed and enclosed with a small thread of gold'. The letter officially engaged Anthony's services as knight for a proposed tournament. This charmingly elaborate invitation was surely orchestrated by the Queen's winsome hand. Elizabeth had brought to her court the ceremony of the medieval romances she had read and loved.

No wonder Edward IV fell in love with this delightful, cultured woman. Even the historian Edward Hall, whose *Chronicle* blames the King's marriage for most of his subsequent problems, commends the qualities of the woman he chose:

> ...she was a woman more of formal countenance, than of excellent beauty, but yet of such beauty and favour that with her sober demeanour, lovely looking, and feminine smiling (neither too wanton nor too humble), beside her tongue so eloquent, and her wit so pregnant, she was able to ravish the mind of a mean person, when she allured and made subject to her the heart of so great a King.[31]

Hall repeats the story told by More and Mancini about Elizabeth initially rejecting the King's offer to make her his 'paramour and concubine' and credits her refusals for fuelling Edward's determination to marry. Hall attributes Edward's choice of wife to 'the confidence that he had in her perfect constancy and the trust that he had in her constant chastity'.[32]

If the marriage angered those who lost stature and status and power, the fault must lie with those displaced, not with the charming, virtuous wife Edward chose: Lady Elizabeth Grey, *née* Wydeville. Though not of the 'blood royal' of England, her heritage combined the blood of European nobility with that of the English landed gentry, a patrimony that produced children with wit and charm sufficient to irritate and intimidate the entrenched nobility.

CHAPTER THREE

The Truth About the Wydevilles

If mothers count, Elizabeth Wydeville could take her place among the highest ranks of European nobility.

Elizabeth's mother, Jacquetta of Luxembourg, was the daughter of Pierre de Luxembourg, Count of St Pol, Conversano and Brienne. Jacquetta's mother, Marguerite, was daughter of Francesco del Balzo, Duke of Andrea in Apulia (a dukedom in the kingdom of Naples). Descended from the most noble and powerful families in Europe, Jacquetta could claim Charlemagne as her ancestor.[1]

Jacquetta's father, the Count of St Pol, was a significant player in the ongoing conflicts between France and Burgundy that dominated fifteenth-century Europe. He and his brothers were major supporters of the Duke of Burgundy, who controlled a powerful fiefdom within the Kingdom of France, and had long fought against the Dauphin. When Jacquetta's father was captured and held for ransom by the Dauphin's allies, he was freed by no less than the intervention of Henry V of England. Jacquetta's uncles were powerful men. Jean de Luxembourg, the Duke of Burgundy's chief captain, was the very man who delivered Joan of Arc to the Church prelates for trial. Louis de Luxembourg, Bishop of Thérouanne, became Cardinal and Archbishop of Rouen, Bishop of Ely and chancellor and treasurer for the English in France.[2]

In the mid-fifteenth century, Burgundy extended north almost 500 miles from the southern Duchy of Burgundy and the Franche Comte to include the Low Countries of Holland, Zeeland, Flanders, Artois, St Pol, Hainault, Brabant and Luxembourg. Not only was the Duke of Burgundy as rich and powerful as the King of France, whose principal wealth lay in the relatively weak city of Paris, but the Burgundian court set fashions in architecture, literature, music, pageantry and festivities that were modelled throughout Europe.[3]

Lying directly across the Channel from England and surrounding Calais, Burgundy's financial and manufacturing centres were vital to England's mercantile trade. London merchants always favoured close ties with the port of Bruges, the cloth-manufacturing centre at Ghent and the financial hub of Lille, as well as the wine-, spice-, and olive-growing regions of southern Burgundy. Centrally located between the Hanseatic League and the Italian cities, the Burgundian Low Countries offered England access to all of Europe.

As a daughter of Burgundian royalty, Jacquetta first married John, Duke of Bedford and eldest brother of Henry V, on 22 April 1433. Bedford, almost twenty-seven years older than Jacquetta, was one of three sponsors at the baptism of Henry VI, who was born while Henry V was fighting in France. When Henry V died in 1422, leaving a nine-month-old son, Parliament gave Bedford precedence to rule while he was in England and designated his younger brother, Humphrey, Duke of Gloucester, as Protector of England while Bedford was in France. The continuing battles with France forced Bedford to spend most of his time on the continent, however, and effectively he gave over the governance of England to Humphrey of Gloucester. In 1423 Bedford had married his first wife, Anne, sister of the Duke of Burgundy, a marriage that strengthened the bonds between England and Burgundy, but antagonised the French King, Charles VII.

Anne died in childbirth just before All Hallow's Eve 1432, and the widower Bedford remarried the following April, choosing as his new bride the seventeen-year-old Jacquetta of Luxembourg. The Duke of Burgundy, Anne's brother, resented not only the unseemly haste of the ceremony, but the close liaison it created between Luxembourg and England. Even though Jacquetta's Luxembourg family were his rich and powerful supporters, Burgundy began to shift his alliance from England to Charles VII of France, a shift that contributed to the decline of English fortunes in France.

Bedford and his new young wife soon visited England, where the beautiful Jacquetta was warmly welcomed. As Duchess of Bedford, Jacquetta enjoyed pre-eminence as one of the first ladies of the land. King Henry VI, only eleven years old, was not married, and the dowager queens, Katharine of Valois (widow of Henry V) and Joan of Navarre (widow of Henry IV), could not compete with the young, lively, cultured and beautiful wife of the man who held all the power. In Coventry, the couple were greeted with gifts to Jacquetta of fifty marks and a 'Cup of silver & overgilt' that cost five marks.[4] When Jacquetta's father died in late 1433, a memorial service was held for him in St Paul's Cathedral, a sign that she had won the hearts of the English. In 1435–6, Jacquetta, Duchess of Bedford, was one of the ladies for whom robes of the Order of the Garter were provided.

The declining English fortunes in France forced the couple back to the continent, where the Duke of Bedford died on the night of 14-15 September 1435. Jacquetta was a widow at the age of nineteen, but she retained her dower as Duchess of Bedford by a patent granted on 6 February 1436, which included the provision that 'she do not marry without the king's consent given under the great seal of England'.[5]

The next time we hear of Jacquetta, she was being pardoned by Henry VI on 23 March 1437, 'for intermarrying without the King's consent'.[6] Would that we knew what happened between 6 February 1436 and 23 March 1437! Jacquetta petitioned Henry VI to forgive her the offence of having taken 'but late ago to Husband your true liegeman of your Realm of England, Richard Wydevylle knight not having thereto your Royal license and assent'. The petition claims that the couple had suffered both 'in their persons as in their goods' as a result of the unsanctioned marriage and requested that they be assessed 'a reasonable fine' as punishment and be pardoned for their transgression.

That 'reasonable fine' turned out to be £1,000, an enormous sum in 1437.[7] Jacquetta may have paid that amount by signing over to Cardinal Beaufort her Bedford dower interest in Charleton Camvile manor in Somerset and other property in Dorset and Wiltshire. Entries in the *Calendar of Patent Rolls* transfer property owned by 'Richard Wydevyll and Jacquetta, in right of her dower', to the Cardinal in exchange for his payment of 13,350 marks to the King. In return the King 'pardoned the trespasses herein and granted the said possessions to the use of the Cardinal'.[8] Jacquetta's pardon was dated 24 October 1437.[9]

Jacquetta had no trouble retaining the good will of Henry VI. Numerous entries in the *Calendars of Patent Rolls,* the *Fine Rolls,* and the *Close Rolls* reveal that Henry VI carefully protected Jacquetta's dower, usually a third part of the extensive and enormously rich Bedford manors, when the rest of the property was transferred to others. The *Fine Rolls*, for instance, exempt from transfer to a new holder Jacquetta's rights to 'a third part...

of the manor of Swalowefeld' on 7 May 1439, her dower in the manor of Bradwell on 19 February 1445, and a third part of 'lands in the town of Scotford' on 17 October 1446. When Bradwell was subsequently transferred to John Poutrell and John Croke on 26 October 1447, the grant again excluded Jacquetta's dower, a specification reiterated on 6 May 1451, when the lease was extended to forty years. Similar lifetime rights to her dower property and income appear in grants to John Penecok on 2 March 1457, as well as in innumerable patents issued throughout Henry's reign.[10]

Jacquetta's second husband, Sir Richard Wydeville, was well known in the English court. Sir Richard's father, also named Richard, had been 'Esquire of the body' to Henry V, a relationship that began when Henry was still Prince of Wales (Shakespeare's 'Prince Hal'). In 1408, Prince Henry granted £40 yearly for life to 'Richard Wydevill, his esquire, and Joan his wife', a grant confirmed in 1413 after Henry V became King, and again in 1422 during the first year of Henry VI.[11]

Henry V also appointed Richard Wydeville 'for life' to the 'office of customer and collector of the customs and cokets in all ports of Ireland, and also of the office of searcher', an appointment confirmed by Henry VI's Great Council in 1426.[12] Richard Wydeville, Esquire, frequently served as a 'Commissioner to take muster' of the troops sent to France and as 'Commissioner of Oyer and Terminer' to examine prisoners and hear court cases. During 1421, he was Seneschal of Normandy, administering justice and all other domestic matters in that important province. 'Richard de Wideville, Esq.' earned Bedford's gratitude in 1425 when as Lieutenant of the Tower of London he refused entry to the troops of Humphrey, Duke of Gloucester, who was challenging Bedford's authority.[13] Under Henry VI, Richard served as Lieutenant of Calais, and subsequently as chamberlain to the Duke of Bedford, who was Captain of Calais. In 1446, the town of Drogheda in Ireland was ordered to pay Joan, wife of Richard Wydeville, £20 a year for life, including arrears since 20 May 2 Henry V.[14]

Richard de Wydeville, Esquire, Jacquetta's father-in-law, was not a member of nobility, but his service to the crown and the extensive family estates made him an important man within the newly emerging landed gentry. In the fifteenth century the term 'Esquire' indicated a man of considerable property who ranked immediately below a knight. A marriage settlement between his daughter, Joan, and William Haute of Kent, Esquire, executed on 18 July 1429, carefully delineated the financial arrangements: William Haute made a marriage grant of land or rents valued at 100 marks yearly, plus a dowry of £40 annually. Richard Wydeville, Esquire, granted the husband 400 marks and agreed to pay all costs of the wedding at Calais. In addition, he declared that his daughter Joan would bring to the marriage a 'Chamber as a gentlewoman ought for to have and after the estate of the foresaid Richard Wydevill'. The 'chamber' included the bride's personal effects, jewellery, and frequently furniture for the wife's living quarters.[15]

Richard Wydeville, Esquire, inherited the Grafton estates from his older brother, Thomas. The Wydeville family had held tenancies in the area since the twelfth century, and their increasing value through the generations had elevated the family to one of the most important in Northamptonshire. During the reign of Edward III, a Richard Wydeville had served as sheriff eight times and represented the region in seven different Parliaments. By 1435, when Thomas Wydeville acquired manorial rights from the Earl of Suffolk, the Wydeville holdings were quite substantial. Thomas continued the family tradition of serving frequently as justice of the peace, and as sheriff of Northamptonshire in 1429.[16] Transactions recorded in the *Close Rolls* reflect his substantial land holdings and his frequent appearance as a witness in quitclaim cases.[17]

When Thomas died, his will enumerated many estates in the counties of Northampton, Bedford and Buckingham. It also revealed a compassionate concern for the welfare of the people who lived on his lands. No fewer than seven servants were bequeathed lifetime estates in their home and annuities comparable to that given to 'John Beck my old servant', who received 'a place and six acres of land with the appurtenances in Grafton abovesaid', plus a lifetime annuity of one mark per year.[18] As landlord, Thomas Wydeville cared for the wellbeing of the people who populated his estates. He granted an annuity of 100 shillings, for instance, 'to the father and the mother of master John Aylewurd now parson of the church of the said Stoke in case that the said parson die leaving his said father and his mother or one of them...'.[19]

In this generation, the spellings of the family surname vary from 'Widevill' to 'Wideville' to 'Wydevill'. Earlier versions had included 'de Wivill', 'de Wydevill' and 'Widvile'. The man whom Jacquetta married appears variously as 'Richard Wydevile', 'Richard Wydevyle' and 'Richard Wydevill', spellings that changed to 'Wydeville' in the next generation, when Caxton printed his son Anthony's book, *The Dictes and Sayengis of the Philosophres.* That contemporary published spelling seems best to reflect historical accuracy in the generation of Elizabeth. Today's common spelling of 'Woodville' was never used by the family.

The son of Richard Wydeville, Esquire, was knighted by Henry VI on Palm Sunday, 19 May 1426, at the same ceremony that knighted Richard, Duke of York, father of Edward IV.[20] The five-year-old King Henry VI had himself just been knighted by Bedford, who undoubtedly determined the individuals worthy of receiving similar honours. Sir Richard Wydeville, son, was retained by King Henry VI in 1433 to fight in France, for which he furnished 100 men at arms and 300 archers, an indenture repeated in 1434. He was captured in France in 1435 while fighting with the Earl of Arundel, sufficiently prominent to be mentioned in contemporary chronicles.[21] By 1435, Sir Richard was serving as a knight bachelor in Bedford's court, and in 1436 he joined the Earl of Suffolk's retinue in France. On 25 January 1437, he was granted the office of constable of the castle of Rochester, with its wages, fee and profits.[22]

Strikingly handsome and athletic, the young knight contrasted markedly with Jacquetta's older first husband, the Duke of Bedford. Sir Richard's more humble origins would, nevertheless, have deterred marriage in the class-conscious circles of European nobility, one reason Jacquetta may not have sought the King's approval. Her uncle, the Bishop of Thérouanne, was greatly distressed by the marriage, since the daughter of a count and the sister of Lewis, current Earl of St Pol, could have negotiated a better match. Violating all traditions and expectations, Jacquetta, Duchess of Bedford, courageously married Sir Richard Wydeville, Knight of England, for love, a precedent her son-in-law Edward IV would follow in the next generation. Prudence may also have compelled the hasty marriage. The exact birth date of their first child, Elizabeth, is unrecorded, and even the year of 1437 may be suspect. An impending birth may explain why Jacquetta ignored the King's Patent of 6 February 1436, and was forced to seek his pardon on 23 March 1437.

The popular Wydeville couple did not remain out of favour long. Soon after the pardon, Sir Richard was appointed Rider of the Forest of Saucy, an area near Grafton where the couple returned to live.[23] Frequent commissions authorised him to investigate customs cases[24] and collect the King's taxes.[25] By 1439, he was back in France with the Earl of Somerset, as part of the effort to relieve Meaux. Meanwhile, his popularity in England grew through his skills as a jouster. At Shrift-tide 1439, he and the Duke of Norfolk dominated the carnival celebrations before Lent as featured jousters of a two-day tournament at the Tower of London.[26]

By 1440, Sir Richard was wealthy enough to purchase the Grafton estate from the Countess of Suffolk, and become a landowner rather than a fee-holder.[27] The couple's renown continued to grow. Both dowager queens had died in 1437, making Jacquetta the highest-ranking woman in England. With her dowry as the Duchess of Bedford, she was also one of the richest. If Sir Richard could not match his wife's title and wealth, he earned his way with service to the King and his fame as a jouster. In November 1440, he defended the honour of England in a tournament at Smithfield in response to the challenge of Pedro de Vasquez, a Spanish knight who served the Duke of Burgundy as chamberlain.

By the fifteenth century, chivalric tournaments were no longer the slashing, bloody battles of earlier years, but exhibitions of splendour and sport similar to today's Olympic games. Carefully-staged pomp and ceremony dominated the festivities, which celebrated both tradition and nationality. King Henry chose the kingdom's foremost man in arms and valour to defend English honour, then ordered his treasurer and exchequer to allow

> …all sums of money… to erect lists and barriers of timber at 'Westsmythfelde' in the suburbs of London by 25 November instant, and to cover the ground within the lists with sand for the purpose, so that there be no let or obstacle there by stones or otherwise, and further… to construct a place there for the king suitable to his royal estate.[28]

The hometown audience enthusiastically cheered its hero knight, fighting in the tradition of the medieval romance:

> …The morn after the day of Saint Katharine was a challenge in arms made and proved to before the King within lists in Smithfield, between Sir Richard Wydeville, Knight of England, and a knight of Spain; which knight for his lady love should fight in certain points of armes, that is to say with axe, sword, and dagger.[29]

The three-year-old Elizabeth may not have been aware of her father's fame at this point, but she would surely have sensed the excitement and bustle at Grafton as her father prepared for the tournament. Sir Richard Wydeville fighting for his lady love, Jacquetta, not only represented the romantic ideal of chivalric tradition, but reflected the reality of his ever-increasing family. During their marriage, Jacquetta gave birth to fifteen children, thirteen of whom survived to adulthood. Sir Richard and Jacquetta divided their time between the bucolic and nurturing environment at Grafton, the more exciting life of the court, and the battlefields of France.

The career of Sir Richard kept pace with his growing family's needs. In February 1441, he was commissioned to collect a subsidy in Northampton, and in July he joined the retinue in France of the Duke of York, who was attempting to relieve Pontoise. The year 1444 brought special distinction, when he and Jacquetta were sent to France to escort Margaret of Anjou to England for her marriage to Henry VI. Jacquetta had grown up in Margaret's world and at the age of twenty-nine could provide a comforting and guiding presence to the fifteen-year-old betrothed moving to a strange and different court. The escort was also a family affair, since Jacquetta's sister Isabel was married to Margaret's uncle, Charles of Anjou, Count of Maine.

Sir Richard was appointed Justice of the Peace in Northamptonshire in 1445 and represented the King on business in Calais twice in 1446. That year the King ruled that the Wydeville sons would inherit property in case of their parents' death:

> Grant in survivorship to Antony, Richard, John and John, sons of Richard Wydevyll, knight, and Jacquetta, his wife, duchess of Bedford, of the remainder of all the rents in the counties of Northampton, Huntingdon, and Buckingham granted to Richard and Jacquetta by letter patent dated 18 June, 18 Henry VI, and 13 November, 19 Henry VI. and confirmed to the same by letters patent dated 8 February, 19 Henry VI; and of the remainder of a rent of £20 yearly by the hands of the sheriff of Bedford and Buckingham, by John Hanham, late escheator in those counties, from the issues of the same falling to Richard and Jacquetta in allowance of her dower after the death of John, duke of Bedford, out of the £60 yearly granted to the Duke in tail male.[30]

Service, valour and integrity led to Sir Richard's creation as Baron and 'Lord de Ryvers' on 9 May 1448. Additional grants of manors in the counties of Bedford and Buckingham supported his increased expenses. By 1450, Lord Rivers served as Constable of England.[31]

In June 1450, Lord Rivers was among the leaders who fought Jack Cade and his Kentish rebels.[32] On 4 August 1450, he was created Knight of the Garter, the highest order of the land, and soon became a member of the Privy Council, the King's most private and privileged advisors. Throughout this decade, Lord Rivers served as Seneschal of Aquitaine[33] and Lieutenant of Calais, while making frequent forays into Gascony 'to resist the malice of the King's enemies there'.[34] During the first battle of St Albans, he was in Calais,[35] where he spent most of the early 1450s serving on endless commissions to hear appeals and to investigate piracy, service rewarded by a grant for life to the castle of Rochester on 22 November 1457.[36]

Lord Rivers and the Duchess of Bedford participated in the usual court events when they found themselves in England. In 1457, the names of 'the lord Ryvers and my lady his Wyff' joined the Buckinghams and the Shrewsburys at a Corpus Christi celebration sponsored by Queen Margaret.[37] Throughout the years, Jacquetta and Queen Margaret exchanged gifts on New Year's Day. Surviving records of the Queen's household cite a 'year's gifts' from Margaret to Jacquetta in 1447–8[38] and jewels in 1451–2[39]. On four different occasions in 1445–6, 1446–7, 1448–9 and 1451–2, Margaret tipped servants of Jacquetta (who apparently delivered gifts to the Queen).[40]

In January 1458, Lord Rivers was one of the barons summoned to the Great Council at Westminster to discuss the rebellion being led by Richard, Duke of York. Rivers's personal battles with Warwick were about to intensify. Their first encounter had occurred in 1455 when Rivers was recalled from Calais after Warwick's appointment as captain there. Rivers, Lieutenant of Calais since 1452, refused to vacate his post until Parliament agreed to pay wages long owed to the garrison. In siding with the soldiers and demanding that the accounts be settled before he departed, Rivers delayed Warwick's assumption of control from 4 August 1455 until 20 April 1456.[41] While Rivers's firm stance endeared him to the troops, it also hardened the garrison's opposition to Warwick. The Earl, whose tolerance for defiance was limited, began to harbour a personal animosity toward Lord Rivers, a grudge more insidious than their Lancastrian–York rivalry.

The next confrontation between Warwick and Rivers also originated in matters of state. From his new position as Captain of Calais, Warwick began enriching his personal treasury through piracy. Among his conquests was a salt fleet headed for Lübeck, attacked in gross violation of an existing treaty.[42] King Henry VI appointed 'Richard Wydeville of Ryvers' as first among the commissioners

> …to summon at Rochester and examine on 9 August next [1458] persons having knowledge of a conflict on the sea between Richard, Earl of Warwick, and his retinue and certain of Lubec under the King's friendship, and to certify the King and Council of their examination before 13 August next.[43]

The inquiry held at Rivers's castle of Rochester irrevocably tainted him in Warwick's eyes. For a man of Warwick's ego to be hauled before a tribunal chaired by a mere baron added personal insult to political injury. Warwick's hatred would reveal itself a year later in the *ad hominem* attacks on Rivers and his son Lord Scales after their capture at Sandwich. The Earl's anger festered for a decade, until he killed as many Wydeville men as he could capture. The women he attacked by trying to destroy their reputations.

As the armies of Lancaster and York moved toward open conflict, Lord Rivers's name appeared prominently in commissions to oppose the rebels:

> Commission of array to Richard Wydevyle of Ryvers, knight, and the sheriff of Kent in Kent, to resist Richard, Duke of York; Edward, Earl of March; Richard, Earl of Warwick; and Richard, Earl of Salisbury; and their accomplices, leagued in rebellion against the King and crown… and appointment of the same to arrest all ships and other vessels late of the said Earl of Warwick and all the tackling thereof and to keep the same for the King's use.[44]

In the midst of such turmoil, the Wydeville children grew up nurtured at Grafton and taught to pattern their lives after their parents. In 1457, 'Anthony Rivers' joined the Duke of Somerset and other knights in jousting before King Henry VI and Queen Margaret at the Tower during Thursday of Whitsun week. On the following Sunday, the show was repeated at Greenwich.[45]

Little about Elizabeth's youth is known, and even her service as attendant to Queen Margaret remains unclear. The 'Isabelle Domine Grey' named as one of Margaret's ladies-in-waiting in 1452–3 and 'Domine Elizabeth Grey' in the 1452–3 list of jewels given by Margaret to her ladies-in-waiting probably refers to the fifteen-year-old Elizabeth, already betrothed to Sir John Grey. But that name could also identify Sir John's mother, Elizabeth, or yet another Elizabeth, 'late the wife of Ralph Grey', mentioned in June 1445 as a daily attendant to the Queen.[46] Both Thomas More and Edward Hall, whose proximity to eyewitness accounts lends credibility, state that Queen Elizabeth was in service to Queen Margaret, a logical appointment given medieval courtly practices and the friendship of Margaret and Jacquetta.

The date of Elizabeth's first marriage to John Grey, son and heir to Edward Grey, Lord Ferrers of Groby, is unknown. Neither does the uncertain birth date of Elizabeth's first son provide further clues. The *Complete Peerage* entry for Thomas, Marquis of Dorset cites 1451 as his birth date (which would make Elizabeth a mother at the age of fourteen), but the entry for Lord Ferrers of Groby states merely that he 'was aged 37 and more in 1492', indicating that Elizabeth was aged eighteen at his birth. A second son, Richard, was born in 1456.

Neither is the age of her husband known, but his age of '25 and more at his father's death' in 1457 leads to an assigned birth date of 1432.[47] The Greys traced their lineage to the time of William the Conqueror. John's father, Sir Edward Grey, was a younger son of Lord Grey of Ruthin and had married Lady Elizabeth Ferrers, heir of Lord Ferrers, whose family had held extensive estates at Groby for eight generations. As newlyweds, Sir John Grey and Lady Elizabeth, *née* Wydeville, may have lived first at the Grey's manor house at Astley in Warwickshire[48], but after the death of Sir Edward in 1457, they likely moved to Groby manor, the 'Old Hall' of which is still standing.

The manor house at Groby was described in 1371 as including a chapel with cloister, a great chamber (the 'whyt chambre') with a wine cellar below, 'the bailies chambre', seven other rooms and a dovecote. The decorative patterns still visible in the brickwork of the dovecote's wall near Markfield Road have been dated by Beryl Richardson as earlier than Elizabeth's residence, since they incorporate the family arms of the Ferrers family (a shield shape with seven 'mascles', or diamonds) that would have been replaced by the Grey's 'Barry of six Argent and Azure' when the last of the Ferrers family died on 18 May 1445.[49]

Life at Groby was similar to Elizabeth's childhood at Grafton, except that as lady of the manor she now presided over the many servants necessary to manage a large country estate. Groby manor, with its bake houses, hay barns, sheepcotes and forge house, dominated the surrounding acres of gardens, fields, ponds and forests, including Bradgate Park where Elizabeth's son Thomas would later build the manor house that became the birthplace and home of Lady Jane Grey. Groby manor held markets on Fridays and a three-day annual fair beginning on St George's Day, privileges granted in 1337–8.

Like the Wydevilles, the Greys of Groby were well-known Lancastrian supporters. Sir Edward Grey, Elizabeth's father-in-law, had sworn allegiance to King Henry VI in Parliament on 24 July 1455, after the first battle of St Albans. At that same Parliament, his neighbour, another Leicestershire representative, adhered fervently to the Yorkist cause. That neighbour was Sir Leonard Hastings, Knight, whose estate at Kirby Muxloe lay just five miles south of Groby manor.

The Greys would have known Sir Leonard Hastings well in his capacity as sheriff of the county of Leicester. An intimate of Richard, Duke of York, Sir Leonard presented his son William to the Duke at Fotheringhay Castle when the boy was sixteen. William Hastings rapidly became a favourite of both the Duke and his eldest son, Edward. First serving as page in the Duke's household, William became body squire for the Duke, and by 1455 was appointed ranger of Were Forest and sheriff of the counties of Warwick and Leicester. In a grant dated at Fotheringhay on 23 April 1456, the Duke awarded William, 'his beloved servant', an annuity of £10 'to the end he should serve him before all others, and attend him at all time (his allegiance to the king excepted).'

The bonds of friendship forged early between William Hastings and the Duke's eldest son, Edward, Earl of March, lasted until death. Hastings fought alongside Edward at the decisive battle of Towton. Immediately upon becoming King in 1461, Edward conveyed to Hastings the manor of Ashby-de-la-Zouch, formerly owned by the loyal Lancastrian James Butler, Earl of Wiltshire and Lord-Treasurer for Henry VI. Ashby-de-la-Zouch lay just twelve miles north-west of Groby. The widowed Lady Elizabeth Grey, a near neighbour, surely must have feared for her own Lancastrian estates, now bounded on both sides by the Yorkist strongholds of Hastings.

Elizabeth's vulnerability may explain her move home to her father's estate at Grafton after her husband's death. Though equally Lancastrian, Grafton manor placed some distance between herself and the newly-honoured Yorkist leaders. She also had to solve the problem of her dowry lands being claimed by her mother-in-law, Lady Elizabeth Ferrers, who had recently married a second husband, Sir John Bourchier, son of the Earl of Essex and Isabella Plantagenet, sister of Richard, Duke of York.

Sir John Bourchier and Lady Ferrers petitioned the Lord Chancellor to require the tenants of three manors given to Elizabeth as part of her marriage dower to 'make astate' instead to Lady Ferrers. Lady Elizabeth Grey in turn filed petitions declaring that these estates – the two manors of Newbotell and Brington in Northamptonshire and a third, Woodham Ferrers in Essex – were enfeoffed at her marriage to provide income for Sir John Grey and his family. In response to the competing claims, two of the tenant holders, Robert Isham and William Bolden, stated that the intent of their contracts was, indeed, to provide an annual income of 100 marks to 'the said John Grey and Elizabeth his wife, and to the heirs of the said John's body'. William Fielding, a more politically circumspect tenant, stated merely 'that he was uncertain as to the intent of the assignment'.

In a second petition indicating controversy between wife and mother-in-law, Lord Rivers states that he had paid 200 marks to Sir Edward Grey, John's father, as his portion of the marriage agreement, but that he held the man in such high trust that he did not require a receipt. Now Sir Edward's widow was requesting payment of 125 marks as part of that settlement. Whether these suits between Lady Elizabeth Grey and Lady Elizabeth Ferrers indicate financial default, personal animosity or political provocation by Lady Ferrers's newly acquired Yorkist relatives cannot be determined from available records.[50]

The land dispute was settled in 1463, when William Fielding was ordered to give over to Lady Grey 'and the heirs of the body of John Grey by her… the common of pasture for beasts and swine', along with the products of the land essential for maintenance of the messuages and closes.[51] Elizabeth thus regained her dowry property from her Yorkist in-law, perhaps assisted by the King's intervention. If Edward thought, however, that solving this financial contretemps augured well for ending the battles between Lancaster and York, he was sorely mistaken.

CHAPTER FOUR

The Cousins' Wars

The Wydevilles were caught in the middle when war broke out between Henry VI and his Yorkist cousins – as was all of England. As long as France was the enemy, the English barons, although always jockeying for power and prestige, fought for a common cause. An initial conflict between the houses of Lancaster and York had ended in 1415 when Henry V executed Richard, Earl of Cambridge for attempting to place his brother-in-law, Edmund Mortimer, on the throne. As heir to Lionel, third son of Edward III, Mortimer claimed precedence over descendants of John of Lancaster, the fourth son. After Henry V quelled that rebellion, Richard, Duke of York, son of the executed Cambridge, fought loyally for England as the Hundred Years' War whimpered towards its end.

The Yorkist struggle for the throne had merely been muted, however, by the uncompromising swords of Henry IV and Henry V. When Henry VI began his reign at the age of nine months, English governance relied on the strong and powerful barons who constituted the King's Council. As long as the Duke of Bedford, brother of Henry V and uncle to the baby King, was alive, an uneasy peace prevailed – although Bedford's brother Humphrey was always skirmishing for dominance. After Bedford's death, each baron who controlled vast tracts of lands and many loyal followers sought to increase his personal and political power. They were not about to give up control to a weak and inexperienced King. Neither was Henry VI capable of compelling submission. Hall's *Chronicle* explains much about England's political and economic problems under Henry VI:

King Henry, which reigned at this time was a man of a meek spirit, and of a simple wit, preferring peace before war, rest before business, honesty before profit, and quietness before labour. And to the intent that all men might perceive, that there could be none more chaste, more meek, more holy, nor a better creature. In him reigned shamefastness, modesty, integrity, and patience...[1]

Hardly qualifications for a politician. As Henry VI progressively lost the French territory won by his father, the nation began to lose confidence in its King and to question his capacity to lead. By 1450, England was in big trouble. The nation was in debt; Normandy had been lost, with Gascony to follow within a year; anarchy was fast replacing governance. By 1453, only Calais remained under English control. Henry VI's marriage to Margaret of Anjou, niece of the French King Charles VII, had failed to secure the peace promised by the 1444 truce at Tours. Henry's claim to be King of France amounted to no more than an empty boast.

Such troubles turned into crisis in July 1453, when Henry suffered a bout of insanity that lasted eighteen months. His cousin Richard, Duke of York was appointed Protector of the Realm and began to assert his claim to the throne. As son of Anne Mortimer, descendant of Lionel, York's lineage was more direct than that of Henry VI. York's claim, however, depended on succession through the female line – Philippa, daughter of Lionel, and Anne Mortimer, great-granddaughter – a claim regarded as weak by those who resisted women as regal heirs.

The crisis worsened with the birth of Prince Edward, son of Henry VI and Margaret, on 13 October 1453. The King was so ill that he did not even know that he had produced an heir to the throne. Queen Margaret, concerned about her son's rights, began taking an active interest in politics. At the same time, Richard of York, a better administrator by far than the King, savoured the power he wielded. But his claim to the throne was now thwarted by a direct descendant of Henry VI. A clash between the houses of Lancaster and York was inevitable.

When Henry VI regained a degree of health in early 1455, he was still incapable of governing. In his stead Queen Margaret, intent on securing her son's rights, tightened her control, with the assistance of Lancastrian supporters led by the Duke of Somerset. Hall describes Margaret of Anjou:

> The Queen his wife was a woman of a great wit, and yet of no greater wit than of haut stomach [arrogance], desirous of glory, and covetous of honour, and of reason, policy, counsel, and other gifts and talents of nature belonging to a man, full and flowing: of wit and wiliness she lacked nothing, nor of diligence, study, and business, she was not unexpert: but yet she had one point of a very woman: for often time when she was vehement and fully bent in a matter, she was suddenly like a weathercock, mutable, and turning.[2]

By 1455, Richard, Duke of York and his followers began to challenge openly the King's authority. The baronial families supporting York included the Nevilles, Mowbrays and Bourchiers, families whose wealth both in land and in men constituted an awesome threat to the King's authority. The Nevilles, in particular, led by Richard, Earl of Salisbury and his son, Richard, Earl of Warwick, controlled enormous resources and loyal supporters across much of England.

Actual warfare broke out in May 1455 at the first battle of St Albans, just north of London, when the supporters of Richard, Duke of York attacked the King's troops. Although the skirmish lasted only half an hour, crucial Lancastrian leaders were killed: Somerset, Northumberland and Clifford. This battle would set the pattern for the next thirty bloody years, during which the nobility of England would progressively annihilate itself.

'The Wars of the Roses', the name by which we know these battles, was never used within the lifetime of its combatants. Three centuries later, Sir Walter Scott romanticised the conflicts as 'The Wars of the Roses', perhaps influenced by Shakespeare's *Henry VI, Part I*, where York picks a white rose and Somerset a red one to symbolise their differences.[3] While the House of York did display the white rose as its symbol during this era, contemporary Lancastrians never identified partisans with a red rose. The name used by the people who lived through the next thirty years more accurately describes these bitter internecine conflicts: 'the cousins' wars'.

The first battle of St Albans in May 1455 resulted in a Yorkist victory. Henry VI was not overthrown, but the shift in power caused major changes in governing authority. Richard, Duke of York once more was made Protector of the Realm, Lord Salisbury was appointed Chancellor, and Warwick was named Captain of Calais. Life in Henry VI's court continued with a patina of civility while York remained superficially loyal to the King. When his appointment as Lieutenant of Ireland in 1457 effectively isolated him from the centre of power, however, York's dissatisfaction increased. Margaret tried to retain Lancastrian control by acting behind the scenes, and soon she replaced her husband in name as well as in deed. When armed conflict ultimately broke out, the Lancastrian troops became known as 'Margaret's army'.

Meanwhile, Warwick used his appointment as Captain of Calais to develop enormous power and influence. As commander of the garrison and naval forces, he sent his English ships to attack both the Hanseatic and Castilian fleets in 1458. His success greatly enriched his personal treasury and consolidated Yorkist power. When the Duke of York plotted another active challenge to the King in 1459, Warwick invaded England, marching through Kent towards Ludlow where York and Salisbury were amassing troops. Salisbury's initial victory over a detachment of the Lancastrian army at Blore Heath augured well for the Yorkist cause. But many Englishmen were not ready to rebel against their anointed King and flocked to the Lancastrian side. As troops began to amass just south of Ludlow, Warwick's men from Calais began to have second thoughts. Led by Andrew Trollope, they deserted, and the Yorkist leaders fled in the face of the superior Lancastrian army. Richard, Duke of York escaped to Ireland, abandoning his wife and two youngest sons, George and Richard, who remained in Ludlow Castle.[4] Warwick and Salisbury, with York's eldest son, Edward, Earl of March, fled back to Calais where they regrouped and rebuilt their forces.

By the summer of 1460, they were ready to invade again. At the battle at Northampton on 10 July, Warwick's superior power crushed King Henry's army and brought Richard, Duke of York home from Ireland. In October 1460, Parliament tried to settle the family feud by decreeing that Henry VI would remain King during his lifetime, and that Richard of York or his heirs would succeed to the throne at Henry's death. Prince Edward of Lancaster was excluded from the throne, as rumours began to circulate that he was not, after all, Henry's child, but adulterous Margaret's bastard. Charges of adultery would become the *modus operandi* of Yorkist men, who claimed regal rights by accusing women of infidelity. In later years, York's sons Clarence and Richard would each accuse their own mother of adultery in their quest for the throne. Whether Richard, Duke of York would have modified his propaganda against Margaret of Anjou had he known that his own wife would be slandered by their sons, we shall never know.

The best-laid plans of York and Warwick, however, failed to take into account the wrath of Queen Margaret, who would not tolerate disinheriting her son, Edward of Lancaster. Since his father could not protect his son's rights, the Queen began to fight. 'Margaret's army' captured and killed Richard, Duke of York at Wakefield on 30 December 1460. Unfed and unpaid, Margaret's army then marched south towards London, ravaging the countryside and creating fear and loathing in the people as they passed. Their decisive victory at the second battle of St Albans on

17 February 1461 caused the citizens of London to tremble in terror as they anticipated starving soldiers ransacking their city.

To save London, the Lord Mayor and the city's aldermen mobilised their best defence. They turned to women. Exploiting the long-time friendship between Margaret of Anjou and Jacquetta of Luxembourg, the Lord Mayor of London asked the Duchess of Bedford to intervene on the city's behalf. Several contemporary records describe what happened:

> The Duchess of Bedford and the Lady Scales, with divers Clerks and Curates of the City, went to Saint Albans to the King, Queen, and Prince, for to entreat for grace for the City. And the King and his Council granted that four knights with 400 men should go to the City and see the disposition of it, and make an appointment with the Mayor and the Aldermen.[5]

'The Lady Scales' was one of Margaret's attendants, and the widow of a noted Lancastrian lord. She became the mother-in-law of Anthony Wydeville, Jacquetta's eldest son, who married Lady Elizabeth Scales sometime before 23 July 1461.

The Great Chronicle reports that 'long and many lamentable supplications' were required to appease Margaret.[6] A letter in the archives of Milan, written by C. Gigli on 22 February 1461, describes the situation to Michele Arnolfini of Bruges:

> I wrote of the victory obtained by the forces of the Queen and Prince at Saint Albans on the 17th of this month, and how they recovered the king and have him, and how this town [London] sent to them at Saint Albans to offer the place, provided they were guaranteed against pillage. With them went my Lady of Buckingham, the widow, and my Lady the Regent that was. They returned on the 20th, and reported that the king and queen had no mind to pillage the chief city and chamber of their realm, and so they promised; but at the same time they did not mean that they would not punish the evildoers.[7]

'My Lady the Regent that was' identifies Jacquetta by her title when married to the Duke of Bedford, the title by which she was prominently known in Bruges and Milan. Lady Buckingham was Anne Neville, sister of Salisbury and of the Duchess of York, a relationship which would seem to align her to the Yorkist cause. But she had married Humphrey Stafford,

Duke of Buckingham, a Lancastrian noble who was killed at the battle of Northampton in July 1460.

Almost nothing has been written about the role of women in these wars. Other than Margaret's command of the King's army, a role that has provoked only negative images, the contemporary chronicles focus on battle manoeuvres and body counts, with little attention paid to the personal devastation wreaked on family and friends. Lady Buckingham's situation reveals how families fragmented as their men fought for power as Lancastrians or Yorkists. The remarriage of Elizabeth Wydeville's first mother-in-law similarly reflects the complexity of personal relationships during these conflicts between cousins. Though the Greys of Groby had always been solid Lancastrians, Sir Edward Grey's widow, Lady Elizabeth Ferrers, married Sir John Bourchier, son of Isabella Plantagenet and nephew of Richard, Duke of York. Personal liaisons shifted political loyalties; politics, in turn, shattered families as war divided brother from sister – or in the case of Lady Ferrers, pitted grandmother against grandson in seeking control of property rights.

Women saved London in February 1461, a fact recorded in the contemporary chronicles but ignored in too many accounts of the Wars of the Roses. We can only wonder what Margaret and Jacquetta discussed as they met to decide the city's fate. Did these two friends recall the innocence of 1445 – just sixteen years earlier – when the Duchess of Bedford and Sir Richard Wydeville escorted the fifteen-year-old Margaret across the Channel to her new country and husband? Did they reflect on the ironies of their changed circumstances? Did they lament the hopes dashed by the miseries of men fighting for power? Did they foresee the future of continuing conflict and the annihilation of most of their loved ones? In these wars of the cousins, personal ties were severed with the swing of a sword, yet in the days following the second battle of St Albans, personal trust saved the city of London.

As a result of the feminine parley between Margaret and Jacquetta, Margaret limited Lancastrian entry into London to a symbolic force of four knights and 400 men. That fateful decision destroyed her cause and allowed the troops of Edward, Earl of March to enter the city just days later. On 4 March 1461, Edward IV was triumphantly declared King. Jacquetta would benefit years later when the city fathers remembered her role at St Albans and protected her and her daughter, then Queen Consort

Elizabeth, from accusations of sorcery by Warwick's henchmen. But that victory, too, would be temporary.

Even in 1461, Jacquetta's plea had its touch of irony. Margaret's victory at St Albans had taken the life of the captain of her Lancastrian cavalry. Sir John Grey, husband of Jacquetta's daughter Elizabeth, died leading the cavalry charge against Warwick. The Lancastrian victory left Elizabeth a widowed mother with two small sons, even as it reunited Margaret with her husband, Henry VI, and her son, Edward, Prince of Wales.

The ironies of the cousins' wars were just beginning.

CHAPTER FIVE

Consternation and Coronation

Between Edward IV's pardons for Elizabeth's family in July 1461 and the announcement of his marriage in September 1464, Elizabeth Wydeville lived in obscurity. Edward IV was busy solidifying his claim to the throne and restoring the nation's political, financial and social stability. With Henry VI and his family in exile in Scotland, Edward IV's fame and fortune grew. The Milanese ambassador wrote to Duke Francesco Sforza: 'This new king is young, prudent and magnanimous'.[1]

A report to the Duke of Milan on 30 August 1461 in the aftermath of Towton provides a rare outside glimpse of Wydeville prominence in England:

> The lords adherent to King Henry are all quitting him, and come to tender obedience to this King, and at this present, one of the chief of them has come, by name Lord de Rivers, with one of his sons, men of very great valour. I held several conversations with this Lord de Rivers about King Henry's cause, and what he thought of it, and he answered me that the cause was lost irretrievably.[2]

The Milanese ambassador did not mention the daughter of Lord de Rivers, Lady Elizabeth Grey, *née* Wydeville.

Neither did Edward's counsellors comprehend the importance of this woman to their King. Only Edward's closest confidant, William, Lord Hastings, perhaps knew of the impending marriage. Just eighteen days before her wedding, Elizabeth contracted with Hastings to marry one of her sons by Sir John Grey to a still-unborn daughter of Hastings. This agreement is particularly intriguing in light of the political antagonisms between the Lancastrian Greys of Groby and their Yorkist neighbours, the Hastings of Kirby Muxloe and Ashby-de-la-Zouch. Was the contract designed to make peace between traditional adversaries before the wedding? The indenture of 13 April 1464 reads:

> ...made between Elizabeth Grey, widow of Sir John Grey, knight, son and heir of Edward Grey, late Lord Ferrers, and William, Lord Hastings for the marriage of Thomas Grey, her son or in case of his death of Richard his brother, with the eldest daughter to be born within the next five or six years to Lord Hastings; or failing such a daughter with one of the daughters to be born within the same period to Ralph Hastings, his brother, or, failing such a daughter with one of the daughters of Dame Anne Ferrers his sister. If any manors or possessions once belonging to Sir William Asteley, knight, called 'Asteley lands' or any of the inheritance of dame Elizabeth 'called Lady Ferrers of Groby' (save all manors, lands and tenements in Nobottle and Brington, co. North hants. and Woodham Ferrers, co. Essex) were at any time recovered in the title and right of Thomas or Richard from the possession of any other person having an interest in them, half of the rent and profits thereof while Thomas or, if he died, Richard, was under the age of twelve years was to belong to Lord Hastings and half to dame Elizabeth. Lord Hastings to pay her the sum of 500 marks for the marriage, but if both Thomas or Richard died before such marriage, or if there was no female issue as above she to pay him the sum of 250 marks.[3]

This contract would achieve in Northamptonshire the unity of Lancaster and York that Edward was pursuing on a national level.

No evidence proves that Hastings knew of the impending marriage between Elizabeth and the King, or that Edward IV was aware of this indenture. But it is inconceivable to think that either was uninformed. As Lord Chamberlain and intimate friend to Edward IV, Hastings was the logical one to facilitate the King's visits to Grafton, keeping the larger court ignorant of Edward's *inamorata*. Someone within his court had to explain the King's absences and cover his tracks. Who else but his chamberlain? Similarly, the King surely knew about – perhaps even arranged – the Hastings-Grey indenture. Elizabeth would never have endangered her impending marriage by excluding the King in negotiating such an important bond. It is equally inconceivable that Hastings would have contracted with Elizabeth without the King's approval.

Edward's other advisors responded with amazement and consternation when he announced his marriage during a Council meeting at Reading in September 1464. Jean de Waurin wrote in his *Chronique* that Lady Elizabeth Grey 'was not his match, however good and however fair she might be... He must know well that she was no wife for such a high prince as himself'.[4] Dismissing the qualities of goodness and fairness as irrelevant to a Queen, as Waurin does, reflects the attitude of subsequent gossips and historians who not only ignore the positive influence Elizabeth exerted on her husband, but the aristocratic lineage of her mother and baronage of her father. Ignoring Lord Rivers's standing and service in the court and the Duchess of Bedford's rank among peers, Waurin's quote tarnished the Wydeville reputation forever after. The family became falsely and unfairly labelled as 'popinjays' who overreached their designated place in the established order. Opinion replaced fact.

The element of surprise – of being excluded from the King's intimate business – infuriated those who found themselves uninformed. Warwick, in particular, was politically humiliated, not merely by the thwarting of his negotiations for a French wife, but by his protégé making a decision and acting without consulting the master. Clearly, Warwick's authority had been undermined, his expectations betrayed. His hatred focused on the Wydevilles, the cause of Edward's rebellious behaviour. Warwick's anger would fester until it erupted in open rebellion against his young cousin.

Edward was undeterred. He proudly and formally introduced his Queen to his court on St Michael's Day, 29 September 1464. Elizabeth was led into the chapel of Reading Abbey for presentation to the King's Council on the arms of the King's brother George, Duke of Clarence and his cousin, Richard Neville, Earl Warwick. If Warwick was unhappy at the honour, he was much too politically astute to rebel just yet. The couple spent their honeymoon at Reading Abbey, the first of many times that Elizabeth would retreat to a religious setting for privacy and seclusion. While the newlyweds resided within the Abbey, the third largest and the wealthiest in England at the time,[5] news of the marriage swept across the land. Advisors and friends were stunned.

Knowing the value of symbolism, Edward IV planned a coronation for his Queen that would signify his reign's stability and solidify its permanence. At his own coronation hard on the heels of Towton, Edward's empty coffers had forced him to borrow money to fund the limited ceremonies. Four years later, Edward's treasury had been augmented by lands and manors seized from Henry VI and the defeated Lancastrians. His Queen's coronation offered an opportunity to display his wealth, glory and grandeur to his nation and the world. Edward staged a splendid celebration that presented his beautiful Queen as a jewel ensconced in a setting of regal pomp and circumstance. The King himself began the rituals at the Tower of London on Ascension Day, 23 May 1465, by inducting forty-three worthy men into the Knights of the Bath. Included among the newly designated Knights were the Queen's brothers Richard and John Wydeville, along with nobles who already were or would be married into the Wydeville family: the Duke of Buckingham, Anthony Grey de Ruthin and Lord Maltravers.[6]

The next day, the Queen made her way from Eltham Palace near Greenwich to the Tower of London in a procession that was then, as it would be now, majestic and grand. Silk covered the Queen's chair, saddle and pillion. Jewels and precious stones adorned her clothing. Citizens crowded the roads to cheer their Queen as she passed by. As she neared Southwark, London's Lord Mayor and aldermen, dressed in flaming scarlet, joined the procession at Shooters Hill to escort her across London Bridge.

The bridge, lined with houses and shops on both sides, had been carefully prepared for the occasion. For days carpenters and painters had built stages and prepared scenery for the pageants that greeted the Queen as she entered the city of London. The Bridgemaster's accounts cite purchases of paint that included 11lb of vermillion, ½lb of indigo, 1lb of verdigris, 6lb of white lead, 6lb of red lead and 18lb of black chalk. Red and purple buckram covered one stage floor. Other decorations required 3 gross tinfoil, 900 'party gold', 200 'party silver', plus reams of gold, red, green, white and black paper. 12lb of glue held all the decorations in place. In completing their work, the painters bought 'pots and dishes of earth', pig's bristles for making brushes, four pairs of scissors, flour to make paste, and 4lb of candles for working at night.[7]

Eight images representing two angels and six virgins provided the background setting for one pageant. Hazelwood rods created the frames for the female figures, adorned by 3lb of flax for hair, 2oz of saffron to dye the flax, eight pairs of gloves for their hands, 1lb of flock to stuff the gloves, plus a thousand pins to hold the clothes in place. Six kerchiefs adorned the virgins, while 900 peacock feathers created wings for the angels.

John Genycote received 3s for writing and limning (illuminating) six ballads presented to the Queen on her approach, and John Thompson 8d for writing '6 ballads on tablets fixed to the pageant on the bridge'. The workers who made the announcement, placed on the bridge before the Queen's arrival, lightened their labours with 'one kilderkin of ale' (half a barrel). Another 46s 10d paid the workmen's expenses incurred at the Crown alehouse next to the Bridgehouse gate. Just before the day of the coronation, the bridge was fumigated and covered with forty-five loads of sand to hide the mud, dirt and droppings of its incessant traffic of people and horses.

The Queen crossed the bridge accompanied by the singing of groups stationed along the way. Clerks had hired a room at the Staple of the bridge from which they greeted her with song. A choir of twenty-five, led by the Master of the Society of Clerks, sang at the drawbridge. The Clerk of the Church of St Magnus led his boys' choir in singing as the Queen passed by. Another choir of boys sang at the door of the Chapel of St Thomas à Becket, patron saint of the city of London.

The pageant that greeted the Queen featured Robert, Clerk of the Church of St George, playing the role of St Paul. Edmund Herte acted the part of Mary Cleophas, whose vigil day it was. Salamon Batell represented St Elizabeth, patron saint of the Queen, and delivered the official speech welcoming Queen Elizabeth to the city of London. The Queen then progressed to the Tower of London, where monarchs historically spent the night preceding their coronation. Edward IV, who had arrived two days earlier, greeted his Queen.

On Saturday 25 May, the procession, augmented by the newly made Knights of the Bath, departed from the Tower. Riding in front of Elizabeth, the bright blue gowns and white silk hoods of the Knights created brilliant expectations for the Queen who followed. Elizabeth, seated on a litter carried by two bay horses, regally made her way through Cheapside to Westminster Palace where she spent the night of Saturday 25 May.

On Sunday 26 May 1465, Elizabeth Wydeville was crowned Queen of England.

A contemporary manuscript, edited by George Smith in 1935, records with remarkable detail the coronation rituals and subsequent banquet. The ceremonies began with the Duke of Clarence, Edward IV's brother and Steward of England, riding into Westminster Hall on horseback, 'his courser richly trapped head and body to the ground with *crapsiur* richly embroidered and garnished with spangles of gold'. Clarence was accompanied by the Earl of Arundel, Constable and Butler for the Feast, and by the Duke of Norfolk, Marshall of England, both on horses 'richly trapped in cloth of gold to the ground'. Their job involved crowd control, as they rode around the hall opening a corridor for the entrance of the Queen.

The Queen entered, walking under a canopy held at its corners by four Barons of the Cinque Ports. Clothed in a mantle of purple and with a coronal upon her head, Elizabeth carried in her right hand the Sceptre of St Edward and in her left the Sceptre of the Realm. She walked between the Bishop of Durham on her right and the Bishop of Salisbury on her left. Behind the Queen, and also under the canopy, walked the Abbot of Westminster.

At the lower step of the door leading to Westminster monastery, Elizabeth removed her shoes and walked barefoot 'upon ray cloth [striped fabric] into the monastery'. Here she was met by the Archbishop of Canterbury and 'divers Bishops and abbotts'. Going before her, now on foot, were the Duke of Clarence, the Earl of Arundel and the Duke of Norfolk. The ten-year-old Duke of Buckingham, traditionally Constable of England but too young to fulfil that role, was carried on the shoulders of a squire.

Following the Queen into the monastery were her attendants. The Duchess of Buckingham 'the elder' (Anne Neville, sister of Edward IV's mother) carried the Queen's train. Next followed the Duchess of Suffolk (Elizabeth Plantagenet, sister of Edward IV), Lady Margaret of York (Edward IV's sister who later married Charles the Bold, Duke of Burgundy), and the Duchess of Bedford (Elizabeth's mother). Elizabeth's ten-year-old sister, Katherine, child bride of the Duke of Buckingham, was carried on the shoulders of an unnamed person. They were followed by a richly-dressed procession of thirteen duchesses and countesses in red velvet and ermine, fourteen baronesses in scarlet and miniver (fur, perhaps squirrel), and twelve ladies baronettes in scarlet.

The procession entered through the north door of Westminster monastery and moved through the Choir to the High Altar, where the Queen kneeled while the Archbishop of Canterbury 'read over her' the appropriate solemnities. Then she 'lay before the altar while certain supplications was said over her'. After anointing her head, the Archbishop crowned her, assisted by the Archbishop of York who held the 'holy unction'. She was then conveyed to her throne 'with great reverence and solemnity', with the Abbot of Westminster carrying the Sceptre Spiritual and the Earl of Essex the Sceptre Temporal.

At the beginning of the gospel, the sceptres were given Elizabeth to hold during its reading. They were then returned to the Abbot and the Earl, who carried them before the Queen as she walked to the Altar for the offering. The Duchess of Suffolk and the Duchess of Bedford accompanied her to attend to the crown, holding it on her head during her responses to the Mass. All this while, the Queen was barefoot. The Mass concluded with the Queen returning to her throne where she 'sang solemnly *Te Deum*'. Then 'from the Monastery she was led crowned between the said two Bishops under the Canopy and the said Abbot with them under the same'. The Duke of Suffolk on her right carried the Sceptre of St Edward, and the Earl of Essex on her left carried the Sceptre of England. The entire procession exited the monastery through the Great Hall, whereupon Elizabeth was led to her chambers where she 'was new revested in a surcoat of purple' for the traditional coronation banquet.

The rituals of the banquet began as the Queen returned to the Great Hall, conducted by the two Bishops. First, 'the Queen did wash', with the Duke of Suffolk standing at her right hand and the Earl of Essex at her left, bearing the Sceptres. The Earl of Oxford served the water for washing, with the Duke of Clarence holding the basin and testing the water's purity before the Queen dipped her fingers.

The Queen sat crowned 'in her estate' at the high table flanked by the sceptre bearers, kneeling. The Archbishop of Canterbury sat on the Queen's right, the Duchess of Suffolk and Lady Margaret of York on her left. Kneeling on the Queen's left were the young Countess of Shrewsbury and the Countess of Kent, who held a veil before the Queen when she ate. Elizabeth herself removed her crown while eating and replaced it when she had finished.

Below the Queen, three long tables of guests were arranged in precise seating patterns. At the middle table on the right side sat, in descending order, thirteen bishops and abbots, beneath whom sat the chief judges of the King's Bench and of the common pleas, the Chief Baron and fellow judges, and 'Barons, Sergeants and divers others'. On the left side sat the Duchess of Bedford, the Countess of Essex, the Duchess of Norfolk (the elder), the Duchess of Buckingham (the elder), the Duchess of Buckingham (the younger), and 'of Countesses and Baronesses many others'. Beneath them at the same table were 'the Knights of the Bath new made'.

The table next to the right wall included the Barons of the Cinque Ports and their fellowship dressed in 'their livery of ancient time due and accustomed for the day'. Beneath them sat the Clerk of the Rolls, and the Masters of the Chancery. At the table next to the left wall sat the Mayor of London along with the aldermen, officers and distinguished citizens of the City.

The serving of each of the three courses began with elaborate ceremony and processionals. Trumpets sounded as the earls, barons and knights entered on foot, followed by Clarence, Steward of England, the Earl of Arundel, Constable, and the Duke of Norfolk, Marshall, riding on horses 'richly trapped to the ground'. The 'Knights of Bath new made' followed with the procession of dishes, of which the first course had seventeen. Splendour and clatter created an exciting atmosphere as the Knights made their way to each table with sufficient platters to serve the hundreds of diners.

Similar processions, horses and all, preceded the second course with its nineteen dishes, and the third with a mere fifteen. The Queen's brother, Anthony, Lord Scales, had the pleasure of serving as official cupbearer and dispensing hippocras (spiced wine). Music played throughout the banquet. Between courses, the King's minstrels, as well as the minstrels of other lords, played and piped 'their instruments great and small before the Queen full melodiously and in the most solemn wise'. As a final treat, 'the knights of Bath new made brought the spice plates unto the cupboard'. Sir John Say delivered a spice plate to Sir William Bourchier, who served the Queen. Clarence 'delivered the assay of the spice plate' while the Mayor of London held 'the cup with wine of void', the last drink before departing from the banquet.

The ritual concluded as the Queen's almoner and chaplain 'folded up the Table Cloth unto the middle of the Table and before her reverently took it up and bore from the Table'. At the 'washing after dinner' the Queen was attended by Sir John Howard, who placed a napkin before her while the Duke of Norfolk, Marshall of England, 'went before and commanded'. The Earl of Oxford carried in the basin for washing, and Clarence, Steward of England, again held it and tested the water before the Queen touched it. In departing to her chamber, the Queen walked between the bishops of Durham and Salisbury with the sceptres of St Edward and of England carried before her by the Duke of Suffolk and the Earl of Essex.

The traditional tournament on the following day Monday, 27 May, was anticlimactic for participants in the coronation ceremonies. But the jousting and games held on the green next to Westminster Abbey permitted the common citizens of London to share in the nation's celebration. Viewers rented space in the belfry at Westminster Abbey to watch the action on the field below, where Lord Stanley won the honours and received the tournament prize of a ring set with rubies.[8]

Not mentioned in the contemporary manuscript describing the coronation are the King, Lord Rivers, Earl Warwick and the Duchess of York. The King traditionally would not have attended, since his presence would have distracted from the honours paid to the Queen. Lord Rivers's presence might have been so ordinary that the unknown contemporary observer made no notes. Warwick was in Burgundy on a diplomatic mission. The absence of the Duchess of York, however, has led to speculation that she deliberately stayed away to express her disapproval of Elizabeth as Edward's wife. The prominent participation of Edward's sisters, however, indicates that some members of the York family, at least, had accepted the King's decision.

The coronation ceremonies reflected Edward IV's ongoing efforts to include former Lancastrians in his reign. The Bishop of Durham, who escorted the Queen on her right, had been suspended from his office for supporting Henry VI, but by 1464 this long-time Lancastrian had been restored to his position and assumed the Bishop's traditional role in crowning the Queen.

Whatever the sentiments of others, Elizabeth Wydeville was now Queen of England. As her next responsibility, she needed to establish her royal household and assume her duties as Queen Consort.

CHAPTER SIX

Setting Up Housekeeping

As Queen, Elizabeth moved to Ormond Place, a great stone house in Knightriders' Street in the parish of St Trinity, Smithfield.[1] A former town house of the Lancastrian Earls of Ormond, the property was given by Edward to his new Queen, along with a grant of his manor of 'Plesaunce, alias Greenwich' in 1465.[2] He transferred his manor at Sheen (now Richmond) to the Queen in 1466.[3] The Queen also spent time at the royal residence at Eltham near Greenwich, and at the palaces of Windsor and Westminster.

The medieval household was an elaborate business, in which a flotilla of attendants served the needs of a few principal residents who moved frequently among their various estates. From gentry to royalty, status depended on display, extravagance, magnificence and hospitality offered to others. Nobles, in particular, employed enormous retinues to operate and maintain their numerous residences, including a kitchen staff to prepare food and drink for the household (where eating consumed one-third of each day), attendants to supervise wardrobes, clerks to keep records and conduct ceremonies, auditors to track expenses and income, grooms to tend horses, and stewards to manage the entire operation. In the fourteenth century, the royal household employed between 400 and 700 servants,[4] and although the Black Death had diminished the size of such establishments, they still remained huge in the fifteenth century.

In 1458, the Duke of York's household in London alone included 400 followers and 140 horses, while Warwick's housed 600 men, who required six oxen roasted daily just for breakfast. When travelling, retinues diminished somewhat, but Salisbury's arrival in London with eighty knights and squires required 400 horses for transport of people and supplies.[5] Even Thomas Bourchier, Archbishop of Canterbury, retained a household in 1459 that averaged sixty-eight persons in daily residence, including pages, grooms, cooks, valets, butlers, stewards and marshals. His small stable of sixty horses provided transportation for ecclesiastical journeys, where every man needed a horse to ride and several packhorses for luggage.[6]

Queens traditionally maintained households separate from the King, to serve the needs of the family while the King travelled through the realm dispensing justice, establishing authority and fighting wars. Often, of course, they lived and travelled together, but the Queen's household was financed and managed separately from the King's. When Henry VI suffered his first bout of insanity in 1454, his council had tried to control household expenses by reducing his staff of officials and servants to 424, Queen Margaret's to 120, and Prince Edward's to thirty-eight. In 1453, Margaret had paid wages to 151 servants.[7]

The Black Book, compiled between June 1471 and September 1472, describes the awesome organisation of Edward IV's household with its list of employee positions and job descriptions.[8] Chamberlain, chancellor, secretary, chaplain, surveyor, squires of the body, wardrobers, yeomen of the crown, yeomen of the chamber, grooms, pages, jewel-house clerks, physician, surgeons, apothecary, barber, henchmen, heralds, pursuivants, sergeants at arms, minstrels, clerks, stewards, household treasurer, clerks of the greencloth (accountants), bakers, pantry staff, butlers, wine purveyors, cellar staff, ale servers, wine butlers, spicery staff, confectioners, chandlers, ewers (providers of basins and dishes), nappery staff (tablecloth staff) and laundry workers begin the incomplete list, which breaks off before the compiler moves outside the palace to the gardens and stables.

The Queen's household replicated the King's on a smaller scale. To cover expenses, queens traditionally received dower grants of lands and income from rents, fees and patents. When Henry V married Katharine of Valois, he wrote to his Viscounts: 'The said Katherine shall take and have dower in our realm of England, as queens of England hitherward (hitherto) were wont to take and have. That is to say, to the sum of forty thousand crowns, by the year of the which twain algates [always] shall be worth a noble, English money'.[9] Joan of Navarre received a dowry of 10,000 marks when marrying Henry IV in 1403, but that amount was a pittance when compared to the £13,000 income of Queen Isabella in 1327. Eleanor of Castile regularly collected 'Queen's gold', a 10% surcharge added to every voluntary fine paid to the King, and in 1289–90 this assessment produced £1,564, more than Eleanor received from her lands.[10]

Most of Queen Elizabeth's income derived from dower lands and fees provided in successive grants from Edward IV. On 16 March 1465, for instance,
she received a 'Grant for life' of fourteen manors, several towns and castles,
and many parks and forests, all of which paid annual fees to her receiver-
general. Cash assessments added a diversified, if minor, source of income:

> 102£. 15s. 6d. yearly from the farm of the town of Bristol, 20£. yearly from
> the fee farm of the town of Norwich,... 10£. yearly from the chancellor of the
> University of Cambridge from the custody of the assize of bread and ale there,...
> 9£. 16s. 9d. yearly from the heirs male of Michael de la Pole, earl of Suffolk.[11]

While some of Elizabeth's dower lands came from the King's estates, many
were manors seized from the Duchy of Lancaster after the Yorkist victory.
In some cases, Elizabeth shared the income with other grantees: from
Swallowfield, for instance, she received two-thirds of the income, since
the other third went to her mother, who held dowry rights as Duchess
of Bedford.[12] To manage the Lancastrian lands, Elizabeth retained many
of the same officials who had served Henry VI, a transition smoothed by
the long association of the Wydevilles with the Lancastrian court. A careful
and meticulous businesswoman, the Queen set up offices at Westminster
in the New Tower, next to the King's exchequer, where her officials could
consult with the King's treasurer in conducting business.[13]

A.R. Myers's study of Elizabeth's household accounts refutes all claims
that she was 'extravagant'. Indeed, Myers proved that Elizabeth was relatively parsimonious and thrifty, especially when compared to her predecessors Isabella, Philippa and Margaret (Queen Consorts to Edward
II, Edward III, and Henry VI). Whereas Queen Philippa paid her general attorney £6 13s 4d in 1337 and Margaret paid hers £10 in 1452–3,
Elizabeth paid £5 in 1466–7.[14] Elizabeth dramatically changed the lax
policies and extravagances of Queen Margaret, who was infamously prof-
ligate in spending money and equally dilatory in paying debts. Perhaps
Elizabeth observed the disastrous consequences of fiscal disarray while
attending Margaret's court. Or perhaps her life in the large family at
Grafton had taught her careful management of limited resources. In any
case, Elizabeth was a perfect match for her husband, imposing the same
frugality on her household that Edward IV brought to the nation after
the dangerously insolvent reign of Henry VI.

The only household accounts extant from each reign record Margaret's income and expenditures for 1452–3 and Elizabeth's for 1466–7. These annual accounts reveal that Elizabeth imposed fairly dramatic economies to reduce Margaret's lavish expenditures. Margaret's income in 1452–3 amounted to £7,563, while Elizabeth's in 1466–7 was only £4,541. Yet, in spite of the smaller income, Elizabeth ended the year with a balance of £200, while Margaret had a deficit of £24.[15] Much of each Queen's income covered the considerable expenses of maintaining and managing properties – from paying wages to footmen to repairing castle walls. Many of Elizabeth's economies reduced wages for those accustomed to Margaret's largesse, a decrease that must have caused distress – perhaps even anger – among the recipients. Margaret's clerk in charge of the stables received £418 19s 3½d, for example, while Elizabeth's received £208 6s 9d.[16]

In her personal life, too, Elizabeth lived more frugally than Margaret. In 1454, Margaret's household staff included 120 individuals, while Elizabeth limited hers to 100.[17] Where Margaret had ten ladies-in-waiting, Elizabeth had five. Margaret's five apprentices-in-law compared with Elizabeth's two. Margaret employed both a clerk of the signet (the writer of documents sealed with her signet) and a secretary. Elizabeth assigned both tasks to one John Aleyn. From total income, Margaret spent £1,719 on her chamber while Elizabeth spent £919.[18]

That is not to say that Elizabeth ignored pleasures and presents. Her 1466–7 accounts cite payments of £14 for sable furs, £54 to her goldsmith, and £1,200 for her wardrobe (a sum that would have paid seamstress wages, bought cloth and thread, and arranged for storage when she moved from one palace to another). In comparison, Margaret's 1452–3 expenditures included £73 to a Venetian merchant for cloth, silk, and gold, £125 for jewels and goldsmith's work, £733 to the keeper of her jewels, and £2,073 to the keeper of her wardrobe.[19]

In staffing her household, Elizabeth has been criticised for including relatives among her attendants. Yet that time-honoured practice (hardly unknown today) served her well. Her brother John Wydeville was Master of the Horse, and both her sister Anne and sister-in-law Lady Scales were among her ladies-in-waiting. In-laws of her sister Anne served as Elizabeth's chamberlain and as one of her stewards. A cousin, James Haute, was her second steward. Since each position provided essential household needs, none entailed extraordinary expenditures, and all evidence points to loyal service, the accumulated criticism is difficult to comprehend.

The Queen's two principal ladies-in-waiting – Anne, Lady Bourchier, and Elizabeth, Lady Scales – received £40 each, while Lady Alice Fogge, Lady Joanna Norreis and Lady Elizabeth Ovedale received £20 each. Among the other nine ladies who attended the Queen, income ranged from £10 to 56s.[20] The annual salary reflects only part of the benefits provided by royal service, of course, since members of the household lived with the court and ate at its tables.

Other household employees included the Queen's chamberlain, Lord Berners, and physician, Dominic de Serigo, each of whom earned £40 per year. Two stewards or carvers, Humphrey Bourchier and James Haute, earned 40 marks (about £26).[21] The Queen's confessor, Edward Story, Chancellor of Cambridge University, received £10. The Queen's household also included a receiver-general (who collected income and paid bills), chancellor, attorney-general, solicitors, and many clerks. A host of yeomen and other servants worked in the stables and the larder.[22] Three minstrels provided music, for £10 shared between them. (The King's household had nineteen minstrels in 1466–7.) An apothecary was paid £18 17s 6d for various medicines.

Edward IV had entrusted to Elizabeth the care of the young Henry, Duke of Buckingham and his brother Humphrey, who were wards of the King during their minority. In August 1465, he granted to the Queen 500 marks yearly from five of his estates in South Wales, for the care of the boys, who 'have for some time been maintained at her expense'. A month later, another patent clarified that the grant was retroactive to the past Easter and would continue during the minority of the boys.[23]

Her household organised, Elizabeth turned to educational and charitable interests. The Queen's College of St Margaret and St Bernard, established at Cambridge University twenty years earlier, had fallen on hard times along with its Lancastrian founders. Initially created by charter of Henry VI on 3 December 1446, the College of St Bernard aspired to educate 'fit persons, who should shine like stars in their courses, and, by learning and example alike, instruct the people'. Queen Margaret had petitioned Henry VI to become the founder of the College and to rename it:

Beseecheth meekly Margaret Queen of England, your humble wife: Forasmuch as your most noble Grace hath newly ordained and established a college of Saint Bernard in the University of Cambridge... in the which University is no college founded by any Queen of England hitherto, please it therefore unto Your Highness to give and grant unto your said humble wife the foundation and determination of the said Collage to be called and named the Queen's College of Saint Margaret and Saint Bernard, or else of Saint Margaret, Virgin and Martir, and Saint Bernard, Confessor, and thereupon for full evidence thereof to have license and power to lay the first stone in her own person or else by other deputy of her assignment.[24]

Margaret desired this Queen's college 'to laud and honour [the] sex feminine', following the precedent set by the Countesses of Pembroke and of Clare who had founded Pembroke Hall and Clare Hall (now colleges of the University of Cambridge). King Henry VI granted his Queen's petition by patent on 30 March 1448, creating 'the Queen's College of St. Margaret and St. Bernard'.[25] Beginning with just four fellows, the College steadily grew through grants and gifts negotiated by its entrepreneurial president, Andrew Doket.

By 1465, four years of Yorkist rule had threatened the survival of Margaret's college, and President Doket appealed to Elizabeth for continued support: '...Closely connected with queen Margaret, Elizabeth Wydeville was doubtless well acquainted both with Andrew Doket and Queens' College'.[26] Elizabeth had been eleven years old when Margaret prevailed on Henry VI to create 'the Queen's College' – old enough to share in the excitement of Margaret's dream. Now she took up where her predecessor left off. On 25 March 1465, the 'College of St. Margaret and St. Bernard in the University of Cambridge' received a licence to hold property worth £200, equivalent to that provided by Henry VI. The institution continued under 'the patronage of Elizabeth, Queen of England'.[27] Cooper's *Memorials of Cambridge* states that Elizabeth 'set aside a portion of her income for the endowment of the college'.[28] Searle adds that 'in the early part of [1465] she appropriated a part of her income to completion of this college'.[29] Unfortunately, President Doket's papers have not survived to verify these claims, a woeful loss since records of that agile administrator who secured patronage from three successive queens – Margaret, Elizabeth and Anne (consort to Richard III) – could provide fascinating insights into medieval fundraising.

A contemporary *Miscellany containing the host foundation of the college* lists first among its benefactors 'Edward IV Rex Anglie' and 'Elizabeth, Regia Anglie', followed by other contributors from the York family, including Cecily, Duchess of York, George, Duke of Clarence, Richard, Duke of Gloucester and Anne, Duchess of Gloucester. A patent entry in 1477 recording the transfer of the manor of Fulmere to Andrew Doket identifies the institution as 'the Queen's college of St. Margaret and St. Bernard in the University of Cambridge, of the patronage of the King's consort Elizabeth, Queen of England'.[30] No details regarding specific contributions, however, have survived.

Eton College, too, benefited from Elizabeth's intercession. During his first Parliament at Westminster in 1461, Edward IV had revoked all endowments made by Henry VI to Eton College[31] and planned to merge it with St George's Chapel across the river at Windsor Castle. In 1463, a bull from Pope Pius II authorised the abolition of Eton, and in 1465 its bells, jewels and furniture were ordered to be removed to Windsor. The King's houses and buildings in the parish of Eton, opposite the College, were granted to the Bishop of Salisbury with 'license to pull down and carry away the same'.[32] In 1467, however, the King changed his mind, restored the College lands, and in 1469 petitioned Pope Paul II to revoke the bull merging Eton and Windsor.

If Edward's early animosity to Eton derived from its founding by Henry VI, the example of Elizabeth in saving Queens' College may have caused him to reverse his decision. No other rationale explains his change of heart. By 1471, Edward and Elizabeth were visiting Eton College rather frequently. During the second week of July, they were attended by a retinue of thirty, only to return the next week in company of more than a hundred. During September, their visit included foreign ambassadors.[33] Here, too, the records provide few facts about Elizabeth's influence, but her contributions during the tenure of Provost Henry Bost indicate significant interest in the welfare of the College. The epitaph on Bost's memorial specifically acknowledges the Queen's contributions: '*Illius auspiciis elemosina conjugis uncti Edward Quarti larga pluebat opem.*' ('For his [Bost's] benefit, the abundant generosity of the wife of the anointed Edward IV showered wealth.')[34]

Indeed, patronage of Eton College became a family affair. Elizabeth's brother Anthony became such a generous patron that a daily Mass was said at the altar of Our Lady every morning at 7.15. The bell tolled for sixty strokes 'so that well disposed people may have knowledge to come to the said mass', where the priest prayed for 'our sovereign lord King Edward the IVth, our sovereign lady Queen Elizabeth, the prince their son, and the lords and ladies his brethren and sistern, the said Earl Rivers and all his brethren and sistern, his father, and his mother, the well-known Jaquinet of Luxemburg, and other relations'.[35] In gratitude, Eton College kept a solemn anniversary for Lord Rivers and his family on 30 October, a tradition that began in 1475 and continued until the reign of Edward VI.[36]

Endowments to educational and religious causes characterised the charities of Elizabeth and the larger Wydeville family. On 5 March 1466, Queen Elizabeth founded a fraternity of sixty priests in London, to be called 'the fraternity of the Holy Trinity and the Sixty Priests of London'.[37] On 12 July 1466, the city of London gave Elizabeth permission to build a chapel or college on Tower Hill, a project that apparently never developed. In later years, she founded and funded a chapel of St Erasmus in Westminster Abbey.

Yet the Queen's deep involvement in spiritual and educational matters did not deter her from paying attention to secular and temporal needs. Among the latter was the wellbeing of her family. Her brothers and sisters, in particular, needed to marry to assure family prosperity and success. The King and Queen turned to that worthy goal, as they found appropriate partners for Elizabeth's Wydeville siblings.

CHAPTER SEVEN

Marriages Made in Court

If the union of Edward and Elizabeth dramatically broke with royal custom by choosing passion over politics, the marriages of Elizabeth's brothers and sisters reverted to tradition. In the fifteenth century, marriage among the nobility generally placed financial and hierarchical status at the centre of the partnership. Marriage was a business aimed at finding an eligible spouse with money and title, and fathers frequently secured their children's future by contracting marriages well before the groom and bride reached puberty. Love, as the medieval romances reveal, was reserved for adulterous liaisons, courtly affairs and dream visions – not for the serious business of a lifelong liaison.

Nothing caused such damage to Elizabeth's reputation as the marriages of her brothers and sisters to members of established nobility. The Queen Consort has been charged with matching her siblings to spouses far beyond their own rank – of 'overreaching' beyond the Wydeville place in the social order. Such charges not only ignore Lord Rivers's stature as Knight of the Garter and his long-term service on the King's Council, but the significant weight of Jacquetta's title and privileges as Duchess of Bedford. The criticism also fails to take into account the history and traditions of medieval marriage.

The fact that Anthony married Lady Elizabeth Scales well before his sister could influence Edward IV – perhaps as early as April 1461 – indicates that the Wydevilles could do well enough on their own. Lady Scales was daughter and heir of Thomas, Lord Scales, a prominent Lancastrian who had fought with Bedford and Talbot in France. When Lord Scales was killed in 1460, his daughter Elizabeth inherited his estates, and Anthony Wydeville subsequently gained his title in right of his wife. Anthony was summoned to Parliament as Lord Scales on 22 December 1462, years before his sister's marriage.[1] Elizabeth's own marriage to Sir John Grey, Lord Ferrers, also indicates sufficient family status and rank to contract an advantageous liaison, especially when so few eligible husbands were available in the fifty or so families of English nobility.

The scarcity of eligible partners was a problem that contributed to the dismay of those left behind when Elizabeth's siblings rapidly diminished the available pool. And when they married into families descended from royal ancestors, the nobility – Warwick, in particular – took umbrage. Because the Wydevilles lacked the 'blood royal' of England (though not of Luxembourg), that issue later became the focus of the Earl's attacks against the Queen's family. What initially infuriated Warwick, however, was the threat to his own power. Several of the Wydeville marriages united Lancastrian and Yorkist families across a political divide still palpable after three years of Edward's governance, decisions made by the King without consulting Warwick. Others who were pre-empted in the marriage market sneered that the King was a besotted fool who gave his wife whatever she asked – ignoring the fact that Edward regularly disregarded Elizabeth's wishes when she objected to his concubines. The fact that the Queen was blamed for the marriages, when they clearly required the King's participation and approval, remains a curiosity of perspective.

The truth is that the King was beating Warwick at his own game. No dynastic family had built fortune and power through marriage as successfully as the Nevilles, a point emphatically made in J.R. Lander's seminal scholarship investigating marriage and politics of the fifteenth century.[2] Between 1412 and 1436, the Nevilles had contracted marriages for thirteen children under the age of sixteen. At nine, Eleanor, a daughter of Ralph Neville, Earl of Westmoreland, was married to a twelve-year-old husband, who left her a widow after two years, whereupon she immediately married the twenty-one-year-old Earl of Northumberland. Cecily Neville, Edward IV's formidable mother, was married at the age of nine to Richard, Duke of York, aged thirteen, a privilege for which her father paid 3,000 marks.

Most egregiously, William, a Neville son by Westmoreland's second marriage, married Joan Fauconberg, heiress to the barony of Fauconberg. The only problem was that Joan had been an idiot since birth, an impediment made irrelevant by her extensive estates.[3] Such marriages were imperative because the children of Westmoreland's first marriage inherited his title and wealth, while those of his second marriage had to earn their way through well-endowed spouses.

Richard Neville, the eldest son of Westmoreland's second marriage to Joan Beaufort (daughter of John of Gaunt, Duke of Lancaster), secured his future by marrying Alice Montacute, daughter and heir of the Earl of Salisbury, thus inheriting both titles and estates by right of his wife. To assure that his son, also named Richard, would not have to wait until his father's death to obtain a title, the Earl of Salisbury contracted the six-year-old boy to the nine-year-old Anne de Beauchamp, heir of the Duke of Warwick. Richard Neville, junior, thereby became Earl Warwick by right of his wife. In fact, four of the six Nevilles who sat in Parliament's House of Lords had inherited their titles through their wives. Such cunning did not, however, prevent Salisbury and Warwick from berating the captured Lord Rivers in Calais for being 'made by marriage' to the Duchess of Bedford. Hypocrisy hardly pertains in politics, war and marriage, especially since Warwick's envy was surely stoked by Jacquetta's superior rank.

Whether Edward IV deliberately plotted to displace the Nevilles and lessen the power of Warwick is irrelevant. That was the result. And the older man could not tolerate the pre-empting of his authority. It was, after all, the wealth, power and experience of the thirty-three-year-old Warwick that had placed the nineteen-year-old Edward IV on the throne. Now that the King was twenty-two and flaunting his royal prerogatives, the older man's ego was bruised beyond repair.

The marriages began just weeks before Edward IV married Elizabeth, with the indenture between Hastings and Elizabeth to join her eldest son, Thomas Grey, with Hastings's yet unborn daughter. That marriage never occurred because two years later Sir Thomas Grey, then eleven, married Anne Holland, daughter of the Duchess of Exeter (eldest sister of Edward IV). Elizabeth paid the Duchess of Exeter 4,000 marks to dissolve a previous contract of marriage between Anne Holland and George Neville, nephew to Warwick.

Warwick was apoplectic. Anne Holland was the only child of the Duke of Exeter, the next Lancastrian claimant to the throne after Edward, Prince of Wales, only child of Henry VI. Marriage to Anne placed her husband close to the Lancastrian throne, a relationship that appealed to Warwick, whose lust after power and the crown was ever growing. Instead, a Neville had been displaced by Elizabeth's son. Worse, Warwick had been outwitted by a woman. Humiliating. Intolerable.

Marriage between Sir Thomas Grey and Anne Holland equally benefited Edward IV, of course, who was still childless. Further, the King welcomed the Lancastrian connection, which strengthened his position in the still unsettled nation. Given those political advantages, it is difficult to explain why Elizabeth, alone, has been blamed for arranging the marriage in an unseemly grasping after status, power and money.

As other marriages followed, those pre-empted in the marriage market began to resent the Queen's family. In October 1464, six months after the Queen's marriage, her eldest sister Margaret married Thomas, Lord Maltravers, heir of the Earl of Arundel and nephew to Warwick. In January 1465, her brother Sir John Wydeville, probably twenty years old, married Catherine Neville, Duchess of Norfolk, aged somewhere between sixty-five and sixty-six – a union that really set gossipy tongues wagging. William of Worcester, a decidedly pro-Neville chronicler, slandered the Duchess by adding twenty years to her age when he sarcastically called her a '*juvencula*' around the age of eighty and snidely sneered that the union was a '*maritagiam diabolicum*'. The Duchess herself didn't seem to mind. She had made her fortune with her first marriage to the Duke of Norfolk, who left her a rich widow at the age of thirty-five. Her dowager rights to the Norfolk estates had given her the freedom to remarry twice already, flouting all conventions with her third marriage to Thomas Strangeways, a mere 'Esquire'! Her son, John Mowbray, 3rd Duke of Norfolk, had died in 1461 without ever receiving his estates, and his mother's tenacity in holding onto property displeased all the Mowbray heirs. Now, with a new, young fourth husband so closely connected to the King, they might never regain their inheritance. No wonder they resented her new husband.

For Edward IV and Elizabeth, intangible benefits accompanied the Duchess of Norfolk's wealth and rank. The bride was the elder sister of the King's mother, Cecily. Thus, the marriage not only made Sir John Wydeville an uncle to the King, but brother-in-law to the Duchess of York, who had so vehemently opposed Edward IV's marriage. Neither were Earl Salisbury, brother of the bride, and Earl Warwick, her nephew, amused. Too rich to be bothered by scandal, the Duchess of Norfolk must have regarded her fourth liaison to the handsome, charming Sir John Wydeville as quite the marriage of convenience.

Did Edward chortle at his mother's discomfort, a subtle revenge for objecting to his own marriage? Did the King and Queen indulge in delighted pillow talk as they conceived the idea of this strange Wydeville-Neville conjugality? If so, their euphoria was short-lived. This marriage ended just four years later when Warwick took his revenge by murdering the groom.

In 1466, the Queen's sister Katherine Wydeville married Henry, Duke of Buckingham, first cousin and ward to Edward IV. Both were around the age of twelve, but the marriage must have been contracted prior to the Queen's coronation, since the contemporary record identifies Katherine as 'the Duchess of Buk the younger'. Both she and her young husband participated in the coronation carried on the shoulders of squires, and the marriage gave Katherine sufficient prominence to be seated at the coronation feast with her mother, the Duchess of Bedford, and three of the King's aunts.

Commonplace speculation credits this marriage with causing the alienation between Buckingham and the Wydevilles that developed later in Edward's reign, an alienation that supposedly began with Buckingham's resentment at being forced to marry beneath his rank. Katherine's rank as sister of the Queen and daughter of the Duchess of Bedford was not trivial, however, and the King, whose wardship of the Duke gave him both legal and traditional authority for contracting the marriage, obviously believed it appropriate. Further evidence points to Katherine's personal charm and attractiveness throughout her life. Years later, after Buckingham's execution in 1483 and sometime before November 7 1485, Katherine married Jasper Tudor, uncle to Henry VII, at a time when Wydeville fortunes were at their absolute nadir. Clearly, Jasper Tudor, son of a Queen and uncle to a King, did not find his wife's supposed lack of status to be a deterrent. And after Jasper Tudor's death, Katherine married a third time to Sir Richard Wingfield.

To blame Buckingham's alienation on a festering resentment of his marriage to the Queen's sister is to oversimplify the complex nature of court politics, as well as the Duke's own character. In later years, Buckingham did join the court faction led by Hastings, and he initially collaborated with Richard of Gloucester after Edward's death. By October 1483, however, he joined forces with the Wydevilles to lead a rebellion against Richard III. Lacking evidence about the marriage between Katherine and Buckingham, and knowledge of the psychological complexity of Buckingham himself, it is disingenuous to blame his political disaffections and affiliations on his wife.

Other Wydeville marriages followed rapidly, but not unusually so by the standards of medieval England. In September 1466, Mary Wydeville married William Herbert, second Earl of Pembroke and heir to Lord Herbert, one of Edward's strongest supporters. The new Lord Herbert was rewarded with the title of Lord Dunster. Mary's sister Anne married Lord Bourchier, heir to the Earl of Essex, sometime before August 1467. Jacquetta married John, Lord Strange of Knockyn, and Joan (sometimes called Eleanor) married Anthony, Lord Grey of Ruthin, cousin to the Greys of Groby. Nothing is known about Martha, who married Sir John Bromley of Bartomley and Hextall, and subsequently disappeared from history.

Of the Queen's brothers, Richard apparently never married, Lionel entered the Church, and Edward's marital state is unknown. All died without issue. Two brothers, Lewis and John, died in childhood.

Malicious gossip denigrating the Wydeville marriages distorts the reality, given contemporary practice and the Neville precedents. Warwick, however, was angry and he began to target the Queen and her family with revenge-inspired gossip and accusations. He tipped his hand when he founded a chantry in the parish church of SS Peter and Paul in Olney and failed to include the Queen in the divine service offered daily. The licence for the chantry stipulates that prayers be offered for 'the good estate of the King and for his soul after death'.[4] The phrasing is extraordinary in its omission: similar licences typically – virtually invariably – call for prayers 'for the good estate of the King and his Consort Elizabeth, Queen of England'.[5] The exclusion of the Queen from daily prayers foretells, with a chilling premonition, the future actions of Earl Warwick.

Meanwhile, the Wydevilles and their spouses settled down to serve their King and their country.

CHAPTER EIGHT

The Queen's Churching

Elizabeth knew well that her principal responsibility as Queen Consort was to produce the children who would assure a long line of Yorkist kings. That first happy event occurred on 11 February 1466, with the birth of an heir to Edward's throne. The occasion was one of national import, with all estates – clergy, nobles and commoners – understanding that continued prosperity and peace required orderly governance and the lawful transfer of power from one generation to the next. The entire nation followed the progress of the Queen Consort's pregnancy with great interest.

Near the time of birth, Elizabeth took to her private chambers. The walls and ceiling had been covered with rich tapestries to add warmth. Carpets on the floor and a canopy over the bed protected her against breezes and damp chills. The windows were covered with hangings so that she might lie in darkness or light according to her preference. When the birthing pains began, the Queen first went to a nearby chapel to receive communion, then returned to her lying-in chamber attended only by women, including her midwife. All supplies for the birth had been laid in, and any additional provisions were passed through the carefully guarded door to the women within the chamber.

All men – including husband, priest, and her physician Domenico de Serigo – were excluded from the birthing chamber, not to assure the mother privacy, but to protect men from the unclean act of giving birth. Childbirth resulted, after all, from the sin committed by Adam and Eve, and both mother and newborn child were considered fallen until purified by religious rites.

Fabyan's *Chronicle,* in its only entry for the fifth year of Edward's reign, records the anticipation and gossip that surrounded this birth of the first York heir:

This year, that is to say the 11th day of the month of February, was Elizabeth princess, and first child of King Edward, born at Westminster, whose christening was done in the Abbey with most solemnity; and the more because the king was assured of his physicians that the Queen was conceived with a prince; and especially of one named Master Dominic, by whose counsel great provision was ordained for christening of the said prince.

Wherefore it was after told, that this Master Dominic, to the intent to have great thanks and reward of the king, he stood in the second chamber where the Queen travailed that he might be the first that should bring tidings to the King of the birth of the prince; and lastly when he heard the child cry, he knocked or called secretly at the chamber door, and frayned [asked] what the Queen had. To whom it was answered by one of the ladies, 'Whatsoever the Queen's grace hath here within, sure it is that a fool stands there without'. And so confused with this answer, he departed without seeing of the King for that time.[1]

While the desire of Master Dominic for a prince was shared by all, Edward IV welcomed his new daughter with love and royal rites.

The Lady Princess was christened Elizabeth, the first time that name was used for a female child born into English royalty, but a name destined to become famous in subsequent centuries. The christening was conducted by George Neville, Archbishop of York and brother to Earl Warwick. Her godfather was Earl Warwick himself. Perhaps Edward was attempting to mollify the Neville clan by conferring these great privileges on them, and perhaps they in turn were hiding their growing animosity to the King and Queen. In 1466, harmony seemed to prevail throughout the House of York. Even the Duchess of York overcame her anger at Edward's choice of wife to stand as godmother to the Lady Princess, along with the child's maternal grandmother, the Duchess of Bedford.

In late March, the churching of Queen Elizabeth took place. An elaborate ritual that usually occurred a month after the birth of a child, 'churching' cleansed the mother of the sin that medieval religion attached to the body and to sex. The month of sequestration and abstinence permitted both physical recovery and reflection by the unclean and unholy woman about the curse of Eve and the sinful act that had created the newborn child. Eve's curse had caused the fall of man, and every new mother had to expiate her share in that sin before rejoining society.

The churching ceremony required the new mother to wear a veil to hide her shame, and to sit in a special pew, usually attended by her midwife. The ceremony of penance and purification began with the mother kneeling at the altar and making offerings. It ended in communal thanksgiving that welcomed – indeed, allowed – the woman back into the Church and into society. Blessed for surviving the perils of childbirth and cleansed of all impurities, the mother could now resume her role in the world and once more engage in sexual relations with her husband.

This joyous religious ceremony was followed by as great a celebratory feast as a family could manage. At the lower end of the social scale, celebrants would adjourn to the local tavern for hours of eating and drinking. The elaborate and sometimes raucous revelries caused the town of Leicester to pass regulations in 1568 to control churching celebrations: 'For the eschewing of the superfluous charge and excess of the inhabitants... there shall be no feasts made at any churching within the said town saving only one competent mess of meat provided for gossips and midwives'.[2]

The revelry was amplified by the fragility of life in a world where childbirth was perilous for both mother and baby. In the absence of medical knowledge and general sanitation, the postpartum mother was vulnerable to infections that frequently led to sepsis and death. Wealth and rank offered no protection, as the death of Isabel Neville after giving birth to Clarence's son would soon remind the nobility. Even fifty years later, all the Tudors' potency could not save Jane Seymour, who died after delivering Henry VIII's long-awaited son. Royalty offered no immunity to childbed fever.

Equally problematic was the creation of a healthy newborn child, in an era when prenatal care was nonexistent. A diet of meat and ale failed to provide vitamins and minerals essential to healthy babies. The wives of Edward IV's brothers, Clarence and Gloucester, suffered several miscarriages and stillborn babies and together produced only three children who survived the perils of birth and early childhood. Two generations later, multiple miscarriages, three stillborn babies and two infant deaths cost Catharine of Aragon both her husband and her crown. The miscarriages of Anne Boleyn led to accusations of witchcraft, treason, and ultimately to the executioner's axe.

The birth of a healthy, beautiful royal child, therefore, was cause for special jubilation. And no one knew how to celebrate better than Edward IV. He would announce to the world that the Yorkist dynasty had begun. The timing was propitious, since the Queen's churching coincided with a visit to England by a group of Bohemian travellers, who could spread the news throughout Europe on their way home! Even without the visitors, the King of England would have planned a churching and banquet for his Queen that displayed the English court in all its plenitude and promise.

The Bohemian visitors recorded their wonder and awe at the wealth and ceremony they encountered throughout all of England. The travel diary of Gabriel Tetzel of Nuremberg, part of the retinue of Leo, Lord of Rozmital, who was brother to the Queen of Bohemia, fairly quivers with hyperbolic compliments: 'We saw with what extraordinary reverence [the King] was treated by his servants. Even mighty counts had to kneel to him... The King is a handsome upstanding man and has the most splendid court that could be found in all Christendom'.[3] Tetzel was equally impressed with the Queen's churching:

> The Queen left her child-bed that morning and went to church in stately order, accompanied by many priests bearing relics and by many scholars singing and carrying lights. There followed a great company of ladies and maidens from the country and from London, who had been summoned. Then came a great company of trumpeters, pipers, and players of stringed instruments. The king's choir followed, forty-two of them, who sang excellently. Then came twenty-four heralds and pursuivants, followed by sixty counts and knights. At last came the Queen escorted by two dukes. Above her was a canopy. Behind her were her mother and maidens and ladies to the number of sixty. Then the Queen heard the singing of an Office, and, having left the church, she returned to her palace in procession as before. Then all who had joined the procession remained to eat. They sat down, women and men, ecclesiastical and lay, each according to rank, and filled four great rooms.[4]

The Bohemian visitors were conducted into the King's hall, where the nobles, but not the King, were dining. There were

> …carvers, buffets and side tables in profusion… Everything was supplied… in such costly measure that it is unbelievable that it could be provided… While we were eating, the King's gifts were distributed among his trumpeters, pipers, jesters and heralds, the heralds alone receiving 400 nobles. All those who had received gifts went about the tables crying out what the King had given them.[5]

After the nobles had eaten, the visitors were conducted to 'an unbelievably costly apartment where the Queen was preparing to eat'. Tetzel's description of that dinner caused much damage to Elizabeth's subsequent reputation:

> The queen sat alone at table on a costly golden chair. The Queen's mother and the King's sister had to stand some distance away. When the Queen spoke with her mother or the King's sister, they knelt down before her until she had drunk water. Not until the first dish was set before the Queen could the Queen's mother and the King's sister be seated. The ladies and maidens and all who served the Queen at table were all of noble birth and had to kneel so long as the Queen was eating. The meal lasted for three hours. The food which was served to the Queen, the Queen's mother, the King's sister and the others was most costly. Much might be written of it. Everyone was silent and not a word was spoken. My lord and his attendants stood the whole time in the alcove and looked on.
>
> After the banquet they commenced to dance. The Queen remained seated in her chair. Her mother knelt before her, but at time the Queen bade her rise. The King's sister danced a stately dance with two dukes, and this, and the courtly reverence they paid to the Queen, was such as I have never seen elsewhere, nor have I ever seen such exceedingly beautiful maidens. Among them were eight duchesses and thirty countesses and the others were all daughters of influential men. After the dance the King's choristers entered and were ordered to sing. We were present when the King heard mass in his chapel. My lord and his company were let in and I do not think that I have heard finer singing in this world...[6]

Malcolm Letts, the translator of this account, comments: 'Elizabeth Woodville's head must have been turned by her sudden elevation in rank. I have sought in vain for confirmation of this picture of extravagant etiquette at this time'.[7] Harsher critics have jumped to conclusions about Elizabeth's hauteur, extravagance and arrogance, pointing especially to her own mother kneeling before her.

Such conclusions ignore both the elaborate rituals of the English court and the religious significance of churching the Queen who had just produced the first Yorkist heir to the throne. Kneeling before the Queen was not unusual, as indicated by Raffaelo de Negra's letter to the Duchess of Milan in 1458. In describing Margaret of Anjou's court, he lists nine noblemen in attendance, then reports:

> Their wives are at Court also, and when the wife of the Duke of Petro a Baylito, the king's son, and all the duchesses speak to the queen, they always go on their knees before her.[8]

Instead of criticising Queen Elizabeth for her mother's kneeling, critics might note that 'at time the Queen bade her rise', perhaps in consideration for her mother's discomfort and a desire to release her from ritualistic requirements. To place such ceremony firmly in its medieval context, it is useful to note Tetzel's report of a subsequent dinner at the home of two earls who served 'an indescribably splendid meal with sixty courses according to their custom'. Medieval ceremony defies modern comprehension. When George Neville was enthroned as Archbishop of York in 1465, his banquet required sixty-two cooks to prepare a dinner of

> one hundred and four oxen, six wild bulls, a thousand 'muttons', three hundred and four 'veals' and as many 'porks', two thousand pigs, more than five hundred stags, bucks, and roes, a dozen porpoises and seals, four hundred swans, a hundred and four peacocks, two thousand geese and as many chickens, a hundred dozen quails, four thousand pigeons, and many other unlucky birds and beasts... while the jellies and tarts and custards numbered thirteen thousand.[9]

This food was washed down with three hundred tuns of ale, a hundred tuns of wine, and a pipe of hippocras. [The pipe of spiced wine amounted to about 125 gallons.] As another instance, Margaret of Anjou's journey to England for her marriage to Henry VI cost £5,563 17s 5d for the fifty-six ships filled with provisions of men and supplies, including 'five barons and baronesses, thirteen knights, forty-seven esquires (each with his own valet), eighty-two valets, twenty sumptermen, and others'.[10] Seven trumpeters announced exits and entrances. A lion was added to the Queen's collection of exotic animals in the Tower of London. A new hall was built at Eltham Palace for the scullery, saucery and serving areas, and a new gatehouse and garden wall were added at Sheen Palace. Westminster Palace was remodelled, including the Great Chamber, the Queen's Lodging, the Parliament Chamber and the Painted Chamber. A coronation scaffold was erected in Westminster Abbey. Money spent on jewels and clothing alone for Margaret's coronation amounted to £7,000.[11]

Pomp, circumstance and splendour have always defined British royalty – to the great delight of commoners, nobles and critics alike. And the birth of Elizabeth of York in 1466 mandated an extraordinary and symbolic display of Edward IV's dynastic power. Queen Elizabeth would give birth to ten royal children, but this first deserved a very special ceremony.

Had the Bohemian visitors known that the newly born Lady Princess Elizabeth would marry King Henry VII and give birth to the Tudor dynasty, they might better have appreciated the gratitude and respect that honoured her mother. The blood of this newborn child flows in the veins of every subsequent English monarch – even until today. In retrospect, the grand celebration after the churching of the baby's mother seems merely appropriate.

CHAPTER NINE

Fun, Games and Politics at Court

Ayear would go by before another magnificent occasion excited all of England. Just before the Queen's coronation, her ladies-in-waiting had set in motion a chivalric tournament when they tied a gold collar around the thigh of her brother, Anthony, Lord Scales, and asked him to issue a challenge to a worthy opponent. Anthony's challenge was accepted by 'Messire Antoine Bastard de Bourgougne, Comte de la Roche en Ardenne', more popularly known as the Bastard of Burgundy. Wars on the continent delayed the event, but by spring 1467 both opponents were ready for the encounter. Edward had used the intervening years to develop ideas about his foreign policy, and now he shrewdly used the tournament to strengthen England's alliance with Burgundy.

The Comte de la Roche, an illegitimate son of Philip the Good, Duke of Burgundy, enjoyed a status and stature in northern Europe second only to his legitimate brother, Charles, Count of Charolais. Bastardy was neither disreputable nor degrading on the continent, where Philip's many illegitimate children enjoyed high status at court, received their own livery of grey, and collected generous allowances from the richest duchy in Europe. The Duke's illegitimate daughters married high nobles of the duchy, and his bastard sons achieved influential positions in the court, the military, and especially the Church.

The most illustrious and erudite of Philip's bastards was Anthony, Comte de la Roche. Renowned for his military prowess, he was made Knight of the Golden Fleece in 1456. His stipend of £3,840 in 1462 allowed him to patronise the arts by augmenting his impressive collection of illuminated manuscripts, even while leading a crusade on behalf of Philip. The crusade ended after the death of Pope Pius II in 1464 and never went beyond the south of France, but the Bastard exemplified the chivalrous knight of medieval legend by serving both his lord and his Church in war and peace.[1] In later years, he would become a loyal member of his brother's court, with custody of the ducal seal and key to the ducal bedchamber.[2]

The tournament with Anthony, Lord Scales was delayed because the Bastard was fighting in a civil war between King Louis XI of France and the Dukes of Burgundy and Brittany. During that conflict, Edward IV negotiated with both France and Burgundy to increase trade with England, playing the two powerful states against each other politically and economically. The London merchants preferred a close alliance with Burgundy, a lucrative market for their cloth trade and a source of money from the financial centres of Bruges and Lille. At the same time, France also offered great commercial potential. The residual hatred of the English for the French and Edward's proclaimed title as 'King of France', however, created barriers to an alliance with France. The French civil war ended with Louis XI gaining the upper hand, although Burgundy and Brittany retained much of their power and even gained territory ceded by Louis XI to achieve peace.

With the war concluded, the games could begin. Edward IV, ever the politician, used the magnificent festival of pomp and pleasure to display England's wealth and civility to this influential Burgundian knight. The splendid event so caught the popular imagination that every contemporary chronicler mentioned it. Sir John Paston, an ever-enterprising and upwardly mobile lawyer from Norfolk, commissioned a detailed account for his edification and records. Probably written by Thomas Whiting, Esquire, Chester Herald, the narrative gives us a ringside seat to observe the elaborate rules and rituals that governed medieval tournaments, from the initial challenge to the jousting on the tilting field.

Comparable to the modern Olympic Games in promoting national pride and popular interest, this tournament involved as much politics as fun and games. Edward IV co-ordinated the event with the opening of Parliament, thus assuring that all estates were present in London to witness England's splendour after six years of Yorkist rule. The Bastard of Burgundy arrived at Greenwich on Saturday 30 May 1467, accompanied by 400 'noble lords, knights, squires and others'.[3] The Constable of England, with a flotilla of seven barges and a galley filled with 'lords, knights, squires, and many aldermen and rich commoners of the City of

London', escorted the Bastard from Greenwich to the City, where the Bishop of Salisbury housed him and his retinue at his London home in Fleet Street and his country house in Chelsea.

On Tuesday 2 June, the King rode from his palace at Sheen towards the city, where he was met two miles outside of London by 'many Princes, Dukes, Earls, Barons, Knights, Esquires, the Mayor, Aldermen, Sheriffs, and Commoners of the City,... Kings of Arms, also Heralds and Pursuivants in coats of arms... with the sound of clarions, trumpets, shawms and other'. The Constable carried the King's staff of office on the right hand with the Earl Marshall on the left. Anthony, Lord Scales, bore the King's sword between the two. The group rode to St Paul's, where the King was met by a 'procession solemn of bishops, many mitered, with incense' who escorted him to the altar where he made an offering.

From St Paul's, the procession rode through Fleet Street with Anthony, Lord Scales bearing the sword before the King. Sensing that the Bastard of Burgundy was watching, Anthony 'turned his horse suddenly and beheld him, the which was the first sight and knowledge personally between them'. The procession rode on to Westminster, where Parliament began the next day.

On 3 June, the Bastard attended the opening of Parliament in the Painted Chamber at Westminster, where he and Lord Rivers, representing his son Anthony, asked the King to set the date for the tournament. The King consulted his counsellors, scheduled the games to begin on St Barnaby's Day, Thursday 11 June 1467, and recessed Parliament from the Wednesday before until the Monday after, so that all could attend. The King then commanded the Constable of England to marshal the Kings of Arms and Heralds in providing lists for the combat. The Mayor and sheriffs of London prepared a tilting area in Smithfield ninety yards long and eighty yards wide, surrounded by a fence with posts sunk three feet into the ground and extending seven feet high. Between the posts ran three rails, each five inches wide and three-and-a-half inches thick, details carefully specified by the King's orders.

At one side was the King's box, from which he judged the combatants. Olivier de la Marche of the Burgundian party describes the King's *maison* as very great and spacious, ascended by steps to the upper part where the King sat with his counsellors and friends. Below him on both sides of the steps sat the knights, then the esquires, then the archers of the crown.

At the foot of the steps sat the Constable and the Marshall who imposed order and controlled the crowd. On the opposite side of the lists was a box for the Lord Mayor and aldermen of London.[4] John Stow, a sixteenth-century historian, adds that 'faire and costly galeries [were] prepared for the ladies and other', but he does not indicate where.[5] *The Great Chronicle* states that the Queen attended along with 'most of the great estates of this land'.[6] At this point, Elizabeth was seven months pregnant with Edward's second child.

In keeping with the splendour of the occasion, Anthony, Lord Scales made his official entrance to the city as the nation's champion on Friday. Arriving by barge from Greenwich, he was met at St Katharine's beside the Tower of London by the Constable, Marshall, Treasurer, and a host of other nobles, knights and squires. Riding on horseback and wearing a long gown of 'rich cloth of gold tissue', with a herald and pursuivant carrying his coat of arms before him, he arrived at the home of the Bishop of Ely in Holborn, where he stayed temporarily. On 10 June, he moved to St Bartholomews near Smithfield to spend the night, this time accompanied by a retinue of dukes, earls, barons, knights, squires and minstrels.

As the games began, the field was prepared for the King's entrance by setting a guard at every other post around the field and a King of Arms at every corner. The King, wearing purple robes and the Garter on his thigh, carried his staff of office as he ascended to his box. 'Truly he seemed a person well worthy to be King, for he was a very fine Prince, and tall, and well mannered', wrote Paston's scribe.[7] An earl stood at the King's side holding the sword before him, and twenty or so counsellors, 'all with white hair', gathered around him. After the King was seated, the Mayor, aldermen, and 'persons of the law' entered. The Mayor's sword of office was borne before him but pointed downwards, in respect, as the procession passed the King. All kneeled to salute the King on their way to the Mayor's box at the opposite side of the lists

Anthony, Lord Scales entered next, preceded by the Duke of Clarence and the Earl of Arundel, each carrying a helmet. The weapons of the day, two spears and two swords, were borne by the Earl of Kent, Lord Buckingham, Lord Herbert and Lord Stafford. After asking and receiving permission from the Constable and Marshall, Anthony entered the lists on horseback, followed by nine richly-dressed horses. He 'came before the King's highness and did him reverence as appertained', then retired to his pavilion constructed in the south-east corner of the field, to await the start of the jousting.

The Chester Herald's account describes this pageantry in great detail. Anthony's own horse wore trappings 'of white cloth of gold, with a cross of Saint George of crimson velvet, bordered with a fringe of gold half a foot long'. His second horse was trapped in tawny velvet 'accomplished with many great bells'. The third had russet damask to his feet, with two heraldic markings worked in gold; the fourth wore purple damask decorated 'with gentlewoman's girdle enforced with goldsmith's work, bordered with blue cloth of gold and half-foot broad and more'. The fifth was trapped to the foot in blue velvet, with pleats of crimson satin along the trapper, worked with gold and bordered with green velvet. The sixth's cloth of gold crimson was bordered for a foot and a half with fine sable fur. The green, foot-length trappings of the seventh horse were decorated with 'the attire of gentlewomen of France in gold, bordered with russet cloth of gold a half-foot wide'. The eighth wore tawny damask. The ninth horse splendidly concluded the parade with a long trapper of ermines, bordered with crimson velvet and tassels of gold. Pages mounted on each horse wore mantles of green velvet, 'embroidered with goldsmith's work, richly made'.[8]

The pavilion to which Anthony retired was made of 'double blue satin, richly embroidered with his letters'. A banner of his arms flew from the top, with a total of eight banners flying from his tent. St George's banner flew beside the King's tent, and banners depicting the arms of other lords flew from every other post around the field.

The entrance of the Bastard of Burgundy was equally splendid. The horse he rode wore crimson trappings hung with silver bells alternating with gold. A second horse carrying his arms was led by four knights. The third wore trappings of foot-length ermine, with reins of fine sable. The fourth wore leather trappings covered with cloth of gold. The fifth was covered with crimson velvet to the feet, and was decorated with a device of eyes filled with teardrops, in goldsmith's work. The sixth wore cloth of silver and fine purple to the feet. The seventh's green velvet was decorated with 'barbacans richly made'. The eighth was trapped 'in fine sables to the foote', with reins of ermine. His pages wore gowns of velvet, with two pleats in white and 'one yellow garnished with goldsmith's work'. The Chester Herald may scant the Bastard of Burgundy's retinue, for Olivier de la Marche mentions twelve horses and a small tent to which he retired, while the English scribe states that the Bastard had no pavilion but armed himself in the open. The rich and colourful pageantry of both accounts still build excitement today.

As the knights prepared for battle, the Constable and Marshall forbade the crowd from approaching the lists during the jousting and from making

> …any noise, murmur, or shout, or any other manner token or sign whereby the said right noble and worshipful lordes and knights which this day shall do their armes within these lists, or either of them, shall move, be troubled or comforted, upon pain of imprisonment and fine and ransom at the King's will.[9]

The silence of a golf match, rather than the raucous cheering of a football game, accompanied this contest of champions.

After such splendour, the jousting itself was almost anticlimactic. In the first encounter, each rider on horseback ran towards the other with lance aimed at his opponent. Accounts vary, but apparently both champions missed their marks on the first run. The second contest was fought on horseback with swords. In the close fighting, Anthony first struck the Bastard on the neck and received in turn a blow on the helmet. But the horses collided and the Bastard's horse fell to the ground with his rider. The accounts differ regarding the cause of the collision. *The Great Chronicle* reports that the bay courser of the Bastard ran into a steel spike on the harness of Anthony's grey courser that 'struck the blind horse so sharply in the nostrils that with pain of that stroke he mounted so high that he fell with his master in the field'. A steel spike would have violated the rules of chivalry and discredited Anthony. The Chester Herald contradicts that report, stating that Anthony 'rode straight and light before the King, and made take off his trapper, showing that his horse had no chamfron [armour] nor piercer of steel'. The Burgundian Olivier de la Marche also exonerates Anthony:

> Monsieur the Bastard fell under his horse, with his sword in his hand. And quickly the King of England made them raise him up; and he [the Bastard] showed himself much enraged against the said Lord Scales, for that he thought that he had committed falseness in the furniture of his horse: yet he had not, but this stroke and this fall happened by mischance.[10]

The rules of combat allowed the Bastard a fresh horse, but the King decided that the day's games should conclude at that point.

The second day of combat took place on foot, with weapons of casting spears, axes and daggers. The ceremonies began with another procession of horses in trapped finery and pages wearing their gold embroidered garments. The King forbade fighting with spears, however, saying that he 'would not have no such mischievous weapons used before [him]'. In the combat with axes, Anthony, Lord Scales struck the first blow and rapidly gained the advantage:

> But when the king saw that the Lord Scales had advantage of the Bastard, as the point of his axe in the visor of his enemy's helmet, and by force thereof was likely to have borne him over, the King in haste cried to such as had the rule of the field that they should depart them and for more speed of the same, cast down a warder which he then held in his hand. And so were they departed to the honour of the Lord Scales for both days.[11]

The Chester Herald adds that no more than three or four strokes were exchanged before the King 'with high voice cried *Whoo!*'

Edward IV clearly did not want his political overtures to Burgundy ruined by an English victory over Burgundy's champion. The combatants were brought before the King:

> He commanded each to take other by the hands and to love together as brothers in arm; which they did. And there they immediately gave each to other as courteous goodly and friendly language as could be thought and went together into the middle of the field and so departed each man to his lodging.[12]

Jousting between lesser knights continued for three more days, with the English continuing to win the honours. Meanwhile, the King settled down to the more serious business of strengthening England's ties with Burgundy. Following the second day's combat, Edward IV and Elizabeth hosted a banquet at the Mercer's Guildhall which suitably impressed Olivier de la Marche: 'I assure you that I saw sixty or four-score ladies, of such noble houses that the least was the daughter of a baron. And the supper was great and plentiful; and Monsieur the Bastard and his people feasted greatly and honourably.'

Edward may have chosen the Mercer's Company as the site of the celebration because of its extensive cloth trade with Burgundy. Their foreign agent, William Caxton, had been a pivotal figure for the past thirty years in negotiating contracts between merchants, and would soon become even more important as Edward sought more personal connections between the two courts. The King's supper served its purpose in winning the Bastard's goodwill, and he reciprocated in kind: 'Monsieur the Bastard prayed the ladies to dine on Sunday, and especially the Queen and her sisters; and he made a great rout and a great preparation.'

All festivities abruptly ended, however, when word arrived that the Duke of Burgundy had died on 15 June. The Bastard immediately departed for home to support his brother Charles, the new Duke of Burgundy. The groundwork laid by Edward in hosting the tournament between Anthony, Lord Scales and the Bastard of Burgundy would soon begin to pay off. In late 1465 or early 1466, Charles, while still Count of Charolais, had proposed a marriage between himself and Margaret of York, the nineteen-year-old sister of Edward IV. The marriage had been delayed in part because Margaret had been promised, if not betrothed, to Don Pedro of Portugal, but now that Charles was the Duke of Burgundy, marriage to him became quite desirable.

Not everyone agreed. Warwick, Edward's powerful cousin, preferred an alliance with France, an alliance he had first tried to arrange through the marriage of Edward IV to Lady Bona of Savoy. When Edward chose Elizabeth Wydeville instead, Warwick experienced his first public humiliation at the hands of the King. Warwick had not given up, however, and even as the tournament between Anthony and the Bastard of Burgundy proceeded, he was in France discussing economic treaties with Louis XI. Gifts lavished on the English ambassadors and marriages plotted to strengthen the Anglo-French alliance persuaded Warwick that he was the centre of power.

Edward, who clearly preferred the Burgundian alliance, knew that he had to diminish Warwick's personal and political influence. While the Earl was in France, George Neville, Archbishop of York and Chancellor of England, represented Warwick and the family interests. On 8 June, just three days before the tournament began, Edward, with his brother Clarence and eleven other men, rode to George Neville's residence at Charing Cross and demanded that the Chancellor surrender the Great Seal of England. The personal presence of the King during this encounter was extraordinary. Moreover, Edward IV stayed until the Seal was delivered, emphasising his presence and authority. Making that point even more emphatic, the next day Edward concluded a treaty with Brittany, another traditional antagonist of France, promising English assistance in case of enemy attack.

Edward was clearly aligning England with Burgundy and Brittany against France, a point that the tournament between Anthony, Lord Scales and the Bastard of Burgundy symbolically demonstrated to the entire nation. For the first time, Edward was strong enough to challenge the power of the Nevilles: he had stabilised the economy, brought peace to the nation, and cultivated powerful supporters to counteract the wealth and popularity of his powerful Yorkist cousins. Prominent among his supporters were the Wydeville family members.

Indeed, the Wydevilles were becoming as central to the Yorkist court as they had been to that of Henry VI. Elizabeth's father, Lord Rivers, was appointed Treasurer of England on 4 March 1466, and created Earl Rivers on 24 May of that year. On 24 August 1467, his appointment as Constable of England provided an annual income of £200, plus 'all other accustomed profits'. At his death, the office would revert to his son, Anthony, Lord Scales, for life. Following the tournament, Anthony's stature and prestige could not have been higher in both popular and courtly circles. Combined with Jacquetta's connections to the Burgundian court, the Wydevilles were now significant players in helping Edward develop commercial and political ties between England and Burgundy.

Curiously, David MacGibbon, one of Elizabeth's biographers, slanders the Queen in blaming her for what was happening: 'Like *la Pompadour* after her, Elizabeth made her influence felt even in the foreign policy of the time, and it would appear that more credit should be given to her for the Burgundian Alliance and all that it entailed than has hitherto been the case.'[13] '*La Pompadour*', a rhetorical slur Elizabeth does not deserve, ignores the political and economic context in which Edward made his decisions.

The London merchants definitely preferred the Burgundian alliance, which they hoped would lift trade barriers against English cloth. Further, the nation as a whole retained a residual distrust, if not hatred, of the French after 100 years of war. Proof that Edward ignored Elizabeth's desires when he wished lies in his appointment of Hastings, instead of Anthony, to become Captain of Calais, a position that Anthony desired. The King also sought and followed advice from his council in ways that J.R. Lander shows has been 'unduly underestimated'.[14]

Perhaps most importantly, Edward IV knew that Warwick's influence had to be thwarted. Warwick took credit for placing Edward on the throne, even though the Earl's disastrous defeat at the second battle of St Albans almost lost the entire war. It was Edward's victory at Mortimer's Cross, his march to London and declaration as King, and his heroism at Towton that gained the upper hand for York. The Earl's overweening ego, however, could not tolerate a position secondary to his young cousin.

Edward IV recognised Warwick's preference for France and took actions during the Parliament and tournament of 1467 to thwart it and to establish the King's personal authority. Edward had sent Warwick to France to discuss the marriage of Margaret of York to Philip of Bresse. Whether he timed the trip to remove Warwick from London while the Burgundians were in town is unclear. That was, however, the result. In France, Warwick and his entourage of 300 men received a munificent welcome from Louis XI. His negotiations were so successful that Louis offered to cover all costs of Margaret's wedding, including her dowry, and to award Edward IV a pension.[15] Louis also gave Warwick presents fit for a king: a gold cup encrusted with gems, and the keys to the city of Honfleur. Such magnificent honours from a King encouraged Warwick to think that he himself should be one.

When Warwick returned on 24 June puffed up with preference and presents, he expected to be quite the man of the hour in London. Instead, he found his brother dismissed as Chancellor, the marriage of Margaret to Charles of Burgundy almost a certainty, and Anthony Wydeville, Lord Scales, the nation's champion knight. Just as George Neville's removal as Chancellor was a very public power play, so was the King's humiliating treatment of Earl Warwick. Twice now in his French negotiations for royal brides, Warwick had been pre-empted – and he blamed the Wydevilles.

Nearing the age of forty, the Earl saw himself being replaced by a younger generation. Attractive, cultured, erudite men – and even worse, women – were winning their positions through merit, rather than birth. The older man, so proud of his royal blood, could not tolerate such political and personal insults from those whom he regarded as upstarts. The Warwick-Wydeville antagonism thus leapt another giant step towards its inevitable clash. Temporarily outmanoeuvred, Warwick retreated to his Middleham estates in the north, where his resentment festered into revenge. It was only a matter of time before Earl Warwick would renew the Cousins' Wars.

CHAPTER TEN

Enemies Within

Soon after the tournament, the Queen retired to Windsor to await the birth of the second royal heir. Her mother, the Duchess of Bedford, joined her on 16 July, and the second princess, Mary, was born at Westminster on 12 August 1467. On 9 October 1468, the King granted Elizabeth £400 a year to support their two daughters, Elizabeth and Mary, who lived at the Palace of Sheen under the governance of Margaret, Lady Berners.[1] Elizabeth's royal duties included visits throughout the realm, where the citizens welcomed her warmly. Over the years, the city of Coventry, in particular, developed a special relationship with the Queen, one that began in December 1467 when the Mayor and citizens greeted her visit with a gift of 100 marks.[2]

Elizabeth's brother, Anthony, Lord Scales, now became one of the King's most trusted and successful ambassadors. When Edward IV appointed a team of negotiators to finalise the marriage contract between Margaret and the Duke of Burgundy, it was headed by Anthony, Lord Scales, and included the Bishop of Salisbury, Lord Hastings and several mercantile representatives. This new embassy set off in September 1467 to complete the complicated business deal, which included issues of defence, trade, currency exchange, fishing rights and travel. The bargaining moved rapidly enough for Edward to announce the marriage to his council at Kingston-upon-Thames on 1 October.

The Wydeville family connections to Burgundy made them natural ambassadors, and the King began to reward Elizabeth's siblings with small favours. In August 1467, Sir William Bourchier and his wife Anne (the Queen's sister) received £100 yearly from the royal manor lands.[3] In July, Elizabeth's brother Lionel, a clerk, was granted 'all issues of the arch-deaconry of Norwich'[4], and in November Anthony was granted for life the custody of the King's castle and town of Porchester and governance of the town of Portsmouth.[5]

As the Wydevilles thrived, Warwick nursed his anger in the north. Not only had the Earl failed in his efforts to promote France over Burgundy, but he was now displaced as the pre-eminent English ambassador. *The Croyland Chronicle,* whose author was a member of the King's Council and in a position to know, attributes the cause of the increasing alienation between Edward IV and Warwick to the Burgundian alliance:

> This, in my opinion, was really the cause of the dissensions between the King and the Earl, and not the one which has been previously mentioned – the marriage of the King with Queen Elizabeth. For this marriage of the King and Queen (although after some murmuring on the part of the Earl, who had previously used his best endeavours to bring about an alliance between the King and the Queen of Scotland, widow of the King of that country, lately deceased), had long before this been solemnly sanctioned and approved of at Reading, by the Earl himself, and all the prelates and great lords of the kingdom.
>
> Indeed, it is the fact, that the Earl continued to show favour to all the Queen's kindred, until he found that her relatives and connections, contrary to his wishes, were using their utmost endeavours to promote the other marriage, which, in conformity with the King's wishes, eventually took place between Charles and the Lady Margaret, and were favouring other designs to which he was strongly opposed.[6]

Not until a reconciliation was negotiated by Warwick's brother, the Archbishop of York, and the Queen's father, Earl Rivers, did Warwick return to the court in January 1468. He was sufficiently mollified to lead Margaret of York's procession when she departed for her new home in Burgundy on 18 June 1468. The procession out of London was grand. First stopping at St Paul's Cathedral to make an offering, Margaret mounted her horse with the Earl of Warwick riding before her and other earls, barons, duchesses, ladies and gentlewomen following. The Mayor of London and the aldermen met her and presented her with a 'pair of rich basins, and in the said basins a £100 of gold'.[7] The first evening she lodged at the abbey of Stratford where the King and Queen were also staying. Then Margaret and her large entourage departed for the shrine of St Thomas of Canterbury, before boarding their ships.

Once embarked, the Wydevilles dominated the English contingent accompanying Margaret. Anthony, Lord Scales and Sir John Wydeville sailed aboard Margaret's ship.[8] In Bruges, Margaret's chief presenter was Anthony, whose continental manners learned at his mother's knee smoothly bridged any divide between the two cultures. Both Wydeville knights participated in the wedding tournament, and after nine days of feasting and fighting, Sir John Wydeville was declared the Prince of the Tournay. Lord d'Argueil, brother of the Prince of Orange, was named Prince of the Joust as the wedding celebrations concluded in diplomatic, as well as marital, harmony.[9]

Problems were developing in England, however. Edward had difficulty in raising Margaret's first dowry payment of 50,000 crowns and ultimately had to secure a bond from merchants and prominent citizens. The honour of contributing to the elaborate royal marriage somewhat cooled national enthusiasm for the enterprise. At one point, the marriage bond was placed at risk by the arrest of Sir Thomas Cook, a principal guarantor, for treason. As long as Margaret of York was in the country, she protected Sir Thomas for helping to secure her marriage bond, but after Margaret arrived in Burgundy, Cook was rearrested.

Until this charge of treason, Sir Thomas, a former Lord Mayor and current alderman, had received great favours from Edward, including his creation as Knight of the Bath at the Queen's coronation. Details of his case are incomplete and the witnesses not always objective, but the Queen and her family have been long and loudly vilified for their part in his prosecution. The most detailed account of the incident appears in *The Great Chronicle* of London whose author identifies himself as Sir Thomas's apprentice at 'about the age of 17 or 18 years and thereabouts' when the trouble began. The author's close relationship to the accused provides details otherwise unrecorded, but it also assures his partisanship toward Sir Thomas.

The story began when John Hawkins, a servant of Lord Wenlock, approached Sir Thomas Cook to request a loan of 1,000 marks. When Sir Thomas asked for whom and what the money would be used, Hawkins disclosed that it was intended for Queen Margaret of Anjou. That exiled Lancastrian Queen! Well aware of the treasonous waters in which he was treading, Sir Thomas denied the loan, even though Hawkins reminded him of Queen Margaret's earlier favours in appointing Cook as her 'wardrober' and making him a 'customer of Hampton to his great advantage'. Hawkins dropped his request to £100, but Sir Thomas sent him away empty-handed.

Hawkins continued his Lancastrian subversions and was arrested two or three years later, taken to the Tower, and tortured for information about other traitors. Among the King's counsellors who questioned Hawkins were Earl Rivers (Treasurer and Constable of England) and Sir John Fogg (Treasurer of the King's Household and husband of the Queen's cousin Alice Haute). When Hawkins implicated Sir Thomas Cook, the alderman was immediately arrested and sent to the Tower. The jury that tried Sir Thomas in July 1468 included Clarence, Warwick, Rivers, Sir John Fogg and other members of the council. *The Great Chronicle* did not commend the process:

> The Mayor being a replete and lumpish man sat for Chief Judge and slept, where-fore the Duke [Clarence] sitting upon his Right hand seeing his misdemeanour said openly in his derision, 'Sirs, speak softly for the Mayor is on sleep.'[10]

Sir Thomas was acquitted of treason by this jury, but as Charles Ross points out, such juries always resisted convicting one of their own: 'The legal records themselves show that, whilst the London juries of presentment were willing to indict known Lancastrian agents, such as Hawkins, whose evidence under torture involved Cook, they would not accept charges of treason against prominent and respectable London citizens.'[11] Cook was acquitted but not freed, and another jury was appointed.

Sent to prison at the King's Bench in Southwark, Cook successfully petitioned to be released into the custody of Sir Robert Brandon, whom he paid 'for his board and bedding'. His wife joined him at Sir Robert's lodgings, since their own house had been confiscated by the crown. When the house was restored to the wife, she found it heavily damaged:

> [The wife] with her friends got again the possession of her own place, the which she found in an ill pickle, for such servants of the Lord Rivers and of Sir John Fogg as were assigned to keep it made such havoc of such wine as was left. In the cellars that what they might not drink and give away, they let run in the cellar, and sundry pipes that they had broached to chose the best, they suffered to stand open vented and lost thereby the wine of sundry vessels which were so pallid that they came to no good. So that by these means eight of nine tuns of Gascony wine lying in one cellar were lost, and over that much stuff of household, as well bedding and other, was bribed and lost.[12]

Worse havoc occurred at Sir Thomas's estates in Essex where his deer, rabbits and fish were destroyed 'without reason', and the house spoiled 'without pity, so that brass, pewter, bedding, and all that they might carry was riffled clean, for the which might never after one penny be gotten in recompensement'.

Efforts to free Sir Thomas continued into 1469, by which time the writer of *The Great Chronicle* specifically blames the Wydevilles for his former master's troubles. He mentions the displeasure of the Duchess of Bedford 'which ever was extremely against the said Sir Thomas, and all was because she might not have [a] certain arras at her pleasure and price belonging unto the said Sir Thomas'.[13] Jacquetta may indeed have admired the arras, which was 'wrought in most richest wise with gold of the whole story of the Siege of Jerusalem, which I heard the foreman of my Master's say that it cost in barter when my said master bought it £400'. But to blame the Duchess of Bedford and an arras for the troubles of Sir Thomas seems a bit far-fetched.

Sir Thomas was ultimately freed when his offence was reduced from treason to misprision (concealment of treasonable activity). The value of his losses while jailed was deducted from his fine of £8,000, and he 'came again to his own dwelling place, and builded and purchased as he did before'.

Queen Elizabeth entered the story when she tried to collect her share of Cook's fine through a provision allowed 'by a statute made of old time' known as 'Queen's Gold', a 10% assessment added to fines paid to the King. This traditional assessment dates at least to the twelfth century, when Eleanor of Aquitaine obtained most of her income from Queen's Gold. In recent years, however, it had become harder and harder to collect. Queen Margaret of Anjou had little success: her account books for 1452–3 record fifty-nine assessments of Queen's Gold, several of which were unpaid after eight years and forty-three still uncollected. Elizabeth improved on Margaret's record by collecting ten of eleven claims in 1466–7.[14] Four queens later, Anne Boleyn was still collecting *aurum reginae* in 1534.[15]

Elizabeth's pursuit of the 'Queen's gold' in the Thomas Cook case has become primary evidence of her 'greedy and grasping' character. What has been overlooked, however, is the fact that the Queen forgave the fine. According to *The Great Chronicle*, Sir Thomas sued for dismissal of the assessment, and 'by the favour of one master page, then solicitor unto the Queen, had his end, how well there was no open speech of it after'. Although Fabyan's *Chronicle* claims that the fine was paid, the greater detail of *The Great Chronicle* makes it a more reliable source, especially in light of the partisanship of its author. His concluding statement about the Queen forgiving Cook's fine resonates ironically even today: 'there was no open speech of it after'.[16]

Even worse, too many historians have ignored the context of the times in which the Cook episode occurred. In 1468, treason was afoot and advancing in England. Queen Margaret was inciting incursions across the always insecure Scottish border, and Lancastrian supporters were fomenting rebellion within. Warkworth's *Chronicle* lists the annual threats in succinct order: in the fifth year of Edward's reign, the rebellion of the Earl of Oxford and his son Lord Aubrey (both executed); in the sixth year, Lord Hungerford's treason; in the seventh, Thomas Cook, John Plummer and Humphrey Howard's arrests. Warwick's rebellion and Margaret's invasion would soon prove the dangers imminent and real.

Further, if Sir Thomas was not guilty of treason, he was certainly guilty of not reporting Hawkins's efforts on behalf of Queen Margaret, a treasonable act. Indeed, Sir Thomas's Lancastrian leanings were more substantial than he admitted during his trial of 1468. When Henry VI was restored to his throne in 1470, Sir Thomas prominently appeared among his supporters. During the November Parliament that disinherited Edward IV and proclaimed him 'usurper of the Crown', Cook requested restitution of his property:

> Sir Thomas Cook then being one of the knights of the shire for London... made him more busy than was for his advantage, for he being an excellent and well-spoken man and a profoundly reasoned, showed in the open Parliament of the great wrongs and losses that he had sustained for the fidelity that he bare unto King Henry and Queen Margaret, and required restitution of 22,000 marks that he had lost by force of the foresaid wrongs.[17]

Other London officials were more circumspect during the Lancastrian readeption. The Mayor, for instance, feigned illness rather than minister his office. But 'the said Sir Thomas casting no perils executed the uttermost of his power to the hurt and indemnity of such as he knew bore any favour unto King Edward'. His former apprentice reports the consequences: 'He repented full sore after'.[18]

King Edward's advisors rightly pursued, therefore, Cook's involvement in Lancastrian plots. Lord Rivers, as Treasurer and Constable of England, and Sir John Fogg, as Treasurer of the King's Household, appropriately investigated the factions endangering the King – actions that, of course, provoked anger and resistance from the accused and their advocates.

In its partisanship, *The Great Chronicle* not only supports Cook, but clearly and explicitly favours Warwick. In reporting that 'many murmurous tales ran in the City atween the Earl of Warwick and the Queen's blood', the writer reveals why Warwick was the popular choice of so many people:

> …by reason of the exceeding household which he daily kept in all countries where-ever he sojourned or lay, and when he came to London he held such a house that six Oxen were eaten at a Breakfast, and every tavern was full of his meat, for who that had any acquaintance in that house, he should have had as much sodyn [boiled meat] and roast as he might carry upon a long dagger...[19]

The well-fed commoners happily believed the slanderous tales about the Queen and her relatives disseminated by Warwick's propaganda: bribery too frequently buys loyalty. But tales told by partisans should not be permitted to distort historical truth.

Such tales typify the methods that have demeaned the Wydeville reputations. Another infamous example, concocted several generations later, blamed Elizabeth Wydeville for the execution, on 14 February 1468, of Thomas FitzGerald, 7th Earl of Desmond. During the reign of Henry VIII, the grandson of Desmond petitioned the Privy Council for restoration of the manor of Dungarvan, by presenting a memoir that accused Queen Elizabeth of causing his grandfather's death. The Desmond affair offers several sorry insights into how unfounded claims create historical reputation.

The Earl of Desmond, Deputy Governor of Ireland, was a somewhat hapless administrator whose defeat in an expedition against County Offaly jeopardised English control of the Pale. Edward IV replaced Desmond with the Earl of Worcester, a notoriously mean-spirited and violent administrator, who convened the Irish Parliament at Drogheda to attaint and subsequently execute Desmond. More than seventy years later, Desmond's grandson claimed that the Earl's execution occurred because Queen

Elizabeth was angry with Desmond for urging Edward IV to annul his marriage and to find a more appropriate foreign bride. In revenge, the Queen stole the King's signet ring, sealed an execution order for Desmond, and sent it off to Ireland.

Although this story first appeared in a grandson's memoir written two generations after the events in 1464, it was included by David MacGibbon in his 1938 biography of Elizabeth:

> A striking example of Elizabeth's influence over Edward is to be found in her treatment of Thomas FitzGerald, 7th Earl of Desmond, who, in 1463 had been appointed Deputy Governor of Ireland. Desmond *is said* to have told the King that he ought to divorce Elizabeth and marry some foreign princess whose connexions would help stabilise his throne. When in May 1467 the Earl of Worcester was made Deputy Governor in Desmond's place*, it was commonly reported* that Worcester's new office had been obtained for him by the Queen, who intended through him to avenge herself on Desmond… In everything he did in Ireland Worcester *appears to have been acting* for Elizabeth, *who is said to have* secretly procured a privy-seal warrant for Desmond's arrest and execution.[20]

Passive verbs lacking attribution turn rumour into fact. While MacGibbon's footnotes cite Desmond's grandson as the source of this slander, along with a note that 'G.H. Orpen disputes the authenticity of this episode in *The English Historical Review*', the footnote cannot undo the damage done by the text. Neither does MacGibbon fairly represent Orpen's clear exoneration of Elizabeth:

> The story will not bear examination… Earl Thomas [Desmond] had many enemies in the anglicized regions about Dublin, who resented his Irish methods, had repeatedly accused him of illegalities (*Statute Roll 3 Edw. IV*, p. 96; *Annals of Duald MacFirbis*, p. 253), and feared his great influence with the 'Irish enemy'. Moreover, his recent rule had been disastrous. Irish writers inform us that in 1466 the earl was taken prisoner by O'Conor Faly, that the country from Naas to Tara was repeatedly plundered by the Irish, and that the earl had purchased peace from O'Brien by a concession of lands and an annuity. The attainder is grounded on treasons committed by the earl 'as well in alliance, fosterage, and alterage with the Irish enemies of the king, as in giving them horses and harness and arms and supporting them against the king's faithful subjects'.[21]

Thomas, Earl Desmond, hardly needed Elizabeth Wydeville to cause his demise, but his grandson needed someone to blame. And Elizabeth Wydeville, long dead, could not defend herself. In 1974 Charles Ross, Edward's biographer, dismissed the accusation as a 'Tudor fabrication', and Anne Sutton and Livia Visser-Fuchs have soundly refuted it in their account of Elizabeth as a 'most benevolent Queen'. Yet the legend lives on in the false reputation of Elizabeth as a 'cold and calculating woman'.

Instead, while the Cook and Desmond affairs were ongoing, Queen Elizabeth was pursuing her many charitable and educational interests. In 1468, she visited the Queen's College at Cambridge, the institution she had rescued after Margaret's defeat. During that visit, she would have seen the Old Court of red brick buildings very much as it appears today. Completed in 1448–9, this medieval college was the first where students could live, study, eat, sleep and worship within its walls. Elizabeth would have entered the College through the east gatehouse, where the figures of St Bernard and St Margaret still decorate the bosses. Directly ahead were the dining hall and kitchens. To the left, students lived in residence halls, and to the right they worshiped and studied in the chapel and library. President Doket would have welcomed her to his lodgings in the corner between the library and dining hall.

By the time of this visit, Elizabeth had been Queen four years and Margaret had been deposed for seven years. In continuing patronage to the College begun by her benefactor and her mother's close friend, Elizabeth must surely have reflected on the hand that fortune deals the 'sex feminine' – and humanity in general.

As the decade of the 1460s drew towards its end, the Queen and her family were serving their King and country in ways that benefited its commerce and its educational and religious institutions. The presence and power of the Wydevilles was undeniable. At one point, Edward's fool, whose wit made him a favourite of the King, appeared in court one hot, dry summer day wearing long boots and carrying a walking staff. When the King inquired why he was dressed so inappropriately for the season, the fool replied, 'Upon my faith, Sir, I have passed through many counties of your realm, and in places that I have passed, the Rivers been so high that I could hardly scape through them.' The King laughed at the joke about 'Lord Rivers and his blood'.[22]

Those displaced by Lord Rivers and his family were not, however, amused. The Yorkist nobles who saw their former Lancastrian enemies reap rewards became increasingly resentful, angry and vindictive. Warwick, the King's cousin who flaunted his 'blood royal', took particular umbrage at this family so recently converted to the Yorkist cause. In plotting his return to power, the Earl sought to discredit the Wydevilles. His propaganda spread to the continent when Luchino Dallaghiexia described the Queen as 'a widow of this island of quite low birth' in a letter to the Duke of Milan.[23] The Italian correspondent deplores Elizabeth's influence with details he could have obtained only from an informant:

> Since her coronation she has always exerted herself to aggrandise her relations, to wit, her father, mother, brothers and sisters. She had five brothers and as many sisters, and had brought things to such a pass that they had the entire government of this realm, to such an extent that the rest of the lords about the government were one, the Earl of Warwick, who has always been great and deservedly so.[24]

His endorsement of Warwick perhaps identifies the source of Dallaghiexia's information. At the least, he had been talking to those displaced by the Queen's family.

Warwick strengthened his position by soliciting support from the King's brother, George, Duke of Clarence, who similarly resented his own loss of prestige and power. Within months, the two joined forces and attacked Edward IV, the Yorkist King whose throne Warwick had helped win. Instead of York fighting Lancaster, the battles turned inward. The Yorkist brothers and cousins took up swords against each other. The family feud turned into another bloody war.

CHAPTER ELEVEN

War Within the Family

Earl Warwick was irrevocably alienated from Edward IV by the treaty with Burgundy and the growing influence of the Wydevilles. He blamed the Queen and her family for Edward's foreign policies and for the personal estrangement developing between himself and his cousin the King. No matter that Warwick was the one harbouring – and nurturing – his resentments and that Edward himself felt no animosity towards his cousin. Indeed, the King apparently remained oblivious to Warwick's growing hatred. The personal passions and political aspirations of Warwick would, however, dominate the next several years of Elizabeth's life. She would have to live with Warwick's ambition and murderous rampages against her family every day for the next four years.

Older than the King by fourteen years, Warwick had always believed he was better able to rule England than the handsome boy addicted to self-indulgent pleasure and games. At the age of forty, Warwick realised that time for achieving his dream was growing short. The Earl, who was so proud of his 'blood royal', traced his lineage to John of Gaunt, who had sired four children by Katherine Swynford while still married to Constance of Castile, children subsequently legitimised by Richard II. Although Henry IV specifically excluded Beaufort descendants from succession to the throne, they retained all other royal privileges and the sons occupied important positions in the court of Henry V. Gaunt's daughter Joan Beaufort married Ralph Neville, 1st Earl of Westmoreland, and their nine children built enormous fiefdoms through shrewd marriages and skilful politics.

Since Ralph Neville's son from his first marriage inherited the title and rights of Westmoreland, the eldest son from his Beaufort marriage made his way in the world by marrying Alice, daughter and heir of the Earl of Salisbury, and inheriting his father-in-law's title. Their eldest son, also named Richard, similarly married well to Anne Beauchamp, heiress of the Earl of Warwick, from whom he inherited his title. The youngest Neville daughter, Cecily, married Richard, Duke of York and grew into the formidable Duchess of York who tried to stop her son from marrying Elizabeth Wydeville. Warwick and Edward IV were first cousins, with Edward claiming the throne as a descendant of Lionel, Duke of Clarence, an older brother of John of Gaunt.

Without question, Warwick's power, money and political skills had helped his young cousin gain his footing as the leader of the Yorkist faction. After the death of the Duke of York at Wakefield on 30 December 1460, Warwick sent reassuring letters to Burgundy and France to control damage done to the Yorkist cause. His leadership was not flawless, however, and he almost lost everything at the second battle of St Albans. Warwick's personality was that of the classic bully, and now that he was not getting his way, he openly defied the King.

Warwick began by suborning the King's brother George, Duke of Clarence. As Steward of England, Clarence had led the procession at Queen Elizabeth's coronation and had ridden beside the King when George Neville was removed as Chancellor. But by 1469, Clarence, too, had become disaffected. Personally miffed by the glory heaped on Anthony Wydeville, and generally discontented with his diminished influence at court, he aligned himself with Warwick, who returned to Calais to build a powerful military base as captain of that crucial port.

Edward did not comprehend the depth of Warwick's hatred and hostility. In June 1469, the King began a progress through East Anglia on pilgrimage to Bury St Edmunds and the shrine at Walsingham. Elizabeth, who had given birth to their third child, Cecily, on 20 March, did not accompany him, but met him at Fotheringhay Castle in late June or early July. On 7 July, Edward left Fotheringhay for the north where Lancastrian rebels were causing disturbances. Elizabeth prepared to fulfil a promise Edward had made to the town of Norwich where he had told its citizens that he would return for another visit, this time with the Queen. With Edward in the north, Elizabeth planned to visit alone with her small children.

John Aubrey, Mayor of Norwich, wrote to Sir Henry Spelman, the City's Recorder in London, on 6 July 1469, to inquire about receiving and entertaining the Queen during 'her first coming hither'. The Sheriff of Norfolk had told Mayor Aubrey that 'she will desire to be received and attended as worshipfully as ever was Queen afore her'. Those words have often been quoted as proof of Elizabeth's demanding arrogance, even though they emanated from the sheriff who was cautioning an admittedly naive fellow administrator to be appropriately ceremonious in receiving royalty. The Mayor, clearly pleased to be hosting the Queen, wanted her visit to reflect credit on the city of Norwich and asked Sir Henry to return home for the occasion: 'and I trust in God, that either in rewards, or else in thankings, both of the King's coming, and in this, ye shall be pleased as worthy is'.[1]

The Mayor, who well knew that entertaining a Queen was no trivial affair, wanted his city to do it right. Pageants had to be written and performed, stages erected, decorations purchased and musicians engaged. Reports of the visit indicate that the people warmly welcomed their Queen, who was a good sport not only in carrying out her husband's wishes, but in ignoring the unpleasant weather.

The Mayor took great pains in his preparations. He sent a man named Lyntok to Windsor to gather information about the Queen's plans. Finding that she was not at Windsor, Lyntok made subsequent trips to Bury St Edmunds and to 'divers parts of Norfolk' to learn of the Queen's progress. Robert Horgoner rode out to find the road the Queen would take, and John Sadler followed to tell the Queen's servants to enter the city by 'Westwyk Gates'.[2] Parnell and his servants from Ipswich were hired for twelve days as consultants to prepare the pageants and ceremonies. A freemason was paid 6d to repair the crest of the conduit on the north side of St Andrew's churchyard.

When the Queen entered Norwich on 18 July through Westwick Gate, the 'Corporate Body' received her. A stage had been built, covered with red and green worsted, and decorated with figures of angels, scutcheons and royal banners. Two giant figures of wood and leather, stuffed with hay and crested with gold and silver leaf, were placed on stage. The angel Gabriel (played by a friar) greeted the Queen, along with two patriarchs, twelve apostles, and sixteen virgins in mantles with hoods. 'Gilbert Spirling exhibited a pageant of the Salutation of Mary and Elizabeth, which required a speech from him in explanation.' Clerks sang accompanied by organs.

The Queen next visited the house of the Friars Preachers, where a second pageant on another newly built stage greeted her. The Friars Minor had lent their 'Tapser work' to cover this stage, along with vestments for the pageant. The great chair of St Luke's Guild had been moved from the cathedral for the Queen's comfort while listening to the singing of Mr Fakke's choir of boys. Unfortunately, heavy rains cut short the ceremonies, forcing the Queen and her small daughters to their lodgings at the Friars Preachers. The dignitaries and performers rushed to the Guildhall, where they changed to dry clothes. Workers scrambled to move stage coverings and ornaments to a house near Westwick Gates, but much damage had already been done. The bills for using the articles included extra allowances for damage.

This inauspicious beginning to the Queen's visit was followed by devastating news. While the Queen was at Norwich and the King at Nottingham, Clarence and Warwick strengthened their alliance through Clarence's marriage to Warwick's daughter, Isabel. Both men had much to gain from the union. Warwick moved his family a step closer to the throne of England, since Clarence was the next male in the Yorkist line as long as Edward had no sons. In addition, Clarence had his eye on the enormous fortune of land and money Isabel would inherit from her father.

Several problems had delayed the marriage. As first cousins once removed, Clarence and Isabel required a papal dispensation to marry. Edward IV had earlier forbidden the marriage, knowing the political danger it would constitute to his own children, and had directed the Pope not to approve it. But Warwick had his own means of influencing the Pope, who granted a dispensation on 14 March 1469. In July 1469, while Edward IV was in the north, Clarence crossed to Calais and married Isabel, the ceremony conducted by George Neville, Archbishop of York, brother of Earl Warwick and uncle of the bride.

The day after the wedding, Warwick, with the support of Louis XI of France, returned to England with Clarence. They gathered forces in Kent and marched north, where they captured Edward IV on 29 July 1469, while he was making his way back to London.[3] First imprisoned in Warwick Castle, Edward IV was soon moved north to Middleham in Yorkshire, the ancestral home of the Nevilles. Warwick's men captured the Queen's father, Earl Rivers, and her brother, Sir John Wydeville, near Chepstow in the Welsh Marches. Rivers and Sir John were taken to Coventry where, on 12 August 1469, they were beheaded without a trial.[4] The horrifying news that her beloved father and brother had been murdered reached Elizabeth while she was still residing in Norwich.

Elizabeth had been married to Edward IV just five years. She had given birth to three daughters: Elizabeth in 1466, Mary in 1467, and Cecily in 1469. Warwick's hatred for her family took its revenge through murder. The widows left by this outrage were Jacquetta, Duchess of Bedford, and Katherine Neville, Duchess of Norfolk and aunt to both Warwick and Edward IV. Worse would come.

A document dated 12 July 1469 fulminates with hatred for the Queen's family. Issued in the names of 'The Duke of Clarence, the Archbishop of York, and the Earl of Warwick', it cites

> …the deceivable, covetous rule and guiding of certain seditious persons: that is to say, the Lord Rivers; the Duchess of Bedford, his wife; Sir William Herbert, Earl of Pembroke; Humphrey Stafford, Earl of Devonshire; the Lords Scales and Audeley; Sir John Wydeville, and his brothers; Sir John Fogg, and other of their mischievous rule, opinion, and assent, which have caused our said sovereign Lord and his said realm to fall in great poverty of misery, disturbing the ministration of the laws, only intending to their own promotion and enriching.[5]

Here lies the source of the slander that has created the myth of the 'grasping, greedy' Wydevilles. In a political document crafted by rebels – Clarence, Warwick and the Archbishop of York – the Wydevilles were accused of motives that have become enshrined in the historical record. Blaming the Wydevilles of 'intending… their own promotion and enriching', the screed goes on to claim that they had no concern for the commonweal of the land, 'but only to their singular lucre and enriching of themselves and their blood'.[6]

The document is obsessed with the concept of blood heritage and compares the reign of Edward IV to the historical precedents of Edward II, Richard II and Henry VI:

> First, where the said Kings estranged the great lords *of their blood* from their secret Counsel, and not advised by them; and taking about them others *not of their blood*, and inclining only to their counsel, rule, and advice, the which persons take not respect nor consideration to the weal of the said princes, nor to the commonweal of this land, but only to their singular lucre and enriching of themselves *and their blood*, as well in their great possessions as in goods; by the which the said princes were so impoverished that they had not sufficient

of livelihood nor of goods, whereby they might keep and maintain their honourable estate and ordinary charges within this realm.[7]

Warwick's claim that he was impoverished to the point that he 'had not sufficient of livelihood nor of goods' to maintain his estate would be laughable if its consequences were less deadly. To that blatant lie he adds the accusations that the Wydevilles caused England's excessive taxes, change of the coinage, diversion of money from 'our holy father' (the Pope), and the general lawlessness of 'great murders, robberies, rapes, oppressions, and extortions.' He then returns to his recurring obsession with blood relationships:

> Also the said seditious persons have caused our said sovereign lord to estrange the true lords of his blood from his secret Counsel... The said seditious persons above named... by their subtle and malicious means have caused our said sovereign lord to estrange his good grace from the Counsels of the noble and true lords of his blood...[8]

Resonating with resentment at Edward's preference for his wife's family over his own, the document clearly reveals the authors' intent and technique. The rebels intended to annihilate the Wydevilles – those whose veins carried merely the blood of an English nobleman and a European duchess. Their technique exploited slander and unproved accusations, lies they would repeat until frequency conferred validity. Their logic began with false premises and their rhetoric rationalised murder. The executions of Rivers and Sir John Wydeville marked merely the beginning of Warwick's schemes.

In August, Queen Elizabeth left Norwich and returned alone to London, where she kept 'scant state' with her three small daughters.[9] The next attack focused on her mother, Jacquetta, who was accused of witchcraft. Earlier allegations that Jacquetta had used charms to bewitch Edward IV into marrying Elizabeth had been forgotten. Now, in 1469, the Duchess of Bedford was officially charged by Thomas Wake, Esquire, with practising witchcraft and sorcery. The evidence provided by Wake was 'an image of lead made like a man of arms of the length of a man's finger broken in the middle and made fast with a wire'.[10] Her accuser tried to suborn John Daunger, parish clerk of Stoke Brewerne in Northampton, into claiming that two other images made by Jacquetta were intended to destroy the King and the Queen (her beloved daughter!).

Charges of sorcery were not trivial and had been used against royal women with great effect in the past. When the men of the family were too powerful to attack head-on, their more vulnerable women became victims. In 1419, Joan of Navarre, Queen Dowager of Henry IV, was accused of witchcraft and briefly imprisoned. More infamously – and malevolently – Eleanor Cobham, wife of Humphrey, Duke of Gloucester, had been charged in 1441 with using witchcraft to shorten the life of Henry VI.

Jacquetta and Eleanor Cobham were sisters-in-law while Jacquetta was married to the Duke of Bedford. Eleanor was arrested in the same year that Sir Richard Wydeville defended England's honour at Smithfield against the challenge of Pedro de Vasquez of Spain, and the two events dominated London news for the year.[11] The Duchess of Bedford must have followed Eleanor's trial closely, not only as a former in-law but as a member of Henry VI's court. Convicted of sorcery, the Duchess of Gloucester was sentenced to the public penance of walking barefoot through the streets of London on three designated market days when the maximum number of shoppers, tradesmen, citizens and visitors would witness her humiliation.

Whether Jacquetta and her four-year-old daughter, Elizabeth Wydeville, watched the three astonishing parades is unknown, but they could not have avoided hearing the sensational accounts. On each day of her penance, Eleanor was brought by barge from Westminster to a London landing where she was met by the Mayor, the sheriffs, and the craftsmen of London. On Monday 13 November 1441, she landed at Temple Bar, where two knights led her, dressed in black and carrying a two-pound lighted candle, as she walked barefoot along Fleet Street to St Paul's Cathedral, where she offered her taper at the high altar. On Wednesday 15 November, she landed at the Swan on Thames Street and walked barefoot through Bridge Street, Grace Church Street, East Cheap, and on to Christ Church at Aldgate. On Friday 17 November, she walked from Queen Hithe along Broad Street to Cheapside and St Michael's Church at Cornhill. Eleanor was then imprisoned until her death sixteen years later. First sent to Chester, she later was moved to Kenilworth and the Isle of Man. Eleanor Cobham died at Beaumaris Castle in North Wales on 7 July 1452, still in captivity.[12]

Among Eleanor's convicted accomplices, Thomas Southwell, a canon of St Stephen's Chapel at Westminster, had the good fortune to die in the Tower. Roger Bolingbroke, an Oxford priest, was hanged, beheaded, disembowelled and quartered. His head was spiked above London Bridge, and the four quarters of his body disbursed to Hereford, to Oxenford, to York and to Cambridge, to warn their citizens against sorcery. Margery Jordemaine, the 'Witch of Eye', was burned at Smithfield.

Twenty-eight years later, the Duchess of Bedford faced the same charges. But Jacquetta had both personal and political allies. Recalling her visit to Queen Margaret after the second battle of St Albans – the meeting that saved London from Lancastrian pillaging – the Duchess asked the Mayor and aldermen of the city to intervene. The investigation proceeded, but even though her accuser Thomas Wake could not persuade John Daunger to corroborate his testimony, Jacquetta's fate remained unresolved. The entire experience must have terrified Queen Elizabeth. She was alone in London with three daughters, aged three years, two years, and five months. Her husband imprisoned, her father and brother murdered, and her powerful, elegant mother charged with sorcery, the Queen could not have been more vulnerable.

Warwick's initial success faded after Parliament refused to support his coup. The London merchants and citizens, afraid that commerce with Burgundy would suffer, began to riot, and the Duke of Burgundy prepared to defend his wife's brother. As Edward IV gathered supporters at Pontefract and began to reassert his authority, Warwick freed him from imprisonment on 10 September 1469. By the end of the year, Edward IV returned to London where he once more ruled as King.

Edward commanded that the charges against Jacquetta be examined by the Bishop of Carlisle, the Earl of Northumberland, Lord Hastings, Lord Mountjoy and Master Roger Radcliff. At the hearing, Thomas Wake testified that he had received the lead image from John Daunger, who admitted sending it to Wake at his request but insisted that 'he heard no witchcraft of the Lady of Bedford'. The two men fell to accusing each other, and the investigating council cleared the Duchess of Bedford of 'the said slander' on 19 January 1470. The King's Great Council endorsed that action in the Parliament chamber on 10 February.[13] The six months between accusation and exoneration, however, must have been harrowing for both Jacquetta and Elizabeth.

Cecily Neville, Duchess of York, then threw her considerable influence into reconciling the brothers and cousins. Edward IV, for reasons hard to discern, issued a general pardon that brought Clarence back into the family fold and aligned Warwick once more with Edward IV's court. Edward naively tried to appease his older cousin by betrothing the three-year-old Lady Princess Elizabeth to Warwick's nephew. The liaison did not come close to satisfying Warwick's overweening ambition, and even while pretending loyalty, he began plotting his next coup.

Rebellion broke out almost immediately in Lincolnshire. When both Warwick and Clarence were implicated, Warwick fled to Calais in April 1470. As he passed through Wiltshire, his men captured Anthony Wydeville and John, Lord Audley, sending them to the Castle of Warder to await execution. But a Dorset man named John Thornhill learned of their capture and during the night 'with a good company of hardy fellows…found the means to deliver these two Lords from captivity'.[14]

Edward IV, finally suspicious, ordered that Warwick not be admitted to the port of Calais. The defenders of the city followed their King's order, stunning Warwick, who had dominated the region for so many years. While his ship lay off the coast deciding where to go, a storm arose that brought tragedy to his family. Among the passengers was his daughter Isabel, who gave birth in the midst of the storm to a stillborn child fathered by Clarence.

Ultimately Warwick's ship landed in Honfleur, where the Earl sought out the French King, Louis XI. Having burned his English bridges, Warwick now committed the unthinkable. On Louis XI's urging, Warwick and Clarence aligned themselves with Margaret of Anjou. The Earl of Warwick and the Duke of Clarence, cousin and brother of the first Yorkist King, plotted to restore the Lancastrian Henry VI to the throne of England. The way these Yorkist warriors turned their coats to Lancastrian colours defies ordinary comprehension.

Queen Margaret was rightly suspicious of the Yorkist traitors and resisted their initial proffers of assistance:

> Up to the present the queen [Margaret] has shown herself very hard and difficult, and although his Majesty [Louis XI] offers her many assurances, it seems that on no account whatever will she agree to send her son [Prince Edward of Lancaster] with Warwick, as she mistrusts him. Nevertheless it is thought that in the end she will let herself be persuaded to do what his Majesty wishes.[15]

To allay Margaret's suspicions and provide a guarantee of loyalty, Warwick's youngest daughter, Anne, was proposed as a wife for Prince Edward of Lancaster, an alliance that, not incidentally, moved Warwick close to the Lancastrian throne. Warwick had apparently forgotten the rumours of Edward's bastardy that circulated at his birth in 1453. Margaret's chancellor, Sir John Fortescue, writes in his notes presented to Louis XI:

> The marriage will take place between the Prince of Wales and the daughter of the Earl of Warwick. By means of which marriage the said Earl of Warwick and his friends will live in security and the said earl will have the principal role in government of the kingdom; and by favour of him and the friends and loyal subjects of King Henry, the queen and the prince will be able to enter more easily into the kingdom.[16]

As Clarence discovered to his dismay, the agreement between Margaret and Warwick moved him further away from any crown. As brother to King Edward IV, he had a much better chance of obtaining the throne than as brother-in-law to the Lancastrian heir, Prince Edward, now married to Warwick's daughter Anne. Ever the slow learner, however, Clarence transferred his support to the House of Lancaster and plotted to invade England to regain the crown for Henry VI.

In the midst of such turmoil, it is amazing to learn that some business as usual was transpiring in England. Whether Queen Elizabeth or the ever-vigilant President Andrew Doket brought the needs of Queens' College to Edward's attention, the King issued a pardon to the college on 1 September 1470. The pardon covered

> …all offences committed before 25 December 1469, with the proviso that it should not extend to his enemy Henry VI, late *de facto*, but not *de jure* king of England, nor to Margaret his wife, nor to Edward son of the said Margaret, nor to any persons who were with Margaret and Edward out of England, or who adhered to them.[17]

The pardon implies that the College had supported Warwick, or at least had accommodated itself to the rule of the rebels while Edward was imprisoned in the north. Clearly, someone was watching over the interests of Queens' College and interceded to secure its pardon at a time when the King was focused on restoring his power and authority. The logical intercessor would be his Queen, responding to the request of President Doket. The respite would be short-lived, however.

Late in July, Edward accompanied his troops north to Yorkshire to quell a rebellion led by Warwick's brother-in-law, Henry, Lord Fitzhugh. For safety, he moved Elizabeth and their daughters to the Tower. While Edward was still in the north, Warwick and Clarence landed their Lancastrian troops at Dartmouth and Plymouth in mid-September 1470. Warwick announced his support for Henry VI, gathered around him Lancastrian supporters in Devon and Cornwall, marched to London, and freed the hapless Henry VI from his long sequestration in the Tower.

Edward IV, outmanoeuvred and outmanned, received word that his own capture by Warwick's supporters was imminent. Leaving Doncaster with a small band of followers, the King almost drowned while crossing the Wash. Arriving at King's Lynn, they secured ships through the influence of Anthony Wydeville, who had property in the area, and set sail for Holland on 2 October 1469. The King was accompanied in exile by his brother Richard, Duke of Gloucester; his best friend and chamberlain, William, Lord Hastings; and the Queen's brother, Anthony Wydeville, who now carried his dead father's title, Earl Rivers.

Word of Edward's plight reached Elizabeth in the Tower. Eight months pregnant with their fourth child, the Queen recognised her extreme vulnerability. The day before Edward sailed off to exile, Elizabeth gathered her family and fled into sanctuary in Westminster Abbey.

CHAPTER TWELVE

Elizabeth in Sanctuary

S urvival of her family depended on Elizabeth. Her husband and her brother Anthony (now head of the Wydeville family) were in exile, her father and brother John murdered. Warwick's intentions were luminously clear. In the dark of night on 1 October 1470, the Queen left the Tower with her children and boarded a barge that rowed the small group up river to sanctuary at Westminster Abbey.[1] The Duchess of Bedford joined her there, while the Bishop of Ely and others entered sanctuary at St Martin's.[2]

Sanctuary was a right guaranteed by the medieval church to anyone who needed protection from secular powers. Criminals athwart of the law could enter a church, register in the sanctuary book, and escape further pursuit. Murderers, common thieves and debtors commonly used sanctuary to escape punishment for their misdeeds, causing distress among their victims who could not pursue justice as long as the criminal stayed within the church's boundaries. London merchants particularly disliked sanctuary, since it protected felons and debtors, but the privilege usually prevailed, with canon law asserting its power over secular authority. The kings of England, as anointed representatives of God, traditionally supported sanctuary, and Richard II had affirmed the rights in 1388. Only the crimes of sacrilege and treason were not protected by sanctuary.

Queens seldom sought sanctuary not only because they could retreat to fortified palaces such as the Tower, but because chivalric tradition generally preserved royal women from execution. The decision of Queen Elizabeth to join the motley crew in sanctuary at Westminster Abbey indicated not only the extraordinary mayhem in the nation, but her profound distrust of Warwick. Fortunately, the compassionate and courageous Abbot Thomas Millyng became her protector.

The exact quarters where the Queen lived during her first sequestration in Westminster Abbey are unknown, but if she resided in one of the fifty or sixty tenements within the sanctuary grounds, her home was dark, cramped and surrounded by a hubbub of cacophonous sounds and noxious smells that would intimidate any modern visitor. The area known as sanctuary lay just north and slightly to the west of the main door to the abbey's nave, bounded by a path aptly named 'Thieving Lane', since thieves were led that way to the gatehouse.[3] The Great West Gate leading outside to Tothill Street was nearby, next to the Almonry and its public latrine, whose stench was so overwhelming that it made renting the adjacent shops difficult.[4] The marshy land surrounding the abbey created drainage problems, although it provided running water for the washerwomen who plied their trade in Long Ditch, which forked off Thieving Lane.

Within the sanctuary area, residents lived side-by-side with shops set up to serve the extensive enterprise that constituted the medieval abbey, with its fifty or so monks, 100 servants, and countless visitors. The 400 residents at nearby Westminster Palace kept business especially brisk, a commercial advantage that the printer Caxton exploited in 1488–9 when he moved to a new stall between the abbey and the palace.

On Fridays and religious feast days, fishmongers set up shop within the North Gate to sell oysters, mussels and fresh fish delivered from London or brought by local fishermen from the nearby Thames. Indeed, the shop-keepers – butchers, brewers, bakers, tailors, barbers/bloodletters, carpenters, smiths, tavern keepers – may have been preferable neighbours to the horse thieves, counterfeiters, heretics, beggars, bankrupts and debtors who sought refuge in sanctuary.

The monks had realised the commercial potential of their valuable property early on and by 1400 rented houses in Westminster Sanctuary for 'upwards of £80 a year', an amount that had decreased by mid-century because of a national recession caused by the plague and by decreased immigration.[5] The monks had recently begun leasing their land to developers, who built and maintained the tenements rented for profit. In 1475, Robert Powle, a chandler, leased 'a row of eight old tenements in the sanctuary', with the promise that he would build seven new ones within four years. Entrepreneur Powle actually added ten new tenements on the site, which measured only 112 foot by 28 foot 7 inches. Each residence, built on a footprint of 10 by 20 feet, included a cellar, a ground floor (frequently used as a shop), and a kitchen above.[6] If the Queen lived

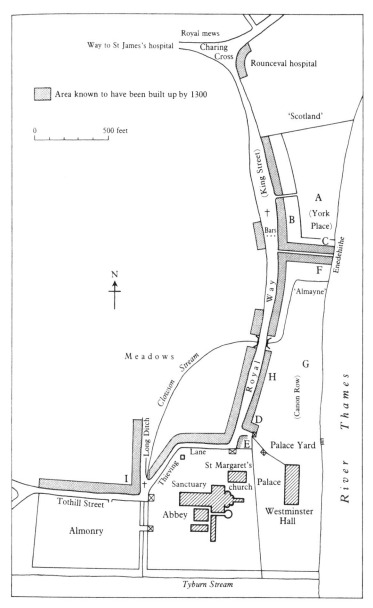

Medieval Westminster, c.1300. The sanctuary was situated just north of the main door to the abbey's nave.

elsewhere than these typical sanctuary quarters, the tenements were just around the corner and the Almonry, with its latrine, was next door.

From sanctuary, the Queen attempted to defend her husband's rights while tending to the needs of her three tiny children and awaiting the birth of her fourth. Elizabeth sent Abbot Millyng to the Mayor and aldermen of London, asking them to take command of the Tower in the name of the King. The City Council's minutes reveal that Elizabeth feared that Warwick's men would invade Westminster sanctuary and 'despoil and kill her'. The citizens of London were no match, however, for the rebels invading from Kent, and they soon surrendered the Tower. They managed only to secure an agreement allowing residents to seek sanctuary before the rebels took it over.[7]

Immediately after Warwick's men seized the Tower, they released Henry VI from his quarters there, an imprisonment that had lasted five years. John Warkworth describes the King as 'not worshipfully arrayed as a prince and not so cleanly kept as should seem such a prince'. The rebels 'new arrayed' Henry VI and took him to Westminster Palace where, on 15 October, he was restored to his crown. The King was totally dependent on Warwick and little more than a puppet. In one of the minor ironies of these wars between cousins, Henry VI returned to the Tower and moved into the quarters that had been prepared for Queen Elizabeth to give birth to her fourth child.

Though no longer Queen, Elizabeth and her daughters did not want for basic necessities. A London butcher provided half a beef and two muttons a week to sustain her household. Neither was she without attendants. Henry VI's council appointed Elizabeth, Lady Scrope, to wait on Elizabeth and paid her a salary of £10. On 2 November 1470, with her husband in exile, Elizabeth gave birth to a son, a birth assisted by midwife Marjory Cobbe and physician Dominic de Serigo. Perhaps Elizabeth had brought these trusted attendants with her into sanctuary. Margaret Cobbe, wife of John Cobbe, had received a grant of '£10 yearly for life' on 15 April 1469, following the birth of Cecily, and would receive another lifetime grant for £10 on 8 November 1475, indicating long-term and dedicated service to the Queen.[8] Dominic de Serigo had been present at the birth of her first daughter. Characteristically, Elizabeth would have planned ahead when facing the harrowing and dangerous ordeal of giving birth in such unknown quarters and uncertain circumstances.

The newborn baby was christened Edward after his father in a cere-mony in Westminster Abbey. Abbot Millyng and the Abbey Prior stood as godfathers, with Lady Scrope as the prince's godmother. No one could know that the inauspicious beginnings of this newborn baby would also foretell his end. At this bleak moment in Elizabeth's life, the child's very arrival on earth must have provided his mother with her one glimmer of hope. She had produced a male heir for the Yorkist throne.

The next six months were spent in Westminster Close, where mother, newborn son, and three daughters under the age of four were largely confined within their rooms. Communications between Holland and England were uncertain, and from her sequestration inside the Abbey Close, Elizabeth must have wondered about the future for her husband, herself and the four children under her care. She drew comfort from her knowledge that Edward IV was in Burgundy where his sister Margaret of York was the Duchess.

Margaret's husband, Charles the Bold, was not pleased, however, with hosting a penniless, deposed King whose presence complicated his own uneasy relations with France, where Margaret of Anjou and Edward, Prince of Wales, were living in exile. Edward IV and his few followers were housed at the Hague under the care of Louis, Lord of Gruuthuyse. Their poverty was so great that Richard of Gloucester had to borrow money to pay for his personal expenses, and Gruuthuyse had to send men into the countryside to catch rabbits for their food.

Fearing outright war with France, Charles the Bold and Margaret kept their distance from the English exiles, although Charles sent money to cover their expenses and Margaret sent secret letters via messengers. Louis XI, exultant in his renewed alliance with Lancastrian England, declared open war with Burgundy on 3 December 1470. At that point, Charles was forced to support Edward IV, who was finally invited to join the Burgundian court at Hesdin. Charles and Edward IV met on 2 January to plan an invasion of England, funded by a £20,000 grant from Burgundy. Three days later, Duchess Margaret met her two brothers, Edward IV and Richard, and began to take an active role in gathering support for them. At her request, merchants and bankers in Flanders, Holland and Zeeland lent money and ships to the expedition. On 24 February, five Dutch towns approved a loan of 6,000 florins to 'my gracious lady of Burgundy and the King Edward of England, her brother, if my gracious lord [Charles] will approve'.[9]

The seven months spent in the Low Countries produced unexpected benefits for the English exiles. Edward IV and his brother-in-law Anthony, Earl Rivers encountered the artistic and literary renaissance already underway in this most erudite of European duchies. Their host, Lord Louis of Gruuthuyse, owned one of the finest libraries in Europe, which after his death was bought by Louis XII of France and ultimately became the basis of the French Royal Library. Bruges was a centre for the bookmaking business, an enterprise in which Edward's sister Margaret took great delight. Duchess Margaret had hired William Caxton, the English governor of the Merchant Adventurers at Bruges, to supervise her financial and commercial dealings, and when she learned that he was translating Lefevre's *Recueil des Histoires de Troie* into English, she asked to read it. A learned and cultured woman, Margaret's excellent knowledge of French and English immediately caused her to correct parts of Caxton's text. Caxton writes rather charmingly in his prologue:

> …anon she found a default in mine English which she commanded me to amend and moreover commanded me straightly to continue and make an end of the residue then not translated. Whose dreadful commandment I durst in no wise disobey because I am a servant unto her said grace and receive of her yearly fee and other many good and great benefits and also hope many more to receive of her highness…[10]

Anthony, Earl Rivers met Caxton while visiting Margaret in early 1471, a relationship that would flourish in just a few years to the great benefit of England. During this sojourn in Burgundy, Edward IV, too, became interested in books and resolved to build his own library. That would have to wait, however, until he regained his throne.

In early March, Edward IV boarded the *Anthony*, a ship belonging to a brother-in-law of Gruuthuyse who was an Admiral in the Burgundian navy. A small fleet of thirty-six ships set sail for England. Prevented from landing at Cromer by the Earl of Oxford's men, the ships sailed on to Ravenspur on the north bank of the Humber, where the King landed on 14 March 1471. Storms had separated the fleet, and Gloucester with his 300 men landed four miles away, while Rivers with his 200 men landed at Powle near Hull, about fourteen miles from the King.[11]

Claiming that he was returning only to regain his lands as Duke of York, Edward was admitted to the city of York only after he swore allegiance to the Lancastrian 'King Harry and Prince Edward' and declared before the High Altar in York Minster that 'he never would again take upon himself to be king of England'. Immediately thereafter, he began to assemble followers, including his brother Clarence, to attack the Lancastrian army.

Family pressure and political reality caused Clarence, once more, to change sides. The Duchess of York, the Duchesses of Exeter and Suffolk (his two sisters in England), and the Duchess of Burgundy (his sister Margaret) had besieged Clarence with letters and messengers urging reconciliation with his brother. Clarence began to have second thoughts about his alliance with Warwick. The marriage of Anne Neville to Prince Edward of Lancaster had moved Clarence farther than ever from any claim to the throne. Even the weak and wayward Clarence could see that he was no more than a pawn used to strengthen Warwick's position.

Even worse, with Henry VI restored to his crown, Clarence would lose much of his personal wealth, which had been funded from Lancastrian spoils won by the Yorkists in 1461 after the battle of Towton. A victory for Henry VI would reverse attainders and bring home a flood of Lancastrian followers to their restored lands, causing Clarence to lose the estates given him by Edward IV. His greed for money and power had positioned Clarence to lose more than he could possibly gain by his attachment to Warwick.

Thus, by the time Edward IV left York to march south to engage Warwick's troops, Clarence had once more turned his coat and marched north to meet his brother. A contemporary chronicler records the encounter:

When they were together within less than half a mile, the King set his people in array, the banners [displayed], and left them standing still, taking with him his brother of Gloucester, the Lord Rivers, Lord Hastings, and [a] few others, and went towards his brother of Clarence. And, in like wise the Duke for his part, taking with him a few noble men, and leaving his host in good order, departed from them towards the King. And so they met betwixt both hosts, where was right kind and loving language betwixt them two, with perfect accord knit together for ever hereafter, with as heartily loving cheer and countenance as might be betwixt two brethren of so great nobility and estate.[12]

Edward IV should have known better. But forgiveness of his younger brother's waywardness seemed to be inbred in the King. In spite of Clarence's disloyalty and folly, Edward embraced his brother's return to the Yorkist camp, restored all his possessions, and appointed him Great Chamberlain of England. Such reluctance to look beneath appearances to discern reality would later contribute to the chaos that followed Edward's death.

Edward IV marched straight towards London without encountering any resistance. On Tuesday 9 April, he sent 'comfortable messages to the Queen' at Westminster and to his supporters in London.[13] Edward IV entered the city on 11 April 1471 to the cheers of merchants and citizens, who were already anticipating restored trade with Burgundy. Phillippe de Commynes snidely commented from his French perspective that Edward IV was welcomed so warmly because of 'the great debts he owed in the city, which made his merchant creditors support him' and because 'several noblewomen and wives of the rich citizens with whom he had been closely and secretly acquainted won over their husbands and relatives to his cause'.[14]

Londoners were pleased to welcome home their handsome and affable Edward IV, whose tall, energetic figure contrasted sharply with the frail and languid Henry VI, whose very appearance, always in the same old blue gown, 'rather withdrew men's hearts than otherwise'.[15] The pitiful Henry VI, perhaps anticipating relief from the six months he had dealt with Warwick and the council, greeted his cousin: 'My cousin of York, you are very welcome. I know that in your hands my life will not be in danger'.[16] For the moment he was correct. Edward IV sent Henry VI back to his quarters in the Tower.

Edward IV stopped by St Paul's Cathedral to give thanks, then headed up river to Westminster. In the abbey he prayed, 'gave thanks to God, Saint Peter and Saint Edward', and had the crown placed on his head by the Abbot.[17] Appropriately sanctified, Edward IV went directly to Westminster Sanctuary to greet his wife, his three daughters, and his six-month-old son. Fleetwood's chronicle summarises Elizabeth's experience:

> The Queen... had a long time abode, and sojourned at Westminster (assuring her person only by the great franchise of that holy place) in right great trouble, sorrow, and heaviness, which she sustained, with all manner (of) patience that belonged to any creature, and as constantly as hath been seen, at any time, any

of so high estate to endure; in the which season, nevertheless, she had brought into this world, to the King's greatest joy, a fair son, a prince wherewith she presented him at his coming, to his heart's singular comfort and gladness, and to all them that him truely loved, and would serve.

From thence that night the King returned to London, and the Queen with him, and lodged at the lodging of my lady, his mother, [Baynard's Castle, home of the Duchess of York] where they heard divine service that night and upon the morrow, Good Friday.[18]

But the Cousins' Wars were only slightly delayed. Warwick was marching towards London. On Good Friday, Edward IV convened his council and prepared to depart the next day to fight the enemy. Queen Elizabeth, her children, the Duchess of Bedford, and the two archbishops once more moved home to the Tower.

CHAPTER THIRTEEN

York Restored

On Easter Sunday 1471, the troops of Edward IV engaged those of his cousin Earl Warwick at Barnet, in one of the more bizarre encounters in these wars of the cousins. On Saturday night, the King's troops camped so close to Warwick's army that Warwick's artillery firing throughout the night overshot Edward's men. On Sunday morning, a dense fog shrouded the field, causing commanders, despite their military experience and expertise, to position troops so poorly that Warwick's line outflanked Edward's at one end, and Edward's outflanked Warwick's at the other.

As the battle began, Edward's left wing was destroyed. Survivors retreated to London, spreading the word that Warwick had won. But the centre of the line under command of Edward and Clarence held, and the right flank, led by Gloucester, moved ahead. Then Fortune spun her wheel, with consequences unintended by mere mortals. The Earl of Oxford, whose Lancastrian troops had destroyed Edward's left wing, returned from pursuing the fleeing Yorkists. As they rejoined the battle in the fog, they mistook the badge of their own men, a flaming star, for the badge of York's flaming sun. They attacked their own men. Warwick, sensing defeat, tried to escape on horseback. But as he rode through the nearby woods, he was recognised, captured and killed on the spot.

The death of Warwick, 'the Kingmaker', whose sword had placed Edward IV on the throne and then replaced him with Henry VI, now assured the ascendancy of Edward IV. By ten o'clock in the morning, the battle of Barnet was over. Edward was back in London in time to celebrate Easter Sunday Mass at St Paul's. On Easter Monday, the body of Warwick was brought to St Paul's, where it was displayed on public view for three days, 'open and naked' except for a loin cloth. No doubt would remain in anyone's mind that the Kingmaker was dead.

Still, the mopping-up of Margaret's army remained. Funded by Louis XI, Margaret had departed from France and landed at Weymouth on that same fateful Easter Sunday. Her troops marched north through Exeter, Taunton, Glastonbury, Wells and Bath, gathering support from the traditional Lancastrian counties of Devon and Cornwall. Moving on into Gloucestershire, Margaret's army arrived at Tewkesbury. In this last battle, on 4 May 1471, Margaret lost everything. Most crushingly, she lost her hope and claim for the future: her son, Edward, the Lancastrian Prince of Wales, was 'taken fleeing to the town and slain in the field', according to the Yorkist account.[1] Lancastrian versions of his death claim that the prince was murdered after the battle. In any case, the son of Henry VI and Margaret was dead. With nothing left to live for, Margaret, who had sailed with such splendour and promise to England at the age of fifteen to marry the twenty-three-year-old King Henry VI, surrendered to Edward IV on 14 May 1471.

The Neville family attempted one last hurrah. Thomas Neville, son of the Earl of Kent and popularly known as the Bastard of Falconbridge, attacked London while Edward IV was consolidating his victory after Tewkesbury. Arriving from Calais with 300 men, Falconbridge gathered followers as he marched through Kent to invade the city. The Mayor and alderman wrote to Edward to come

> …in all possible haste… to the defense of the Queen, then being in the Tower of London [with] my Lord Prince, and my Ladies, his daughters [and] likely to stand in the greatest jeopardy that ever they [had] stood [in].[2]

Edward IV dispatched 1,500 men to defend the city, but Falconbridge attacked before they arrived, setting fires at Aldgate, Bishopgate and London Bridge, where his men burned over sixty houses in an effort to clear a path into the city.

Anthony Wydeville, the Queen's brother, saved London. Bivouacked in the Tower, he mobilised his troops to counter-attack Falconbridge's rebels:

> …After continuing of much shot of guns and arrows, a great while upon both parties, the Earl Rivers, that was with the Queen in the Tower of London, gathered unto him a fellowship right well chosen and habiled [able] of four or five hundred men, and issued out at a postern upon them, and, even upon a point came upon the Kentish men, being about the assaulting of Aldgate, and mightily laid upon them with arrows, and upon them with hands, and so killed and took many of them, driving them from the same gate to the waterside.[3]

The Croyland Chronicle particularly commends the heroism of Anthony:

> [The Londoners] were especially aided... by a sudden and unexpected sally,
> which was made by Anthony, Earl Rivers, from the Tower of London. Falling, at
> the head of his horsemen, upon the rear of the enemy while they were making
> furious assaults upon [Bishopgate], he afforded the Londoners an opportunity
> of opening the city gates and engaging hand to hand with the foe; upon which
> they manfully slew or put to flight each and every of them.[4]

A poem 'On the Recovery of the Throne by Edward IV' devotes three
stanzas to celebrating and thanking Anthony, including:

> The erle Revers, that gentill knight,
> Blessed be the time that he borne was!
> By the power of God and his great might,
> Through his enemies that day did he pass.
> The mariners were killed, they cried 'Alas!'
> Their false treason brought him in woo,
> Thus in every thing, Lord, thy will be doo.[5]

With the defeat of Falconbridge, the way was clear for Edward IV's return
to London. He entered the city on 21 May 1471 in a procession of state,
preceded by Richard, Duke of Gloucester and followed by George, Duke
of Clarence. The former Queen Margaret of Anjou brought up the rear, displayed in defeat. She was sent to the Tower but not permitted to visit Henry
VI who was also imprisoned there. She never saw her husband again.

That night, King Henry VI died. Whether he died because of the 'pure
displeasure and melancholy' caused by his son's death and wife's capture, as recorded in the *Arrival*, or whether he was killed by the hand
of Richard, Duke of Gloucester, as reported by the *Chronicle of London*,
Fabyan, Commines, and common gossip, will never be known. Henry VI's
body was displayed in St Paul's to inform the world that his departure from
this earth was beyond doubt. With only his face exposed, any wounds were
hidden. Witnesses declared that in his lying he bled upon the pavement.

By July, Edward IV began to secure the future of the Yorkist monarchy.
On 3 July, the seven-month-old Prince Edward of York was created Prince
of Wales with two archbishops, eight bishops, and the nobility of England

swearing allegiance to him as the next heir to the throne. If anyone doubted Edward IV's trust and respect for his Queen, the appointment of Elizabeth as head of the Prince's Council put all such doubts to rest. The other council members – the Archbishop of Canterbury, the Bishop of Durham, the Bishop of Bath and Wells, the Duke of Clarence, the Duke of Gloucester and Earl Rivers – were appointed 'to be of council unto the said Prince, giving unto them, and every four of them, with the advice and express consent of the Queen, large power to advise and council the said Prince' until he was fourteen years old.[6]

So, too, Edward IV rewarded those individuals who had helped Elizabeth survive his exile. Abbot Thomas Millyng of Westminster Abbey was appointed chancellor to Prince Edward. William Gould, the butcher who had supplied the weekly 'half of beef and two muttons' while the Queen was in sanctuary, and sent a hundred oxen to the meadow near the Tower following the battle of Tewkesbury, was given a ship called the *Trinity of London* to fill with ox-hides, lead, tallow and all other merchandises except stapleware (wool), for trading in whatever parts of the sea he desired. Marjory Cobb, midwife, received a grant for life of £10 and Doctor Serigo was awarded £150 from the Venetian wine trade.[7]

In September, King Edward IV and Queen Elizabeth went on pilgrimage to Canterbury to give thanks for their survival. In less than two years, Elizabeth had lived through the murder of her father and brother, the witchcraft trial of her mother, the exile of her husband, the birth of her son in sanctuary, and a siege within the Tower. The poem 'On the Recovery of the Throne by Edward IV' acknowledges the Queen's trials, and concludes with a three-stanza tribute to her:

> O queen Elizabeth, of blessed creature,
> O glorious God, what pain had she?
> What languor and anguish did she endure?
> When her lord and sovereign was in adversity.
> To hear of her weeping it was great pity,
> When she remembered the King, she was woo,
> Thus in every thing the will of God is doo.
>
> Here after, good lady, in your felicity,
> Remember old troubles and things past,

And think that Christ himself is he
That is King of kings, and ever shall last,
Knit it in your heart surely and fast,
And think he hath delivered you out of woo,
Heartly thank him, it pleaseth him so to doo.

And ever, good lady, for the love of Jhesu,
And his blessed mother in any wise,
Remember such persons as have been true,
Help every man to have justice.
And those that will other manner matters devise,
They love not the King, I dare say soo,
Beseeching ever God that his will be doo.[8]

With such praise and good wishes from the people of her country, the future must have looked bright for the Queen. Finally, she could relax, as the royal court began governing the nation. The prosperous reign over which they presided would last just twelve years.

The court spent Christmas 1471 at Westminster, in public displays of their royal presence. On Christmas Day, the King and Queen, wearing their crowns, celebrated Mass sung by the Bishop of Rochester in Westminster Abbey. Following the Mass, the King sat in state at Whitehall, with the Bishop of Rochester sitting on his right and the Duke of Buckingham on his left. On New Year's Day, the King and Queen went in procession without their crowns. On Twelfth Day, yet another procession showed 'the King crowned, and the Queen not crowned because she was great with child'.[9]

Queen Margaret's fate was less happy. Elizabeth took pity on the Queen she had served as lady-in-waiting: 'The imprisonment of Queen Margaret was at first very rigorous, but it was, after a time, ameliorated through the compassionate influence of Edward's Queen, Elizabeth Woodville, who probably retained a grateful remembrance of the benefits she had formerly received from her royal mistress'.[10] Margaret's first imprisonment was in the Tower, but she was soon moved to Windsor. On 8 January 1472, John Paston wrote that she was 'removed from Windsor to Wallingford, nigh to Ewelm, my Lady of Suffolk's place in Oxfordshire'.[11] Alice Chaucer, Dowager Duchess of Suffolk, had been a favourite friend of Margaret in happier days. Now her custodian, Lady Suffolk received eight marks each week for the former Queen's maintenance.[12] Margaret lived with Lady Suffolk until Louis XI ransomed her in 1475, when she returned to France to live in poverty and pain until her death on 25 August 1482, aged fifty.[13]

In February 1472, the court moved to Sheen, the Queen's dower palace that she particularly loved for its pleasant and peaceful setting. The proximity of this palace to the Carthusian charterhouse and to the Bridgettine Abbey of Syon, both of which Elizabeth patronised, provided easy access to the spiritual sustenance she frequently sought. But any simple pleasures that the Queen hoped to enjoy with husband and children were soon shattered by conflicts between her brothers-in-law. Instead of a peaceful and long-overdue holiday, the Queen had to contend with the anger and antagonisms of Clarence and Gloucester, brotherly battles in which Edward was forced to arbitrate. The ingratitude of Clarence, in particular, grated against Elizabeth's desire for family harmony.

Although Clarence's alliance with Warwick and Henry VI had constituted nothing less than treason, Edward completely forgave him after his exemplary service at Tewkesbury and, always indulgent of his younger brother, welcomed him back into the family.[14] Now, with Warwick's death, Clarence was anticipating the huge inheritance that his wife, Isabel Neville, would receive from her father. But the youngest of the York brothers, Richard, Duke of Gloucester, had proposed marrying Isabel's younger sister, Anne, a widow since the death of Prince Edward of Lancaster at Tewkesbury. To Clarence's dismay, Gloucester expected his half of the Warwick family fortune. Furious at the thought of dividing Warwick's estates, Clarence responded with devious plots that would foretell his ultimate and sad end. Victory in the wars of the cousins now led to a new battle between two Yorkist brothers.

Both Clarence and Gloucester had grown up as childhood friends of the Neville sisters. At the age of nine, Gloucester moved to his cousin Warwick's Middleham estate, where he lived for three years.[15] At that point, Isabel was ten years old and Anne five. In 1472, when Gloucester was proposing to marry Anne, he was nineteen and she, already widowed, was fifteen. Clarence and Isabel, who had been married for three years, were twenty-two and twenty. These brothers with such bright, wealthy futures ahead turned their passions against each other. Perhaps too many battlefields during their childhood and adolescence had created a character that glorified conflict and nurtured rancour. Whatever the cause, Clarence resorted to combat tactics and kidnapped Anne to prevent his brother from marrying her. He disguised his sister-in-law as a servant and hid her in a house in London. Gloucester found Anne and took her to sanctuary.

Edward IV was called upon to negotiate peace. Concerned that the entire Neville inheritance in Clarence's hands would lead to more mischief, he approved the marriage of Richard to Anne and decreed that the inheritance should be divided between the daughters. Missing from the negotiations was the girls' mother, Anne, Countess of Warwick, who legally retained all rights to the property during her widowhood. The Countess had fled to sanctuary at Beaulieu Abbey after Warwick's death, and from there she wrote desperate pleas in her own hand, trying to regain her property. In one letter, the Countess directs her

> …labours, suits, and means to the King's Highness, soothly also to the Queen's good Grace, to my right redoubted Lady the King's mother, to my Lady the King's eldest daughter, to my Lords the King's brethren, to my Ladies the King's sisters, to my Lady of Bedford mother to the Queen, and to other Ladies noble of the realm.[16]

The women of the realm, however, could not counteract the avarice and ruthlessness of Clarence and Gloucester.

The Warwick inheritance provides a useful touchstone for evaluating the charges of greed levelled against the Wydevilles, a family easily outclassed by the avarice of the York brothers who were declared sole heirs to

> …possess and enjoy as in the right of the said wives all possessions belonging to the said Countess [Warwick's wife, Anne Beauchamp] *as though she were naturally dead and that she should be barred and excluded therefrom*, that they should make partition of the premises and the same partition should be good in law, that *the said dukes should enjoy for life all the possessions of their wives if they should outlive the latter*.[17]

After cautioning the brothers not to meddle in each other's inheritance, the settlement provides that Richard, even if he divorced Anne and did not remarry, 'should enjoy as much of the premises as should appertain to her during his life'.[18]

Richard also became 'Constable of England' and 'Warden of the Forest north of the Trent'. To compensate Clarence for his losses, Edward IV appointed him 'Great Chamberlain and Lieutenant of Ireland' and granted him a slew of manors, castles, tenements and mills.[19] It was not enough. Clarence's resentment at losing half of the Neville fortune simmered towards boiling point, and he would soon take steps that would cause him to lose all.

In the wrangling, no one paid any attention to the violations of canon law and biological imperative that these marriages flouted. Both husbands and wives were first cousins once removed; worse, they descended from ancestors whose intermarriages placed the health of any children at serious risk. While the medieval world lacked knowledge of modern genetics, the Church knew enough about the consequences of consanguinity to forbid marriage among close relatives. Unfortunately, the Church often ignored its own precepts when powerful, rich men petitioned for marriages aimed at preserving their fortunes within the family. It would be only a matter of time until the children produced by the two ill-advised unions of the cousins York and Neville would suffer the folly of their fathers' greed. The blood royal of which Warwick was so proud produced grandchildren of limited vigour.

Throughout these contretemps within the family, Queen Elizabeth was preparing for the arrival of the fifth royal heir, Margaret, who was born at Windsor on 19 April 1472. The choice of the baby's name is interesting: was Elizabeth paying tribute to her predecessor Queen, who was living in Oxfordshire under the supervision of the Duchess of Suffolk? Within a month, on 30 May, Elizabeth's beloved mother, the Duchess of Bedford, died at the age of fifty-six. She had outlived her husband by just three turbulent years. With both parents gone, Elizabeth's personal loss was profound, but the absence of Jacquetta's loving presence and astute intelligence must have been particularly devastating.

Royal duties required the Queen's attention, however, and in autumn 1472 she helped Edward IV repay the hospitality he and his small band of exiles had received while in Burgundy. Lord Louis of Gruuthuyse, Governor of Holland and host of the English exiles at his Bruges Palace, was invited to England, where the royal household reciprocated in kind. Remembering the tapestries and paintings, the library of books and manuscripts at Gruuthuyse Palace, Edward tried to exhibit equivalent luxury at Windsor Castle where the Burgundians began their royal visit. Unfortunately, the chapel of St George at Windsor, newly commissioned to replicate the Flemish architecture Edward had so admired during his exile, was not yet built.

The Gruuthuyse visit, described in 'The Record of Bluemantle Pursuivant', provides a rare and fascinating glimpse into the ritual and everyday activities of Edward's court. After greetings by the King and Queen, the Gruuthuyse party dined in 'two chambers richly hanged with cloths of Arras and with beds of estate', before revisiting the King in his chambers. Edward immediately escorted the visitors to

…the Queen's chamber, where she sat playing with her ladies at the morteaulx [a game similar to bowls], and some of her ladies and gentlewomen at the Closheys of ivory [ninepins], and dancing. And some at divers other games according. The which sight was full pleasant to them.

Also the King danced with my Lady Elizabeth, his eldest daughter. That done, the night passed over, they went to his chamber. The Lord Gruuthuyse took leave, and my Lord Chamberlain [Hastings] with divers other nobles accompanied him to his chamber, where they departed for the night.[20]

The next day began with Mass in the King's private chapel, following which Edward IV lavished gifts on his former host: a cup of gold garnished with pearl, in the midst of which was 'a great piece of an Unicorn's horn to my estimation vii inches compass. And on the cover was a great sapphire'. After breakfast, the King went into the quadrant with Prince Edward, almost two years old, who was carried by his chamberlain, Sir Thomas Vaughan, to greet Lord Gruuthuyse. They rode off to the King's nearby park, where Edward let Lord Gruuthuyse ride his horse before making a gift of the horse to his visitor. He also presented Gruuthuyse with 'a royal Crossbow the strings of silk, the case covered with velvet of the King's colours, and his arms and badges thereupon'. The heads of the crossbow bolts were gilt. Before dinner at the hunting lodge, a captured doe was given to the servants of Lord Gruuthuyse. After dinner, the hunt resumed with half a dozen bucks slain and given to Lord Gruuthuyse himself. Before returning to the castle, Edward showed his visitors his garden and 'vineyard of pleasure'. Then:

After hearing Evensong in their chambers, the guests joined the Queen who had ordered a great Banquet in her own chamber. At the which Banquet were the King, the Queen, my lady Elizabeth the King's eldest daughter, the Duchess of Exeter, my Lady Rivers, and the Lord Gruuthuyse, sitting at one mess; and at the same table sat the Duke of Buckingham, my lady his wife, with divers other Ladies,... my Lord Hastings Chamberlain to the King, my lord Berners Chamberlain to the Queen, John Gruuthuyse son of the foresaid Lord, master George Bartte secretary to the Duke of Burgundy, Lois Stacy usher to the Duke of Burgundy... also certain other nobles of the King's own court.

Item, there was a side table, at which sat a great view of ladies, all on the one side. Also in the outer chamber sat the Queen's gentlewomen, all on one side. And at the other side of the table against them, sat as many of the lord of Gruuthuyse's servants...

And when they had supped, my lady Elizabeth the King's eldest daughter, danced with the Duke of Buckingham, and divers other ladies also. And about nine of the clock, the King and the Queen, with her ladies and gentlewomen, brought the said Lord Gruuthuyse to three chambers of Pleasure, all hanged with white silk and linen cloth, and all the floors covered with carpets. There was ordained a bed for himself, of as good down as could be gotten, the sheets of Raynes, also fine fustians [blankets]; the counterpoint cloth of gold, furred with ermine, the Tester and the Ceiler [canopy] also shining cloth of gold, the curtains white sarsenet; as for his bed sheet and pillows [they] were of the queen's own ordinance.

In the second chamber was another [bed] of estate, the which was all white. Also in the same chamber was made a Couch with feather beds, hanged with a Tent, knit like a net, and there was a Cupboard.

Item, in the third chamber was ordained a Bayne [bath] or two, which were covered with Tents of white cloth. And when the King and Queen, with all her ladies and gentlewomen, had showed him these chambers, they turned again to their own chambers, and left the said Lord Gruuthuyse there, accompanied with my lord chamberlain, which dispoiled [undressed] him and went both together in the Bayne... And when they had been in their Baynes as long as was their pleasure, they had green ginger, divers Syrups, Comfits and Hyppocras [spiced wine]; and then they went to bed.

And on the Morn he took his Cup of leave of the King and the Queen, and turned to Westminster again, accompanied with certain knights, esquires, and other of the King's servants, home to his lodging. And the Sunday next following the King gave him a gown of cloth of gold furred.[21]

The court also moved to Westminster for the opening of the October Parliament which would honour Lord Gruuthuyse:

> On the feast of St. Edward, our most dread and liege lord the King Edward the iiiith, which was the xii year of his most noble Reign, kept his Royal estate in his palace of Westminster. And about 10 of the clock afore noon, the King came into the Parliament Chamber in his parliament robes, and on his head a cap of maintenance, and sat in his most Royal majesty, having before him his lords spiritual and temporal, also the speaker of the Parliament, which is called William Alynton.[22]

After ritual greetings, Speaker Alynton especially praised Queen Elizabeth for her conduct during Edward's exile:

> The intent and desire of his Commons specially in the commendation of the womanly behaviour and the great constancy of our Sovereign Lady the Queen, the [King being] beyond the sea. Also the great joy and surety to this his land [by] the birth of my Lord, the Prince.[23]

The Speaker then praised 'the constant faith of my lords Rivers and Hastings', along with other nobles and yeoman who had accompanied Edward into exile. After formal thanks from the Commons to Lord Gruuthuyse for his hospitality to 'his Highness when he was in the counties of Holland and Flanders', the Commons adjourned, and preparations began for the King to create Lord Gruuthuyse as Earl of Winchester:

> This done the King went into the Whitehall, whether came the Queen crowned. Also my Lord the Prince in his robes of estate, which was borne next after the King by his Chamberlain called Mr. Vaughan and so proceeded forth into the Abbey church and so up to the shrine of St. Edward, where they offered.[24]

After giving thanks to St Edward, all returned to Whitehall for a celebratory banquet.

The splendour of this ceremonial visit masked the harsh reality of life in the fifteenth century. As the end of 1472 neared, Edward and Elizabeth's newborn daughter Margaret died, on 11 December 1472, before reaching eight months of age. Like most children of the era, the baby was buried with no knowledge of what might have caused her death. Even if the illness were diagnosed, no medicine existed to treat it. As the royal couple settled into their married life, they had to confront the eternal problems that afflict all humanity. Family and human nature would bring more pain to the Royals.

CHAPTER FOURTEEN

Problems in Paradise

Married eight years, the royal couple could just now begin to settle into life together. As with all couples everywhere, the relationship was not consistently ideal. While Edward IV always treated Elizabeth with utmost respect, treasured her intelligence and good sense, and perhaps loved her as deeply as it is possible for man to love woman, he also exercised his royal and masculine prerogative to live the life that pleased him best. The King's closest associates, most notably William, Lord Hastings, constituted a rival interest to Elizabeth and her family. Thomas More describes Hastings as the 'Lord Chamberlain against whom the Queen especially grudged, for the great favour the King bore him, and also for that she thought him secretly familiar with the King in wanton company'.[1]

Edward IV had always possessed a roving eye and boasted about his bastard children. It is unfair, therefore, to blame Hastings for the King's indiscreet escapades. But Hastings undoubtedly accompanied the King in his pleasure-seeking forays, and perhaps served his master in arranging them. Edward's infamous and long-term mistress, Elizabeth Shore, popularly known as 'Jane Shore', was acquainted with both men, and after Edward's death became Hastings's mistress. Described by More as 'honestly brought up' but married when too young, Mistress Shore's unhappiness initially

…made her incline unto the King's appetite when he required her… The respect of his royalty, the hope of gay apparel, ease, pleasure and other wanton wealth was able soon to pierce a soft, tender heart. But when the King had abused her, anon her husband (as he was an honest man and… not presuming to touch a King's concubine) left her up to him all together. When the King died, the Lord Chamberlain took her. Which in the King's days, albeit he [Hastings] was sore enamoured upon her, yet he forbare her, either for reverence, or for a certain friendly faithfulness.[2]

Hastings's complicity in the King's sexual excursions undoubtedly caused Elizabeth concern.

Yet the degree of animosity between the Queen and Hastings is unclear and may be exaggerated by historical tradition. The 1464 indenture that betrothed Elizabeth's eldest son to Hastings's unborn daughter was, indeed, abrogated when Sir Thomas Grey instead married Anne Holland. But if that change in plans created any alienation, Elizabeth and Hastings apparently reconciled their differences. In July 1466, Elizabeth appointed Hastings and his brother Ralph as 'overseers of vert and venison' in her forest at Rockingham.[3] When Anne Holland died in 1467, Thomas Grey married Hastings's stepdaughter Cecily Bonville, aged thirteen, in July 1474. Further, that agreement stipulated that his brother Richard Grey would marry Cecily if Thomas died 'without carnal knowledge of her'.[4] The Hastings and Grey families were thus united by marriage contract at the midpoint of Edward IV's reign. In 1476, Hastings nominated both Sir Thomas and Sir Richard Grey for membership in the Order of the Garter.[5]

The Queen's feelings about Edward's sexual adventures are unknown – and difficult to ascertain from our differing perspectives. Illegitimate children were commonplace among nobility and were frequently awarded familial status, if not inheritance rights. At Elizabeth's own funeral in 1492, her body was attended by 'Mistress Grace, a bastard daughter of King Edward', one of only two women in the small funeral cortege.[6] Mistress Grace appears nowhere else in historical references, and this sudden mention of her existence suggests that other bastards of Edward IV remain unknown. Certainly, all of England knew about Edward's profligacy, and Elizabeth surely must have regretted her husband's boasting about his exploits:

> The King would say that he had three concubines, which in three diverse properties diversely excelled. One the merriest, another the wiliest, the third the holiest harlot in his realm, as one whom no man could get out of the church lightly to any place, but it were to his bed.[7]

While More identifies the merriest as Elizabeth Shore, he declines to identify the other two 'somewhat greater personages'. Others have suggested that Elizabeth Lucy, the mother of Edward's illegitimate son Arthur

Plantagenet, was the holiest, but given Edward IV's propensities, a number of women unknown to history might equally qualify.

The Queen's own family may have participated in Edward's debauchery. After the King's death, Gloucester accused Thomas Grey, Marquis of Dorset, of inheriting Elizabeth Shore as his paramour, a claim that may, however, have originated in Richard's propaganda discrediting the Queen's family as he pursued the throne.[8] Polydore Vergil's Tudor chronicle refers to Dorset as a 'good and prudent man'. Rumours that the Queen's second son, Sir Richard Grey, and her brother Sir Edward Wydeville indulged in the general dissipation of the court must remain exactly what they are: rumours unsubstantiated by evidence.

The royal family interacted with the gentry in ways that are tantalisingly obscure in the fragmented evidence that survives from the period. The Stonors, for instance, were a family of established country gentry and merchants, who grew rich from their extensive estates and the wool trade. A letter probably written by Jane Stonor to her daughter discusses the girl's distress at being placed with a noble family at the request of Queen Elizabeth. Mother Stonor hopes that her daughter knows how to conduct herself in her new home, believed to be that of the Duchess of Suffolk, sister of Edward IV, since 'you wot [know] well you are there as it pleased the Queen to put you'.[9] The Stonor mother and father are concerned about maintaining good relationships with the Queen, who was 'right greatly displeased with us both; all be it we know right well it came not of her self'. The source and cause of the Queen's displeasure remain a mystery, as does the statement that the Queen's actions 'came not of her self'. Despite that, the mother offers to have her daughter return home if 'my husband or I may have writing from the Queen with her own hand, and else he nor I neither dare nor will take upon us to receive you, seeing the Queen's displeasure before; for my husband sayeth he hath not willingly disobeyed her commandment here before, nor he will not begin now'.[10]

The problem between the Stonors and the Queen was apparently worked out, since one of the younger males was subsequently knighted. Sir William Stonor also fell in and out of favour with the Queen through the years. In a letter of 19 August 1481, Queen Elizabeth charges her forester of Blakmore to deliver a buck to 'our trusty and well beloved Sir William Stoner, Knight', but another letter in August 1482 threatens to sue Sir William for hunting and slaying deer in her forests at Barnwood Chace and Eggshill Common.[11] Apparently Sir William took advantage of his favoured position and provoked action from the Queen.

More troubling problems arose from the continuing resentment and envy harboured by long-term Yorkists, who were angry at the power and influence of the formerly Lancastrian Wydevilles, now so central to Edward IV's life and court. Even though realignments of loyalty were commonplace in this small kingdom – Warwick and Clarence were certainly proof of that – the military expertise, chivalric prominence and cultured intelligence of the Wydevilles caused particular resentment among those who lacked their *savoir faire*. Still, the extent of hostility to the Queen's family may be greatly exaggerated. Those critics who claim that Edward IV's appointment of the Queen's father as Treasurer of England alienated Sir Walter Blount, the man he replaced, ignore the contemporary evidence that Blount named Earl Rivers and his son Sir John Wydeville in his will as deceased friends for whom Masses were requested.[12] No one disputes that Rivers served Edward IV well as Treasurer of England, faithfully carried out the King's orders and helped the nation achieve the solid financial standing it lacked under Henry VI. Neither does anyone doubt that Rivers paid the highest price for serving the King when he was executed by Warwick in 1469.

Leading the opposition to the Wydeville faction were Edward IV's brothers, Clarence and Gloucester, supported by Hastings and Buckingham, all long-time Yorkists of the blood royal. The differences between the two factions originated in personal, as well as political, ideals. Anthony Wydeville's undisputed military and administrative skills were matched by a scholarly and pious propensity that set him apart from others. As soon as English governance began to stabilise, for instance, Anthony determined to make a pilgrimage to Santiago de Compostela in Spain, a shrine second only to Jerusalem in attracting devout Christians during the medieval era. Anthony believed such a pilgrimage to be particularly appropriate for an English warrior who had spent the past twelve years in hand-to-hand killing.

If a letter from Sir John Paston to his mother is accurate, Edward IV responded in anger when he heard Anthony's request to make the pilgrimage:

> The King is not best pleased with him [Anthony] for that he desireth to depart; in so much that the King hath said of him that whenever he hath most to do, then the Lord Scales will soonest ask leave to depart and weeneth that it is most because of cowardice.[13]

Hardly cowardice. Whatever Anthony's faults, cowardice was not one of them. At the age of seventeen, this man was captured at Sandwich by Dynham and carted off to Calais where Warwick imprisoned him; in 1461 he fought at Towton only to be captured and imprisoned; in 1463 he helped direct the siege of Alnwick Castle; in 1470 he defeated Warwick and Clarence at Southampton; in 1470 he helped Edward IV escape Warwick's troops and accompanied him into exile; in 1471 he rode out from the Tower to defeat Falconbridge; in April 1472 he led 1,000 archers to the relief of Brittany which helped repel the latest invasion from France.[14] While at sea, his men were decimated by the 'flux and other epidemics', and his ships had to return home in November.[15] Anthony's military service was matched only by his chivalric prowess, renowned in the tournament lists of both England and Burgundy.

If Edward IV ever uttered the hasty words reported by John Paston, he soon issued an order of safe conduct in which Anthony, Earl Rivers was termed *Carissimus ac Dilectissimus Consanguinius* (our most dear and beloved brother). In the preface to his translation of *The Dictes and Sayengis of the Philosophers*, Anthony states his reason for making the journey:

> Where it is so that every human Creature by the sufferance of our Lord God is born and ordained to be subject and thrall unto the storms of fortune and so in diverse and many sundry wises, man is perplexed with worldly adversities of the which I, Antoine Wydeville, Earl Rivers, Lord Scales... have largely and in many different manners have had my parte, and of them relieved by the infinite grace and goodness of our said Lord through the mean of the Mediatrice of Mercy, which... exhorted me to dispose my recovered life to his service in following his lawes and commandments. And in satisfaction and recompense of mine iniquities and faults before done, to seek and execute the works that might be most acceptable to Him. And as far as mine frailness would suffer me, I rested in that wit and purpose during that season I understood the Jubilee and pardon to be at the Holy Apostle Saint James in Spain which was the year of grace 1473.[16]

This reflective humility symbolises the differences between Anthony and the rapacious rivalries of Edward's court. Cynics who may question the sincerity of Anthony's words need only look to his actions for proof. Within months of his pilgrimage, this most accomplished of courtiers departed for the Welsh Marches to spend the rest of his life as governor to the three-year-old Prince Edward, heir to the throne.

None of the Wydevilles, in fact, built personal fortunes or accumulated great power from their closeness to the King – certainly not in the grand tradition established by the Nevilles and pursued by Clarence and Gloucester. Neither did the Wydevilles receive vast grants of land and lucrative offices such as the King conferred on William, Lord Hastings; William, Lord Herbert; Humphrey, Lord Stafford; and a host of other preferred intimates. Nor did any Wydeville ever display the greed of Clarence and Gloucester, who dispossessed the Countess of Warwick of her lawful rights and property, most of which she had inherited from her own father. Beyond the marriages of Elizabeth's siblings to noble spouses, the Wydevilles profited little by their sister's marriage to the King.

Whatever the Wydevilles did receive, they earned through meritorious service. The appointment of Elizabeth's father as Treasurer of England, Constable of England, and member of the King's Council, for instance, earned him £1,330 per year.[17] Beyond his creation as Earl Rivers, Elizabeth's father gained no extraordinary grants of land or money from Edward IV. So, too, Anthony Wydeville received his principal income from his wife's inheritance, a marriage made years before Elizabeth became Queen. When the King granted Anthony the lordship of the Isle of Wight and the castle of Carisbrooke in November 1466, and made him Keeper of the Castle of Porchester in Hampshire in 1467, that recompense was hardly extraordinary considering his military service and his diplomatic expertise in negotiating the marriage of Margaret of York to the Duke of Burgundy.

Among the other Wydeville brothers, John and Richard were knighted at the Queen's coronation in 1464. Richard was Edward IV's candidate to become Prior to the Knights Hospitaller in 1468, but was thwarted by Warwick's supporter, John Langstrother, proving that the Queen did not always win her will.[18] Although Richard did serve as Justice of the Peace in Bedfordshire from 1473–87, he exists as little more than a hard-to-find footnote in fifteenth-century history. John, married to the Duchess of Norfolk, died with his father at the hands of Warwick in 1469.

Neither did the Queen's youngest brothers, Edward and Lionel, receive unusual preference during Edward IV's reign. Edward Wydeville became a naval officer, but his notoriety did not develop until after the death of Edward IV. Lionel graduated from Oxford with a Doctor of Divinity degree and entered the Church. He became Dean of Exeter in November 1478, Chancellor of the University of Oxford in 1479, and Bishop of Salisbury in 1482. Lionel was somewhere between the ages of twenty-nine and thirty-six when he became Bishop (his birth year is uncertain), as compared to Robert Neville who obtained that post at the age of twenty-three, two years before canonical age.[19] In short, preferences given to the Wydevilles never exceeded traditional norms for the era.

Only Anthony figured prominently in court politics during the reign of Edward IV. His contributions were enormous. After appointment as governor to Prince Edward in 1473, Anthony spent much of his time at Ludlow supervising the young prince and bringing order to the lawless and unruly Welsh Marches. While there, he also translated moral and phil-osophical texts already popular on the continent into English. Anthony periodically left Ludlow to serve in diplomatic missions, where his know-ledge of continental traditions served England well – most notably, an effort to persuade Charles the Bold to abandon the siege of Neuss and join the English campaign against Louis XI of France – but he soon returned to Ludlow to govern the Marches, supervise the extensive estates inherited from his father-in-law, and translate more texts. There is no question that he was 'different' from the typical member of Edward's court.

That 'difference' may be exactly why Edward IV appointed Anthony as governor of Prince Edward, heir to the throne. In his September 1473 'Letters of Instructions from King Edward IV. to the Earl of Rivers, and John... Bishop of Rochester, for the education of his son Edward, Prince of Wales', Edward IV made it absolutely clear that the objective of his son's education was 'the virtuous guiding of the person of our dearest first-begotten son, Edward, Prince of Wales, Duke of Cornwall, and Earl of Chester, for the politic, sad [serious] and good rule of his household'.[20]

To that end, the King gave absolute power to Anthony in supervising every detail of the prince's life:

Ordinances, touching the guiding of our said Son's person, which we commit to the said Earl Rivers.

First. We will that our said first-begotten son shall arise every morning at a convenient hour, according to his age; and, till he be ready, no man be suffered to come into his chamber, except the right trusty the Earl Rivers, his chaplains, and chamberlains, or such others as shall be thought by the said Earl Rivers convenient for the same season...[21]

The King specified the nature of the boy's instruction during meal times, another reason for selecting Earl Rivers as governor:

Item. That no man sit at his board, but such as shall be thought fit by the discretion of the Earl Rivers; and that then be read before him such noble stories as behooveth to a prince to be understand and know; and that the communication at all times in his presence be of virtue, honour, cunning [knowledge], wisdom, and of deeds of worship, and of nothing that should move or stir him to vice.[22]

A separate 'Item', addressing the education of the prince and other children living in his household, similarly emphasises both moral and intellectual instruction:

Item. We will that the sons of noble lords and gentlemen being in the household with our said son, arise at a convenient hour, and hear their mass, and be virtuously brought up and taught in grammar, music, or other training exercises of humanity, according to their births, and after their ages, and in nowise to be suffered in idleness, or in unvirtuous occupation.[23]

King Edward IV wished his son to be educated in the new humanism that was changing the world from medieval parochialism into the renaissance of learning that was already sweeping the European continent. The King chose the best man in the realm to govern that education: Anthony Wydeville, Earl Rivers.

Rivers's appointment was confirmed by patent issued at Westminster on 10 November 1473:

Appointment, during pleasure, of the earl Ryviers, brother of the queen, as governor and ruler of the king's first-begotten son the prince of Wales, duke of Cornwall and earl of Chester, that he may be virtuously, cunningly and knightly brought up.[24]

The elaborate instructions of the 'Letters' leave no doubt that the King had carefully considered what constituted an appropriate education for the next King of England. Above all, he was concerned for the prince's moral wellbeing. Much of the day was spent worshipping at divine services – Masses, Matins, Evensong – for which the Bishop of Rochester was responsible. Governance of the prince's daily schedule by Earl Rivers demonstrated not only the King's enormous respect and trust for the Queen's brother, but his ideals for his son's education and character. Unfortunately, Edward IV's values did not extend to others in his kingdom, who still believed that personal gain was the *raison d'être* of political power.

To assure that his son lived in a household governed by culture and by moralistic principles, the King surrounded him with his Wydeville relatives. The Queen's brother Lionel became the prince's chaplain. Brothers Sir Edward Wydeville and Sir Richard Wydeville were appointed counsellors to the prince. Sir Richard Grey, Elizabeth's son by her first marriage, was Prince Edward's comptroller, assisted by Elizabeth's cousin, Richard Haute.[25] The Master of the Horse was Lord Lyle, Elizabeth's brother-in-law by her first marriage. If the prince's long-time chamberlain, Sir Thomas Vaughan, was not a relative, he was close friends with the Wydevilles. The overwhelming presence of the Wydevilles infuriated other factions of Edward's court. They dared not, however, oppose the will of the King.

Thus, at the age of two-and-a-half, Prince Edward and his entourage moved to Ludlow Castle, where his father had grown up. To avoid the personal distress that Edward IV had endured when a child at Ludlow, Queen Elizabeth accompanied the prince, moving to Ludlow with him in March 1473, even before Edward IV issued his formal letter of instructions.[26] The journey could not have been easy for the Queen, who was five months pregnant with the King's sixth child. Perhaps she welcomed the bucolic retreat, away from the pestilences of London and the politics of the court, as she set up her son's home before preparing to enter the birthing chamber for her eighth child.

CHAPTER FIFTEEN

Life at Ludlow

Medieval Ludlow was a bustling market town surrounded by the rich farms of Wales, Shropshire, Worcester and Herefordshire. Every Thursday, the streets filled with merchants, shoppers and visitors attending the weekly market. Livestock sold at the Bull Ring spilled over into Corve Street and Old Street where pigs, cattle, horses and sheep jostled with people coming and going about their business. Merchant stalls along High Street sold wine, ale, fish, salt, oats, peas, bread – produce from the surrounding farms and necessities imported from elsewhere.

Wool drove the region's economy, with sheep raised along the Welsh border producing the finest fibre available in the world. The river Teme provided power to drive fulling mills – two at the end of Mill Street and two at Old Street – turning Ludlow into a cloth-manufacturing centre which exported goods to London and abroad. The wool and cloth industry required a wealth of other tradesman – carpenters and sawyers, masons and stonecutters, tilers and thatchers – to provide the infrastructure for the expanding economy. Taverns and friaries housed and fed scores of people who came long distances to do business in Ludlow.

Three fairs added to the prosperity of the region: the feast of St Philip and St James on 1 May, St Laurence's Fair on 9, 10 and 11 August, and St Catherine's Fair on 24, 25 and 26 November. Tolls collected at the seven gates to Ludlow provided income to fund the leper hospital of St Giles and the Hospital of St John the Baptist. Rich burgesses became alderman and councillors as town governance brought order to the growing community.

Religion thrived, with friars preaching and teaching and tending the needs of their parishioners. The Dominicans, or Blackfriars, had arrived in 1254, and the Carmelites, or Whitefriars, in 1350. Members of the Palmers' Guild, established in the mid-thirteenth century, appear prominently as figures in the stained-glass windows of the parish church of St Laurence.

The soaring Perpendicular splendour of St Laurence's was extensively remodelled between 1433 and 1471, reflecting even today the economic vigour of Ludlow during this era.

To this vibrant community, Queen Elizabeth and her son Edward, Prince of Wales, moved in March 1473. Taking up residence in Ludlow Castle, a particularly appropriate home for the 'Prince of Wales', the entourage established a royal presence in the Welsh Marches. Located approximately twenty-five miles south of Shrewsbury, Ludlow Castle dominated a country that Thomas More characterised as 'far off from the law and recourse to justice', where robbers walked at liberty, uncorrected. The first castle at Ludlow, built by Roger de Lacy, son of Walter de Lacy who accompanied William the Conqueror to England, was a Norman stronghold that not only protected England from the unconquered Welsh but launched expeditions into Ireland. De Lacy descendants had married into the Mortimer family, another powerful Norman dynasty, through which Richard, Duke of York inherited Ludlow Castle. When Edward IV became king in 1461, Ludlow became a royal castle, similar to Windsor and Balmoral today.

To bring this region under royal control, Edward IV created the 'Prince's Council' to govern Wales and the border counties through courts that heard criminal, civil and ecclesiastical cases. Prince Edward, though a mere child, represented the King's authority, which otherwise resided with the Privy Council in far-off London. The King appointed to the Prince's Council astute politicians and loyal supporters, chief among whom were the Queen, the Archbishop of Canterbury, Clarence, Gloucester, Rivers, Hastings, and Sir Thomas Vaughan (the prince's chamberlain). Other members included the Bishop of Bath and Wells, the Abbot of Westminster, Lord Dacre, Sir John Fogge, Sir John Scotte, John Alcock and Richard Forster.[1] On occasion, the council met at Tickenhill in Bewdley (the prince's summer home), Shrewsbury and Worcester, but Ludlow was the headquarters of the King's authority.

The Prince's Council had its work cut out for it. Its investigation of robberies and murders in the counties of Hereford and Salop compelled the prince and his court to remain in Wales during Easter 1473.[2] In February 1474, Anthony, Earl Rivers and ten other knights and a sheriff were commissioned to array the county of Hereford against three Herberts and two Vaughans for refusing to appear before the King and for stirring up insurrection.[3] In 1475, Thomas, Marquis of Dorset and Sir Richard Grey, the

Queen's sons, were commissioned to array all men between sixteen and sixty to quell the 'robberies, murders, manslaughters, ravishing of women, burning of houses by the inhabitants of the Marches', along with thieves of Oswestry hundred and Chirksland.[4]

In 1476, the King commissioned the prince and his council to

…be at Ludlow on 24 March next to discuss with the lords of the Marches, to whom the King has written separately, the ways and means for the punishment of many homicides, murders, robberies, spoliations and oppressions in Wales and the Marches of the same, for which the King is going in person to those parts after Easter.[5]

Gradually, the council began to establish order among the individual Marcher lords, and to impose a lawful peace in Wales.

The prince and his entourage lived in the castle, situated high above the river Teme. The castle's fortifications of thick walls and towers (with spectacular views of the surrounding countryside) provided protection for the adjacent town. By fifteenth-century standards, the castle was luxurious. A Great Hall sixty feet long and thirty feet wide, with an open hearth on the floor near the dais table, provided warmth for the large number of people who gathered for meetings and meals. Private apartments for the lord and lady of the castle adjoined the Great Hall, with a hooded fireplace in the first-floor chamber. An arched doorway in the second-storey chamber provided access directly to the Great Hall gallery. The private apartments had windows to provide brightness within the rooms, although the light would seem dim by modern standards.

Adjacent to this chamber block was a three-storey block of rooms with circular staircase, where Prince Edward lived. Between the two chamber blocks was constructed the truly luxurious feature of Ludlow Castle: the garderobe tower (toilets), built with chutes leading outside the Norman curtain wall. Most remarkably, four of the eight garderobe chambers had windows.[6]

The Chapel of St Mary Magdalene was the most important religious site within the castle. Located within the inner bailey, its circular nave, imitating the Church of the Holy Sepulchre in Jerusalem, included decorative chevrons and arches and a stone bench for the comfort of worshippers. Though the chancel has been destroyed, the ornate arch leading from the nave to the chancel reflects the elaborate design and careful workmanship of the entire castle complex.[7] The Chapel of St Peter in the outer bailey, built by Roger Mortimer in the fourteenth century to celebrate his escape from the Tower of London, indicates the importance of religion in the daily life of castle inhabitants.

Far removed from the political intrigues of London, Ludlow offered protection to the young prince. Although the town had suffered greatly during the Black Death epidemics of the previous century, it was safer than the teeming, disease-breeding streets of London. Beyond the plague, other diseases transmitted by close contact with others – smallpox, measles, whooping cough, influenza, diphtheria – threatened both children and adults alike. With no medications to treat such afflictions, death generally claimed its victim.

Both Edward IV and Elizabeth tried to assure that the young Prince Edward had a happier childhood home than his father, who had lamented 'the odious rule and demeaning of Richard Crofte and his brother'. His mother supervised the setting-up of the household, and Edward IV joined them in June, before the official establishment began on 29 September 1473. The King's 'Letters of Instructions' specified that the prince's household 'be set up and begun at the Feast of Saint Michael the Archangel next following'. The day was propitious. St Michael's flaming sword tossed Satan out of Heaven and forever after protected God and his Church. His feast day, celebrated with thanks for the fruit of harvest, provided an auspicious beginning for the education of the next King of England. By modern standards, the prince's schedule was rigorous:

1   Awakening 'at a convenient hour, according to his age'.

2   Matins said in the prince's chamber by the chaplains.

3   Mass in the prince's chapel or closet, 'and in no wise in his chamber without a cause reasonable; and no man to interrupt him during his mass-time'. On holy days, the prince made offerings at the service. On feast days sermons were delivered.

4   Breakfast.

5   'Virtuous learning', appropriate to the prince's age.

6   10 a.m. Dinner, a meal with meat, served by 'worshipful folks and squires' wearing livery and accompanied by the reading of noble stories that encouraged virtue, honour and wisdom. On fast days, dinner was scheduled at 12 noon.

7   Instruction in grammar, music, and humanities.

8   Sports and exercises.

9   Evensong.

10   4 p.m. Supper

11   Sports and recreation

12   8 p.m. Bedtime. At this hour, the prince was to be in his chamber, the
     curtains drawn, and all persons excluded except those designated as night
     attendants.

The prince's household attendants followed a similar schedule, with Mass
scheduled in the hall at 6 a.m. for the prince's officers, followed by Matins
in the chapel at 7 a.m., and a Mass with music at 9 a.m.

Prince Edward's attendants were huge in number. The outer bailey
was filled with the buildings, supplies and people necessary to serve the
needs of the royal household: ostlers, stable hands, horses; delivery men
with meats and grains for the castle's kitchen and bakery; carpenters,
masons; garderobe cleaners; servants gathering rushes for the castle floors;
stewards supervising the teeming mass of workmen. The inner bailey was
equally busy with cooks, bakers, cleaning servants, candle tenders, chamber
grooms, seamstresses, wardrobe supervisors – all necessary to serve the
needs of the prince, his council members, scribes, accountants, chaplains,
musicians, minstrels, treasurer and stewards.

Those in intimate contact with the prince included his three chaplains:
an almoner who distributed gifts to the poor and served as confessor to
the household, and two others who said divine services for the prince. A
physician and surgeon, 'sufficient and cunning', was present at all times.
Explicitly prohibited from the presence of the prince was any person
who might be a 'swearer, brawler, backbiter, common hazarder [gambler],
adulterer', or user of ribaldry.[8] Fighting was strictly forbidden, and anyone
who drew any weapon in the presence of the prince would 'the first time...
sit in the stocks, and there to sit as long as shall be thought behoveful by
our said son's council: and at the second time... lose his service'.[9]

The gates of the castle opened between 6 and 7 a.m. and closed at 9
p.m. from Michaelmas to 1 May. From 1 May to Michaelmas, the gates
opened between 5 and 6 a.m. and closed at 10 p.m. The porters were
charged to take any weapons from men entering the castle and to assure
that 'no stuff... be embezzled out of the gates'. Every Saturday, the treasurer
and comptrollers made a strict accounting of all expenses and charges to

the Prince's Council. Expenses were paid from income received from the Duchy of Cornwall, the towns of Chester and Flint, and the regions of North Wales and South Wales. The prince's treasury was kept in a chest under three keys, one held by 'our dearest wife, the queen', another by the Bishop of Rochester, and the third by Earl Rivers. The prince's signet, also kept in the chest, could be used only by the advice of his council.

In light of events following the King's death, his concluding instructions regarding the prince's safety are particularly poignant:

> Item. For the weal, surety, and profit of our said son, we will, and by these presents give authority and power to the right reverend father in God, John Bishop of Rochester, and to our right trusty and well-beloved Anthony Earl Rivers, to remove at all times the same our son, as the case shall require, unto such places as shall be thought by their discretion necessary for the same season; and ever, that for the sure accomplishment of these statutes and ordinances, they have the like authority to put them, and every of them, in execution accordingly, to the effect and intent of the articles and the premises above expressed and rehearsed, and to punish the breakers of the same.[10]

Such absolute authority to move the prince for his safety and protection indicates the total trust the King placed in Anthony Wydeville and the Bishop of Rochester. Unfortunately, Edward IV could not control those who forcibly seized the boy after the King's death.

Every word of the King's 'Letters of Instruction' reflects the loving care taken by both father and mother in raising their children, the number of which was increasing regularly. By 1473, Elizabeth had presented the King with four daughters and one son, of which only Margaret had died, at the age of eight months. By midsummer, Queen Elizabeth was preparing for the arrival of their sixth child, and she moved to nearby Shrewsbury for the birth of their second son, Richard, on 17 August 1473.

Twice the size of Ludlow, Shrewsbury was surrounded by a loop of the Severn river, whose wharfs made the town a vigorous shipping and mercantile centre. Elizabeth stayed in the royal quarters of the Dominican community, the oldest settlement of friars in Shrewsbury. Royalty had favoured the Blackfriars since their arrival in May 1232, when Henry III granted them the stone that lay in the Severn river under the bailey of Shrewsbury Castle to build their church, along with thirty oak trees from

Under this Oak. Elizabeth Grey. the widow of Sr John Grey. presented a Petition to King Edward 4th. praying the King to restore her late Husband's Lands. The King fell in love with her, and married her presently at Grafton Regis. The next year she was crowned queen at Westminster.

1 'The Queen's Oak'. According to oral tradition Lady Elizabeth Grey, *née* Wydeville, met King Edward IV under an oak tree in Whittlewood Forest, Grafton, to request restoration of property rights granted as part of her dowry. The encounter began a courtship that led to their marriage.

2 Edward IV, 1442–1483.

3 Elizabeth Wydeville, 1437–7/8 June 1492.

Above: 4 The church of St Mary the Virgin, built in the early thirteenth century on the ancestral Wydeville estate in Grafton. The tower was added by Sir John Wydeville in the early fifteenth century.

Left: 5 The tomb of Sir John Wydeville, great-grandfather to Queen Elizabeth, in the church of St Mary the Virgin, Grafton Regis.

Opposite page:
Above left: 6 Medieval jousters. Richard Wydeville, Elizabeth's father, and Anthony Wydeville, her brother, were famed jousters throughout England and Burgundy during the fifteenth century.

Above right: 7 Medieval tournament. The chivalric skills of the Wydeville men made them popular participants in the tournaments that celebrated royal weddings and national holidays.

8 Queen Elizabeth as a member of the Worshipful Company of Skinners' Fraternity, *c.*1472. The roses of the background depict the Yorkist symbol of Edward IV. The gillyflower, or carnation, pattern symbolises the love, motherhood and purity of the Virgin Mary, ideals to which Queen Elizabeth aspired.

9 Edward IV. Stained-glass window in the Martyrdom Chapel, Canterbury Cathedral. It was commissioned by King Edward IV, probably in 1465, and completed between 1475 and 1483.

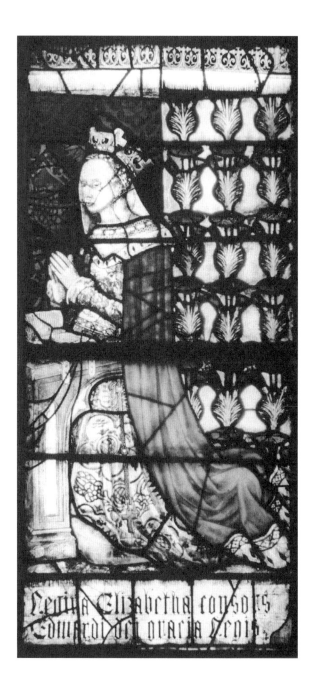

10 Queen
Elizabeth.
Stained–glass
window in the
Martyrdom
Chapel,
Canterbury
Cathedral.

Left: 11 Richard, Duke of York. Stained-glass window in the Martyrdom Chapel, Canterbury Cathedral.

Above: 12 Edward, Prince of Wales. Stained-glass window in the Martyrdom Chapel, Canterbury Cathedral. The Croyland Chronicler commended the royal court for 'a point in which it excelled all others… boasting of those most sweet and beautiful children, the issue of [Edward's] marriage with queen Elizabeth'.

Above: 13 The Lady Princesses Elizabeth, Cecily and Anne. Stained-glass window in the Martyrdom Chapel, Canterbury Cathedral.

Right: 14 The Lady Princesses Katharine and Mary. Stained-glass window in the Martyrdom Chapel, Canterbury Cathedral. The inclusion of their children in the series of stained-glass portraits reflects the importance of family to Edward IV and Elizabeth.

15 The Royal Arms and Supporters of Queen Elizabeth. The dexter impalement displays the Royal Arms of Edward IV, her husband. The sinister chief impales the heraldry of St Pol of Luxembourg (1), Baux of Andria (2) and Cyprus (3). The sinister base impales Ursins (4), St Pol (5) and Wydeville heraldry (6). The dexter supporter is the black bull, sometimes used by Edward IV as supporter of the Royal Arms. The sinister supporter is the greyhound, collared and chained, of Wydeville.

16 Facsimile of Anthony Wydeville's arms from *Writhe's Garter Book*, c.1480. The shield of six quarterings displays the fess and a quarter gules of the Wydeville arms (1), semy of escallops of Scales (2), lion rampant of Luxembourg (3), sun rayonny of Baux (4), griffin of Rivers (5), and vair of Beauchamp.

17 The Throne of the Holy Trinity with Bishop Thomas Rotherham in the foreground and Edward IV and Queen Elizabeth kneeling opposite each other at prie-dieux. From *The Luton Guild Book*.

18 Anthony Wydeville, Earl Rivers kneels as he presents a manuscript of *The Dictes or Sayengis of the Philosophers* to Edward IV. Queen Elizabeth sits to the King's left and Prince Edward stands before her.

19 On Sunday 22 June 1483, Ralph Shaa, Doctor of Divinity, delivered a sermon at Paul's Cross entitled 'Bastard Slips Shall Never Take Deep Root', in which he alleged that Edward IV was illegitimate and Richard III the rightful heir to the throne of England. 'The Preaching at St. Paul's Cross' by John Gipkyn.

20 Elizabeth's signature at the end of a receipt certifying partial payment of her annuity from Henry VII, her son-in-law. The text, written by a scribe, reads: 'Be it remembered that I queen Elizabeth late wife to the excellent prince King Edward the iiiith have received the xxi day of May the vith year of King Henry the viith of John Lord Denham Treasurer of England [by] the hands of Thomas Stolys [one] of the receipt xxx£ in part of payment of CC£ due to me at Easter last past as it appeareth be my annuity granted be the King. In witness whereof I have endorsed this bill with my hand the day and year above said.'

Opposite above: 21 Photocopy of a lost drawing of the 'Abbey Church of Bermondsey'. Queen Dowager Elizabeth spent the last five years of her life in the convent at Bermondsey.

Opposite below: 22 Inscription on the tomb of Edward IV and Elizabeth Wydeville, St George's Chapel, Windsor.

Abbey Church of Bermondsey   S. Gilbert

King Edward IIIJ and his Queen Elizabeth Widvile

ELISABETH WYDVILLE

Queen-Consort of Edward 4ᵗʰ of England.

Married to King Edward 1464.
Died 1488.

An authentic portrait engraved
exclusively for the Court Magazine

VOL XX.   Nᵒ 96 of the series
of ancient portraits.   1841

Nᵒ 11 Carey street
Lincoln's Inn. London.

23 Queen Elizabeth as depicted in 1841 for the *Court Magazine*.
Her demure, modest expression reflects 'her sober demeanor,
lovely looking, and feminine smiling', described in Edward
Hall's sixteenth-century *Chronicle*.

the forest of La Lye and ten hardwood trees from the forest of Hagenia. In 1241–2 when the town walls were being rebuilt, Henry III ordered the bailiffs and sheriff of Shrewsbury to give the Blackfriars 200 cartloads of surplus stone and 100 loads of lime. In 1244, Henry himself contributed ten marks for the church building.

By the mid-fifteenth century, the Dominican priory extended from St Mary's Water Lane on the north to the English Bridge on the south, bounded by the banks of the Severn on the east and Dogpole Street on the west. Edward, when Earl of March, had spent Christmas at the priory during the fateful year of 1460 – his father was beheaded just five days later. The bailiffs of Shrewsbury had welcomed Edward then with a pipe of ale (105 Imperial gallons) 'for the honour of the town'.[11]

Now in 1473, Edward IV's wife came to this Dominican community to give birth to their sixth child. The prosperous, highly educated and scholarly Blackfriars were popular for their preaching against avarice and gluttony. Concerned about the growing number of poor people in the midst of prosperity, they admonished the rich that true wealth resides in the spiritual value of charity.[12] Once more, Elizabeth found comfort and care in the midst of a strict and ascetic religious community.

Edward spent part of 1473 in Shrewsbury as well, and may have been there when Richard was born. The royal family was close-knit, with the same warmth that characterised the family of Sir Richard Wydeville and Jacquetta. If that warmth first attracted Edward IV to Elizabeth, she now provided the same devotion and care to his own growing family. The newborn Richard would grow to become one of his mother's favourites. Described as 'nimble and merry', Richard was a son in whom Elizabeth took special delight – during his brief years on earth.

On 28 May 1474, the infant Richard was created Duke of York, an occasion celebrated by the usual tournament featuring Anthony Wydeville, Earl Rivers. When the costs of the royal event proved burdensome, other participants protested, as noted in an interesting inscription written on the list of contents of a medieval manuscript, next to the title 'The Challenge of six gentlemen at the creation of Richard, Duk of York, son of King Edward the IVth':

The challenge of the Earl of Rivers. – At which jousts there were certain gentlemen which showed the King that the fees to his servants was so great that if they should enter the field to his honour and to the honour of his Realm, the charges would be too much for them to bear, and besought the King that they might be at some reasonable fine.

Whereupon for that time it was ordained by the Judges... [that the] Earl should pay for that time of his entry to the Office of Arms 10 marks, a baron £4, a knight 40s, and an Esquire 26s. 8d of which composition the officers of arms were but so contented. And whereas the noble lord the Earl of Rivers was taxed by the Judges at 10 marks, he sent of his benevolence to the officers of arms 20 marks like a noble man and desired them to be contented for him and his hermitage to whom God send good life and long amen. And the trumpets had for their duty half of the sum appointed for heralds according to every estate and degree as before he rehearsed.[13]

Anthony's generosity at least earned the admiration of the anonymous author of this note.

The pageantry of such celebrations became an integral part of Yorkist governance. At the age of three, Prince Edward made a royal visit to Coventry, where he entered the city on horseback seated in a chair. He was greeted by the 'Mayor and his brethren', who gave the prince 100 marks in a 'gilt cup of 15 ounces with a kerchief of Pleasaunce upon the said cup' and then entertained him with a series of pageants representing English and biblical history. Five days later 'the Mayor and his Brethren were sent for to come before my lord Prince', where they swore an oath accepting Edward, Prince of Wales, as 'first begotten son of our sovereign lord Edward the IVth, King of England'.[14]

Such loyalty received its reward later that year, when the city fathers arrested one of the King's servants for quarrelling and disturbing the peace. Their actions elicited a personal letter of thanks from Queen Elizabeth who endorsed their actions:

We intend not in any wise to maintain support nor favour any of my said Lord's servants, nor ours, in any their riots or unfitting demeaning among you, nor elsewhere to our knowledge.[15]

The Queen also thanked the city for the affection and devotion shown to 'our dearest son, the Prince; and in like wise to all our children... and namely unto our right dear son, The Duke of York, in this time of our absence from them'.[16] In further appreciation, Elizabeth sent a gift of venison from her forest of Fekenham to the Mayor, with explicit instructions that the twelve bucks be divided equally: 'that is to say six of the said bucks unto the said Mayor and his brethren, and the other six of them unto their said wives'.[17]

The careful records maintained by the city of Coventry reveal a positive and mutually beneficial relationship between the Queen and the citizenry. Other surviving documents from the era indicate that both the King and the Queen acted in the best interests of the nation and its institutions. Certainly, both continued their commitment to educational causes. In March 1473, President Andrew Doket and fellows of Queens' College received the sum of thirteen marks yearly from an alienation in mortmain of a manor in Kent.[18] On 29 May 1473, Edward IV pardoned Queens' College of all offences committed before 30 September 1471, a pardon that protected the college from any Lancastrian affiliations it may have made during Henry VI's readeption. A year later, the King's mandamus, dated 4 October 1474, ordered his treasurer and Barons of the Exchequer not to molest Queens' College.

Letters in the name of King Edward, Queen Elizabeth and Prince Edward to the Mayor, bailiffs and commonalty of the town of Cambridge resulted in a deed dated 6 October 1474, that transferred a large plot of common land to Queens' College in the name of 'Andrew Doket the president, and the fellows or scholars for ever'. As a result, 'the president and fellows undertook to lengthen the Smalebrigge next the college twelve feet, and to widen the river on the east of the said soil to the breadth of fifty-one feet, and had liberty to throw a bridge over the river on the east part of the soil, so that the arch of such bridge stretched as far as the arch of the bridge of King's college'.[19] The ever-vigilant President Doket surely instigated these actions, but his ability to secure the King's support required a sympathetic intercessor – almost certainly the Queen.

Eton College also received a grant of several priories, messuages (building sites) and cottages in March 1473.[20] Considering that Edward had once ordered Eton closed, this support also suggests an intercessor devoted to educational philanthropy. While Queen Elizabeth's role in these actions is unproved, someone had to provoke the King's interest in small, struggling colleges far removed from the military and political issues that were beginning to consume him. Edward IV was preparing for war with France and deeply engrossed in raising money and assembling an army to attack England's hundred-year enemy. The most likely intercessors for Queens' College and Eton College, especially in light of subsequent tributes from the institutions, were Queen Elizabeth and her brother Anthony, Earl Rivers.

CHAPTER SIXTEEN

War and Peace

Early 1475 found England preparing for war. Edward had first announced his intention of invading France during the Parliament of October 1472,[1] and in the meantime had been raising funds from citizens willing to attack the enemy, but reluctant to pay the cost of the invasion. Naval preparations had been ongoing for several years, with ships bought or hired, officers commissioned, and crews assembled. Archers, still nine-tenths of the army, were summonsed, and hundreds of thousands of arrows were made by craftsman. Cannon, powder, sulphur and artillery were stored at the ports for shipment to the continent. The King himself planned to lead the largest English army ever to invade France.

In the midst of these military preparations, Queen Elizabeth pursued her charitable and educational interests. On 10 March 1475, she issued the first set of statutes to Queens' College, Cambridge. From her first intercession in 1465, when Edward was dissolving institutions created by Henry VI, the Queen had been central in saving Queens' College and securing pardons after Margaret's defeat at Tewkesbury. A college historian writes about Elizabeth: 'Piety, natural reason and her duties as queen combined to make her "specially solicitous concerning those matters whereby the safety of souls and the public good are promoted, and poor scholars, desirous of advancing themselves in the knowledge of letters, are assisted in their need."'[2]

In issuing the statutes, Elizabeth formalised the administrative structure of the institution, providing for such essential details as the election of the president, the establishment of his residence, office and authority, the supervision of the land, and the designation of stipends for the president and scholars. By this time, Queens' College had grown from four fellows to twelve, and a new college seal incorporating Elizabeth's coat of arms with those of England replaced the coat of arms of Margaret, who was still imprisoned in the Tower.

A contemporary handwritten account of the college's founding refers to Queen Margaret as '*fundatrix nostra prima*' (our first founder), while a second account, apparently written after the death of Andrew Doket in 1484, refers to Queen Elizabeth as the '*vera fundatrix*' (true founder), who, according to the law of succession, completed the founding of the college when Margaret was unable to finish the task. This historian credits Elizabeth with leading the college to its end, issuing its statutes, and obtaining many privileges from the King.[3] The designation of Elizabeth as *vera fundatrix* has led subsequent critics to accuse her of trying to displace Margaret and take exclusive credit for founding the college. Such a view misconstrues the evidence, since the historical account not only gives due credit to Margaret, but was written by an anonymous cleric sometime after the death of Edward IV in 1483, when Elizabeth was in no position to influence anyone – even college historians.

A copy of the *Statuta Collegii Reginalis* in the collection of the University of Cambridge Library (QCV 65) names the 'Co-Foundresses of this College': 'Queen Margaret of Anjou, wife to K. Henry the sixth' and 'Queen Elizabeth, wife to K. Edward the fourth'. Erasmus, who resided at the college from 1511 to 1514, referred to the institution as '*Collegium Reginae*', or 'College of the Queen', implying that a single founder was credited. The issue was resolved in 1823, when the apostrophe was placed after the 's', crediting both Margaret and Elizabeth as the joint founders of Queens' College. Today, the most famous portrait of Elizabeth Wydeville hangs proudly in the Great Hall of the Old Court. The portrait's place of honour over the hearth, surrounded by stained glass windows displaying coats of arms of England's noble families, provides a stately and honoured setting for the Queen who held this institution so close to her heart.

That Elizabeth took such interest in education and domestic matters is significant, for Edward IV's mind was focused on war. As assessed 'benevolences' slowly accumulated the money necessary to invade France, Edward secured the northern borders of England by arranging a marriage between his daughter Cecily, aged five, and Prince James of Scotland, aged three. To govern in his absence, the four-year-old Prince Edward moved from Ludlow to London on 12 May, assumed the title 'Keeper of the Realm', and became head of a regency government. The prince lived with his mother, Queen Elizabeth, who received £2,200 for his annual maintenance, in addition to her own allowance of £2,200.

Edward left London for Sandwich on 30 May 1475, to prepare for the voyage across the Channel. Elizabeth once more took charge of the family at home. Her brother Anthony, Earl Rivers, head of the Wydeville family, accompanied the King with two knights, forty lances and 200 archers, as did her eldest son, Thomas Grey, Marquis of Dorset. Elizabeth was left alone with five children, the eldest of which was the Princess Elizabeth at nine years of age and the youngest Richard at twenty-two months. The Queen was four months pregnant with the King's seventh child. Surely she must have felt some qualms about her husband's enterprise, while stoically repressing her feelings of abandonment.

At Sandwich where the troops were gathering, Edward IV made his will, signed on 20 June 1475, 'the year of our Reign the xvth'. In his will, he acknowledges the enormous debts he had accrued for the foray into France and gives repetitive instructions that they be repaid in case of his death. But the King also paid specific and meticulous attention to the welfare of his children and his 'dearest Wife the Queen'. His two eldest daughters, Elizabeth and Mary, were each bequeathed 10,000 marks as a marriage dowry, as long as 'they be governed and ruled in their marriages by our dearest wife the Queen and by our said son the Prince, if God fortune him to come to age of discretion'. If either of the daughters married 'without such advice and assent so as they be thereby disparaged', the dowry money would be diverted to paying Edward IV's debts.[4]

Similarly, he provided for the child the Queen was then expecting, by allocating a dowry of 10,000 marks if the child was a daughter, 'so always that she be ruled and guided in her marriage as afore is declared in the article touching the marriages of our said daughters Elizabeth and Mary'.[5] Those protests seem a bit much, given his own defiance of tradition in making a happy marriage, but as a father Edward IV decreed that similar actions by his daughters could cost them their dowries.

Cecily, already betrothed to the son and heir of the King of Scots, was bequeathed a dowry of 18,000 marks, over and above the 2,000 already paid, but the King's Council would have to agree that the marriage would advantage the realm. If Cecily married 'any other [husband] by the counsel and advice of our said Wife and any other afore named', the 18,000 marks – or what remains – would be paid to that husband. To make sure that all the dowries were funded, the will designates specific properties in the Duchy of Lancaster responsible for paying the money.

The will conveys to Richard, Duke of York, when he reaches the age of sixteen, all the traditional York lands that had belonged to his grandfather, with the provision that the Duchess of York have a lifetime interest in the estates. In addition, Richard would receive the Bolingbroke lands currently enfeoffed to Thomas, Cardinal and Archbishop of Canterbury. Prince Edward, of course, would assume the crown of England. References to him are poignantly ironic in light of subsequent events. In the language that characterises wills, the naming of 'Edward the Prince' is always followed by 'or such as shall please almighty God to ordain to be our heirs' or 'if God fortune him to come to age of discretion', phrases that eerily foreshadow the disasters to ensue in just eight years.

Queen Elizabeth received consideration equal to their children: 'our said dearest Wife' received 'during her life all the revenues, issues, and profits' of the lands and manors she currently possessed. After her death, half of her estate would pay the King's debts and the other half her own, with any remaining monies going to the unborn child, if a son, when he reached sixteen years or to Richard, Duke of York, if the newborn was a daughter. The Queen also received all personal property of the royal household, including 'bedding, arrases, tapestries, verdours, stuff of our household, ornaments of our Chapel with books appertaining to the same'. Specifically excluded, however, were the plate and jewels, designated to pay burial costs of Edward IV, as well as those ornaments and books bequeathed to the College of Windsor. Curiously, the will twice mentions the Queen's rights to her personal goods:

> And over this we will that our said wife, the Queen, have and enjoy all her own goods, chattels, stuff, bedding, arrases, tapestries, verdours, stuff of household plate and jewels, and all other things which she now hath and occupieth, to dispose it freely at her will and pleasure without let or interruption of our Executors.[6]

The reiteration ironically calls attention to the inappropriate actions of the executors, who seized these goods following Edward's death, and to the meagre possessions owned by Elizabeth when she died seventeen years later.

In appointing his executors, Edward IV names first and foremost 'our said dearest and most entirely beloved wife Elizabeth the Queen'. Nine additional executors follow, including bishops and high officials of the kingdom, but the will reiterates that it is 'our said dearest Wife in whom we most singularly put our trust in this party'. This formal declaration speaks eloquently of Edward's respect and love for his wife of eleven years.

The army amassed by Edward IV was one of the best prepared that England had ever placed on the field. With peace at home, the nation was delighted to take up arms against an enemy abroad, and its citizens ultimately contributed generously to Edward's solicitations for money and men. But the Duke of Burgundy, who had first summoned Edward's aid, was fighting in Germany and ill-prepared to help take on the French. Neither did Louis XI wish to engage in battle, much preferring to negotiate a compromise. Surreptitious efforts began to settle the quarrels diplomatically. In one of the most curious encounters of antagonists ever to occur, the kings of England and of France met on 29 August 1475, on a bridge over the river Somme at Pécquigny, to conclude a treaty:

> In the middle of the bridge a strong piece of trellis-work, such as lion's cages are made from, was erected. The holes between the bars are just big enough for a man to push his arm through easily. The top alone was covered with boards to keep off the rain and it was big enough for ten or twelve people to get under it on either side. The trellis-work stretched right across the width of the bridge so that no one could cross from one side to the other.[7]

Louis XI offered Edward IV an immediate payment of 75,000 crowns (£15,000 sterling) and an annual stipend of 50,000 crowns (£10,000) if he would return to England and leave France unmolested. Edward's closest advisors, including the Chancellor, Lord Chamberlain (Hastings), and the Marquis of Dorset (Elizabeth's son by Sir John Grey), would receive 16,000 crowns, plus an annual pension.[8] A free-trade agreement would abolish tolls and fees between merchants of the two countries.

What sealed the deal for Edward IV, however, was the betrothal of the Dauphin, heir to the French crown, to the Princess Elizabeth – or to her sister Mary, if Elizabeth should die. Why fight, if France could be achieved via marriage rather than by bloodshed? Why attack French cities, if stipends paid to the King of England turned France into a fiefdom – and paid off Edward's enormous debts in the bargain? Edward IV could not refuse. The past fifteen years of bloodshed and intrigue had produced an older and wiser Edward IV:

The missal was brought and the two kings placed one hand on it and the other on the Holy True Cross. Both swore to keep what had been mutually promised, that is to say, a truce of nine years which included the allies of both parties, and to complete the marriage of their children on the terms agreed in the treaty.[9]

Edward IV went home, where the French tribute, paid faithfully until Louis XI signed the Treaty of Arras with Burgundy on 23 December 1482, made him a rich king.

Not everyone was happy. The soldiers, always ill-paid, had expected to line their pockets with French booty. They gained nothing for their efforts except the time lost from their farms and trades. Now they had to sail home with no gains and no glory. From their perspective, English honour had suffered a serious blow. Richard, Duke of Gloucester angrily opposed the treaty at Pécquigny, a stance that made him popular with the soldiers who went home empty-handed and with the citizens who had paid taxes to fund an expedition that now seemed futile.[10]

Queen Elizabeth sustained a personal loss from the whole encounter. Her uncle, the Count of St Pol, lost his life because of duplicitous promises to support both sides of the conflict. St Pol's position as Constable of France compelled loyalty to Louis XI, but his blood ties to the Queen of England and political alliances with Burgundy aligned him with Edward IV. Promising aid to each, he succeeded only in alienating both. After the English had gone home, Louis XI expeditiously beheaded him.

Margaret of Anjou's fate remained unresolved. Edward had taken her to France with him to prevent her from causing trouble in England during his absence.[11] The former Queen was imprisoned at Calais, then returned to England with Edward's troops. Later that summer Louis XI offered to pay Edward IV £10,000 in ransom for the deposed Queen. Margaret renounced all claims to her title and property in England, and on 13 November 1475 Edward released her to the custody of his counsellor, Thomas Montgomery, for delivery to Louis of France.[12] Margaret returned home, where she lived in poverty and penury until her death on 25 August 1482.

Edward IV returned to England two months before the birth of the child who had been anticipated in his will. With Anne's birth on 2 November 1475, the royal household settled down to the business of raising its growing family, a business always intertwined with the nation's best interests. Within three years, Anne was betrothed to the son of Archduke Maximilian of Austria. Her dowry of 100,000 crowns, larger than that of her older sisters, indicates both the relative wealth that Edward IV was accumulating and the expanding political agenda of England.

To mollify some of the ill feelings harboured by those who regarded the Treaty of Pécquigny as capitulation to the French, Edward IV spent liberally on public events that displayed his royal presence as King. No occasion was more elaborately staged than the reburial of his father, Richard, Duke of York and his brother Edmund, Earl of Rutland, who had been killed at Wakefield in 1460. York's body, initially desecrated when his head was stuck above Micklegate Bar in York, had been interred by Edward at the family estate at Pontefract after his victory at Towton in 1461. Now with money and stature sufficient to bury his father properly, Edward used the occasion to demonstrate not merely his wealth and prestige, but the lineage through which he claimed the throne of England.

The splendour of the Duke of York's reburial especially engaged the north of England.[13] As King, Edward did not participate in the ten-day procession from Pontefract to Fotheringhay, which was led by Richard of Gloucester as chief mourner and attended by nobles, officers of arms and 400 'poor men' on foot carrying torches. The King met the procession at the family estate of Fotheringhay where he, Queen Elizabeth, and two daughters gathered for the reburial ceremonies.

Fotheringhay had been granted to Edmund Plantagenet, founder of the House of York, by his father, Edward III, and had become a principal residence of his descendants. The Duke of York and Cecily spent much time at the castle, where three of their sons were born, including Richard, Duke of Gloucester. After the death of her husband, Cecily had lived there until 1469. Now the family gathered to pay tribute to the father of the first Yorkist King.

When the procession arrived at Fotheringhay on 29 July 1476, the King met it at the entrance to the cemetery of the collegiate church of St Mary and All Saints. Unlike the other mourners dressed in black, the King wore a blue habit, with mourning hood furred with miniver. The large group of mourners included the King's brothers Gloucester and Clarence, the Queen's brother Anthony Wydeville, her eldest son, Thomas Grey, Marquis of Dorset, and her chamberlain, Lord Dacre. The effigy and coffin were removed from its carriage and placed inside the church, on the hearse especially constructed for the occasion.

The hearse was the size of a small house, with pillars at the four corners rising high to hold an ornamental roof and candelabra that illuminated the coffin and its effigy. Fifty-one wax images of kings, painted and gilded, and 420 gilded angels decorated the pillars of the hearse, which was itself gilded and 'powdered with silver roses and a gold sun'.[14] Pennons displayed symbols of the Duke, including 'two with a white lion, and two with a black bull'. Twenty banners depicted 'diverse saints and arms', along with 150 streamers and '218 scutcheons of paper beaten with gold and silver with the arms of the said late duke of York [and] 120 scutcheons of paper in the colours of the same arms'. Lining the ceiling was 'le maieste cloth', painted with the image of Christ sitting on a rainbow. Barriers along the side of the hearse allowed mourners of rank to stand next to the coffin, separated from the less eminent mourners who stood outside the barriers. The coffin placed in the centre of the hearse was covered by a blue cloth of gold, with a white satin cross. A lifelike effigy of the Duke, dressed in a gown of dark blue furred with ermine, lay atop the coffin. A purple cap of maintenance was on the effigy's head, behind which a white angel held a crown to indicate the Duke's royal right to the throne he had never possessed.

Services began on the evening of 29 July where, during the Magnificat, Lord Hastings, representing the King, offered to the body seven pieces of cloth of gold, each five yards long. Lord Dacre, the Queen's chamberlain, offered five yards for Queen Elizabeth, each piece laid across the body in the shape of a cross. The Queen attended the service dressed in mourning and accompanied by two daughters and many other ladies wearing mourning.

On Tuesday 30 July, three High Masses were sung by the Bishop of Lincoln. During the gospel, the Queen's brother Anthony, Earl Rivers offered to the body three pieces of cloth of gold five yards long, followed by similar offerings by Essex, Kent, Northumberland, Lincoln, Suffolk, Gloucester and Clarence. The King offered seven pieces and the Queen six, all of which were placed in the form of a cross. Symbolic offerings reflecting the Duke's knighthood followed, after which a black horse in full-length black trappings decorated with the royal arms was led to the choir by barons, knights and heralds. Lord Ferrers, holding an axe with its point downwards, rode on the horse. The King then offered the Mass penny and:

…in passing did his obeisance before the said body. Next the queen came to offer, dressed all in blue without a high headdress, and there she made a great obeisance and reverence to the said body, and next two of the king's daughters came to offer in the same way.[15]

After offerings from the ambassadors of France, Denmark and Portugal, the common people followed with their pennies.

The account recorded by the Chester Herald states that 5,000 people came to receive alms. Others enjoyed the ceremonies in

…tents and pavilions and halls of canvas where people could sit and rest and there were as many as 1,500 places where they could sit and eat, besides other, reserved, places; and apart from the court of the king there were counted on the said day as many as twenty thousand persons; and there was enough to drink and eat of wine and meat for everybody.[16]

Provisions for feeding such a mass of people required slaughtering 49 beef, 210 sheep, 90 calves and 200 pigs, supplemented by unknown, but obviously enormous, quantities of fish and poultry. Thirty-one tuns of ale and forty pipes of wine provided liquid refreshment.[17]

Noteworthy is the presence of the king's daughters', who were unnamed in the contemporary accounts. Most likely they were Princess Elizabeth, aged ten, and Mary, almost nine. Edward and Elizabeth were grooming their children for their roles as royal adults, even as their already good-sized family continued to increase. If not during their stay at Fotheringhay, it was at some point close in time that their eighth child was conceived. Elizabeth gave birth to a third son, who was named after his uncle George, Duke of Clarence, sometime before 12 April 1477. The name, for those who believe in sympathetic correspondences, proved unpropitious. The child died as an infant, perhaps from the plague epidemic that struck London in 1479.

The days at Fotheringhay were the last the family York would spend together in harmonious celebration. Storm clouds were gathering over the life of George, Duke of Clarence. They would soon burst, with disastrous and lasting consequences for the Royals.

CHAPTER SEVENTEEN

George, Duke of Clarence: Perpetual Malcontent

If Queen Elizabeth disliked Clarence, who could blame her? He was part of Warwick's rebellion in 1469, which had executed her father, Earl Rivers, and her brother, Sir John Wydeville. Clarence had helped Warwick depose her husband during the Lancastrian readeption of Henry VI. Following Edward's victory over Warwick, the brief moments of family repose and leisure had been disrupted by the conflict between Clarence and Gloucester over their Neville wives and inheritances. Now Clarence once again shattered the peace of both nation and family during the prosperous years that followed the invasion of France. Elizabeth lived with the machinations and malevolence of Clarence every day of her life. Her dislike of the man was both reasonable and right.

Even though Clarence had been welcomed back into the family after his treason with Warwick and his quarrel with Gloucester, he remained a malcontent. His marriage to Isabel Neville had produced two surviving children, a daughter, Margaret, and a son, Edward. Six weeks after giving birth to another child, Isabel died on 22 December 1476. She was twenty-five years old. Left a widower at the age of twenty-seven, Clarence was once more an eligible bachelor and began looking for a new wife.

Having made a fortune with his first marriage, he held hopes for even more success with a second. Clarence looked towards Burgundy, where the recent death of Charles the Bold had left his daughter, Mary, a very rich and powerful Duchess of Burgundy. Mary's stepmother, Margaret of York, had always favoured her younger brother Clarence and supported a marriage between him and her stepdaughter. Edward IV objected, knowing well his brother's overreaching ambitions and disloyal tendencies. The King of England could not countenance Clarence having power in

Burgundy, where he could cause endless trouble with France and Brittany. Croyland records the King's displeasure at such a marriage:

> He threw all possible impediments in the way, in order that the match before-mentioned might not be carried into effect, and exerted all his influence that the heiress might be given in marriage to Maximilian, son of the emperor, which was afterwards effected.[1]

Perhaps to buy time, Edward IV proposed another suitor: Anthony, Earl Rivers, the cultured and recently widowed brother of Queen Elizabeth. The best-educated and most urbane of the English candidates, Anthony's status, however, was insufficient to interest a duchess. As Philippe de Commynes sniffed from his French perspective: 'he was only a minor earl and she was the greatest heiress of her time'.[2] Edward IV very well knew the importance of rank and perhaps was trying to send his sister Margaret the message that their brother Clarence did not have his approval.

At the same time, Louis XI of France offered the eleven-year-old Dauphin as husband to the twenty-year-old Mary, never mind the previous betrothal of the Dauphin to Princess Elizabeth of York. The Duchess of Burgundy herself settled the issue by marrying Archduke Maximilian of Austria, in accordance with an agreement made earlier by her father and the Holy Roman Emperor.

Clarence responded with all the petulance that thwarted ambition and a disturbed mind could produce. He blamed Queen Elizabeth and her brother Rivers for obstructing his marriage, although clearly Edward IV was the one who had sent Sir John Donne and John Morton to Ghent, in February 1477, to formally propose the marriage of Anthony and the Duchess Mary.

Clarence's revenge took twisted, quite astonishing turns. His actions are somewhat murky, given incomplete historical records, but the certain facts begin with two bizarre trials in April and May 1477, both of which involved Clarence. The first, held at Warwick Castle, accused three defendants of causing the death of his wife, Isabel, by poisoning. Ankarette Twynyho, servant to Isabel, was accused of serving her mistress poisoned ale on 10 October, which caused her death on 22 December 1476. John Thuresby was accused of giving poisoned ale to the baby Richard on 21 December 1476, leading to the infant's death on 1 January 1477. Sir

Roger Tocotes was accused of helping the other two carry out their dastardly deeds.[3]

The trumped-up charges were ridiculous, especially given the absurdly long time between the alleged poisonings and the ensuing deaths. Nevertheless, Clarence's men seized Ankarette at her manor at Cayford, and took her seventy miles across three counties to Warwick, the seat of Clarence's power. They took from her 'all her jewels, money and goods, and also in the said Duke's behalf, *as though he had used King's power…* kept Ankarette in prison unto the hour of nine before noon on the morrow, to wit, the Tuesday after the closing of Pasche [Easter]'.[4] In three short hours on 15 April 1477, Ankarette was indicted, tried and found guilty by a jury which determined that 'she should be led from the bar there to the gaol of Warwick and from thence should be drawn through the town to the gallows of Myton, and hanged till she were dead'.[5] Ankarette and her alleged accomplice, John Thuresby, were executed on the spot by the sheriff. Sir Roger Tocotes had the good sense to be absent.

Rigged from start to finish, the trial was conducted by justices and a jury of Clarence's tenants, who dared not cross their lord. In a subsequent petition to the King, Ankarette's kinsman, Roger Twynyho, stated that 'the jurors for fear gave the verdict contrary to their conscience, in proof whereof divers of them came to the said Ankarette in remorse and asked her forgiveness, in consideration of the imaginations of the said Duke and his great might'.[6] After her death, Roger asked that the record, process, verdict and judgment be voided, but that the justices and sheriff 'not be vexed', since the entire process was done 'by the command of the said Duke'. Edward IV's official response was *pro forma*: 'Soit fait come il est desire.' ('Let it be done as desired.') Perhaps the best explanation for this sorry episode is Professor J.R. Lander's: 'the accusations were so fantastically implausible that only a seriously disturbed mind could have produced them'.[7]

Within a month, another trial occurred in London involving three conspirators – John Stacy, Thomas Blake and Thomas Burdet – indicted for 'seeking the death and destruction of the King and Prince'.[8] The three men were accused of disseminating rhymes, ballads, complaints and seditious arguments against the King, actions intended to provoke rebellion and to cause 'the final destruction of the King and Prince'. The defendants were tried by a jury of nobles, including ten members of the Order of the Garter and seven from other ranks of English nobility – one-third of the English nobility. This powerful and authoritative jury convicted all of the accused.[9] Blake was later pardoned, but Burdet and Stacy were hanged at Tyburn on 20 May 1477, each declaring his innocence before execution.

Because Burdet was a close associate of Clarence, the one who would most benefit from the death of the King and the prince, the Duke immediately fell under suspicion of conspiring with the traitors. Such suspicion might have remained mere gossip, had Clarence not committed a very strange and inexplicable act. While the King was at Windsor, Clarence and a Franciscan friar, Doctor William Goddard, attended a meeting of the King's Council at Westminster, where Goddard read the declarations of innocence made by Burdet and Stacy before their executions. After making that statement, Clarence and Goddard left the council.[10]

Not only did the visit call attention to Clarence's close relationship with the traitors, but it provocatively challenged the King and the system of justice that had convicted them. Twice within two months, Clarence had acted irresponsibly, first using his power as if he were King and then defying a ruling of the courts. Edward IV had no choice but to arrest his brother. In June 1477, Clarence was sent to the Tower accused of 'conduct... derogatory to the laws of the realm and most dangerous to judges and juries throughout the kingdom'.[11]

Clarence was tried by Parliament during the sessions, which began on 16 January and ended on 21 February 1478. Convicted by Parliament, he was sentenced to death. When Edward hesitated for ten days in carrying out the death sentence, the Speaker of the Commons formally asked the House of Lords to impose the punishment. Clarence died on 18 February 1478, at the Tower of London – whether drowned in the infamous barrel of Malmsey wine or executed in some more direct manner remains obscured in myth and history.

All this would seem to have little to do with Queen Elizabeth, except that subsequently she was accused of instigating the actions taken against Clarence! Five years later – after the death of Edward IV – Dominic Mancini reported that Elizabeth resented Clarence for 'his bitter and public denunciation of Elizabeth's obscure family'.[12] Only a foreigner ignorant of the prominence of the first Earl Rivers and the Duchess of Bedford in the courts of both Henry VI and Edward IV, as well as of the stature of Anthony, the second Earl Rivers, could call the Wydevilles 'obscure'. An Italian who spoke limited English, Mancini depended on informants for his analysis of English politics and the complex personalities at its centre. He gathered his information during the anxious period after Edward IV's death, when Richard of Gloucester was claiming the crown and disseminating propaganda that demeaned and denigrated the Wydevilles. As good as he was at gathering intelligence, Mancini inevitably recorded what he heard on the streets of London. His conclusions must be weighed against other evidence.

Mancini claims that Clarence's insults and calumnies caused Elizabeth to believe 'that her offspring by the king would never come to the throne, unless the duke of Clarence were removed; and of this she easily persuaded the king'.[13] In Mancini's account, the Queen arranged to have Clarence 'accused of conspiring the king's death by means of spells and magicians'. Mancini also alleges that after Clarence's death, 'Richard duke of Gloucester was so overcome with grief for his brother, that he could not dissimulate so well, but that he was overheard to say that he would one day avenge his brother's death', providing a motive for Richard's actions against Edward's children and wife.[14]

Ever since, some historians have blamed Queen Elizabeth for Clarence's death. M.A. Hicks, Clarence's biographer, doubts the justice of Clarence's trial and questions Edward's intent to execute his brother. Based on the delay between Clarence's arrest and execution – and on reports of the King's subsequent regrets – Hicks speculates that Edward IV ultimately acted against Clarence only because of 'the instigation of others'.[15] Those 'others' were the Wydevilles, who supposedly stacked the Parliament of 1478 that convicted Clarence. As evidence, Hicks points to Wydeville dominance of Prince Edward's household, and their overwhelming presence in London during Clarence's trial and imprisonment.

The Wydevilles were, indeed, prominent in London during Clarence's trial because Edward IV had, in typical fashion, scheduled a magnificent royal event to coincide with the meeting of Parliament. What better opportunity to display to the nobles and citizens of his realm the King's wealth, prestige and progeny? The occasion featured the wedding of the four-year-old Prince Richard to Anne Mowbray, an older woman at the age of five. All the Wydevilles attended the wedding and the tournament, while Clarence was conspicuous by his absence, imprisoned as he was in the Tower.

The marriage, on 15 January 1478, was a splendid affair – as were all royal events during these years. Anne was heiress to the enormous wealth of the recently deceased John Mowbray, Duke of Norfolk, a bride worthy of a royal prince. At the wedding ceremony, the Wydevilles fulfilled their roles as relatives of the groom's mother, but they certainly did not displace Edward IV's family. If during the bride's presentation in the King's great chamber at Westminster, on the day before the wedding, she was 'led by the right noble Count Rivers', on the morning of the wedding, Princess Anne:

> …came out of the Queen's chamber at Westminster, and so proceeded through the King's great chamber, and into the White Hall, and so proceeded into Saint Stephen's Chapel, being attended by great estates and many ladies and gentlewomen, my lord the noble Count of Lincoln led her on the right hand, and upon the second hand the noble Count Rivers.[16]

The Count of Lincoln was the King's nephew, John de la Pole, in the place of honour on the bride's right. The rest of the royal family sat under a canopy of 'imperial cloth of gold' and included 'the King, the Queen, and my Lord the Prince, and the right high and excellent Princess and Queen of right, Cicely Mother to the King, the Lady Elizabeth, the Lady Mary, the Lady Cicely, daughters to the King and our Sovereign Lord'.

The King himself escorted the bride to the altar, and 'the high and mighty Prince the Duke of Gloucester' brought in golden basins filled with coins of gold and silver to cast among the common people.[17] After the ceremony, Princess Anne was led to the feast by Gloucester on her right hand and the Duke of Buckingham on her left, both relatives of the King. The Wydevilles were present, but the King's blood relatives took precedence during the wedding ceremony.

The Wydevilles, as always, dominated the 'Jousts Royal' held at Westminster on the following Thursday, where they captured the public's attention through their splendid chivalric display. The Marquis of Dorset entered the lists first, with his helmet carried by the Duke of Buckingham (a courtesy that contradicts reputed and repeated claims of Buckingham's long-standing antagonism toward the Wydevilles). Sir Richard Grey, the Queen's second son, followed next with his retinue of knights and esquires, clothed in blue and tawny, and three horses trapped in crimson cloth of gold and tissue. 'The victorious Earl Rivers' made a dramatic entrance in 'the house of an Hermit walled and covered with black velvet'. Exploiting the pageantry of the celebration, Rivers was 'armed in the habit of a White Hermit', a costume of 'pleasance' which he removed before the tournament began. His servants also wore livery of blue and tawny, embroidered with columbines and embellished with drops and flames. Sir Edward Wydeville participated, with horses trapped in cloth of gold and tissue.[18]

After all the spears were broken and strokes exchanged, the tourney prizes went not to the Wydevilles, but to the opposing team. Thomas Fynes was declared the best jouster, Richard Haute the best runner of the 'Ostinge Harnesse', and Robert Clifford the best of the Tourney. In a characteristic act of *noblesse oblige*, Earl Rivers 'rewarded the said Kings of Arms and Heralds with twenty marks'.[19]

Certainly, Clarence's absence from the wedding celebrations emphasised his isolation from the family. But to assert that the Wydeville presence at the wedding and prominence at the tournament caused Parliament to convict Clarence is to ignore Clarence's history of perfidy and treason, while shifting blame for his crimes to his victims. Innuendo, suggestions and subjunctive verbs in modern histories distort the facts: '...the Wydevilles *probably* pulled every available string. But in happier circumstances, if ascendant, Clarence *might have* commanded support which in adversity he was denied.'[20] Reiterated allegations, such as 'The Wydevilles and their allies strove to influence elections', and negative sneers about 'the Wydeville connection'[21] and 'the Wydeville coalition'[22] rhetorically demean the family beyond any substantiating evidence.

Hypothetical speculation cannot obscure Clarence's lifetime of treacheries. Nor should it transfer Clarence's crimes and greed to Queen Elizabeth and her family. The profound irony of such displaced blame lies in the contrast between Clarence's wealth, all obtained through marriage or grants from the King, and the quite modest holdings of the Wydeville brothers and sisters. After Warwick's death, for instance, Clarence had become the second richest man in the kingdom by denying inheritance rights to the Duchess of Warwick. Never satisfied with what he had, he always grasped for more – the crown itself – until he finally overreached his bounds. That Edward IV may, indeed, have regretted the death of his younger brother merely accentuates the King's infinite patience with Clarence in spite of his disloyalty and treasons. Regret and sorrow for a lost brother, however, hardly proves domination – or even undue influence – by the Wydevilles.

A modern psychologist might analyse Clarence as a privileged individual with a sense of entitlement who finds himself outclassed by those he considers inferior. Resultant anger, exacerbated by instability, rapaciousness and envy, led to actions that were no less than criminal. When Clarence finally confronted his death and the fate of his soul, his last thoughts tried to set right the evils he had perpetrated on the Wydevilles. His final wishes, in essence, confessed his sins against the Queen's family. Accordingly, on 19 November 1478, the King granted to

> ...the king's kinsman Anthony, Earl Ryvers, and his heirs and assigns for six years from Easter last, *in consideration of the injuries perpetrated on him and his parents by George, late duke of Clarence, and because the said duke on the day of his death and before intended that he should be recompensed*, of the manors of Sweyneston, Brighteston, Thoruey and Wellowe with their members with knights' fees and advowsons of churches in the Isle of Wight, reserving to the king escheats, wards, marriages and reliefs.[23]

Clarence's contrition perhaps amounts to a confession of his part in the deaths of the first Earl Rivers and Sir John Wydeville. No evidence of the 'injuries perpetrated' on Anthony survives to explain the recompense Clarence requested. The Wydevilles were not the only victims of Clarence's greed. When Edward learned of Clarence's extortion of Lord Dynham, the King granted Dynham an annuity of £100 for six years 'for the safety of the soul of the said duke'.[24] To the end, Edward's love for his brother tried to save Clarence's soul from perdition.

Edward awarded custody and wardship of Clarence's son, Edward, including the right to arrange the boy's marriage, to the Queen's son, the Marquis of Dorset, in return for £2,000 paid to the King. That grant included several of Clarence's lucrative estates and manors, including 'the borough, town, hundred and liberty of Tewkesbury' and 'the great court of Bristol... called Earles Court, co Gloucester', along with their knights' fees, marriages, courts, fairs, markets, parks, forests and waters.[25] Dorset also received a grant for life as master of game and steward of Clarence's properties in the counties of Somerset, Devon and Cornwall.[26]

No doubt such preferences shown towards the Wydevilles were resented by the King's Yorkist relatives, who had been born to title and privilege and took offence when others intruded on those rights. Such conflict remains intrinsic to human nature. In fifteenth-century England, where heredity, rank and wealth counted for everything, the ascendancy of the Wydevilles was not welcomed by those who were displaced. But the world was changing faster than the feudal lords could recognise, and within a generation the next dynasty of Tudor kings would elevate merit, rather than heritage, to the prime qualification for its ministers. Social order was being challenged as the medieval world gave way to the Renaissance.

In England, the most significant harbinger of such change was the Queen's brother, Anthony Wydeville, Earl Rivers. Noted for his military service, chivalric triumphs, intellectual achievements and moral character, this 'Renaissance man' had arrived before England was ready for him. Anthony Wydeville would suffer the consequent fate.

CHAPTER EIGHTEEN

Anthony Wydeville: Courtier *Par Excellence*

Sometime between 1508 and 1519, at the height of the Italian Renaissance, Baldassare Castiglione wrote *Il libro del cortegiano,* a manual describing the qualities of the ideal courtier. It swept through European courts with the popularity of a bestseller: 'The principal and true profession of a Courtier ought to be in feats of arms'. No mere warrior, however, this new 'Renaissance man' was courteous, urbane, artistic, scholarly, pious and chivalrous. A gentleman of exemplary conduct, the ideal courtier possessed wisdom and integrity, learning and diplomacy, social skills and eloquence – all to the purpose of fulfilling his major obligation in life: serving his prince as a loyal soldier and wise counsellor.

Anthony Wydeville, Earl Rivers, Lord Scales could have been the prototype for Castiglione's courtier. Beyond his appointment as governor to the Prince of Wales, Anthony provided his King exemplary service as military commander, political leader, diplomatic ambassador, estate administrator and scholarly translator. Even the harshest critics of the Wydevilles have nothing bad to say about Anthony. Dominic Mancini, who otherwise describes the Wydeville family as 'ignoble'[1] and 'obscure'[2] commends Anthony, Earl Rivers as 'a kind, serious and just man, and one tested by every vicissitude of life. Whatever his prosperity he had injured nobody, though benefiting many; and therefore he had entrusted to him the care and direction of the king's eldest son.'[3]

Elegant, well read, and deeply pious, the young Anthony first earned his reputation through service. After his pardon by Edward IV in 1461, he was summoned to Parliament as Lord Scales in December 1462, then joined Edward's siege at Alnwick two years before his sister married the King. After the marriage, the tournament at Smithfield and Anthony's diplomacy in Burgundy earned him the custodianship of Porchester Castle and appointment as governor of the town of Portsmouth in November 1467. (He resigned his rights in Porchester Castle to his brother, Sir Edward, in 1479). In midsummer 1468, Anthony contracted to serve the King with five knights, fifty-five men-at-arms, 2,945 archers, twenty-four shipmasters, and 1,076 mariners.[4] On 7 October 1468 he was appointed Captain of the King's Fleet with 5,000 men, two ships and several galleys that patrolled the waters between England and France.[5] With each increasing responsibility, Sir Anthony solidified the trust placed in him by Edward IV. His fluency in French, his urbane manners and his chivalric skills particularly enhanced the image of England during Anthony's service on the continent.

After Warwick executed Richard Wydeville, Earl Rivers in April 1469, Anthony inherited his father's title and became the respected head of the Wydeville family, second only to the Queen in prominence. Troops commanded by the new Earl Rivers were instrumental in scattering the ships of Warwick and Clarence as they fled to France in late 1469.[6] During Edward's exile, Anthony remained by the King's side. In June 1471, Anthony was appointed Lieutenant of Calais, a position he never filled because Edward subsequently appointed Hastings to that post. Some historians believe that the animosity between the Wydevilles and Hastings began at that point.[7] Anthony vacated the Calais office to Hastings in July 1475 after his appointment as governor to Prince Edward, but the ill feeling may have rippled outward and contributed to the developing factions in Edward IV's court.[8]

As governor to Prince Edward, Anthony not only provided the young boy with a humanistic education, but also helped to quell the disorder and unruliness of the Welsh Marches west of Ludlow, through his prominence on the Prince's Council. In controlling the Marcher lords, each of whom was a law unto himself, the council had to centralise authority under the crown through Commissions of the Peace, which Anthony headed as they met throughout the border counties. In April 1478, for instance, the Commission developed ordinances for the town of Shrewsbury.[9]

When his diplomatic skills were needed by Edward, Anthony departed Ludlow to serve the King. Before the French campaign, the King sent Anthony to Charles the Bold's camp at Neuss to persuade him to lift his siege and to fight in the war against France, as the recalcitrant Duke had promised.[10] While Anthony succeeded in his mission, Burgundy's troops were so battered that by the time they reached France they could provide no help at all to the English, a factor in Edward's decision to negotiate peace. After the truce at Pécquigny, Anthony did not return directly to England, but departed on another religious pilgrimage, this time to Rome and the shrines of southern Italy.

His letter of safe conduct from Edward IV to the Duke of Milan, dated 1 October 1475, did little good, for after leaving Rome, Anthony's group of English pilgrims was robbed at Torre di Baccano, about twelve miles north of the city.[11] Anthony lost all of his jewels and plate, which John Paston valued at 1,000 marks.[12] The pilgrims returned to Rome to seek remedy and apply for restitution of their property, and Queen Elizabeth sent Anthony letters of exchange for 4,000 ducats in Rome. When some of the stolen goods appeared in Venice for sale, the Signoria there graciously restored Anthony's losses 'out of deference for the king of England and his lordship'.[13]

On his way home, Anthony stopped on 7 June 1476 to visit the Duke of Burgundy, who was encamped at Morat. On his arrival, the Duke 'made much of him and sent to meet him'. At Anthony's departure days later, the Duke accused him of leaving to avoid combat with the enemy who was near: 'This is esteemed great cowardice in him, and lack of spirit and honour', writes the Milanese ambassador.[14] It was hardly cowardice, however, to avoid engagement with Charles the Bold in his disastrous military campaigns. Still fresh in Anthony's memory was the Duke's duplicity in promising aid to Edward IV but keeping his troops at Neuss until England's invasion of France was seriously compromised. Anthony also remembered the English march through Picardy, where the Duke refused to allow English troops inside his cities. Rather than let himself be taken in by Burgundy's faithless promises and reckless schemes, Anthony headed home to serve his own King. His good judgment was proved when Charles the Bold was slain just months later on 5 January 1477, laying siege to Nancy during the dead of winter.

During Anthony's pilgrimage, Pope Sixtus IV honoured him with the title of 'Defender and Director of the causes apostolique for the holy father the Pope in... Englande'.[15] Beyond the spiritual enlightenment of his journey, his grand tour of the continent steeped Anthony in the architecture, sculpture and painting of the Italian Renaissance just as it was reaching its apex. He returned to England filled with images of continental culture, and imbued with the new humanism that was exciting western thought.

Anthony's scholarly and artistic impulses, stimulated during the months with Edward IV in Burgundy, were ready to flourish. In Flanders, Anthony had become friends with William Caxton, an English merchant adventurer in service to Margaret of Burgundy. Caxton set up his first printing press at Bruges in 1473, but he moved to Westminster in 1476, where Anthony became his patron. The timing was propitious, since Anthony's governance of Prince Edward encouraged him to translate texts from French into English to educate his young charge. He chose texts that provided the prince with an education in religion and moral philosophy, the essential foundation for enlightened leadership.

Anthony's translation of *The Dictes or Sayengis of the Philosophres* was the first book published in England by Caxton in 1477. Anthony first encountered this text on his pilgrimage to Santiago de Compostela in 1473, when a fellow pilgrim, Louis de Bretaylles, gave him a French translation of the Latin original. Anthony's English translation contains 143 pages of philosophical instructions for living a moral and useful life, followed by a six-page addendum written by Caxton that takes Anthony to task for omitting parts of Socrates.

In his preface, Anthony reflects upon the human condition, 'subject and thrall unto the storms of fortune... and perplexed with worldly adversities', and states that his own 'iniquities and faults' compelled him to make the pilgrimage to the shrine of St James. The book he received as a gift offers a guide to all pilgrims as they journey through life:

> When I had heeded and looked upon it [*The Dictes*] as I had time and space, I gave thereto a very affection, and in especial because of the wholesome and sweet sayings of the paynems [pagans] which is a glorious fair mirror to all good Christian people to behold and understand.[16]

The Dictes begins with the sixteen virtues of 'Sedechias' (probably Zedekiah, King of Judah), which mixes the admonitions of the Ten Commandments with moral precepts such as 'have patience... love Justice... be liberal and not covetous'. Anthony quotes Sedechias on the obligations of rulers of kingdoms:

As it appertains to the people to be subject and obedient to the Royal majesty of their king or prince, right so it behooveth their king or prince to intend diligently to the weal and governance of his people, and rather to Will the Weal of them than his own proper lucre [profit]... If a king or a prince enforce himself to gather money or treasure by subtle exhortation or other ends... he doth amiss, for such treasure may not be gathered without the sequel be to his danger or depopulation of his Realm or country.[17]

The Dictes marches diligently through twenty-two pre-Christian philosophers who have instructed their followers in living the virtuous life. Hermes of Egypt (equated with Mercury and the Hebrew Enok) admonishes to 'let truth be always in your mouth' and 'to employ not your time and your mind in falsehood nor in malice'.[18] Hermes's emphasis on 'science', or knowledge, endorses the new learning that would soon challenge the faith-based traditions of the contemporary medieval Church:

He that will not teach that he understands in science and good conditions, he shall be partner to the ignorance of froward [obstinate] folk. And he that denies to teach science to him that it is covenable [appropriate] unto, he ought to be deprived of his benefice in this world... Liberality and largess is better in science than in riches, for the renown of a wiseman abideth and the riches abideth not.[19]

Carrying on through the philosopher 'Tac' ('he that cannot refrain his ire hath no power over his wit') to Salon (the most difficult thing in a man is 'to know himself') and Sabyon ('a Wiseman ought to beware how he weds a fair woman, for every man will desire to have her love and so they will seek their pleasures to the hurt and displeasure of her husband'), the homilies soon weary the modern reader.[20]

Didactic to the final sentence, Alquinus, Homer, Hippocrates, Pythagoras, Diogenes, Socrates, Plato, Aristotle, Alexander the Great, Ptolemy, Assaron, Legmon, Anese, Sacdarge, Thesille, St Gregory and Galen point out human shortcomings and the need to serve one's fellow man. The book was so popular that it appeared in three editions in 1477, 1479 and 1489.[21]

The content of *The Dictes* takes on special significance because of Anthony's governance of the young prince. While we all know that mere words do not guarantee virtuous actions, the education that Edward V received must surely provoke speculation – and regret – about the enlightened leadership that might have resulted from the youth who had studied such a text. Perhaps the character of the precocious Edward, Prince of Wales, portrayed in Shakespeare's *Richard III*, originated in knowledge about the education the prince received under the supervision of his enlightened governor.

The Dictes also suggests something about the character of its translator. While translators do not necessarily follow the precepts they record, this translation required hundreds of hours devoted to contemplating human frailty and to defining moral principles. This was the first of three such works that Anthony translated, requiring similar labour, intelligence, devotion and contemplation of an imperfect human nature.

After 143 pages of pious instruction, Caxton adds an epilogue that contributes some greatly appreciated comic relief. With tongue firmly in cheek, the printer gently chides the translator for not recording the misogynistic ideas of Socrates, a lapse that the printer feels compelled to correct. Properly deferential, Caxton reiterates several times that Lord Rivers urged him to oversee the work, 'and where as I should find fault, to correct it'. Caxton gladly seized the opportunity.

Commending his 'said Lord' for his excellent translation from French to English, Caxton then launches into extensive speculation about why the translator deleted Socrates's antifeminist sentiments: 'I suppose that some fair lady hath desired him [Anthony] to leave it out of his book'. Or perhaps Lord Rivers was himself 'amorous on some noble lady for whose love he would not set it in his book'. Or perhaps the faults Socrates found in Greek women do not exist in English women who are:

> …right good, wise, pleasant, humble, discrete, sober, chaste, obedient to their husbands, true, secret, steadfast, ever busy and never idle, temperate in speaking and virtuous in all their works or at least should be so, for which cause so evident my said Lord as I suppose thought it was not of necessity to set in his book the failings of his author Socrates touching Women.[22]

Or perhaps this part of *The Dictes* was missing in Lord Rivers copy: 'peradventure… the wind had blown over the leaf at the time of translation'. The printer, therefore, was obliged to correct the translator's omission, especially since his 'said Lord' so often commanded him 'to correct and amend where as I should find fault'.

Either the 'said Lord' had a tin ear for irony or he possessed a sense of humour that allowed Caxton to play such games in print. Protesting more than a little too much, Caxton printed Socrates's misogynistic musings: 'He saw a young maid that learned to write, of whom he [Socrates] said that she multiplied evil upon evil'; 'Whosoever will acquire and get science [knowledge], let him never put him in the governance of a woman.' Whether Earl Rivers omitted this text because of his chivalrous nature or because he disputed the content, we shall never know.

Six weeks after *The Dictes* appeared on 18 November 1477, an illuminated manuscript of the printed text was completed by a scribe, on 24 December 1477. Prepared as a presentation copy for the King, the illumination that introduces the text shows Earl Rivers kneeling on his right knee and presenting the manuscript to the King, who is sitting on his throne and wearing his crown. The Queen sits on the King's left, with the prince standing in front of his mother. A dedicatory verse appears below the illumination:

> This boke late translate here in sight
> By Antony Erle [erasure] that vertueux knyght
> Please it to accepte to youre noble grace
> And at youre convenient leysoure and space
> It to see reede and understond
> A precious Jewell for alle youre land
> For therin is taught howe and in what wise
> Men vertues shuld use and vices desuse
> The Subjette theire Princes ere obeye
> And they therein in right defendng
> Thus to do every man in his degre
> Graunte of his grace the Trinite[23]

The most remarkable thing about this dedication is the erasure of Anthony's title from the page. Throughout the manuscript, Anthony's surname and titles have been carefully excised from each folio where they originally appeared. The first sentence of the preface, where Caxton's printed book identifies the translator as 'Antoine Wydeville Erle Ryuyeres, lord Scales', has been vandalised in the handwritten manuscript with carefully excised deletions: 'Antoine W[erasure] Erle [erasure] [erasure]'. Even in the end note, his title has been obliterated: 'Thus endeth the boke of the dictes and notable moral sayenyes of philosophres late translated out of the Frenssh unto Englissh by my forsaide lorde Th erle of [erasure] and by his comaundment seete in forme and emprinted in right substantiall maner.'

Anne Sutton and Livia Visser-Fuchs suggest that 'perhaps all the erasing was part of an ill-informed Protestant cleaning-up', a practice commonly followed, especially in deleting the names of Popes from books.[24] But Protestants would hardly have taken umbrage at the secular names of 'Wydeville', 'Rivers' and 'Scales', especially in a text of unassailable moral teachings. The care taken to erase Anthony's surname and titles argues for a more specific focus on this particular man. Did someone hate Earl Rivers so much that he attempted to obliterate him from history?

The erasures become poignantly ironic in light of a marginal note in late-sixteenth- or early-seventeenth-century handwriting[25] to the left of the dedicatory inscription:

This Erle was the most
lernyd valyant and
honorable knight of
the world for his tyme
yet all was exersid wth
adverse accydentes in
his lyfe. At length cam
to atcheeve the honor
of an undesarvid death.[26]

The last flyleaf contains another erasure of what once was a signature, perhaps an owner of the manuscript. M.R. James speculates: 'I have wondered whether it was not that of Richard III'.[27] Sutton and Visser-Fuchs reject that possibility, however, based on an examination of the flyleaf signature under ultraviolet light.

Ownership of this manuscript cannot be traced, even during Edward's lifetime. And while the events following Edward's death encourage intriguing speculations about Richard III excising the name of the man he executed, no proof exists to assign ownership or responsibility for the erasures. The enigma only deepens the mysteries surrounding the Wydeville reputation. Someone certainly wished to erase all evidence of the moralistic Anthony Wydeville, Earl Rivers from this earth.

Anthony's devotion to issues philosophical and moral resulted in a second book, *The Morale Proverbes of Christyne*, printed by Caxton at Westminster, 'in February the cold season' 1478.[28] Just eight pages long, this moral tome translates the proverbs of Christine du Castel (de Pizan) into rhymed couplets which, again, guide readers to an exemplary life:

> A prince's court without a governour
> Being prudent can not last in honour.

★   ★   ★

> Great diligence with a good remembrance
> Doth a man oft to high honour advance.

★   ★   ★

> He that seeketh often others to blame
> Giveth right cause to have of him the same.

★   ★   ★

> Worldly richess for to win wrongfully
> Doth in danger bring the soul and body

The irregular rhythms and contrived rhymes fall far short of poetic success. As with *The Dictes*, these rhymed aphorisms, didactic to a fault, are best read in small doses – and with an added tolerance for poetic dissonance. A moralist, yes. A poet, Anthony was not.

During this period, James III of Scotland proposed a marriage between his sister Margaret and Earl Rivers, aimed at strengthening the ties between the two countries. A marriage treaty was drawn up in December 1478, and a safe-conduct pass was sent to Margaret on 22 August 1479. The Scots Parliament approved a dowry of 20,000 marks, and Edward himself planned to attend the wedding, scheduled for October 1479 at Nottingham. The marriage was postponed, however, when the Scots began to send raiding parties into northern England, and Edward prepared to invade Scotland. Open warfare ultimately led to the cancellation of two proposed marriages: Anthony, Lord Rivers to Margaret of Scotland, and Cecily, the King's nine-year-old daughter, to James III's son.

In the midst of marriage proposals and war preparations, Anthony continued translating and in 1479 published the *Cordiale siue de quatuor nouissimis*, a consideration of the 'four last things' whose remembrance will keep man from falling into sin.[29] Another 149 pages teach about the possibility of salvation. In his prologue, Anthony thanks God for the mercy and grace that enables man to survive his present transitory life, which is afflicted with frailty, inconstancy, feebleness and 'insufficiency of self to resist the fraudulent malice and temptation of our ancient enemy the fiend'. Reason must be man's 'lantern', and 'remembrance' the guiding force to man's salvation.

The four sections of the *Cordiale* discuss in sequence 'the holy remembrance of death', 'the last and final day of Judgment', Hell and its painful places, and 'the blissful Joys of heaven'. Each section is subdivided into three parts. The remembrance of bodily death, for instance, should cause man to 'be meek and humble himself', 'despise all vain worldly things', and 'do penance and to accept it with glad heart'. Reflections on the Day of Judgment explain that accusation is a 'thing to be dread', Judgement Day is 'terrible and not without cause for there must be given a due reckoning and account of every thing', and 'the extreme sentence causeth doubts to be had of the Judgement'.

The section on Hell discusses the diverse and many names of Hell in Holy Scripture, 'the great and sundry paines' that afflict those who descend into Hell, and 'the diverse conditions of grievance in the pains of Hell. The last section, describing the Joys of Heaven, celebrates the beauty, clearness and light of the 'Royalme of Heaven', 'the manifold goodness that be abundant therein', and 'the perpetual and infinite Joy and gladness therein'.

Caxton's three-page epilogue once more commends the translator:

> This book is thus translated out of French into our maternal tongue by the noble and virtuous lord Anthoine Earl Rivers, Lord Scales & of the Isle of Wight, Defender and director of the causes apostolic for our holy father the Pope in this Realm of England. Uncle & governor to my lorde prince of Wales.[30]

Caxton recalls 'the time of the great tribulation and adversity of my said lord', who has since gone on pilgrimages to St James in Galicia, St Bartholomew in Rome, St Andrew in Amalfi, St Matthew in Naples and St Nicolas in Bari. Caxton also commends Anthony, not only for his service to the King and Prince of Wales, but for using his time to translate this text rather than for leisure.

Caxton also mentions Anthony's 'diverse ballads against the seven deadly sins', poems which have been lost to posterity. In commending his translator and patron, Caxton describes a character which 'conceiveth well the mutability and the unstableness of this present life and... desireth with a great zeal and spiritual love our ghostly help and perpetual salvation. And that we shall abhore and utterly forsake the abominable and damnable sins', including 'pride, perjury, terrible swearing, theft, murder, and many others'.[31]

Anthony may also have assisted Caxton in the printing of *Le Morte D'Arthur*. Lotte Hellinga's meticulous tracing of the manuscript – from its likely owner Richard Followell, who lived in Litchborough in Northamptonshire, just ten miles from the Grafton home of the Wydevilles, to the printing press of Caxton – presents a convincing case for Earl Rivers as the 'instigator of the printing of this book'.[32] Because the printed text was completed on 31 July 1485, during the reign of Richard III, who had already executed Anthony, Caxton could not name his patron and merely credits 'a certain gentleman' who delivered the manuscript to him.[33]

Even as Anthony immersed himself in religious and philosophical contemplation, he continued supervising his worldly affairs. Papers surviving in the files of his lawyer and business agent, Andrew Dymmock, reveal a man with sharp business acumen and a clear mind, who personally supervised the affairs of his estates. He wrote with authority and knowledge as he issued instructions for paying bills, discussed wheat prices, and arranged the London sale of sheep brought from Wales. A political realist, he discussed means of electing his preferred candidates to the Parliament of January 1483, and he requested a copy of his recently renewed patent to govern the prince's household.

When fortune turned against him in 1483, Anthony resorted to poetry to record his philosophical acceptance of life's end. In a short ballad composed in prison at Pontefract Castle while awaiting execution at Gloucester's order, Anthony's resignation to his fate is clear.

> Me thinks truly
> Bounden am I
> And that greatly

> To be content;
> Seeing plainly
> That fortune doth awry
> All contrary
> From mine intent.

While the final stanza welcomes Fortune, he laments:

> But I neer went
> Thus to be shent [killed]
> But so it meant.
> Such is her wont.[34]

In this case the jarring rhythms and failed rhymes reflect the reality of the axe about to descend on his neck.

Anthony Wydeville's published work and his lifelong deeds eloquently refute the modern reputation of the Wydevilles as unprincipled, conniving schemers devoted to personal aggrandisement. As head of the royal in-laws, Anthony's *contemptus mundi* musings bespeak a profound and sincere rejection of things worldly. Pious and contemplative devotion, recognition of worldly sin and a desire for redemption define this devout man. Yet his modern critics remain unpersuaded – and somewhat bemused – by perceived contradictions in Anthony's behaviour. M.A. Hicks, who condemns the 'grasping' Anthony for retaining his first wife's inheritance and pursuing reversion rights to other estates, muses:

> Strangely Anthony waited eight years from the death of his first wife until his second marriage to Mary Lewis, a teenager with modest estates in Essex. Stranger yet, after painfully accumulating estates, Anthony planned to divide them between his brothers, neither of whom was married. The three brothers' apparent unconcern about the future prosperity of their family, or even its continuance, contrasts with their personal greed. One wonders what was the point.[35]

Perhaps sharing – in the tradition inspired by Anthony's philosophy and religion – was the point. In any case, Anthony cannot logically be condemned as 'grasping', then criticised for marrying modestly and for giving away his estates.

Sharing their property fairly and equally was a tradition followed by other Wydevilles. In 1485, Sir Edward Wydeville designated an inheritance priority for his annuity that was absurdly complicated, considering its paltry value of £50. Sir Edward designated his first heir to be his brother, Sir Richard Wydeville. If Richard died without heirs, the annuity was divided among their sisters Anne, Margaret and Joan, and their niece Elizabeth (daughter of deceased sister Mary). If those four beneficiaries died without heirs, the annuity went to two other sisters, Queen Dowager Elizabeth and Katharine, Duchess of Buckingham.[36] Sir Edward's intent seems clear. Beyond the male prerogative of inheritance, the money was split equally among the family members who needed it most. Only if they lacked heirs did it go to the Queen Dowager and Duchess of Buckingham, who enjoyed resources of their own.

Among the five Wydeville brothers, Anthony, John and Lionel benefited from their connection to Edward IV. Anthony earned his rewards through service. John was murdered for his audacity in marrying the Duchess of Norfolk. Lionel became Chancellor of Oxford University and Bishop of Salisbury, venerated positions to be sure, but ones that produced no notable wealth. Neither Richard nor Edward Wydeville has ever been charged with untoward seeking of wealth, and beyond an occasional tournament honour, they remain footnotes in Edward IV's annals. Given that record, where is the evidence of 'greed' and 'grasping' for which the Wydevilles have been castigated by modern critics?

When such accusations are traced to their source, the propaganda of Warwick, Clarence and, later, Gloucester always rears its ugly head. Once Warwick and Clarence were out of the picture, the King's youngest brother took up their cause in asserting dominance of the blood royal. The hatred and envy that incited Warwick and Clarence to execute the first Earl Rivers now simmered – and was fast approaching boiling point – in the soul of Richard, Duke of Gloucester. The first act Gloucester would commit when beginning his coup against Edward V would be the seizure and imprisonment of Anthony Wydeville, Earl Rivers, Lord Scales. Gloucester held his prisoner for fifty-six days before he dared to order Anthony's execution on 25 June 1483. Twelve days later, Gloucester was crowned King Richard III. His purification of the 'blood royal' from the contaminating influences of the elegant, cultured and pious Wydevilles would last just two years.

CHAPTER NINETEEN

The Queen's Happy Years, 1475–1482

W hile the rivalry between Anthony, Earl Rivers and Richard, Duke of Gloucester was growing, Queen Elizabeth was enjoying seven happy years of family prosperity. She shared with Anthony his love of books and his deep piety. Both had been influenced by their mother, Jacquetta, who had grown up surrounded by the bibliophiles of the Burgundian courts. Jacquetta's first husband, the Duke of Bedford, had purchased the French royal library in June 1425, after he became Regent of France, and Richard Griffith postulates that many of the 800 volumes in that collection were inherited by Jacquetta at Bedford's death and passed on to Anthony.[1] Only one surviving manuscript originally from the French royal family reveals Wydeville ownership, however, and it was not listed in the inventory of books purchased by Bedford. That illuminated manuscript of *Oeuores poètiques de Christine de Pison* displays a handwritten 'Jaquete' and the motto and autograph of Anthony on its flyleaf.[2]

Elizabeth, too, treasured books. The final entry in her 1466–67 household accounts lists £10 spent for a book, title unknown, purchased from 'Willelmi Wulflete', Chancellor of Cambridge University.[3] Autographs in the illuminated manuscript of the *Romance of the Saint Graal* – 'E Wydevyll', 'Elysabeth, the kyngys dowther', 'Cecyl the kyngys dowther', 'Jane Grey', 'Thys boke is myne dame Alyanor Haute' – trace the family's love of books through successive generations.[4] A late-fifteenth-century inscription on the back folio of a copy of Caxton's first printed book, *Recuyell of the Histories of Troy*, associates that volume with Elizabeth:

This boke is mine quene elizabet late wiffe unto the
moste noble king edwarde the forthe off whose

bothe soolis y be seche almyghty Gode ~~Take~~
Take to his onfinyght mercy above. Amen.
Per me Thoma
Shukburghe iuniorem[5]

Thomas Shukburghe, from a family whose members were in Elizabeth's service, may have obtained the book and recorded its previous ownership by the Queen.[6]

A religious text, *Hours of the Guardian Angel*, almost certainly belonged to Elizabeth, whose name is spelled out with an acrostic 'ELISABETH', each letter of which introduces the first nine lines of a dedicatory poem to a 'Lady sovereyne princes'.[7] The presentation miniature depicts a woman kneeling before a crowned princess who has 'red-gold hair beneath a pearl-decorated, open crown' and is dressed in a crimson surcoat trimmed in ermine. Analysis by Sutton and Visser-Fuchs of the clothing depicted on both donor and Queen convincingly establishes Elizabeth as the 'Sovereign Princess'. The gift of this volume would have pleased the Queen, whose piety was an essential, deeply felt and constant part of her nature.

Caxton also mentions Elizabeth in a book he gave to Edward, Prince of Wales, containing the story of Jason and the Golden Fleece, printed around 1477. Caxton states that the gift was made with the King's 'licence and congye [permission] and by the supportacion of our most redobted liege lady, most excellent princesse the Quene'. Caxton's 'Prologue' hopes that the young prince will 'begin to learn [to] read English, not for any beauty or good endyting [composition] of our English tongue that is therein, but for the novelty of the histories which as I suppose have not been had before the translation hereof'.[8] The Queen, who became a patron of Caxton along with her brother Anthony, clearly believed the printing of books to be essential for knowledge and education. They were right. It changed the world.

How much influence Elizabeth had in encouraging the King's bibliographic interests is less certain. During his exile in Flanders, Edward IV became interested in the libraries of Lord Gruuthuyse and of his sister, Margaret, Duchess of Burgundy. After his restoration, Edward began to buy books and manuscripts that ultimately became the core of the royal library of England. That the Queen promoted such purchases to the King, who was immersed in the demands of governing the realm, is probable, but not provable.

With the number of royal children increasing, education became increasingly important to the Queen. Elizabeth gave birth to ten children between 1466 and 1480, with four born after the King's return from his foray into France. There were moments of sadness, when Margaret died in 1472 and George in 1477, both within months of their births, but the other children provided great joy for their mother, who took care to educate them in both letters and in courtly traditions. In 1476, Master John Giles, grammar teacher of the princes Edward and Richard, was rewarded with a lifetime grant of £20 yearly.[9]

The protocol of royal responsibility and ritual was an essential part of the children's education. Two daughters, presumably ten-year-old Elizabeth and eight-year-old Mary, experienced firsthand the public ritual of royal life when attending the 1476 reburial of their grandfather, the Duke of York. When the Queen celebrated Mass at the Garter ceremony on St George's Day, arriving on horseback and dressed in a murrey gown of the Order of the Garters, Princess Elizabeth accompanied her 'in a gown of the same livery'.[10]

A more interesting lesson in political and religious protocol occurred during the wedding of Prince Richard to Anne Mowbray, when the seven-year-old Prince Edward and his sisters Elizabeth, Mary and Cecily witnessed the diplomatic and religious manoeuvres necessary to subvert canon law prohibiting the marriage of close relatives. The wedding procession with the four-year-old groom and the five-year-old bride was stopped at the door of the Chapel by one Doctor Cooke, who pronounced that

> …the high and mighty Prince Richard Duke of York ought not to be wedded to that high and excellent Princess, for that they were within degrees of marriage; the one at the fourth, the other at the third; for which cause he defended [forbid] the espousals, without that there were a special license from the Pope, and dispensation from the Pope for the said nearness of blood.[11]

Doctor Gunthorpe, an obviously resourceful Dean of the King's Chapel, produced the Pope's bull of authority, and the marriage proceeded, conducted by the Bishop of Norwich. That carefully staged exchange quelled any gossip and precluded any future questions about the legitimacy of the royal marriage.

During these happy years, the Queen's continuing interest in charitable and religious works led her to endow a chapel dedicated to St Erasmus at Westminster Abbey. On 13 January 1479, Abbot John Estney received a royal charter authorising a new chapel to be erected next to the Lady Chapel, and to be funded by permanent conveyance from the Queen of her property rights to two parts of the manors and lordships of Cradley and of Hagley in Worcestershire. The third part of the manors would revert to Westminster convent at the death of Margaret, widow of Fulk Stafford.[12]

The Queen's selection of St Erasmus, venerated during the fifteenth century as a martyr, may have derived from that saint's tenacity when afflicted by adversity. During the reign of Diocletian, Erasmus converted many pagans to the Christian faith and survived the Emperor's persecutions only by living as a solitary hermit on Mount Lebanon, where he was fed by a raven. Discovered, he was taken to Diocletian, beaten, covered in pitch and set on fire. Miraculously unhurt, he was imprisoned again but rescued by an angel who led him to Illyricum, where he resumed his preaching and teaching. Captured once more, Erasmus was disembowelled in the year 303.

When the plague swept across Europe, St Erasmus became one of 'Fourteen Holy Helpers', saints popular for their endurance during periods of extreme hardship. The Black Death had arrived in England in 1348, with recurring epidemics decimating the population in 1361, 1369 and 1375. The disease remained endemic, with periodic outbreaks during the next several centuries, and some historians speculate that the King and Queen's infant son George died of the plague in 1479.

Dedicating her chapel to a saint who survived adverse circumstances was particularly apt for this Queen, whose own tenacity during adversity had already been tested and proven – with worse to come just beyond the horizon. The endowment for the Chapel of St Erasmus specified that every day two monks who were chaplains of Westminster monastery would say Mass 'for the good estate of the King and Queen and for their souls after death and the souls of their children'. On each anniversary, the Abbot or his representative assembled, with the entire convent singing *placebo* and *dirige*. The ceremony was lit with twenty-four tapers, each made of six pounds of wax. A solemn Mass was sung at the high altar, 'with tapers and candles lit and bells tolled'. Monks in minor orders said a 'whole psalter' and the lay brothers said 'the Lord's Prayer and the Creed, with the Ave Maria, as many times as the abbot and convent shall appoint'. The Prior and convent distributed one penny to each poor person at the High Mass, 'to the number of 240'. Two tapers remained on the altar throughout the year, to be lit 'at the greater feasts of vespers and mass'.[13]

The building of the Chapel of St Erasmus required 21,000 bricks, 302 loads of burnt lime, 20 loads of sand, 100 tiles for covering the wall, and 100 roof-tiles, all installed by two tilers and two workmen. By the time these items were listed in the *Liber Niger Cartulary* of Westminster Abbey in 1486[14], the Queen who endowed the chapel had suffered almost as much adversity as St Erasmus, whose image then stood under a canopy.

At the moment of endowment in 1479, however, the family of Elizabeth and Edward IV – as well as England itself – was thriving. A ninth child, Katharine, was born at Eltham in early to mid-1479, just in time for her father to begin negotiating her marriage to the infant son of Ferdinand and Isabella of Spain. Within the year, Elizabeth became pregnant with the King's tenth child (twelfth for Elizabeth). Her growing family did not deter her engagement in activities traditional for English queens, who frequently acted as intercessors for those who wished to lobby the King.

On 4 September 1479, Edward IV assessed the merchants of London with a subsidy that was approved by an act of Parliament. The Merchant Adventurers' Company were assigned £2,000, a sum they found excessive and resolved to fight. After discovering that the 'two discreet men' appointed to reduce the assessment were inadequate to the job, the company embarked on an intensive lobbying campaign that involved the Queen, the Marquis of Dorset, Earl Rivers and Lord Hastings. If at this point the Wydevilles and Hastings were at odds, they at least worked together in the interest of the Merchant Adventurers, whose records are fulsome in praise of the Queen:

> Very good effort [was] made by mean of the Queen's good grace, the lord Marquess, the Lord Maister, & the Lord Chamberlain & other gentles &. But especially by the Queen. And as William Pratt reports, the Lord Chamberlain is our very good special Lord and aviseth us to apply our labour still unto the Queen's grace & to the Lord Marquess, and he will help when time cometh what he can do or may do for us.[15]

When those efforts did not provide immediate success, Hastings advised them to be 'more secret of their friends… Except the Queen's good grace only, which that is, & always has been, our very good & gracious lady in the said matter.'[16] While 'the Queen's grace' succeeded in reducing the subsidy by 500 marks, the Adventurers wanted more, and sent another delegation to the King asking for additional relief. They soon discovered that they had met their match in Edward IV, who told them that he really intended to assess them 3,000 marks, but 'at the special Instance & prayer of the Queen's good grace he had released 1,000 marks'.[17] Aware that they had encountered a superior negotiator, the Merchant Adventurers went home and assessed their individual members sufficient sums to meet the King's subsidy.

Such ordinary business transactions transpired in the midst of on-going royal celebrations and splendour. In late June 1480, the court prepared for a visit from the King's sister Margaret, Dowager Duchess of Burgundy, a visit that, as always, combined pleasure with politics. Margaret was escorted across the Channel aboard the royal ship *The Falcon* by Sir Edward Wydeville, the Queen's brother who had become a naval officer. Twelve years earlier, Sir Edward, along with his more famous brother Anthony, had accompanied Margaret to Burgundy for her marriage with Charles the Bold. Her visit home – the only one – was equally splendid, with the Burgundians disembarking at Gravesend, where Margaret transferred to a royal barge manned by twenty-four oarsmen who rowed her up the Thames to London. The master and oarsmen wore new liveries in the Yorkist colours of murrey and blue, with white roses embroidered on their jackets. The escort party of knights and squires wore black velvet jackets decorated with silver and purple. Sir Edward Wydeville had been provided 'a yard of velvet purple and a yard of blue velvet' for his own wardrobe.[18]

Margaret had her choice of two residences especially prepared for her three-month visit: the palace at Greenwich where she had lived before her marriage, and the London house of Coldharbor on Thames Street, near the Duchess of York's Baynard's Castle. Both had been renovated with new curtains, screens, tapestries, bed linens and coverlets. A hundred servants wore new 'jackets of woollen cloth of murrey and blue'. Ten horses, with harnesses of green velvet decorated with aglets of silver and gold, and reins of crimson velvet, were provided for Margaret's travels in England, made more comfortable by Edward IV's gift of a pillion saddle in blue and purple cloth of gold, fringed with Venetian gold thread.[19]

Queen Elizabeth welcomed Margaret and introduced her to her large family of royal nieces and nephews. Richard, Duke of Gloucester, who was in the north fighting the Scots, came to London to visit his sister. Edward IV hosted a state banquet at Greenwich honouring Margaret and their mother, Cecily, Duchess Dowager of York. Margaret must have expressed particular delight in the wine, for the next day the King sent her a gift of 'a pipe of our wine' valued at 36s 8d.

Margaret's visit was not merely a pleasure jaunt to see the family. Edward IV's alliance with France had worked to the disadvantage of Burgundy, and Margaret was determined to win back his support. She also hoped to negotiate a marriage between the Burgundian heir Philip, son of Maximilian and Mary (Margaret's stepdaughter), and Edward's daughter Anne, now five years old. Edward was in an awkward position, since such a shift in alliance might forfeit his allowance from Louis XI and abrogate the marriage contract between the Dauphin and Princess Elizabeth.

Margaret was a charming, intelligent and persuasive advocate for restoring Burgundian influence in England, a threat of which Louis XI of France was well aware. While Margaret was in England, Louis sent a delegation to Edward IV to deliver his annuity of 50,000 crowns and to offer an additional annuity of 15,000 crowns to Princess Elizabeth until her marriage to the Dauphin. Edward IV tried to play both France and Burgundy for England's benefit. He offered to support Burgundy by invading France, but only if Burgundy replaced his French annuity. Further, no dowry would accompany his daughter Anne when she married Philip. Such exorbitant demands were beyond Margaret's authority to negotiate, and she was forced to send messengers to Maximilian and Mary for advice.

Weeks of tricky diplomatic negotiations produced an agreement whereby Edward IV would permit Burgundy to recruit English archers for their battles with France, and would provide a loan to cover their wages and transportation to Burgundy. He would also support Burgundy's claims for lands confiscated by France after the death of Charles the Bold and declare war against France if the lands were not restored by Easter 1481. In return, Burgundy would replace Edward IV's French annuity if that were cancelled. Princess Anne and Philip would marry in six years time, with Anne bringing a dowry of 100,000 crowns, half to be paid within two years of the marriage. Since Margaret's own dowry was still unpaid twelve years after her marriage, that promise might have raised a few diplomatic eyebrows, but the deal was sealed with a Burgundian promise to pay Anne an annuity of 6,000 crowns for living expenses, and a wedding ring presented to the five-year-old princess by Margaret.

Just as this agreement was concluded, Margaret received word that Maximilian had himself negotiated a seven-month truce with France on 21 August, to be followed by a peace conference in October. To soothe any English feathers he might have ruffled, Maximilian invited Edward IV to join France and Burgundy at the conference. Margaret was a bit concerned that Maximilian's double-dealing would anger Edward IV, but the King seemed unperturbed and escorted his sister from London as she left to return home.

Before departing from England, Margaret spent a week in Kent, where she visited the shrine of St Thomas à Becket, staying at the private estate of Anthony Wydeville, Earl Rivers. Their shared interest in books and philosophy fostered their friendship. Anthony's patronage of Caxton, Margaret's protégé, must surely have been part of their conversation, along with the three books Anthony had translated and Caxton had printed.

Shortly after Margaret's departure, Queen Elizabeth, aged forty-three, gave birth on 10 November 1480 to the last of her children, Bridget. The christening took place in the chapel at Eltham on the day following Bridget's birth, an elaborate ceremony that began with a procession of knights, esquires and 'other honest persons' carrying 100 torches. Lord Maltravers carried the basin, 'having a towel placed around his neck'. The Earl of Northumberland carried an unlighted taper and the Earl of Lincoln the salt. Under a canopy carried by three knights and a baron, Lady Maltravers (the Queen's sister Margaret) walked with Lady Margaret Beaufort, Countess of Richmond, who carried the baby with the assistance of the Marquis of Dorset (Elizabeth's eldest son).

The Bishop of Chichester baptised the child, placing salt in the baby's mouth to preserve its body and soul, wetting the baby's ears and nostrils with saliva, smearing oil on its breast and back, then totally immersing the child in the font three times – once on the right side, once on the left, and once face downwards. The baby's godmothers at the font were the Duchess of York (paternal grandmother) and the Lady Princess Elizabeth (the baby's eldest sister). Her godfather was the Bishop of Winchester. Among the men present were Lord Hastings, the King's chamberlain, Lord Stanley, steward of the King's house, and Lord Dacre, the Queen's chamberlain, as well as the baby's brother, the Duke of York.[20] Following baptism, Lady Maltravers stood as godmother for the baby's confirmation. Presented before the high altar, the child was then carried into a curtained section of the church where she received gifts from her godparents.

Finally, the new little princess was taken to her mother's bedside, where Elizabeth and Edward named her Bridget in honour of the Swedish nun St Bridget. The name chosen for her daughter foretold the life that Queen Elizabeth would soon choose for herself. St Bridget had served as chief lady-in-waiting to the Queen of Sweden before she and her husband departed on pilgrimage to Santiago de Compostela. Quitting the court completely, Bridget founded the Order of the Most Holy Saviour, the Bridgettines, who devoted themselves to spirituality, study, and a simple lifestyle. Within seven years, Elizabeth Wydeville would make a similar decision.

An inherent sadness marks the life of this last of the royal children. Little is known about Bridget. Apparently no marriages were negotiated for her, and she entered the Dominican convent at Dartford at the age of ten in 1490.[21] Bridget's obscurity and religious seclusion have led to speculation that the child might have been developmentally disabled in ways that precluded participation in courtly activities. On the other hand, Elizabeth's own retreat to Bermondsey convent in 1487 may have persuaded her that the cloistered life offered the most tranquil and ideal future for this youngest of her children.

Her growing family did not prevent the Queen from joining Edward IV on his journeys, and in September 1481 they visited Oxford University, where Elizabeth's brother Lionel served as chancellor. A graduate of Oxford with a Doctor of Divinity degree, Lionel had been appointed Dean of Exeter in November 1478 and Chancellor of Oxford University in 1479. The visit was an extended family affair, with the King's sister Elizabeth, Duchess of Suffolk, visiting her son Edmund de la Pole, who was studying there.

The royal entourage arrived at Oxford on the evening of 22 September 1481, causing a great stir as their carriages entered the city preceded by a crowd of people carrying torches. They were taken to Magdalen

College, where Lionel greeted the party with a speech. The next day offered more speeches and a tour of the college. On the third day, the King attended the public Disputations and heard the Divinity Lecture delivered by Chancellor Lionel Wydeville. After visiting other parts of the University and hearing 'Scholastical exercises', Edward 'departed with great content'.[22]

The years of happiness and splendour, however, were about to change, as the royal family entered a period of mourning and decline. Anne Mowbray, the child bride of Prince Richard, died on 19 November 1481, not quite nine years old, and was buried in Westminster Abbey. Within months, the Princess Mary, recently betrothed to the King of Denmark, died at Greenwich on 23 May 1482, at the age of fourteen.

Mary's funeral procession reflected her royal state and far exceeded the rites to be given her mother a decade later. From Greenwich Church, where a dirge was sung, the funeral train moved to Kingston-on-Thames, where it spent the night. The next morning a canopy, supported at each corner by a gentleman, was placed over the hearse, and the procession continued, augmented by thirty poor men carrying torches. Along the way, villagers in mourning paid their respects to the cortege. When it reached Eton, the Mayor and aldermen of Windsor, dressed in white liveries and carrying torches, met the hearse for the final journey to St George's Chapel at Windsor. Here Mary was buried next to her brother George, who had died four years earlier. Neither the King nor Queen are mentioned in surviving accounts of the burial.[23] Elizabeth was represented at the services by her chamberlain, Lord Dacre, and by her sister, Lady Grey of Ruthin, and several nieces. As King, Edward IV would not have attended the burial.

Almost immediately, Edward left for the north where his brother Richard, Duke of Gloucester was commanding the troops fighting with Scotland. Included in the King's troops were 500 men commanded by Sir Edward Wydeville, who was appointed 'to attend upon my lord of Gloucester'.[24] Edward IV's sojourn in the north was brief, and he returned without personally engaging in the battles that Gloucester efficiently won by August 1482. Bad news from the continent greeted the King in London. The peace conference between France and Burgundy had resulted in the Treaty of Arras, signed on 23 December 1482. Its provisions included the marriage of Margaret, daughter of Maximilian and Mary of

Burgundy, to the Dauphin Charles of France, who had been betrothed to Princess Elizabeth! Not only did Edward IV lose that long-desired union of England and France, but the concord between Burgundy and France caused Louis XI to terminate on Michaelmas 1482 the annual pension he had been sending Edward IV.[25]

The calamities of 1481 and 1482 brought heartache, pain – and per-haps fear – to Queen Elizabeth. The royal family, nevertheless, celebrated Christmas 1482 with stunning displays of wealth, fashion and familial prosperity:

> King Edward kept the following feast of the Nativity at his palace of Westminster, frequently appearing clad in a great variety of most costly garments, of quite a different cut to those which had been usually seen hitherto in our kingdom. The sleeves of the robes were very full and hanging, greatly resembling a monk's frock, and so lined within with most costly furs, and rolled over the shoulders, as to give that prince a new and distinguished air to beholders, he being a person of most elegant appearance, and remarkable beyond all others for the attractions of his person. You might have seen, in those days, the royal court presenting no other appearance than such as fully befits a most mighty kingdom, filled with riches and with people of almost all nations, and (a point in which it excelled all others) boasting of those most sweet and beautiful children, the issue of his marriage... with queen Elizabeth.[26]

The irony of Croyland's description – especially his commendation of 'those most sweet and beautiful children, the issue of his marriage... with queen Elizabeth' – poignantly amplifies the horrors about to begin. Within four months, Edward IV would be dead, Queen Elizabeth would once more flee to sanctuary at Westminster Abbey, and 'those most sweet and beautiful children' would be placed in peril of their lives. Within a year, the two princes – happy, lively, intelligent boys – would disappear. Their fate, even today, is unknown.

CHAPTER TWENTY

1483 Begins

The year 1483 brought profound grief to Queen Elizabeth and the royal family. When Parliament opened on 20 January, life seemed to be proceeding normally. Parliament spent some time discussing the treacheries of France, but more in thanking Richard, Duke of Gloucester for his service against the Scots and rewarding him with hereditary rights to the marches of Scotland, the city and castle of Carlisle, and all crown possessions in the county of Cumberland – plus similar rights to additional lands he might win from the Scots. The grants conferred on Gloucester a degree of power that made him a real threat to any occupant of the throne, causing Scofield to conclude that the Parliament of 1483 'was at the moment completely under Gloucester's thumb'.[1]

Perhaps Gloucester's growing power explains letters written in January 1483 by Anthony, Earl Rivers attempting to elect representatives to Parliament from Norfolk, Yarmouth and Cornwall who were sympathetic to the Wydevilles. In all, Anthony tried to influence the election of five members of Parliament, an effort that, according to E.W. Ives, indicates the growing factions within that body.[2]

Although all seemed in good order on Candlemas Day, 2 February, when the King and Queen walked in stately procession with the court from St Stephen's Chapel to Westminster Hall, such appearances may have masked a more contentious reality. Rivers asked to have his longstanding patent to serve as Prince Edward's governor renewed, which was done on 27 February 1483. In a letter to his business agent, Andrew Dymmock, written on 8 March 1483, Anthony asks for a copy of that newly issued patent, along with another granting him authority to raise troops in Wales:

> Send me by some sure man the patent of my authority about my lord Prince, and also a patent that the King gave me touching power to raise people, if need be, in the march of Wales.[3]

Since Rivers had served as governor of the prince since 1473, these requests are perplexing. The admonition to send by 'some sure man' also indicates something sinister in the state of England.

Around Easter (30 March), Edward IV fell ill and took to his bed. The Croyland Chronicler takes special care to state that the onset of the illness was sudden:

> When the Parliament had been dissolved, the king, neither worn out with old age nor yet seized with any known kind of malady, the cure of which would not have appeared easy in the case of a person of more humble rank, took to his bed. This happened about the feast of Easter; and, on the ninth of April, he rendered up his spirit to his Creator, at his palace of Westminster, it being the year of our Lord, 1483, and the twenty-third year of his reign.[4]

The nature of Edward's sickness is unknown, although contemporaries attributed it to a variety of causes: disappointment at the Treaty of Arras, the broken betrothal between the Dauphin and Princess Elizabeth, the loss of his annual stipend from France, a chill caught while fishing, apoplexy, acute indigestion, poisoning. The King had abused his body for years with overeating and debauchery, but the sudden onset and severity of his illness indicates some cause other than general deterioration. Edward IV died just nineteen days before his forty-first birthday.

The King had time during his illness to reflect on the uneasy politics that dominated his court, and made a futile effort to reconcile the dissident factions. Within the court's circle of advisors, two adversarial groups dominated. At the head of one was Queen Elizabeth, supported by her brothers and her two sons by her first marriage. Anthony, the most respected for his military service, piety and learnedness, spent most of his time in Ludlow with Prince Edward. Lionel, Chancellor of Oxford University, had been elevated to Bishop of Salisbury in 1482. Sir Edward Wydeville, the naval officer, became prominent only after the King's death, when the council appointed him Admiral of the Fleet, in command of twenty ships which took to sea on 30 April or 1 May to protect against a French invasion.[5] Elizabeth's eldest son was a significant member of this faction. Sir Thomas Grey, Marquis of Dorset, had inherited the estates of his father, Lord Ferrers of Groby, and had accompanied Edward during the 1475 invasion of France, where he was important enough to receive a pension from Louis XI.[6] Recently, he had fielded 600 men in the war with Scotland.[7] If contemporary rumours are true, Dorset also joined Edward IV during his debauched forays among the ladies and pleasures of London. The Queen's second son, Sir Richard Grey, attended Prince Edward in his household at Ludlow.

Opposed to the Queen's family were the King's men. Led by William Hastings, Lord Chamberlain and Edward's most intimate friend, this faction included the Duke of Buckingham, the Duke of Suffolk, the Earl of Lincoln and Lord Maltravers. While Richard, Duke of Gloucester headed this group, he had spent recent years away from the court administering the north of England and conducting the war with Scotland. With the exception of Hastings, all of these men shared the 'blood royal'.

Before he died, Edward IV called the leaders of the two factions together. Thomas More recounts a deathbed scene where Edward IV asked Dorset and Hastings to bury their animosity in the interests of his children, whose youth made them especially vulnerable:

> If you among your selves in a child's reign fall at debate, many a good man shall perish and haply he, too, and you, too, ere this land find peace again. Wherefore in these last words that ever I look to speak with you: I exhort you and require you all, for the love that you have ever born to me, for the love that I have ever born to you, for the love that our lord beareth to us all, for this time forward, all griefs forgotten, each of you love other.[8]

Touched by the King's words and his imminent death, Dorset and Hastings declared their reconciliation: 'There in his presence (as by their words appeared) each forgave [the] other, and joined their hands together, when (as it after appeared by their deeds) their hearts were far asunder.'[9]

The earlier amity between Hastings and the Queen, who had contracted marriages between their children, had been replaced by acrimonious feelings. Thomas More attributes the Queen's hostility towards Hastings to the 'great favour the King bare him, and also for that she thought him secretly familiar with the King in wanton company'.[10] Edward's many gifts to Hastings, including his appointment as Captain of Calais when the office had been promised to Anthony Wydeville, also rankled. Croyland suggests that Hastings was at fault:

> [Hastings] was afraid lest, if the supreme power should fall into the hands of the
> Queen's relations, they would exact a most signal vengeance for the injuries
> which had been formerly inflicted on them by that same lord; in consequence
> of which, there had long existed extreme ill-will between the said Lord Hastings
> and them.[11]

Hastings's actions in the next several days would be fatal to the Queen's family – and to himself.

After Edward IV's death, the primary obligation of the nation was to assure the safety of Edward V, a boy of twelve years and five months, who was at Ludlow Castle under the governance of his uncle, Anthony Wydeville, Earl Rivers. The boy received news on 14 April of his father's death. On 16 April, Edward V wrote to the Mayor of Lynn to state his intention of departing to London 'in all convenient haste'.[12] Elizabeth argued at the King's Council that an army should be commissioned, to bring the boy to London as rapidly as possible for his coronation. Hastings and the Duke of Buckingham, both of whom resented the Wydeville governance of the prince, responded that a large display of force would only alarm those of opposing factions, remind them of past differences, and destroy the amity and peace recently achieved at the King's deathbed. Croyland identifies Queen Elizabeth as the peacemaker:

> The Queen most beneficently tried to extinguish every spark of murmuring
> and disturbance, and wrote to her son, requesting him on his road to London,
> not to exceed an escort of two thousand men.[13]

The new King's departure may have been delayed by the council discussions and the celebration of St George's Day in Ludlow, for Edward V did not leave Ludlow until 24 April.

Meanwhile, the boy's paternal uncle, Richard, Duke of Gloucester, 'wrote unto the King so reverently, and to the Queen's friends, there so lovingly, that they nothing earthly mistrusting, brought the King up in great haste'.[14] As the King's party proceeded towards London, Gloucester headed south. Before leaving York, Gloucester took an oath of loyalty to the new King and required all northerners to do the same. Gloucester reached Northampton as Edward V's party arrived at Stony Stratford, eleven miles away. That evening, Tuesday 29 April, Rivers met with

Gloucester and Buckingham for dinner in Northampton. If animosity between Rivers and Gloucester had developed during the Parliament of 1483, Rivers clearly anticipated no danger in dining with Gloucester. Indeed, evidence that Rivers trusted Gloucester exists in an arbitration request he and Roger Townshend had submitted to Gloucester's council sometime after 25 March 1483, requesting settlement of conflicting claims over property rights in East Anglia. Rivers would hardly have asked Gloucester to intervene if he had doubted his fairness.[15]

With Edward V at Stony Stratford, under the protection of his half-brother Sir Richard Grey, his chamberlain Sir Thomas Vaughan, and the treasurer of his household Sir Richard Haute, his two uncles settled down in Northampton for an evening of conviviality. 'So was there made that night much friendly cheer between these Dukes [Gloucester and Buckingham] and the Lord Rivers a great while', and the men parted 'openly with great courtesy'.[16] Rivers went to his lodgings. Gloucester and Buckingham spent the night plotting. The next morning, Gloucester's followers locked the doors of the inn where Rivers was staying and prevented his departure from Northampton. When Rivers protested, Gloucester's men arrested him.

Buckingham and others rode to Stony Stratford, where 'they came to the King, and on their knees in very humble wise, saluted his Grace: which received them in very joyous and amiable manner, nothing earthly knowing nor mistrusting as yet'.[17] In the presence of the young King, Buckingham accused Earl Rivers, the Marquis of Dorset and Sir Richard Grey of attempting to rule the King and the realm, of causing dissension within the kingdom, and of destroying the 'noble blood of the realm'. They also accused Dorset of entering the Tower of London and removing the King's treasure. Mancini corroborates More's version and adds the reaction of Edward V:

> The youth, possessing the likeness of his father's noble spirit besides talent and remarkable learning, replied to this saying that he merely had those ministers whom his father had given him; and relying on his father's prudence, he believed that good and faithful ones had been given him. He had seen nothing evil in them and wished to keep them unless otherwise proved to be evil. As for the government of the kingdom, he had complete confidence in the peers of the realm and the queen, so that this care but little concerned his former ministers.

On hearing the queen's name, the duke of Buckingham, who loathed her race, then answered, 'It was not the business of women but of men to govern kingdoms, and so if he cherished any confidence in her he had better relinquish it. Let him place all his hope in his barons, who excelled in nobility and power'.[18]

Buckingham then took the boy into his custody and arrested Sir Richard Grey, Sir Thomas Vaughan and Sir Richard Haute.

Irony of ironies! Edward V was captured at Stony Stratford, the town where his father had resided when courting and secretly marrying his mother. The date was 30 April 1483, the eve of Edward IV and Elizabeth's nineteenth wedding anniversary.

Gloucester's custody of Edward V was not inappropriate. As the sole surviving brother of Edward IV, Gloucester would traditionally serve as his nephew's 'Protector' until the King reached majority age. Neither had anyone reason to doubt Gloucester's loyalty and motives. He had fought loyally and fiercely at his brother's side through all of the wars with the cousins – from Henry VI to Earl Warwick. Unlike his brother Clarence, Richard never challenged Edward IV's authority or his claim to the throne. During the last years of Edward IV's reign, Gloucester had gloriously won the war with Scotland, capturing Berwick Castle on 24 August 1482, after twenty-one years of Scottish control. His service had greatly enriched the King's coffers and prestige. His administration of England's northern regions had earned him a reputation for honest, just and competent stewardship. He and his wife, Anne, enjoyed both political and personal popularity in northern England.

Still, Anthony's appointment as Prince Edward's governor gave him legal authority to control the boy's movements, at least until the council made Gloucester's Protectorship official. Edward IV had been clear and explicit in his orders:

Item. For the weal, surety, and profit of our said son, we will, and by these presents give authority and power to the right reverend father in God, John Bishop of Rochester, and to our right trusty and well-beloved Anthony Earl Rivers, to remove at all times the same our son, as the case shall require, unto such places as shall be thought by their discretion necessary...[19]

No one could imagine that Gloucester and Buckingham would violate the King's patent and inaugurate the dreadful events of 1483. Anthony – intelligent, erudite and politically shrewd – was completely deceived.

Gloucester attempted to allay the fears of Edward V, who 'wept and was nothing content' at the arrest of his Wydeville relatives and at his own sequestration. At dinner, Gloucester even sent a dish from his own table to Lord Rivers, with a message that all would be well. That gesture was followed, however, by orders to send Rivers, Grey, Vaughan and Haute north, where Rivers was imprisoned at Sheriff Hutton, Grey at Middleham Castle, and Vaughan and Haute at Pontefract. The Wydevilles were isolated in the ancestral territory of the Nevilles, now owned by Gloucester.[20]

Queen Elizabeth feared the worst when hearing about the arrests. Memories of the 1469 murder of her father and her brother, Sir John Wydeville, at the hands of Warwick and Clarence must have flooded her soul with a dreadful sensation of *déjà vu*. The Queen made the only sensible move. She fled into sanctuary:

> The Queen in great flight and heaviness, bewailing her child's ruin, her friend's mischance, and her own infortune, damning the time that ever she dissuaded the gathering of power about the King, got her self in all the haste possible with her younger son and her daughters out of the Palace of Westminster in which she then lay, into the Sanctuary, lodging her self and her company there in the Abbot's place.[21]

Similarly, Anthony must immediately have sensed his impending death once he found himself in prison. He could hardly, however, have imagined the horrors to follow.

Neither can subsequent historians explain Gloucester's change of character. Overnight, Richard, Duke of Gloucester, a loyal younger brother, became an ambitious, power-mad villain who murdered not merely political foes, but his brother's friends and family. Gloucester became a case study of absolute power corrupting absolutely.

Defenders of Gloucester argue that his villainy is unproved. They reject many accounts of 1483 because they were written later under the Tudor dynasty – victors writing history about their defeated enemy. John Morton, Bishop of Ely and a source for More's history, had been arrested by Gloucester and ultimately elevated by Henry VII to Cardinal

Archbishop of Canterbury. A Tudor partisan, indeed. Yet Morton's presence at meetings of Edward V's council, and his service as one of Edward IV's executors, provide invaluable first-hand testimony. Other eyewitnesses supplying More with information included John Argentine, physician to Edward V and later to Prince Arthur (son of Henry VII); John More (father of Thomas), a prominent London judge probably present at the Guildhall when Buckingham argued Richard's claim to the throne; and John Roper, father of More's son-in-law. Validation of any historical perspective must lie in its corroboration by other authorities. For the year 1483, the narratives of More and Mancini, the chronicles of Croyland and of the London writers, and the letters of contemporary citizens record the tragic events with remarkably similar accounts, varying mainly in degree of detail. All offer harrowing glimpses into the suffering of those who lived and died.

Elizabeth was not the only one to panic at the capture of Prince Edward. Wise and rational men acted precipitously and sometimes foolishly when they heard the news. Thomas Rotherham, Archbishop of York, Lord Chancellor of England, and Keeper of the Privy Seal since 1467, heard that the Queen had sought sanctuary at Westminster and immediately went to her:

> He caused in all the haste all his servants to be called up, and so with his own household about him, and every man weaponed, he took the great Seal with him, and came yet before day unto the Queen. About whom he found much heaviness, rumble, haste and business, carriage and conveyance of her stuff into Sanctuary, chests, coffers, packs, fardels, trusses, all on men's backs, no man unoccupied, some lading, some going, some discharging, some coming for more, some breaking down the walls to bring in the next way, and some yet drew to them that helped to carry a wrong way.
>
> The Queen her self sat alone low on the rushes all desolate and dismayed, whom the Archbishop comforted in the best manner he could, showing her that he trusted the matter was nothing so sore as she took it for. And that he was put in good hope and out of fear, by the message sent him from the Lord Chamberlain. 'Ah woe worth him', quod she, 'for he is one of them that labours to destroy me and my blood'. 'Madame', quod he, 'be ye of good cheer. For I assure you if they crown any other king than your son, whom they now have with them, we shall on the morrow crown his brother whom you have here

with you. And here is the Great Seal, which in likewise as that noble prince your husband delivered it unto me, so here I deliver it unto you, to the use and behalf of your son', and therewith he betook her the Great Seal, and departed home again, yet in the dawning of the day.

By which time he might in his chamber window see all the Thames full of boats of the Duke of Gloucester's servants, watching that no man should go to Sanctuary, nor none could pass unsearched. Then was there great commotion and murmur as well in other places about, as specially in the city, the people diversely devining upon this dealing. And some Lords, Knights, and Gentlemen either for favour of the Queen, or for fear of themselves, assembled in sundry companies, and went flockmele in harness [armour], and many also, for that they reckoned this demeanour attempted, not so specially against the other Lords as against the King himself in the disturbance of his Coronation.[22]

With the light of day, the Archbishop regretted his hasty deliverance of the Great Seal to the Queen, who, indeed, had no authority to use it, and he sent secretly to her to have it returned. Meanwhile, Hastings assured the London nobles that Gloucester 'was sure and fastly faithful to his Prince' and that Rivers and Grey had been arrested for actions they had taken against Gloucester and Buckingham. He cautioned all against further opposition, which would disturb the King's coronation. Since the King, with his escort of Gloucester and Buckingham, was nearing London for that very coronation, peace was maintained.

As Edward V approached the city on 4 May, the Mayor and citizens of London rode out to meet his party. The Mayor and aldermen, dressed in scarlet, were accompanied by 500 citizens on horses clothed in violet. The King, in blue, and his lords and servants, in black, made a splendid procession that impressed all who witnessed it. Gloucester obsequiously and deferentially tended to the prince 'in open sight so reverently… with all semblance of lowliness', a public display of obeisance that won back any trust he had jeopardised by arresting Rivers and Grey and seizing the prince. But the King's party arrived in London too late for the corona-tion initially scheduled for 4 May, and the event was postponed until 22 June.

Initially lodged in the Bishop's Palace at St Paul's, Edward V was moved to the Tower of London by 19 May. Residence in the Tower, a royal palace with quarters luxuriously furnished for the King and Queen, was appropriate. Coronation processions always began at the Tower before moving through the City to Westminster Abbey, and both Edward IV and Elizabeth had spent the night there before their coronations.

On 7 May 1483, an extraordinary meeting took place at Cecily Neville's Baynard Castle. In attendance were the King's leading prelates, including the Archbishops of Canterbury and York, the Bishop of Bath and Wells, and the Bishop of Ely. Also present were the powerful nobles who had seized control of Edward V: Gloucester, Buckingham, Arundel, Hastings and Stanley. At that meeting, those present, 'acting on behalf of the deceased King Edward IV and because they were named Executors in his Will', seized control of the goods, jewels and seals of the late King.[23] The jewels were placed in the custody of William Dawbeney, Richard Laurence and Rouland Forster. The Archbishop of Canterbury, by virtue of the prerogative of his ecclesiastical position, took physical possession of all seals that belonged to the King, including the Great Seal and the Privy Seal.

The importance of this meeting cannot be overstated. Not only did this action invalidate the stipulations of Edward IV's 1475 will, but it also stripped all power from the Queen. While the men claimed they were acting as executors of Edward IV, there is no evidence that they were the only executors or that Edward IV had removed Elizabeth – 'our said dearest Wife in whom we most singularly put our trust in this party' – from his carefully designated list of executors in 1475.[24] Both Croyland and Mancini report that Edward IV added deathbed codicils to his will which, among other things, appointed Gloucester as Protector of his son during his minority:

> At his death Edward left two sons: he bequeathed the kingdom to Edward the eldest, who had already some time before been proclaimed prince of Wales at a council meeting of the magnates of the entire realm. The king wished that his second son called the duke of York should be content with his apanage [land and revenue] within his brother's realm. He also left behind daughters, but they do not concern us. Men say that in the same Will he appointed a protector of his children and realm his brother Richard duke of Gloucester, who shortly after destroyed Edward's children and, then claimed for himself the throne.[25]

Mancini's dismissive attitude towards the daughters reflects the general attitude of the men who assumed power after Edward IV's death, the men who excluded the Queen from their deliberations. No evidence, however, indicates that Edward himself ever wavered in the principal trust he placed in Elizabeth, or that he removed the Wydevilles from all positions of power, as some insist his appointment of Richard as Protector proves.

Indeed, Croyland implies that Edward's will of 1475 remained in force, with codicils added to update it, a logical addition since many of the earlier executors had died:

> Long before his illness he had made his Will, at very considerable length, having abundant means to satisfy it; and had, after mature deliberation, appointed therein many persons to act as his executors, and carry out his wishes. On his deathbed he added some codicils thereto; but what a sad and unhappy result befell all these wise dispositions of his, the ensuing tragedy will more fully disclose.[26]

Alison Weir believes that 'Rivers, it seems, was to be removed from his office of Governor, and the Queen was apparently given no power at all.'[27] But the reissue of Anthony's patent as governor on 27 February 1483 argues against the first claim, and the participation of the Queen in the King's Council immediately following Edward's death contradicts the second. If Edward had added codicils to his will withdrawing the Queen's authority, their content would have been known by the time the council met to discuss arrangements for bringing the prince to London. The Queen's participation in council discussions indicates that she remained an active and respected advisor. After she entered sanctuary on 1 May, Elizabeth could not, of course, attend any further deliberations.

The meeting at Cecily Neville's home on 7 May would not have been necessary if the King in his deathbed codicils had removed Elizabeth from her precedency as executor. During this meeting, the powerful men who opposed Elizabeth and her family seized control of Edward's personal goods and treasury, goods that Edward in 1475 had specifically willed that 'our said wife the Queen have the disposition thereof without let or interruption of the other our Executors'.[28] In repudiating this provision, the careful, legalistic phrasing of the 7 May sequestration justifies its action as being 'interposed for the beloved children'. It never mentions the Queen.

To establish its legal authority, the sequestration cites the prerogative of the Archbishop, protesting a little too much, as if those seizing control were hiding behind the prelate's ecclesiastical robes.

The codicils to Edward IV's will have never been discovered, a curious absence if they established Gloucester's authority, since Gloucester could have cited them to his great advantage when he encountered resistance. Only reports of their existence and speculation about their content survive – Mancini's '*Men say* that in the same Will he appointed a protector of his children and realm his brother Richard duke of Gloucester, who shortly after destroyed Edward's children and, then claimed for himself the throne.' In any case, both Edward's will of 1475 and any deathbed codicils were rendered moot by the 7 May meeting. Gloucester had launched a *coup d'état* that now began moving inexorably toward its horrifying end. The Duke was preparing for the meeting of the King's Council on 27 May, where he was chosen as 'the only man… thought most meet to be Protector of the King and his realm'.[29] That same council chastised the Archbishop of York, Lord Chancellor, for delivering the Great Seal to the Queen and removed his authority to use it.

Immediately after the 7 May meeting, Gloucester began acting more aggressively. He reinforced Buckingham's loyalty by promising to marry his own son to Buckingham's daughter and to grant Buckingham his inheritance in the Earldom of Hertford, which Edward IV had never delivered. Then Gloucester began to eliminate his enemies. To regain control of the fleet that Sir Edward Wydeville had taken to sea to guard against French opportunists, the council declared Sir Edward to be an enemy of the state and ordered the soldiers aboard his ships to disband or desert.[30] Gloucester issued orders to Sir Thomas Fulford and John Halwell on 10 May and to Edward Brampton and others on 14 May 'to go to the sea with ships to take Sir Edward Wydeville'.[31] As a consequence, all ships left the fleet except two that fled to Brittany under Sir Edward's direct command.

A letter written by Simon Stallworthe to Sir William Stoner on 9 June reveals the desperate situation of the Wydevilles:

> The Queen keeps still Westminster my Lord of York [Prince Richard], my Lord of Salisbury [Lionel Wydeville], with other more which will not depart as yet. When so ever can be found any goods of my Lord Marquess [Thomas

Grey] it is taken. The Prior of Westminster was and yet is in a great trouble for certain goods delivered to him by my Lord Marquess.

My Lord Protector [Gloucester], My Lord of Buckingham with all other lords as well temporal as spiritual were at Westminster in the Council Chamber from 10 to 2, but there was none that spoke with the Queen. There is great busyness against the coronation which shall be this day fortnight as we say. When I trust you will be at London and then shall you know all the world.

The King is at the Tower. My Lady of Gloucester came to London on Thursday last.[32]

Gloucester next accused Queen Elizabeth of plotting to murder him and his supporters. A letter from Gloucester to the city of York on 10 June, and another to Lord Neville of Raby on 11 June, asked that they send troops from the north:

We heartedly pray you to come up unto us in London in all the diligence you can possible, after the sight hereof, with as many men as you can make defensibly arrayed – there to aid and assist us against the Queen, her bloody adherents and affinity; which have intended and daily doth intend to murder and utterly destroy us and our cousin the Duke of Buckingham and the old royal blood of this realm.[33]

While waiting for those reinforcements, Gloucester targeted Lord Hastings, who was loyal to the children of Edward IV even though he opposed the Wydevilles. The destruction of Hastings required both subterfuge and surprise. On Friday 13 June, Gloucester called part of his council to the Tower to discuss the King's coronation. Gloucester arrived in a congenial mood around 9 a.m., apologising for his late arrival, complimenting the Bishop of Ely on the good strawberries in his garden at Holborn, and asking if he could 'have a mess of them'. The Bishop sent his servant for the berries, and Gloucester departed from the meeting. Between 10 and 11 a.m., Gloucester returned to the council 'all changed with a wonderful sour angry countenance, knitting the brows, frowning and froting, and gnawing his lips'.[34] He asked the council what should those persons deserve who planned 'the destruction of me, being so near of blood unto the King, and Protector of his royal person and his realm'. After a stunned silence, Hastings, who believed his closeness to Gloucester privileged him to speak, replied that any such persons should be punished as 'heinous traitors'.

Gloucester then named 'sorcerers' – including Queen Elizabeth – who were attempting to destroy him. The accusation stunned everyone. Hastings may not have been terribly distressed at the naming of the Queen, but when Gloucester went on to name the 'witch' Mistress Shore, with whom Elizabeth had collaborated, Hastings must finally have comprehended Gloucester's game. Elizabeth Shore, the favourite mistress of Edward IV, was now Hastings's paramour.[35] The charge of witchcraft was preposterous, as Thomas More so eloquently explains:

> The Queen was too wise to go about any such folly. And also if she would, yet would she of all folk least make Shore's wife of counsel, whom of all women she most hated, as that concubine whom the King her husband had most loved.[36]

Gloucester's accusation of Mistress Shore was clearly a means of entrapping Hastings. When Hastings attempted a diplomatic response, Gloucester exploded with anger and arrested Hastings, Lord Stanley, Archbishop Rotherham, Bishop Morton and John Forster (receiver-general to Queen Elizabeth) as traitors. Hastings was permitted a quick confession and beheaded before dinnertime on 13 June 1483.

Other sources corroborate much of More's story:

> Incontinently without process of any law or lawful examination, led the said Lord Hastings out unto the Green beside the Chapel, and there upon an end of a squared piece of timber without any long confession or other space of Remembrance struck off his head. And thus was this noble man murdered for his troth and fidelity which he firmly bare unto his master, upon whose soul and all Christians Jesus have mercy. Amen.[37]

Mancini offers a more concise, slightly different, version of the day. When the council had entered the Tower's innermost quarters:

> The Protector, as prearranged, cried out that an ambush had been prepared for him, and they had come with hidden arms, that they might be first to open

the attack. Thereupon the soldiers, who had been stationed there by their lord, rushed in with the duke of Buckingham, and cut down Hastings on the false pretext of treason: they arrested the others, whose life, it was presumed was spared out of respect for religion and holy orders. Thus fell Hastings, killed not by those enemies he had always feared, but by a friend whom he had never doubted. But whom will insane lust for power spare, if it dares violate the ties of kin and friendship?[38]

After dinner, Gloucester sent a herald throughout the city proclaiming the traitorous actions and evil intents of Hastings. The proclamation, issued within two hours of the beheading, was so elaborately detailed and 'so fair written in parchment in so well a set hand' that suspicions immediately grew that judgement had preceded the accusation.

Mistress Elizabeth Shore was arrested and sent to prison, with all her goods seized by the sheriffs of London. Declared a common harlot, she was made to walk barefoot before the cross in a Sunday procession with a taper in her hand, 'out of all array save her kirtle [gown] only'. Mistress Shore comported herself so demurely that More tells us she evoked pity, rather than hatred, from the people.

The stage was set for a battle of wills between Richard, Duke of Gloucester and Queen Elizabeth.

CHAPTER TWENTY-ONE

The Mother *v.* The Protector

During her second sequestration in Westminster Sanctuary, Elizabeth lived in the Abbot's quarters, the manor of Cheyneygates. Located within Westminster Close, Cheyneygates contained the Abbot's private rooms and a small courtyard. Elizabeth presumably dined in the Great Hall, sitting on the dais at the north end looking over the lower tables to the screen at the far end, with the minstrel's gallery above. Four windows in each side wall and a lantern in the middle of the roof lighted the 52ft by 27ft room. If not as luxurious as her quarters at Westminster Palace, the rooms at Cheyneygates offered much comfort, and Abbot John Esteney provided consoling and loving care.

The Queen may have met with her advisors in the Jerusalem Chamber, named after the tapestry on the walls. That large, commodious room had been the resting place for Henry IV when he became ill while praying at the shrine of St Edward the Confessor. Henry IV died in front of the great fireplace in the Jerusalem Chamber on 20 March 1413, a memory that would have reminded Elizabeth that the Abbot's home offered a place of refuge and ultimate solace.

At Cheyneygates, Elizabeth once more became head of her family, negotiating with the men of the realm for the safety of her sons and daughters. Given subsequent history, the question that burns in the minds of everyone is: 'Why?' Why did Queen Elizabeth deliver her nine-year-old son, Richard, Duke of York, into the hands of his uncle Richard, Duke of Gloucester? As long as the prince remained in sanctuary at Westminster Abbey, the boy was safe. And as long as the second heir to the throne survived, his older brother, Edward V, would be protected from usurpers, who would gain nothing by his death.

After Hastings's execution on 13 June 1483, Gloucester made his next move. At the next meeting of the King's Council, Gloucester in his role as Protector argued eloquently and persuasively that the council should demand custody of Prince Richard. The council had been attempting to persuade Elizabeth to depart from sanctuary since her entry, and now Gloucester insisted that Prince Richard must be present at his brother's coronation. Thomas More summarises their arguments in favour of removing the boy from sanctuary:

1   The Queen's sequestration of her son Richard reflected badly on the council and implied that its members were not to be trusted with the King's brother. Indeed, she was deliberately provoking a bitter hatred among the people against the nobles of the King's Council.

2   The young brother's companionship was essential to the wellbeing of King Edward V, who needed 'recreation and moderate pleasure' beyond that provided by 'ancient persons'.

3   Dishonour within the realm and in foreign lands would redound to the King and the council if his brother remained in sanctuary.

4   If released, the boy would be cherished and honourably entreated. The Queen's resistance derived from obstinacy, malice, frowardness (perversity), or folly. It was 'the mother's dread and womanish fear' that made her oppose the boy's release. 'Womanish fear, nay womanish frowardness', responded the Duke of Buckingham.

5   In depriving her son of liberty, the Queen was like Medea in avenging her enemies at the expense of her own children.

6   If she feared to deliver her son, the council should fear to leave him in her hands, since she must suspect that he would be captured and might send him out of the country.

7   The boy's presence in sanctuary threw him in with 'a rabble of thieves, murderers, and malicious heinous traitors'. Even worse, sanctuary harboured 'men's wives [who] run thither with their husbands' plate, and say they dare not abide with their husbands for beating'. No young boy should consort with such company.

8   Since sanctuary protected those in danger of harm and the boy had done no wrong, there was no reason for him to be there. Those who did not need sanctuary could not claim it.

The reasons were so compelling that Gloucester proposed taking the boy by force, if necessary: 'He that takes one out of sanctuary to do him good, I say plainly that he breaks no sanctuary.'[1] Such logic and eloquence persuaded not only the secular members of the council, but many of its spiritual leaders, to seize the boy if necessary. Nevertheless, the council decided to try persuasion yet once more and sent Thomas Bourchier, Cardinal Archbishop of Canterbury, to meet with Elizabeth.

The Cardinal Archbishop did not visit Elizabeth alone, but in company with other members of the King's Council, whose presence indicated consensus, rather than a mere individual request. The collective weight of those imposing men must have had enormous impact on the Queen. This was, after all, the council which had served Edward IV and Elizabeth so loyally and well during the past nineteen years. The Queen herself had consulted the council frequently about state and household affairs. Moreover, the Cardinal Archbishop was the very man who had presided over the coronations of both Edward IV and Elizabeth, the man whom Edward IV had designated in his 1475 will to assist his executors 'according to the great trust that we have in him'. If not this personal friend and spiritual head of the Church in England, whom could Elizabeth trust?

Alone, Elizabeth had to stand against the combined political and spiritual forces of the realm. More tells us that she held her own with logical rebuttals of the Archbishop's arguments:

1   If Prince Edward needed his young brother for company, why not place them both in their mother's custody, especially considering the 'infancy' of the younger boy?

2   Considering the recent illness of Prince Richard, from which he was 'rather a little amended than well recovered', it would place his health at risk to take him from his mother, who knew best how to care for him.

3   The imprisonment of her brother Anthony and son Richard indicated that enemies were intent on procuring 'their destruction without cause'.

4   Protection of herself and her family could not be assured when 'greedy' men prevailed.

5   Her son had every right to seek sanctuary: 'A place that may defend a thief may save an innocent.'

6   If Edward V needed 'play fellows', could they not be provided by other children, his peers, rather than by his recently ill brother, who as yet had 'no lust for play'?

7   Since the law made the mother the guardian of children, no one had the right to remove her son from her protection.

Elizabeth cited three laws that confirmed her right to keep Prince Richard: man's law allows the guardian to keep the infant, nature's law allows the mother to keep her child, and God's law provides sanctuary to protect her son. She stated that her fears originated in the same fears that the law recognises when it forbids 'every man the custody of them by whose death he may inherit less land than a kingdom'.[2] The Queen refused to deliver Richard, Duke of York to the Protector.

Archbishop Bourchier, whose sincerity no one doubts, saw that he was losing the argument, that the Queen was becoming angry, and that she might say 'sore biting words against the Protector'. He cut short the discussion and used an approach that even Elizabeth could not refute. The Cardinal Archbishop of Canterbury pledged his body and soul, 'not only for his surety but also for his estate', if she delivered Prince Richard to him. Otherwise, he would depart and never entreat her further. Did she think that he and the other men with him lacked both wit and troth? Were their wits so dull that they could not perceive what the Protector intended? Did she doubt their faithfulness, loyalty and honesty in thinking that they would take her son if they perceived any evil intended toward the child?

'The Queen with these words stood a good while in a great study', More reports.[3] Dare she challenge the integrity of the spiritual leader of the Church in England, a personal friend so trusted by her husband and herself? How could she oppose Gloucester's men, who already surrounded Westminster Sanctuary ready to seize the prince by force? How could she find means to convey the boy elsewhere?

At the last she took the young Duke by the hand, and said unto the lords: 'my Lord... and all my lordes, I neither am so unwise to mistrust your wits, nor so suspicious to mistrust your troths. Of which thing I purpose to make you such a proof, as if either of both lacked in you, might turn both me to great sorrow, the realm to much harm, and you to great reproach. For lo here is... this gentleman'.[4]

...And therewithall she said unto the child: 'Farewell, my own sweet son, God send you good keeping, let me kiss you once yet ere you go, for God knoweth when we shall kiss together again. And therewith she kissed him, and blessed him, turned her back and wept and went her way, leaving the child weeping as fast.

When the Lord Cardinal and these other lords with him had received this young Duke, they brought him into the Star Chamber where the Protector took him in his arms and kissed him with these words: 'Now welcome my Lord even with all my very heart'.

...Thereupon forthwith they brought him to the King his brother into the Bishops Palace at Paul's, and from thence through the City honourably into the Tower, out of which after that day they never came abroad.[5]

Prince Richard departed from sanctuary at Westminster Abbey on 16 June 1483. Another contemporary chronicle summarises that fateful day:

The Duke of Gloucester went to Westminster and took with him the Archbishop of Canterbury: where by fair means and for trust that the Queen had in the Archbishop, which said Bishop thought nor intended no harm, she delivered to them the Duke of York, a child about the age of 7 years, whom the said Duke conveyed unto the Tower and there caused him to be kept with the Prince, his brother.[6]

With both boys in his protection, Gloucester could move more aggressively. He next set about discrediting the children of Edward IV by proclaiming them to be bastards, illegitimate children of Edward IV, with no rights to the throne of England. For good measure, the legitimacy of Edward IV and his brother Clarence was also challenged, never mind that such an accusation slandered Gloucester's own mother, the Duchess of York, who was still living.

The purveyor of these claims of illegitimacy was Ralph Shaa, Doctor of Divinity, popular London preacher, and brother of the Lord Mayor. On Sunday 22 June, Doctor Shaa delivered at Paul's Cross a sermon entitled 'Bastard Slips Shall Never Take Deep Root'. First establishing the importance of matrimony, then the unhappiness and 'lack of grace' of bastard children conceived in adultery, he declared that Richard, Duke of Gloucester was the only rightful heir to the throne. Doctor Shaa claimed that both Edward IV and Clarence were illegitimate and he provided proof: neither man resembled their father Richard, Duke of York, but 'their favours more resembled other known men than him'. Only Gloucester, the Lord Protector, 'the very noble prince, the special pattern of knightly prowess, as well in all princely behaviour as in the lineaments and favour of his visage, represented the very face of the noble Duke his father'.[7]

Mancini, More and Polydore Vergil all report Shaa's claim that Edward IV was a bastard, an accusation so outrageous that some modern historians find it hard to accept. Bertram Fields, for instance, rejects the tale as Tudor propaganda, arguing that Gloucester was living with his mother at Baynard Castle during much of this time and would not have slandered her so publicly. Michael Jones, however, not only accepts the claim, but attributes its source to the Duchess of York herself. Jones even identifies the probable father of Edward IV as a handsome French archer named Blaybourne, who took advantage of York's long absences from his wife during the French wars.[8] The rumour of Edward IV's illegitimacy first surfaced in 1469, when Clarence made the same allegation to clear his way to the throne,[9] and Jones believes that Cecily Neville, still seething with anger at Edward IV's marriage to Elizabeth, admitted her indiscretion then to assist Clarence to the throne.

Mancini indicates that the rumour of Edward's illegitimacy was common gossip in the streets of London during the summer of 1483, when no one would have dared repeat it if Gloucester had objected. Allegations do not constitute truth, however, and claims of illegitimacy that slandered mothers were frequently bruited about to challenge the inheritance rights of their children. Margaret of Anjou was accused of adultery when Edward of Lancaster was born in 1453, an accusation that gained credibility from the illness of Henry VI. That story was probably planted by Warwick and the Duke of York, as they plotted to claim the throne for York. Again, in 1469, Warwick and Clarence could have won without fighting if Edward IV and his children had been removed from the York lineage, a powerful motive for gossip about the Duchess of York's infidelity. In 1483, Gloucester was merely following family tradition in slandering his mother.

Solid evidence exists to refute any claims that Cecily Neville was complicit with Gloucester in proclaiming Edward's bastardy. Her will, made in 1495, specifically and lovingly declares the parentage of her son, who had been dead for twelve years:

> I, Cecily, wife unto the right noble prince *Richard, late Duke of York, father unto the most Christian prince my Lord and son King Edward the iiiith*, the first day of April the year of our Lord 1495… make and ordain my testament in form and manner ensuing.[10]

With her final words on this earth, Cecily Neville set the record straight. She twice stated clearly and unequivocally that Edward IV was the son of Richard, Duke of York. Further, not one word in her will mentioned either Clarence or Richard III. Was she still suffering the hurt and humiliation she felt when her sons publicly proclaimed her an adulteress? Cecily's will designated personal items to be distributed to the children of Edward IV and Elizabeth and to the de la Pole descendants of her daughter Elizabeth, Duchess of Suffolk. If the Duchess of York ever harboured resentment at Edward IV's marriage to Elizabeth Wydeville, it was long forgotten in her loving bequests to the Queen and to 'my daughter Bridget… my daughter Cecily… my daughter Anne… my daughter Katharine.' The son and daughter of Clarence, still living, were not mentioned.

Charges of Edward's bastardy were only the beginning of Doctor Shaa's propaganda. The Doctor of Divinity also resurrected the tale of Edward's pre-contract to another woman (whose identity varies from Lady Elizabeth Lucy to Lady Eleanor Butler, both of whom had been mistresses of Edward IV). Any pre-contract would have invalidated Edward's marriage to Elizabeth and made all of their ten children illegitimate, thus disentitling Edward V as King. In all claims of the alleged pre-contract, no one ever mentioned Edward's nineteen years of married life, during which all of England had welcomed and cheered Elizabeth as the King's wife. Nor did the slanderers recall that each of their ten children were welcomed at birth with joyous celebrations and royal rituals proclaiming them princes and princesses.

At the point in Doctor Shaa's sermon where he proclaimed these charges of illegitimacy, Gloucester was supposed to arrive and the people spontaneously cry 'King Richard! King Richard!' But the timing was off and Gloucester didn't show up, forcing Doctor Shaa to move on in his prepared remarks. When the Duke finally appeared, the good Doctor went back to repeat his words and point to Gloucester: 'This is the father's own figure, this his own countenance, the very print of his visage, the sure undoubted image, the plain express likeness of the noble Duke, whose remembrance can never die while he liveth.'

But instead of crying 'King Richard! King Richard!', the people 'stood as they had been turned into stones, for wonder of this shameful sermon', after which the preacher went home in shame and kept 'out of sight like an owl'.[11] Doctor Shaa died within the year, a broken man: 'Doctor Shaa by his sermon lost his honesty, and soon after his life, for very shame of the world, into which he durst never after come abroad.'[12]

But if the Doctor of Divinity was ruined, the Protector pursued his plan with even more daring. On 24 June, the Tuesday following Shaa's sermon, the Duke of Buckingham addressed a Guildhall convocation of lords and knights, the Mayor, aldermen, and commons of the city, to add secular strength to Shaa's religious rant. Buckingham recalled the recent years of civil bloodshed, with its devastation of families and country, then he attacked the recently deceased Edward IV:

> For no woman was there any where young or old, rich or poor, whom he set his eye upon, in whom he any thing liked either person or favour, speech, pace, or countenance, but without any fear of God, or respect of his honour, murmur or grudge of the world, he would importunely pursue his appetite, and have her, to the great destruction of many a good woman, and great dolour to their husbands, and their other friends...[13]

Buckingham reiterated Shaa's lies about the illegitimacy of Edward's children:

> The children of King Edward the Fourth were never lawfully begotten, forasmuch as the King (leaving his very wife Dame Elizabeth Lucy) was never lawfully married unto the Queen their mother, whose blood, saving that he set his voluptuous pleasure before his honour, was full unmeetly to be match with his, and the mingling of whose bloods together, hath been the effusion of great part of the noble blood of this realm. Whereby it may well seem that marriage not well made, of which there is so much mischief grown...[14]

Once more, the theme of 'noble blood' recurs. To claim that the Queen was 'unmeetly to be match' with Edward harks back to Warwick's obsession with his blood royal, and his chiding of Elizabeth's father and brother for their low class origins. Once more, Jacquetta's heritage, titles and rank disappear in xenophobic parochialism and self-interested promotion. How ironic, this claim that Wydeville blood had tainted the realm, when the miscarriages and the sickly children born to the Neville cousin-wives of Clarence and Gloucester demonstrated the sad consequences of incestuous unions, of commingling only 'noble blood'.

In his speech, Buckingham touched only lightly on the bastardy of Edward IV himself, because 'nature requireth a filial reverence to the Duchess his mother'. Nevertheless, he declared that the common law of the land must recognise the Lord Protector as the only 'lawfully begotten son of the fore remembered noble Duke of York'. Added to the general wisdom that 'Woe is that realm that hath a child to their King', Buckingham urged the citizens to petition Gloucester to accept the throne. When the crowd continued its silence, even after the City Recorder repeated the petition, a small claque of Buckingham's servants began crying 'King Richard! King Richard!', sufficient support to schedule a meeting with the Protector the next day.

On 25 June 1483, Buckingham, in company with the Lord Mayor, aldermen, lords and knights, visited Baynard's Castle to petition Gloucester to assume the throne. The Protector first demurred, declaring that the 'entire love he bare unto King Edward and his children' prevented him from accepting the offer. With persuasion, however, he changed his mind.

On that same day, the Queen's brother Anthony Wydeville was executed. Her son, Sir Richard Grey, her cousin, Sir Richard Haute, and the prince's elderly chamberlain, Sir Thomas Vaughan, were either already dead or killed that day as well. In blaming the Protector for the executions, *The Great Chronicle* states the cause was 'more of will than of justice'.[15]

Anthony Wydeville's will, made on 23 June 1483, asks first that his heart be buried in the Chapel of 'Our Lady of Pew beside Saint Stephen's College at Westminster', a chapel he had supported in happier days.[16] He willed the land inherited from his father and his first wife, Lady Scales, to his brother Edward, with 500 marks set aside to pray for the souls of his first wife and her brother, Thomas. He decreed that his 'fee simple land' be sold to fund a hospital at Rochester for thirteen poor folks, and other deeds of charity, such as paying prisoners' fees, visiting the prisons of London and burying the dead.

His will also enumerated debts to be paid, and designated that his plate and personal possessions be given to his wife. All household servants received their wages for the Midsummer's quarter, along with a black gown. His clothing and horse harness were to be sold and the money used to buy shirts and smocks for poor folks, excepting his 'tawney cloth of gold', which went to the Prior of Royston, and his trapper of black cloth of gold, to Lady Walsingham. Certain designated lands remained 'with the manor of Grafton toward the funding of the Priest of the Hermitage'. Tybold, his barber, received five marks and his servant, James, forty shillings.

The will appointed as executors the Bishop of Lincoln, the Bishop of Worcester, the Chief Judge of the King's Bench, the Chief Judge of the Common Place, and six others of whom any three had 'full authority and power'. As if he could foretell the future actions of Gloucester, his will concluded with a plea:

> I beseech humbly my Lord of Gloucester, in the worship of Christ's passion and for the merit and weal of his soul, to comfort, help and assist, as supervisor (for very trust) of this testament, that my executors may with his pleasure fulfill this my last will, which I have made the day abovesaid.[17]

Anthony's executioners discovered that he was wearing a hair shirt next to his skin, a self-imposed penance to remind himself of mortal imper-fections.[18] The Carmelite Friary at Doncaster hung the hair shirt before the statue of the Virgin Mary to symbolise the piety of this virtuous man. Unfortunately, Anthony's penance could not save his family – or England – from two more years of bloodshed.

On 26 June, the Protector proceeded to Westminster Hall in company with a great train of followers to sit in the royal chair in the Court of the King's Bench. The symbolism of that act was unmistakable: the King's Bench was the royal seat of judgement, where the King heard pleas to the crown and dispensed justice. King Richard III dated his reign from this day, rather than from his coronation date of 6 July 1483. Mancini reports that 'the cardinal of Canterbury, albeit unwillingly, anointed and crowned him king of England'.[19] The Archbishop's state of mind is corroborated by his absence at the coronation banquet: 'on the right hand of the King [sat] the Bishop of Durham in the Cardinal's stead'.[20] Perhaps the Cardinal

Archbishop was remembering his pledge of troth to Queen Elizabeth when he persuaded her to give up Prince Richard to his protection.

From sanctuary at Westminster Abbey, Elizabeth heard the pomp and circumstance taking place next door, as the bells rang in joyous pronouncement of Richard III's coronation. Beyond feelings of despair, she must have raged with anger at the slander sweeping the streets of London. When she learned that her nineteen-year marriage had been invalidated and ten of her children declared bastards in a public sermon delivered at Paul's Cross, she must have comprehended that Richard III's coronation annihilated all hopes for her sons' survival.

The fate of the princes remains shrouded in history. Thomas More states quite simply that Richard III planned 'the lamentable murder of his innocent nephews, the young King and his tender brother'.[21] Copious details, including named perpetrators, confer a compelling credibility on More's history: Richard III sent 'one John Green' to Sir Robert Brackenbury, Constable of the Tower, with a letter ordering him to 'put the two children to death'. Brackenbury refused. Richard III then commissioned the deed to Sir James Tyrell, a man with 'high heart, [who] sore longed upward, not rising yet so fast as he had hoped'. A letter from the King commanded Brackenbury to give Tyrell the keys to the Tower for one night.

The thirteen-year-old Edward V and his nine-year-old brother had been shut up in the Tower with only one man, 'called Black Will or William Slaughter', to serve them. Tyrell hired two men, Miles Forest and John Dighton, to commit the murder:

This Miles Forest and John Dighton, about midnight (the sely [innocent] children lying in their beds) came into the chamber, and suddenly lapped them up among the clothes so be wrapped them and entangled them keeping down by force the featherbed and pillows hard unto their mouths, that within a while smothered and stifled, their breath failing, they gave up to God their innocent souls into the joys of heaven, leaving to the tormentors their bodies dead in the bed.

Which after that the wretches perceived, first by the struggling with the pains of death, and after long lying still, to be thoroughly dead: they laid their bodies naked out upon the bed, and fetched Sir James to see them. Which upon the sight of them, caused those murderers to bury them at the stair foot, meetly deep in the ground under a great heap of stones.[22]

This information More 'learned of them that much knew and little cause had to lie'. More's account has been corroborated by many contemporary documents.

Letters by Simon Stallworthe record the unrest in England as early as 9 June 1483. A second letter, on 21 June, recounts the delivery of Prince Richard from sanctuary in an atmosphere of general distrust:

> I hold you happy that you are out of the press, for with us is much trouble and every man doubts other. As on Friday last was the Lord Chamberlain headed soon upon noon. On Monday last was at Westminster great plenty of harnessed [armed] men. There was the deliverance of the Duke of York to my Lord Cardinal, my Lord Chancellor, and other many lords temporal. And with him met my Lord of Buckingham in the midst of the hall of Westminster. My Lord Protector receiving him at the Star Chamber door with many loving words and so departed with my Lord Cardinal to the Tower.[23]

Twenty thousand of Gloucester and Buckingham's men were expected in the city, 'to what intent I know not but to keep the peace'. Stallworthe comments on the imprisonment of the Archbishop of York and the Bishop of Ely in the Tower, and supposes 'they shall come out nevertheless'. He is less certain about the fate of Mistress Shore, who is also in prison: 'what shall happen her I know not'.

Croyland describes similar discontent and worry:

> A circumstance which caused the greatest doubts was the detention of the King's relatives and servants in prison; besides the fact that the Protector did not, with a sufficient degree of considerateness, take measure for the preservation of the dignity and safety of the Queen.[24]

A cryptic document among the Cely Papers, written between the death of Hastings on 13 June and Richard III's assumption of power on 26 June, reiterates Stallworthe's feelings of unrest and cautiously expresses fear for the safety of Edward V and Prince Richard. Mancini records information collected before he left London, sometime after 6 July 1483:

> But after Hastings was removed, all the attendants who had waited upon the king [Edward V] were debarred access to him. He and his brother were

withdrawn in the inner apartments of the Tower proper, and day by day began to be seen more rarely behind the bars and windows, till at length they ceased to appear altogether.

The physician Argentine, the last of his attendants whose services the king enjoyed, reported that the young king, like a victim prepared for sacrifice, sought remission of his sins by daily confession and penance, because he believed that death was facing him.[25]

At that point, Mancini cannot resist describing 'the talent of the youth':

In word and deed he gave so many proofs of his liberal education, of polite, nay rather scholarly, attainments far beyond his age; all of these should be recounted, but require such labour, that I shall lawfully excuse myself the effort. There is one thing I shall not omit, and that is, his special knowledge of literature, which enabled him to discourse elegantly, to understand fully, and to declaim most excellently from any work whether in verse or prose that came into his hands, unless it were from among the more abstruse authors. He had such dignity in his whole person, and in his face such charm, that however much they might gaze he never wearied the eyes of beholders. I have seen many men burst forth into tears and lamentations when mention was made of him after his removal from men's sight; and already there was a suspicion that he had been done away with. Whether, however, he has been done away with, and by what manner of death, so far I have not at all discovered.[26]

Mancini thus corroborates Croyland's boast about the family that 'excelled all others', especially in its 'most sweet and beautiful children, the issue of his marriage... with Queen Elizabeth'.[27] The Wydeville influence – especially Anthony's service as Edward V's governor – had achieved its goal of educating an enlightened and knowledgeable prince. All for naught.

Rumours of the princes' deaths were widespread throughout Europe by the end of 1483, some blaming Richard by name. Weinreich's Danzig *Chronicle* records in 1483: 'Item later this summer Richard, the King's brother, had himself put in power and crowned in England and he had his brother's children killed, and the Queen put away secretly also.'[28] Guillaume de Rochefort, the French chancellor, reported the deaths of the boys in a speech before the States General at Tours on 15 January 1484:

Regard the events which have occurred in that land since the death of King Edward. See how his children already quite old and brave have been murdered with impunity and the crown has been transferred to their assassin by the consent of the people.[29]

In England, *The Croyland Chronicle* reports that the boys were held in the Tower while Richard III made a post-coronation progress through Windsor, Reading, Oxford, Gloucester and Coventry to York, where he invested his own son Edward as Prince of Wales on 8 September 1483. By the time rebellion broke out in late September, Croyland states 'a rumour was spread that the sons of king Edward before-named had died a violent death, but it was uncertain how'.[30] Another chronicle, recorded in *Vitellis A XVI* manuscript, states:

> Anon as the said King Richard had put to death the Lord Chamberlain and other Gentlemen, as before is said, he also put to death the two children of King Edward, for which cause he lost the hearts of the people.[31]

The Great Chronicle reports in 1484 that 'after Easter much whispering was among the people that the King had put the children of King Edward to death...'. By 1485, public anger at Richard III had reached the point where the author of *The Great Chronicle* felt sufficiently safe to return to the fate of the princes:

> Considering the death of King Edward's children, of whom as then men feared not openly to say that they were rid out of this world, but of their deaths' manner was many opinions, for some said they were murdered between two feather beds, some said they were drowned in Malvesy, and some said they were sticked with a venomous potion. But how so ever they were put to death, certain it was that before that day they were departed from this world, of which cruel deed Sir James Tyrell was reported to be the doer, but others put that blame upon an old servant of King Richard's named, _____
> [no name fills in the blank].[32]

In 1489, when Philippe de Commynes was writing his *Memoirs*, he had not the slightest doubt: 'On the death of Edward, his second brother the

Duke of Gloucester killed Edward's two sons.'[33] Polydore Vergil states that Richard III ordered the boys' death on his way to Gloucester, sometime in late July or early August 1483.

The princes were popular in the kingdom, particularly with the Welsh who favoured Edward V because his ten years of residency at Ludlow had brought order and prosperity to that region. As the summer of 1483 progressed and the boys were no longer seen by the many visitors to the Tower, Croyland tells us that 'in order to deliver them from… captivity, the people of the southern and western parts of the kingdom began to murmur greatly, and to form meetings and confederacies'.[34] Plots began to develop opposing Richard III, especially 'on the part of those who, through fear, had availed themselves of the privilege of sanctuary and franchise'.

When she entered sanctuary on 1 May 1483, the Queen had been accompanied by her son Thomas, Marquis of Dorset, and her brothers Lionel and Richard. It is unclear when Dorset left sanctuary, but Mancini dates his departure at around the time of Hastings's execution and reports that Gloucester sent troops and dogs to search around Westminster through 'the already grown crops and the cultivated and woody places', confirming a mid- to late June departure.[35] Lionel, Bishop of Salisbury, protected by his clerical status, left to participate in the commission of the peace during June and July 1483. Sir Richard Wydeville, now the third Earl Rivers, also left sanctuary at an unknown time. Sir Edward Wydeville remained in Brittany with his two ships.

Croyland describes an early plot to spirit the daughters out of sanctuary, so that they could

> …go in disguise to the parts beyond the seas; in order that, if any fatal mishap should befall the said male children of the late king in the Tower, the kingdom might still, in consequence of the safety of his daughters, some day fall again into the hands of the rightful heirs.[36]

Richard's spies discovered that plan, however, and Westminster Abbey was immediately surrounded by 'men of the greatest austerity', under the leadership of Captain John Nesfeld, Esquire. A watch was set up at 'all the inlets and outlets of the monastery, so that not one of the persons there shut up could go forth, and no one could enter, without his permission'. The girls remained in sanctuary.

It is unclear when Elizabeth learned of the boys' deaths, but Polydore Vergil graphically describes her response:

She fell in a swoon and lay lifeless a good while; after coming to herself, she wept, she cried out aloud, and with lamentable shrieks made all the house ring. She struck her breast, tore and cut her hair, and overcome in fine with dolour, prayed also her own death, calling by name now and then among her most dear children and condemning herself for a madwoman for that (being deceived by false promises) she had delivered her younger son out of sanctuary to be murdered by his enemy.[37]

CHAPTER TWENTY-TWO

A Woman Alone

Plotting to overthrow Richard III now began in earnest. Whether Queen Elizabeth or Margaret Beaufort, Countess of Richmond, first suggested marrying Henry Tudor, Earl of Richmond to the Lady Princess Elizabeth hardly matters. The blood relationship between Richmond and Princess Elizabeth had been frequently discussed, as revealed in subsequent depositions to Pope Innocent VIII, certifying that Henry and Princess Elizabeth were related in the fourth and fourth degrees of kindred: Master Christopher Urswyke, the King's almoner, testified that 'he heard the aforesaid degrees lineally recited and declared by the archbishop of York and the bishop of Worcester and Master Richard Lessy, a chamberlain of the pope'.[1] The fact that many witnesses testified that husband and wife were 'related in the double fourth degree of kindred' suggests that their marriage may even have been contemplated prior to Edward's death.

Elizabeth Wydeville and Margaret Beaufort had been friends for years. During the reign of Henry VI, they were loyal Lancastrians. Both had subsequently married powerful Yorkists and had survived the fluctuations of power as the cousins battled for dominance. The Countess of Richmond attended Queen Elizabeth and her daughters at the reburial of Richard, Duke of York at Fotheringhay in 1476.[2] She was prominent at the wedding of Prince Richard to Anne Mowbray in 1478, and she was distinctly honoured when she carried the royal Princess Bridget at her baptism in 1480. Margaret's stepson George (Lord Stanley's heir who was later held hostage at Bosworth) was married to the Queen's niece Joan, daughter of Lord Strange and Jacquetta Wydeville.

Margaret Beaufort was the great-granddaughter of John of Gaunt, Duke of Lancaster, by his third wife, Katherine Swynford. The children of that liaison were born well before Gaunt married Katherine, although they were legitimised by Pope Boniface IX in 1396. King Richard II and Parliament added secular legitimisation in 1397, but the Beaufort descendants were excluded from the throne by Henry IV's patent, issued on 10 February 1407 (the legality of which has been questioned). Their royal blood, combined with astute marriages, had made the Beauforts one of the richest and most powerful families in England.

In 1455, Margaret Beaufort, at the age of twelve, married the half-brother of Henry VI, Edmund Tudor, Earl of Richmond. When Richmond died within the year while imprisoned by the Yorkists at Carmarthen Castle, Margaret was already pregnant. She gave birth to Henry on 28 January 1457, when she was thirteen years old. The young widow soon married Sir Henry Stafford, another prominent Lancastrian who saved his property after the battle of Towton by switching his loyalty to Edward IV. Stafford died in 1471, and Margaret subsequently married the staunch Yorkist, Thomas, Lord Stanley, who served Edward IV as Steward of the Household.

Henry Tudor, Margaret's only child, spent his first eleven years living under the protection of his uncle, Jasper Tudor, at the family estate of Pembroke in Wales. When Jasper's continuing opposition to Edward IV forced him into exile, the King made the young Henry a ward of William, Lord Herbert, a loyal Yorkist. The brief restoration of Henry VI in 1470 brought Jasper back to England, where he introduced his nephew at the Lancastrian court. Edward IV's triumph at Tewkesbury, however, forced both Jasper and Henry Tudor to flee to Brittany, where they had lived in exile since 1471. After the deaths of Henry VI and his son Edward, Henry Tudor was next in the Lancastrian line for the crown of England. Yorkist domination, however, made his chances of sitting on the throne remote.

Richmond had other royal blood in his veins as well. His father, Edmund Tudor, was the son of Katherine of Valois, Dowager Queen of Henry V, who had scandalised English royalty after the death of the King by marrying Owen Tudor, a mere Welsh knight who had been Clerk of the Wardrobe. If his father was disparaged as a mere knight, Henry Tudor was, nevertheless, the great-grandson of Charles VI of France.

The fact that Margaret Beaufort's husband, Lord Stanley, was a high-ranking and trusted advisor to Richard III did not deter her from promoting the interest of her son Henry. She sent her Welsh physician, Lewis Caerleon, 'a grave man and of no small experience', to visit Queen Elizabeth in sanctuary at Westminster.[3] Polydore Vergil states that this visit occurred 'after the slaughter of King Edward's children was known', and perhaps the best evidence that the two princes were dead lies in Elizabeth's complicity in this particular plot.[4] Elizabeth agreed to the proposal that Princess Elizabeth, Yorkist heir if the boys were dead, should marry Henry Tudor, Lancastrian claimant to the throne:

> ...she would do her endeavour to procure all her husband King Edward's friends to take part with Henry [Margaret's] son, so that he might be sworn to take in marriage Elizabeth her daughter after he shall have gotten the realm, or else Cicely the younger if the other should die before he enjoyed the same.[5]

Messengers sent to Brittany informed Richmond of the plan and solicited financial support for invading England.

Meanwhile, Buckingham left Richard III's retinue and returned to his Brecknock estate in Wales, where he held in custody John Morton, Bishop of Ely, who had been released from the Tower at the petition of Oxford University. Buckingham was becoming increasingly alienated from Richard III. Some say that Richard's failure to deliver the promised Hereford inheritance caused the break. *The Great Chronicle* blames the death of the princes:

> The common fame went that King Richard had within the Tower put unto secret death the two sons of his brother Edward IV for the which, and other causes had within the breast of the Duke of Buckingham, the said Duke, in secret manner, conspired against him...[6]

Others claim that Buckingham himself was aiming at the throne, and some even blame him for the princes' deaths. Everyone credits Buckingham's prisoner Morton with considerable influence in persuading him to oppose the King, perhaps provoked by Margaret Beaufort, whom the Bishop served as chaplain. In fact, Margaret may have influenced Buckingham directly, since she was his aunt through her earlier marriage to Sir Henry Stafford. Whatever his reasons, Buckingham soon headed up a group of rebels who openly challenged King Richard. Once more, he embraced the relatives of his Wydeville wife, Katherine.

Among Buckingham's troops were the Queen's son, Thomas, Marquis of Dorset, along with 'Thomas his son, a very child', and the Queen's brother, Edward Wydeville, 'a valiant man of war'.[7] Lionel Wydeville had left sanctuary and was living in Buckingham's manor of Thornbury, twelve miles north of Bristol and close to the action in Wales, from where he continued to conduct his ecclesiastical duties as Bishop of Salisbury.[8] Sir Richard Wydeville, too, joined the rebellion that broke out in October 1483.

Alerted to the danger, King Richard marched his army to the west. Buckingham set out with his troops on 18 October, in the midst of a ten-day storm that flooded the rivers and washed away bridges. With his men scattered by floods and mired in mud, the Duke went into hiding at the cottage of his tenant, Ralph Banaster. A reward of £1,000 and land worth £100 a year in perpetuity enticed Banaster to turn his lord over to the Sheriff of Shrewsbury.[9] Taken to Richard III at Salisbury, Buckingham was executed on All Souls Day, 2 November 1483. His widow, Katherine Wydeville, joined her sister Elizabeth in sanctuary.

Dorset, who was leading the rebellion in Exeter, was denounced in a proclamation issued by Richard III on 23 October:

> Thomas Dorset, late Marquess Dorset, which not fearing God, nor the peril of his soul, hath many and sundry maids, widows, and wives damnably and without shame devoured, deflowered, and defouled, hold[s] the unshameful and mischievous woman called Shore's wife in adultery.[10]

After Buckingham's defeat, Dorset fled to Brittany, where he joined his uncle Edward Wydeville and the forces of Richmond. Bishop Lionel Wydeville entered sanctuary at Beaulieu.[11] Bishop John Morton escaped from Brecknock, made his way secretly across country, stopped at Ely to replenish his supplies, and went into exile in Flanders.

Richmond had tried to leave Brittany on 3 October to invade England, but his ships were thwarted by the same storm that destroyed Buckingham's army. The winds forced his ships back into port, and he could not sail again until 18 October. By the time Richmond's ships reached Plymouth on 2 November, Buckingham was dead. Richmond returned to Brittany to reconnoitre and plan a second attack. On Christmas Day 1483, Henry, Earl of Richmond took a solemn oath in the cathedral at Rennes to marry Princess Elizabeth of York.

Queen Elizabeth's plight in Westminster Sanctuary could not have been more desperate. All male members of her family were dead, attainted, or exiled. Sir Edward Wydeville, newly denounced along with Buckingham and the Bishop of Ely in Richard III's proclamation of 23 October, remained in Brittany. Elizabeth's eldest living brother, Richard, now the third Earl Rivers, was accused of conspiring in the death of the King and attainted by Richard's Parliament, which opened on 23 January 1484. Bishop Lionel Wydeville, in sanctuary at Beaulieu, resisted Richard III's efforts to compel his presence at Parliament in February 1484, and was removed from his bishopric of Salisbury on 15 March 1484.[12] He died sometime before 23 June 1484.[13]

Richard III's men surrounded Westminster Sanctuary, where Elizabeth depended on the Abbot for sustenance. While she alone might have been able to survive, she had five daughters to worry about, ranging from the seventeen-year-old Elizabeth to the three-year-old Bridget. Unlike her earlier residence in sanctuary in 1470, no sympathetic butcher delivered half a beef and two muttons a week to feed the Queen and her family. Elizabeth and her daughters were living under siege, and totally dependent on charity. The Abbot of Westminster remained in 'great trouble' for accommodating his guests.[14]

There was no end in sight. Richard's 1484 Parliament officially humiliated Elizabeth by approving *Titulus Regius: An Act for the Settlement of the Crown upon the King and his issue, with a recapitulation of his Title*. In that document, the three estates of the realm of England (the Lords Spiritual, the Lords Temporal, and the Commons) declared:

> that the said pretended Marriage betwixt the above named King Edward and Elizabeth Grey, was made of great presumption without the knowing and assent of the Lords of this Land, and also by Sorcery and Witchcraft, committed by the said Elizabeth, and her Mother, Jacquetta Duchess of Bedford...[15]

Beyond sorcery and witchcraft, Parliament also declared that the 'said pretended Marriage' was made privately and secretly, without publication of the banns and at a time when Edward was already married to Dame Eleanor Butler, daughter of the Earl of Shrewsbury. If secrecy invalidated the marriage of Edward and Elizabeth, that impediment surely applied equally to any pre-contract between Edward and Eleanor Butler. No one mentioned that logical discrepancy, however, and Parliament decreed:

> Which premises being true, as in very truth they be true, it appears and follows evidently, that the said King Edward during his life, and the said Elizabeth, lived together sinfully and damnably in adultery, against the Law of God and of his Church... Also it appears evidently and follows, that all the issue and Children of the said King Edward, be Bastards, and unable to inherit or to claim any thing by inheritance, by the Law and Custom of England.[16]

The sole authority for Edward's alleged betrothal to Eleanor Butler was Robert Stillington, Bishop of Bath and Wells. That the Bishop had remained silent for nineteen years, during which time the eternal soul of the King was at risk for living in adulterous sin, was ignored. Similarly, no one recalled the fact that Warwick had been negotiating a marriage with Lady Bona of Savoy when Edward's marriage to Elizabeth stunned the court. Warwick, as uncle to Eleanor Butler, would hardly have been seeking a new wife for a King already contracted to the Earl's niece. Nevertheless, Bishop Stillington's belated declaration of Edward's marital pre-contract proved sufficient to convict the King of adultery and to bastardise his children. No one questioned the Bishop's motives.

More politician than prelate, Bishop Stillington had earlier befriended Clarence. Their long-time alliance had enabled the Bishop to intervene during Clarence's dalliance with Warwick, and to persuade the wayward brother to rejoin Edward IV when the King returned from exile in 1471.[17] Later, Stillington had been imprisoned in the Tower during Clarence's trial in 1478, suggesting an association with the Duke's treasons.[18] No one, however, could question a bishop's moral authority – even though this prelate had himself fathered illegitimate children and neglected his seldom-visited diocese.[19] Neither could Eleanor Butler, long dead, speak for herself. Slander now carried the weight of law.

What was Elizabeth to do? Street gossip was devastating enough. With Parliament invalidating her nineteen years of marriage and declaring ten of her children illegitimate, she was publicly humiliated and personally vulnerable. She could only suffer the will of the King, who wielded all the power. Richard III wanted Elizabeth out of sanctuary so that he could gain control over her daughters. The betrothal of Henry Tudor to Elizabeth of York constituted a real threat to the King. Many regarded Princess Elizabeth, a seventeen-year-old beauty with her mother's golden hair and lovely features, as the legitimate heir to the throne. A union between Henry Tudor and Elizabeth of York, eldest surviving child of Edward IV, legally challenged Richard's heritage. She could not be dismissed because of gender, since the entire Yorkist claim to the throne depended on women – beginning with Philippa, daughter of Lionel, and continuing through Anne Mortimer, grandmother of Richard III.

Croyland tells us that during the Parliament of 1484 'frequent entreaties as well as threats... strongly solicited' the Queen to release her daughters from sanctuary.[20] Ongoing negotiations took place, that led to Richard III swearing an extraordinary oath before the assembled estates of clergy, nobles and commons, including the Lord Mayor and alderman of London, on 1 March 1484:

I, Richard, by the Grace of God King of England and of France and Lord of Ireland, in the presence of you, my lords spiritual and temporal and you Mayor and Aldermen of my City of London, promise and swear *verbo regio* upon these holy Evangels of God by me personally touched, that if the daughters of dame Elizabeth Grey, late calling herself Queen of England, that is to wit Elizabeth, Cecily, Anne, Katharine, and Bridget, will come unto me out of the Sanctuary of Westminster, and be guided, ruled and demeaned after me, then I shall see that they shall be in surety of their lives, and also not suffer any manner hurt by any manner person or persons to them or any of them or their bodies or persons, to be done by way of ravishment or defiling contrary their wills, nor them or any of them imprison within the Tower of London or other prison; but that I shall put them in honest places of good name and fame, and them honestly and courteously shall see to be founden and entreated, and to have all things requisite and necessary for their exhibition and findings as my kinswomen; and that I shall marry such of them as now be marriageable to gentlemen born, and every of them give in marriage lands and tenements to the yearly value of two hundred marks for the term of their lives; and in likewise to the other daughters when they come to lawful age of marriage if they live. And such gentlemen as shall happen to marry with them I shall straitly charge, from time to time, lovingly to love and entreat them as their wives and my kinswomen, as they will avoid and eschew my displeasure.

And over this, that I shall yearly from henceforth content and pay, or cause to be contented or paid, for the exhibition and finding of the said dame

Elizabeth Grey during her natural life, at four terms of the year, that is to wit at Pasche, Midsummer, Michaelmas, and Christmas, to John Nesfield, one of the squires for my body, for his finding to attend upon her, the sum of seven hundred marks of lawful money of England, by even portions; and moreover I promise to them that if any surmise or evil report be made to me of them, or any of them, by any person or persons, that then I shall not give thereunto faith nor credence, nor therefore put them to any manner punishment, before that they or any of them so accused may be at their lawful defence and answer. In witness whereof, to this writing of my oath and promise aforesaid in your said presences made, I have set my sign manual, the first day of March, the first year of my reign.[21]

A modern reader finds Richard's oath to be rife with unintended irony, since it was a little late to promise that the girls would 'not suffer any manner of hurt'. One must also ask how Elizabeth could trust Richard to keep his word.

But almost a year had gone by since the death of Edward IV, and if Elizabeth's situation in sanctuary was difficult, that of her young daughters was untenable. They had no future in sanctuary. And there was no way out. Richard III's troops surrounded Westminster and controlled the kingdom. Elizabeth could only hope that public scrutiny and political necessity would compel the King to honour his promises. He could not afford to break his oath, made so publicly before the men on whom he depended for military, economic and regal survival.

Elizabeth and her daughters left sanctuary in March 1484, with John Nesfield taking custody of the former Queen, now dependent on Richard's 700 marks for her support. She was essentially a ward of Nesfield, who did his job so well that no one knows where Elizabeth lived during this period. Richard III confiscated her dowry and denied her title as Queen Dowager. Life, however, had taught Elizabeth patience.

Little is known about the four younger daughters, but Princess Elizabeth re-entered court life and soon regained her former status. By Christmas 1484, she was prominent at court in ways that saddened the Croyland Chronicler:

Many other things... are not written in this book, and of which I grieve to speak, although the fact ought not to be concealed that, during this feast of the Nativity, far too much attention was given to dancing and gaiety, and vain changes of apparel presented to Queen Anne and the lady Elizabeth, the eldest daughter of the late king, being of similar colour and shape; a thing that caused the people to murmur and the nobles and prelates greatly to wonder thereat.[22]

Strict sumptuary laws distinguished rank by dress and required that no one wear clothing in a colour or style similar to the Queen's. For Princess Elizabeth to wear apparel that matched Queen Anne's could only provoke speculation about her relationship to Richard III. Croyland despairs:

…it was said by many that the King was bent, either on the anticipated death of the Queen taking place, or else, by means of divorce, for which he supposed he had quite sufficient grounds, on contracting a marriage with the said Elizabeth. For it appeared that in no other way could his kingly power be established, or the hope of his rival be put an end to.[23]

The idea of an uncle marrying his niece defies modern comprehension. Yet the motives of Richard III, although perverse, can perhaps be explained by the unexpected death of his only son, Edward, earlier that year (around 9 April 1484). In February, the eight-year-old boy had been declared his father's heir in an oath signed by the lords of the realm and the nobles of the King's household. The boy's subsequent and early death caused great suffering to his father and mother, perhaps exacerbating Queen Anne's lingering illness (probably tuberculosis). Anne's poor health made it unlikely that she could bear another heir. Croyland writes: '…the King entirely shunned her bed, declaring that it was by the advice of his physicians that he did so. Why enlarge?'[24] Queen Anne, Richard's wife for fourteen years, died on 16 March 1485, 'the day of the great eclipse of the sun', a phenomenon that in superstitious England caused rumours to circulate that Richard had poisoned her. Anne was not quite thirty years old.

Whatever Richard's intent toward his niece Elizabeth, rumours of a marriage were so prevalent that 'the king was obliged, having called a council together, to excuse himself with many words and to assert that such a thing had never once entered his mind'. His close advisors, Sir Richard Ratcliff and William Catesby, warned him that if he did not deny such a marriage before the Mayor and Commons of London, his northern supporters (inherited through his wife's Warwick ties) would blame him for the death of Queen Anne. Croyland adds, however, that Ratcliff and Catesby also feared that the accession of Princess Elizabeth would place themselves in jeopardy for their part in executing 'her uncle, Earl Anthony, and her brother Richard'.[25]

The King followed the advice of Ratcliff and Catesby and denied any intended marriage, sometime before Easter 1485. He spoke in a 'loud and distinct voice' before the Lord Mayor and the citizens of London, in the great hall of the Hospital of St John. To quiet any lingering suspicions, Richard III sent Princess Elizabeth north into isolation at Sheriff Hutton, where she shared the castle with another York descendant, Edward, Earl of Warwick and son of Clarence. Both enjoyed hereditary rights that placed them closer to the throne than Richard III.

Opinions differ about the role played by Princess Elizabeth and her mother in the rumoured marriage. The seventeen-year-old Elizabeth apparently loved her life at Richard's court and may, indeed, have fallen in love with her powerful uncle, who could be quite charming when he wished. An infamous letter which Sir George Buck claims was handwritten by Princess Elizabeth asks the Duke of Norfolk to intercede in helping to arrange her marriage with the King, 'who, as she wrote, was her only joy and maker in this world, and that she was his in heart and thoughts'.[26] The letter, which expressed her fear that Queen Anne would never die, supposedly resided in the private cabinet of Thomas, Earl of Arundel and Surrey. Unfortunately, only Buck, an apologist for Richard III, mentions this letter, which has disappeared with its authenticity unconfirmed.

Writing 135 years after the event, Buck contradicts the statement of Polydore Vergil, made twenty-six years after the event: 'Richard had kept [Elizabeth] unharmed with a view to marriage. To such a marriage the girl had a singular aversion.'[27] The antithetical views of Vergil, a Tudor historian, and Buck, a Ricardian, reflect the difficulty of finding truth in the stories about both Princess Elizabeth and her mother.

Claims that Queen Dowager Elizabeth left sanctuary anticipating her daughter's marriage to Richard are negated by irrefutable facts: Richard III's son and heir, Edward, did not die until a month after Elizabeth departed from sanctuary. Richard's wife, Anne, died more than a year later. Elizabeth Wydeville left sanctuary because she and her daughters had no alternative.

Richard's biographer, James Gairdner, claims that

> …the queen dowager had been completely won over by Richard, so that she not only forgot her promise to the Countess of Richmond, but even wrote, at the king's suggestion to her son, the Marquis of Dorset, at Paris, to abandon the party of the Earl of Richmond and come to England.[28]

While Elizabeth did request her son to come home, her motives remain unknown. It is possible that she wrote under compulsion by Richard – or that she needed Dorset's physical and emotional support for herself and her daughters. Dorset, who had begun to despair of Richmond's chances, secretly left Paris for Flanders, on his way to England. When his plans were discovered, Richmond sent Humphrey Cheney to intercept and persuade Dorset to stay in France, which he did.

By summer 1485, defectors from Richard III's cause were flocking to Richmond, whose invasion of England was drawing near. Sedition was growing throughout the land. *The Great Chronicle* reports the hanging and disembowelling of a man named Colyngbourn for demeaning Richard III's supporters Lovell, Ratcliff and Catsby with a 'seditious rhyme', which slandered the King and his badge of the white boar:

> The Cat, the Rat, and Lovell our dog
> Rule all England under an hog.[29]

The most damning evidence comes from *The Great Chronicle*: 'the more in number grudged so sore against the King for the death of the Innocents [the two princes] that as gladly would they have been French, as to be under his subjection'.[30]

When Henry Tudor, Earl of Richmond landed at Milford Haven in Wales on 7 August 1485, he had no trouble gathering support as he marched east to meet Richard III in battle. Among the chief men of his army was 'Edward Wydeville, brother of Queen Elizabeth, a most valiant knight'.[31] The two armies met near a small town named Market Bosworth, on 22 August 1485, a battle that has been immortalised in drama and history beyond anything its participants could have envisioned. Richard III died heroically, charging down a hillside to attack Richmond in person, even as his followers failed to support him. Most significantly, the troops of Lord Stanley waited to see which way the tide turned before joining the forces of his stepson, Henry Tudor.

With the death of Richard III, Queen Dowager Elizabeth could once more hope for the future. Her daughter, Elizabeth of York, left Sheriff Hutton for London, where her betrothed was now King of England. Nineteen years old, she was a beautiful woman with golden hair and tall stature, who instantly won the hearts of the people. She had never met Henry Tudor, a man quite different from her father and brothers and uncles. Cautious, parsimonious and dull, Henry VII was exactly the type of King needed by a country battered by eighty-five years of war and political instability.

The union of the houses of Lancaster and York did more than bring peace and economic growth to England. Under the Tudors, the barons progressively lost ground to an increasingly powerful monarch. That transition was made easier by the preceding decades of internecine warfare, in which cousins fighting cousins had destroyed many of the noble families of England. If the ordinary citizens of England were largely untouched by the hostilities, the powerful barons suffered irretrievable losses. The Lancasters and the Nevilles had effectively annihilated themselves. Only two male heirs remained in the House of York: Edward, Earl of Warwick, the reputedly feeble-minded son of Clarence, and John, Earl of Lincoln, the son of Elizabeth (sister to Edward IV, Richard III and Clarence).

CHAPTER TWENTY-THREE

Queen Dowager Elizabeth

Henry VII's treatment of his wife's mother – the role that Elizabeth Wydeville would play for the rest of her life – was honourable, but careful. In 1485, he immediately restored her 'estate, dignity, preeminence, and name', along with all possessions held before the Parliament of Richard III deprived her of them.[1] At the same time, he ordered the defamatory *Titulus Regius* to be 'cancelled, destroyed, and... taken and avoided out of the roll and records of the said Parliament of the said late king, and burned, and utterly destroyed'.[2] Anyone with a copy or even a 'remembrance' of that bill was ordered to destroy it or deliver it to the Chancellor, before 'the feast of Easter next'. Otherwise, imprisonment and 'fine and ransom to the King at his will' would result.[3]

Queen Dowager Elizabeth attended the wedding of her daughter, Elizabeth of York, and Henry VII at Westminster on 18 January 1486, five months after Bosworth Field. On 4 March 1486, the King confirmed the Queen Dowager's dowry rights to six manors in the county of Essex. The following day he added the remainder of her dowry property.[4] During the spring, while Henry VII was in the north quelling a rebellion, the women of the family – the new Queen Elizabeth and her sisters, Queen Dowager Elizabeth, and Margaret Beaufort (the King's mother) – lived at Winchester. Queen Elizabeth was a mother-in-waiting, and her loved ones gathered around during her confinement.

The family dynamics, however, had shifted. Margaret Beaufort, Countess of Richmond, was now mother of the King. And even though the Queen Dowager outranked the Countess, Elizabeth was merely mother of the Queen, whose sweet, retiring nature deferred to her husband and her mother-in-law. Friends though they were, Elizabeth Wydeville may have found Margaret Beaufort's dominance within the household to be a bit overbearing. The Countess was six years younger than the Queen Dowager, and had more energy and vigour than the woman who had lived through three years of sanctuary and sequestration.

Perhaps that change in status explains the lease Elizabeth obtained, on 10 July 1486, from the Abbot of Westminster, for 'a mansion within the said Abbey called Cheyne gate... with all the houses, chambers, aislement and other...'. The indenture between the Abbot and 'the most high and excellent Princess Elizabeth by the grace of God Queen of England, late wife to the most mighty Prince of famous memory Edward the IVth' reflects Elizabeth Wydeville's change of status. Twice the document addresses her merely as 'princess'.[5]

As she approached fifty years of age, Elizabeth Wydeville was entering a period of contemplative reflection, away from the swirling cauldron of court politics. She had always been a deeply religious woman – even choosing Reading Abbey as the site of her honeymoon – and she had twice found solace and sustenance in sanctuary during the most traumatic moments of her existence. In 1486, when she enjoyed the goodwill and grace of Henry VII, as well as her full dowry, the Queen Dowager could have lived anywhere. She chose to sign a forty-year lease for Cheneygate manor within Westminster Close. That residence, close to Westminster Palace, offered proximity both to the family she loved and to the God she worshipped.

When her daughter gave birth to a son, Arthur, on 20 September 1486, Queen Dowager Elizabeth shared in the glory of the moment. At the christening ceremony, she was distinctly honoured by being designated godmother to Prince Arthur, to whom she gave a gold cup. Her second daughter, Cecily, carried the baby to the font. Given the familial closeness Elizabeth had nurtured throughout her life – from the large Wydeville clan to her own royal family – she must have felt warm satisfaction at becoming grandmother to her eldest daughter's firstborn, a prince!

The crown, however, rested uneasily on Henry VII's head. Yorkist sympathisers, particularly Edward IV's sister Margaret, Duchess Dowager of Burgundy, was not pleased with the King, who had killed her brother Richard III. She was ready to fund a rebellion. France and Scotland, always interested in destabilising England, listened sympathetically to proposals that would unseat the new Tudor King. Ireland, a Yorkist stronghold, added resistance to the government of Henry VII.

Conspiracies proliferated, led by pretenders to the throne. In late 1486, a young boy of about eleven appeared on the scene, claiming that he was Richard, Duke of York, the younger son of Edward IV and Elizabeth. Margaret of Burgundy, sister of Edward IV, supported his claim and helped fund an army led by John de la Pole, Earl of Lincoln (son of Elizabeth, sister to Edward IV, Richard III and the Duchess Dowager Margaret) to carry out the Yorkist rebellion. The boy was sent to Ireland, where he changed his identity and claimed to be Edward, Earl of Warwick, son of Clarence, but still a Yorkist male with a more direct claim to the throne than Henry VII. Such a change of identity was foolish, particularly since the real Warwick was imprisoned in the Tower and the claimant clearly an impostor. The growing Yorkist movement nevertheless rallied around 'Warwick' and posed a challenging threat to Henry VII.

On 2 February 1487, Henry VII met with his council of nobles to deal with the rebellion. Polydore Vergil reports on ordinances authorised at that same meeting to deal with 'improvements in public administration'.

> Among other matters, Elizabeth the widow of King Edward was deprived by the decree of the same council of all her possessions. This was done because she had made her peace with King Richard; had placed her daughters at his disposal; and had, by leaving sanctuary, broken her promise to those (mainly of the nobility) who had, at her own most urgent entreaty, forsaken their own English property and fled to Henry in Brittany, the latter having pledged himself to marry her elder daughter Elizabeth.[6]

Vergil blames Elizabeth for endangering the marriage of Henry and Elizabeth, and for condemning the English nobles to perpetual exile: 'she was accordingly deprived of the income from her estates, so that she should offer an example to others to keep faith'.[7]

Vergil's explanations are puzzling, especially since Elizabeth's so-called 'peace with King Richard' and her departure from sanctuary had occurred in March 1484, three years earlier than this February 1487 meeting. It was a little late to punish the Queen Dowager for that action. Further, since Henry VII's victory, the King had treated the Queen Dowager with respect and generosity. Speculation abounds about the 'deprivation' – Vergil's word – of Elizabeth's property, an action endorsed by Parliament on 20 February 1487, along with the grant of an annuity of 400 marks.

Had Elizabeth participated in some activity that caused the forfeiture of her estates? Vergil never connects Elizabeth to the rebellion of the young Yorkist claimant, but that is where speculation has led. Evidence favouring such an allegation might lie in the fact that Elizabeth's eldest son, Thomas Grey, Marquis of Dorset, was held in the Tower during the rebellion and not released until after the battle of Stoke, where the Earl of Lincoln was killed and the impostor captured. Evidence against the theory lies in that fact that Sir Edward Wydeville supplied and led 2,000 horsemen at the battle of Stoke, an array of arms Henry VII would never have permitted if he suspected Wydeville treachery. Furthermore, Elizabeth's sister Katherine had married Jasper Tudor, the King's uncle, sometime before 7 November 1485, solidifying the family ties.

Those who suspect Elizabeth of supporting the 'Warwick' rebellion point to the eleven-year-old boy at its head, whom Elizabeth might have believed was her son Prince Richard. Still, it is difficult to think that she would endanger her daughter, Queen Consort Elizabeth, by favouring any rebel claimant. Once the impostor had changed his identity to Warwick, son of Clarence, it is inconceivable to imagine that Elizabeth Wydeville would support the son of her hated enemy in preference to her own daughter. Equally improbable is her collaboration with another of the rebels, Bishop Stillington – the very man who had declared her marriage adulterous and her children illegitimate!

Perhaps Vergil – writing twenty-six years after the fact – ascribed a motivation to the council's action that was inaccurate. As Sutton and Visser-Fuchs point out, the Queen's dowry was being transferred from mother to daughter, maintaining the tradition that the Queen Consort received her principal income from Lancastrian properties.[8] The transfer is recorded in 'Writs under the Great Seal, Easter Term, 2 Hen. VII':

> To the lady queen, for payment of all profits and issues of all lands, honours, and castles, lately belonging to Elizabeth, late wife of Edward the Fourth.[9]

Henry VII's orders to the treasurer and chamberlains of his exchequer on 1 May 1487 clearly state that all property of 'Queen Elizabeth, late wife to the full noble prince of famous memory Edward the Fourth' be assigned to 'our dearest wife the Queen'.[10] Those transfers were completed on 26 December 1487, when Queen Consort Elizabeth received a grant for life of her mother's six manors in the county of Essex.[11]

At this point in her life, Elizabeth Wydeville may even have welcomed the exchange of her dowry property for a cash annuity. Estate management was a strenuous business that required supervision of officials, settling disputes between tenants, granting leases, collecting rents, supervising sales of timber, wood and wool – all conducted over vast estates scattered throughout the kingdom.[12] While a large administrative staff handled such transactions, the few letters preserved from Elizabeth's reign indicate that she took an active, personal role in estate management. In one letter, for instance, she admonishes Sir William Stonor for poaching deer in her forest and chase of Barnwood and Exhill and threatens a law suit; in another she warns the Earl of Oxford not to deny Simon Bliaunt his inheritance in the manor of Hemnals, in Cotton.[13] Such matters must have seemed trivial and irrelevant to Elizabeth after the horrifying events of 1483.

The recent deaths of a husband, three sons, and two dearly beloved brothers may have led the Queen Dowager to seek out the convent at Bermondsey, a place where she could make peace with reality. With her daughter Queen Consort and her grandson heir to the throne, Elizabeth Wydeville had done her part for family and country. All we know is that sometime around 12 February 1487, she registered as a 'boarder' at Bermondsey Abbey, where she received free hospitality as the widow of a descendant of the Abbey's founder. What she thought, as she gazed from the south bank of the Thames across to the Tower of London, where her life as Queen had begun in such splendour, we shall never know.

Five days later, on 17 February 1487, the leader of the rebellion against Henry VII was officially declared an impostor and his claim thoroughly disproved by a public appearance of Clarence's actual son on 29 February. Henry VII released the ten-year-old Edward, Earl of Warwick from the Tower just long enough to exhibit him throughout London and to let him attend Mass at St Paul's. After Mass, young Warwick met with men who had known him in earlier days, had his identity verified, then returned to the Tower while England prepared for war.

The Earl of Lincoln's troops, in company with the impostor 'Warwick', invaded England in June. A hard-fought, three-hour battle at Stoke on 16 June 1487 resulted in a resounding victory for Henry VII. Lincoln was killed, and the impostor, subsequently identified as Lambert Simnel, taken prisoner. That unfortunate child, used by the Earl of Lincoln and Margaret of Burgundy to reclaim the throne for male Yorkists, was just another pawn in the wars that had destroyed so many noble families during the past century. In a rare bit of uncharacteristic leniency, Henry VII did not execute Simnel, but made him a turnspit in his kitchens – a living lesson to all nobles and commoners of the fate of rebels. No blood ties to royalty have ever been discovered for Simnel, but scullery duties for someone declared a relative by Margaret, Duchess Dowager of Burgundy, sent a powerful and continuing message to all. Simnel, identified in Tudor documents as the illegitimate son of an Oxford organ-maker, apparently prospered in his new duties. Later appointed the King's falconer, he died a quiet death in 1525.

Speculation still runs rife, however, and a 1998 defense of Richard III by Bertram Fields hypothesises that Lambert Simnel was a 'stalking-horse' for one of the two missing princes, who had escaped from the Tower and fled to the continent. Since Margaret of Burgundy supported the rebellion, Fields speculates that at least one of the princes was 'hidden abroad awaiting the moment when he could return and claim the throne'.[14] The defeat of the rebels ended such hopes and poor Lambert Simnel, not the real prince, ended up in Tudor hands. That scenario, Fields claims, explains Queen Dowager Elizabeth's support of the rebellion against the interests of her daughter Elizabeth, Queen Consort to Henry VII. Such speculation about the Queen Dowager's role exceeds any known facts.

With the rebels defeated, Henry VII finally scheduled the coronation of his Queen, Elizabeth of York, on 25 November 1487, almost two years after their marriage on 18 January 1486. Queen Dowager Elizabeth did not attend her daughter's coronation. If she watched the procession of boats as the new Queen left Greenwich, sailed past Bermondsey Abbey, and landed at the Tower to spend the night before her coronation, Elizabeth Wydeville's thoughts must have torn at her soul. Did she look across the Thames at the splendour of her daughter's coronation and recall 25 May 1465 – her own silk-covered chair, the blue gowns of the newly made Knights of Bath, the scarlet cloaks of the Mayor and alderman, the prancing horses, the cheers of the citizens – as she made her way through Cheapside to her coronation at Westminster Abbey? Or did she see only the Tower's foreboding grey walls, which enclosed the graves of her two sons, buried, as rumours insisted, in the middle of the night under a staircase? Was she attempting to find peace through religious seclusion? Or did the King forbid her presence at the coronation?

Evidence that the Queen Dowager remained in good favour with Henry VII resides in his continuing grants. In 1487, a grant of 200 marks was made 'To the Queen Elizabeth, late wife of Ed. IV'.[15] A writ to the Exchequer, dated 10 March 1488, orders payment of 200 marks to the 'right dear and right well beloved Queen Elizabeth, late wife unto the noble prince of famous memory King Edward the IVth, and mother unto our dearest wife the Queen'.[16] Unfortunately, the stylised, official language provides no insight into the King's true feelings. On 30 May 1488, the King made Elizabeth's annuity permanent, granting '100 marks sterling' in advance of the Midsummer term and ordering that quarterly payments continue 'unto time ye have otherwise from us in commandment'.[17] Within the week, a mandate from the King at Windsor Castle ordered payment of £6 to 'right dear mother Queen Elizabeth… for a ton of wine towards her costs and expenses'.[18]

With living expenses covered by her entitlement at Bermondsey Abbey, Elizabeth's simple life required few material goods. In February 1490, her annuity was increased to £400 granted for life, and in mid-December 1490 the King granted her a special sum of fifty marks 'against the feast of Christmas next coming'.[19] Her son Thomas, Marquis of Dorset, had been restored to full favour by 19 July 1488, when the King ordered payment of Dorset's £35 annuity, including arrears of £15.[20]

Except for brief excursions, Elizabeth Wydeville spent the rest of her life in Bermondsey convent. At the age of fifty, she had retreated from the swirling, murderous world of court politics. Experience had taught her the futility of vanity and the imperative of faith, a conclusion supported by her lifelong piety. Throughout her husband's reign, Elizabeth had gladly filled the Queen's traditional role in tending to religious offices and activities. In November 1468, she was granted the next presentation to the hospital or free chapel of St Anthony in London.[21] In 1472, she received the disposition of the next vacant canonry and prebend in the King's Chapel of St Stephen's at Westminster Palace.[22] In 1474 she became patron of the chantry or priory of Flaunsworde[23], and in 1475 she presented George Daune for his confirmation as chaplain in the royal chapel of St Stephen at Westminster Palace, where, in 1476, she was granted the next vacant canonry and prebend.[24] Proof that such offices were not merely *pro-forma* rituals of position resides in her other actions and charities.

Elizabeth's decision in 1473 to give birth to the King's sixth child at the Dominican Friary in Shrewsbury, rather than returning to the royal palaces at Westminster or Windsor, reflects not only a mother's desire to stay close to her son Edward at Ludlow, but a deep-seated trust and belief in the Blackfriars. Highly educated and scholarly, the Blackfriars were well known in Shrewsbury for preaching against avarice and gluttony. They cautioned the fortunate 'to have wealth of the spiritual value of charity' and to avoid accumulating riches beyond reasonable need – a wicked act, the Blackfriars taught, unless those riches were used to help the needy. At the height of her glory as Queen, Elizabeth's retreat to the Dominican Friary speaks volumes about the ideals she embraced.

In 1477, Elizabeth revealed a particular interest in the solitary, ascetic order of the Carthusians, when she obtained a licence to attend services at all Carthusian monasteries founded by the kings and queens of England. Her manor at Sheen enclosed the Great Charterhouse, where the monks studied, prayed, worked, ate and slept in their private cells, congregating only for Vespers and Sunday dinner. On 1 April 1479 she granted its Prior, John Ingelby, forty-eight acres of her land in West Sheen[25], and in 1492 she named Prior Ingelby the leading executor of her will. Many Carthusians wore a hair shirt, as did Elizabeth's brother Anthony at his death.

So, too, the signature device associated with Elizabeth in several portraits has significant religious connotations. The pattern surrounding her figure in the stained glass of Canterbury Cathedral has been identified by Anne Sutton and Livia Visser-Fuchs as a gillyflower, otherwise called a pink or carnation.[26] A similar pattern appears in the background of a painting of Elizabeth in the Book of the Fraternity of Our Lady's Assumption of the Skinner's Company of London, and again in the border of an illuminated manuscript of the poetry of Charles d'Orléans, probably commissioned for Edward IV. The gillyflower symbolised the Virgin Mary, and its choice as a device points to Elizabeth's devotion to the purity, love, motherhood and ideals of the Holy Mother. Her special feelings for the Virgin are confirmed by an indulgence for the general populace issued by the Pope at Queen Elizabeth's request, which states 'that she has a singular devotion for the feast of the Visitation [of] St Mary the Virgin to St Elizabeth'.[27]

Retirement to Bermondsey Abbey, therefore, may have exactly fulfilled Elizabeth's emotional and psychological needs after fifty years of few triumphs and many tragedies. A bucolic retreat with extensive gardens, Bermondsey convent had long harboured royal guests seeking shelter from the outside world. As early as Domesday Book, the site was a royal manor, and the monastery had developed with the support of kings. Past royal visitors had included King Stephen and his Queen, Maud, Henry II (who spent Christmas 1154 there), and Edward III. By 1399 it had become a rich, prestigious and powerful abbey, sequestered from its Clunaic mother house at La Charité-sur-Loire. More recently, the Abbey had provided a resting site for the body of Joan of Navarre, widow of Henry IV, on the way to her burial at Canterbury. Katharine of Valois, widow of Henry V, entered Bermondsey convent in 1436, a forced retreat after the Duke of Gloucester discovered her marriage to Owen Tudor. The current abbot, John de Marlow, had officiated as a Deacon at the funeral of Edward IV and would witness Elizabeth's will two months before her death. Abbot Marlow lived long enough to attend the body of her daughter Elizabeth of York at her funeral in 1503.[28]

In 1487, the enormous convent, which lay about half a mile from the river bank, was dominated by the majestic Romanesque Abbey of St Saviour, with its extensive cloisters, chapter-house, monastic offices, royal lodgings, visitor quarters and infirmary. Its Benedictine monks were noted for their artistic and intellectual pursuits. The parish church of St Mary Magdalene, serving the tenants and servants, lay within the precinct boundary. Modern excavations have revealed a sophisticated system of stone-lined drains, which provided fresh water to a small washroom and latrines.

Queen Dowager Elizabeth moved into the state apartments once used by the earls of Gloucester, an ironic association given the havoc wreaked on her family by the most recent Gloucester. Even at Bermondsey, however, the outside world threatened to intrude. England's continuing skirmishes with Scotland had concluded with the Three Years Truce of 3 July 1486, wherein Henry VII had proposed to marry Elizabeth to James III, a widower fifteen years her junior. James III's eldest son would marry whichever of Elizabeth's daughters he chose, while his second son would marry daughter Katharine.[29] These rather bizarre negotiations ended with the death of James III on 11 June 1488, while he was fighting a civil war with his son. Henry VII's proposal, however, provides further evidence that he did not suspect the Queen Dowager of treason, or he would never have aligned her with the King of the always-troublesome Scots. How Elizabeth felt about being used as a bargaining chip in the proposed treaty remains enshrouded within her soul.

Painful reality intruded yet again into Elizabeth's secluded retreat when one of her two remaining brothers, Sir Edward Wydeville, was killed at the battle of St Aubin du Dormier, on 27 July 1488. Sir Edward, whom Vergil describes as 'an impetuous man, trained to arms and incapable of languishing in idleness',[30] had set to sea in command of the English Navy after the death of Edward IV. When Gloucester ordered the ships back to England, Sir Edward joined the forces of Richmond and landed at Milford Haven. The King rewarded him on 16 September 1485 with a grant of the castle and town of Porchester and governance of Portsmouth, along with the Isle of Wight and its castle of Carisbrooke, property earlier held by Anthony Wydeville.[31] On 13 March 1487, Sir Edward was granted the manors of Swanston, Thorley, Welowe and Brexton, to be held during the minority of Warwick.[32] Such favour disproves yet again any claims that the King was at odds with the Wydevilles.

Indeed, Henry VII may have owed Sir Edward particular gratitude for his conquests as an adventurer-knight. During Henry's reign, Edward's restless spirit had carried him into hazardous enterprises, with far-reaching personal and national consequences. A contemporary Spanish account tells of 'an English lord, a relative of the English Queen, who called himself Lord Scales' arriving in Spain in May 1486 with 300 sol-diers, to join Ferdinand and Isabella's battles against the Moors. The real Lord Scales, Anthony Wydeville, Earl Rivers, was dead, of course, and this impostor has been identified by Roger B. Merriman as none other than Sir Edward Wydeville.[33] Sir Edward had no right whatsoever to call him-self 'Lord Scales', but since Anthony during his lifetime had resigned his grant to the Isle of Wight to his younger brother (a grant reaffirmed by Henry VII), he may have felt free to expropriate his brother's title as well, especially since the Spanish would hardly detect the identity theft.

In an eyewitness account of a battle near Granada in May 1486, Andrez Bernaldez, chaplain of the Archbishop of Seville, describes Lord Scales fighting 'after the manner of his country;... dismounting from his horse, and armed with sword and battle-axe, he charged forward at the Moorish host... slashing and hacking with brave and manly hearts, killing and dismount-ing right and left'.[34] Such valour resulted in Sir Edward being struck by a stone, which knocked him unconscious and broke his teeth. The surgeons saved his life, after which Sir Edward paid homage to Queen Isabella, who sympathised with his misfortune. With dashing charm, the English knight dismissed his lost teeth with a witty reply: 'Christ, who reared this whole fabric has merely opened a window, in order more easily to discern what goes on within.' Pleased with his service and wit, the Queen rewarded him with 'twelve Andalusian horses of the finest breed, two couches with richly wrought hangings and coverings of cloth of gold, a quantity of fine linen, and sumptuous pavilions for Woodville and all his suite'.[35]

Sir Edward returned to England just in time to assist his own King against the rebels at Stoke. But his restless spirit remained unquelled and, in May 1488, Sir Edward requested Henry VII's permission to raise a force to assist the Duke of Brittany against the French. Henry, however, desired peace with France and 'straightly prohibited him to attempt any such strategy or enterprise'.[36] Whereupon Sir Edward sailed to the Isle of Wight, commandeered 400 men, and sailed to Brittany anyway. His arrival caused great consternation to the French and a flurry of ambassadorial activity between England and France. Within a month, Henry changed his mind and decided to augment the army in Brittany. The French attacked before the English reinforcements arrived, however, and slaughtered 6,000 Bretons and most of the English, including Sir Edward Wydeville.

Merriman surmises that Sir Edward's adventures in Spain and Brittany were connected. On 10 March 1488, Henry sent a proposal to Ferdinand and Isabella to marry his eldest son, Arthur, to their youngest daughter, Catherine of Aragon. Formal discussion of the marriage agreement began in London on 7 July, two months after Sir Edward had sailed for Brittany. Merriman suggests that Sir Edward anticipated that Spain would demand English support of Brittany as part of the marriage settlement, not merely to assure Brittany's independence but to force France to cede the provinces of Cerdagne and Rousillon to Spain. Unfortunately, the failure of English reinforcements to reach Brittany in time cost that country its independence.

Sir Edward's adventures, however, had elevated England's worth in the eyes of Spain, the most powerful country in Europe. And his reports to Henry VII of the power and riches of Spain may have encouraged the King to contemplate a marriage of the two royal families. Merriman concludes that Edward Wydeville's contributions were

> …of incalculable importance for Europe and for Christendom;… the first of a chain of events that paved the way for the English Reformation, the defeat of the Spanish Armada, the transference of the sovereignty of the seas from Spain to England, and for the conflicts of these two great powers in the New World.[37]

For Queen Dowager Elizabeth, however, the death of the reckless, adventurous Sir Edward meant that only one brother, Sir Richard Wydeville, remained from the once large, happy family of her childhood. Fortunately, her daughter the Queen Consort soon became pregnant with her second child, and on All Hallows Eve 1489, Queen Elizabeth of York 'took to her chamber at Westminster', accompanied by 'my lady the Queen's mother'. The Queen Dowager, who was at her daughter's side during her confinement, would have recognised the elaborate rituals:

[Queen Elizabeth] was led by the Earl of Oxford and the Earl of Derby. The reverend father in God, the Bishop of Exeter, said mass in his pontificals, and the Earl of Salisbury held the towels when the Queen received the Host, and the corners of the towels were golden...When she arrived at her great chamber she tarried in the anteroom before it, and stood under her cloth of estate; then was ordained a voide of refreshments. That done, the Queen's chamberlain, Sir Richard Pole, in very good words, desired in the Queen's name all her people to pray that God would send her a good hour, and so she entered into her chamber which was hanged and ceiled with blue cloth of arras.[38]

When the Queen Dowager's cousin, François de Luxembourg, arrived at the head of a group of French ambassadors visiting England, Elizabeth graciously took him to visit the current Queen of England in her private chambers, where she was awaiting the birth. Elizabeth Wydeville's second royal grandchild, Margaret, was born on 29 November 1489.

Elizabeth Wydeville was nearing the end of her lifetime of glory and grieving – as was her generation of the Wydeville family. Her last living brother, Sir Richard Wydeville, died on 6 March 1491. The third Earl Rivers never achieved either greatness or notoriety. He had been attainted by Richard III along with all the Wydevilles, an action reversed by Henry VII in 1485. Henry commissioned him to investigate treasons, felonies and conspiracies in the county of Hereford in 1486, and paid him a reward of £33 6s 8d on 8 June 1486 'for his counsel'.[39] Sir Richard also inventoried archers in the county of Northampton, for the expedition to Brittany in 1488.[40] Beyond his service as commissioner of the peace in Bedfordshire and Northamptonshire, his most prominent position seems to be a 1487 appointment to try petitions presented to Parliament.

Richard Wydeville, third Earl Rivers, died without descendants. His will, of 20 February 1491, indicates that only his sisters Elizabeth and Katharine survived in his generation. He bequeathed his land to his nephew Thomas, Marquis of Dorset, and named as his other heirs his sister Katharine and the children of his sisters Anne, Margaret, Mary and Jacquetta. None of Elizabeth's brothers left legitimate sons, and in a touching effort to preserve the family's presence at Grafton, Sir Richard's will directed that 'there might be as much underwood sold, in the Woods at Grafton as would buy a Bell, to be a Tenor at Grafton, to the Bells then there, for a remembrance of the last of the blood'.[41] With his death, the Wydeville name became extinct.

Queen Dowager Elizabeth would live to see the birth of a second grandson, Henry, on 28 June 1491. This grandson would assure that Wydeville blood flowed on to produce the greatest monarchs in English history. This grandson, Henry VIII, and her great-granddaughter Elizabeth I (the first Queen Regnant to use that Christian name) may have been Tudors, but their vigour, intelligence, flamboyance and feistiness owed much to Elizabeth Wydeville.

Whether the Queen Dowager learned of yet another rebellion in 1492, led by someone claiming to be her son Richard, Duke of York, we shall never know. If rumours of a surviving prince reached her at Bermondsey convent, her heart must once more have been broken by a mother's love for a favourite child. In a curious reversal of the Lambert Simnel rebellion, this impostor, ultimately identified as Perkin Warbeck, first declared himself as Clarence's son, Warwick, then switched his identity to that of the younger of the two princes, Richard, Duke of York. Fortunately, Elizabeth would never have to live through the rebellion, which ended with Warbeck's death in 1499.

Queen Dowager Elizabeth, *née* Wydeville, died in Bermondsey Abbey on 8 June 1492. She was fifty-five years old. Anticipating her death, she had written her will two months earlier:

In Dei nomine, Amen. The 10th day of April, the year of our Lord God 1492. I, Elizabeth, by the grace of God Queen of England, late wife to the most victorious Prince of blessed memory Edward the Fourth, being of whole mind, seeing the world so transitory, and no creature certain when they shall depart from hence, having Almighty God fresh in mind, in whom is all mercy and grace, bequeath my soul into his hands, beseeching him, of the same mercy, to accept it graciously, and our blessed Lady Queen of comfort, and all the holy company of heaven, to be good means for me. Item, I bequeath my body to be buried with the body of my Lord at Windsor, according to the will of my said Lord and mine, without pompous entering or costly expenses done thereabout. Item, where I have no worldly goods to do the Queen's Grace, my dearest daughter, a pleasure with, neither to reward any of my children, according to my heart and mind, I beseech Almighty God to bless her Grace, with all her noble issue, and with as good heart and mind as is to me possible, I give her Grace my blessing, and all the foresaid my children. Item, I will that such small stuff and goods that I have be disposed truly in the contentacion of my debts and for the health of my soul, as far as they will extend. Item, if any of my blood will any of my said stuff or goodes to me pertaining, I will that they have the preferment before any other. And of this my present testament I make and ordain my Executors, that is to say, John Ingilby, Prior of the Charterhouse of Shene, William Sutton and Thomas Brente, Doctors. And I beseech my said dearest daughter, the Queen's grace, and my son Thomas, Marquess Dorsett, to put their good wills and help for the performance of this my testament. In witness whereof, to this my present testament I have set my seal, these witnesses, John Abbot of the monastery of Saint Saviour of Bermondsey, and Benedictus Cun, Doctor of Physic. Given the day and year abovesaid.[42]

Her eldest daughter, Queen Elizabeth, was awaiting the birth of her fourth child and unable to attend her mother's funeral.

The funeral procession to Windsor Castle, where Elizabeth Wydeville was buried in St George's Chapel beside her beloved husband, Edward IV, could not have contrasted more starkly with the elaborate processions of her queenly days. The scanty attendance and truncated funeral rites paled beside the elaborate ceremonies at the reburial of Richard, Duke of York – and even the funeral rites for her daughter Mary in 1482. The shabby hearse, the few mourners, the inferior tapers and the slight attention paid by church authorities discomforted the scribe who recorded the events:

On the 8th day of June the year of our Lord 1492 at Bermondsey in Southwark deceased the right noble princess Queen Elizabeth, some time wife of King Edward the IVth and mother to Queen Elizabeth, wife to King Henry the VIIth, which was the Friday before Whitsunday as that year fell.

And the said Queen desired in her death bed that as soon as she should be deceased, she should in all goodly haste without any worldly pomp by water conveyed to Windsor and there to be buried in the same vault that her husband the King was buried in. On Whitsunday she was according to her desire by water conveyed to Windsor and there privily through the little park conveyed into the castle, without ringing of any bells or receiving of the dean or canons in their habits or accompanied as who says, but with the prior of the Charterhouse of Sheen; Doctor Brent, her chaplain; and one of her executors, Edmund Haute; Mistress Grace, a bastard daughter of King Edward; and upon another gentlewoman. And as it told to me, one priest of the college and a clerk received her in the castle. And so privily, about eleven of the clock in the night. She was buried, without any solemn dirge or the morn any solemn Mass done for her obit.

On the morn thither came the Lord Audley, Bishop of Rochester, to do the service, and the substance of the officers of arms of this realm, but that day there was nothing done solemnly for her, saving a low hearse, such as they use for the common people, with four wooden candlesticks about it, and a cloth of black cloth of gold over it, with four candlesticks of silver and gilt, every one having a taper of no great weight, and two scutcheons of her arms crowned pinned on that cloth.

On the Tuesday thither came by water four of King Edward's daughters and heirs, that is to say the Lady Anne, the Lady Katherine, and the Lady Bridget accompanied with the Lady Marquess of Dorset, the Duke of Buckingham's daughter... niece of the foresaid Queen. Also the daughter of the Marquess of Dorset, the Lady Herbert, also niece to the said Queen, the Lady Egermont, Dame Katherine Gray, Dame Guilford... Also that same Tuesday thither came the lords that follow: the Lord Thomas, Marquess of Dorset, son to the foresaid Queen; the Lord Edmund of Suffolk; the Earl of Essex; the Viscount Welles [son-in-law]; Sir Charles of Somerset, Sir Roger Cotton, Master Chatterton.

And that night began the dirge, the foresaid Bishop of Rochester and vicars of the college were rectors of the choir, and no canons. The Bishop of Rochester read the last lesson at the dirges of the canons the other two. But the Dean of that College read none, though he was present at that service. Not at dirge nor at noon... was there never a new torch, but old torches; nor poor man in black gown nor hoods... but... a dozen divers old men holding old torches and torches' ends.

And on the morn one of the canons, called Master Vaughan, sang Our Lady Mass, at which the Lord Marquess offered a piece of gold. At that Mass offered no man saving himself and in likewise at the Mass of the Trinity, which was sung by the Dean, and kneeled at the hearse head because the ladies came not to the Mass of Requiem. And the lords before rehearsed sat above in the choir into the offering time, when that the foresaid lords and also the officers of arms there being present went before my Lady Anne, which offered the Mass penny instead of the Queen, wherefore she had the carpet and the cushion laid. And the Viscount Welles took her offering, which was a very penny indeed of silver, and Dame Katherine Gray bore the said Lady [Anne's] train. In time she was turned to her place again, then every one of the Kings' daughters bore own trains and offered a piece of gold. After the ladies had offered in likewise, the Lord Marquess offered a piece of gold, then the other foresaid lords offered their pleasures; then offered the Dean and the Choir and the poor knights; then Garter King of Armes, with him all his company. Then offered all other esquires present and yeomen and the servants that would offer, but there was none offering to the corpse during the Mass. There was given certain money in alms. After Mass the Lord Marquess rewarded... their costs 40s.

I pray to God to have mercy on her soul. At this same season, the Queen her daughter took her chamber, wherefore I cannot tell what dolent abbey... she goeth in. But I suppose she went in blue in likewise as Queen Margaret, the wife of King Henry the VI, went in when her mother the Queen of Sicily died.[43]

CHAPTER TWENTY-FOUR

Legacy

Elizabeth Wydeville died without knowing with certainty the fate of the two princes, perhaps the saddest aspect of her life. While the death of Prince Richard was officially recognised during her lifetime, there was always the possibility that the boys had been spirited to a safe haven in Europe. A declaration of Richard's death appears six years after his disappearance, in a petition of the Duchess of Norfolk on 27 November 1489, aimed at regaining property he had inherited through Anne Mowbray. A single, stark sentence in the *Calendar of Patent Rolls* states simply: 'The said Richard Duke of York died.'[1] Still, the impossible hope that at least one of the boys survived must have tantalised Elizabeth throughout her remaining days on earth.

Whether Elizabeth was aware of the Perkin Warbeck rebellion that began just before she died, we do not know. That rebellion – again sponsored by Margaret of Burgundy – featured a nineteen-year-old male coached to impersonate the younger of the boys. In March 1492, the pretender visited the French court, which received him as Richard, Duke of York. Elizabeth died three months later, and we can only wonder if this news from France reached her at Bermondsey. If so, her heart once again must have leaped with hope before it broke. This pretender provoked considerable attention, as he travelled through the courts of Portugal, France, Flanders and Scotland, all of which welcomed him as the Duke of York. By July 1493, Henry VII had identified the man as Perkin Warbeck, 'another feigned lad... born at Tournay in Picardy', but that was a year after Elizabeth's death. Warbeck was not captured until 5 October 1497, after his skirmishes through Cornwall and Devon caused quite a stir in England. Imprisoned in the Tower, Warbeck tried to collaborate with Clarence's son, the Duke of Warwick, in planning an escape. The escape plot gave Henry VII a reason to execute both men. Perkin Warbeck was hanged on 23 November, and Edward, Earl of Warwick beheaded on 26 November 1499. The male line of the Plantagenets was thereby rendered extinct.

Five centuries later, questions still persist about the fate of the young princes. The motive for killing them was strong in all the men seeking power: uncle Richard III, uncle Henry Buckingham, and brother-in-law Henry VII, none of whom could claim the throne without eliminating the boys. Instead of providing protection, consanguinity compelled death by those whose ambitions took precedence over family ties. The intra-familial conflicts and the passions that drove these men created a legacy that subsequent generations have tried to comprehend through five centuries of historical study and literary introspection.

Elizabeth Wydeville, after a lifetime of watching ambition ravage her family and kill so many of the persons she loved, must have found her reclusive residence at Bermondsey convent to be a welcome and comforting retreat from the reality of worldly affairs. In her private meditations there, perhaps she reread the books translated by her brother Anthony, and reflected on their *contemptus mundi* insights. She could not possibly have imagined that the events of her lifetime would stimulate so much interest in others trying to understand human motivations and actions.

In retrospect, we can place the Wydeville family at the centre of the cultural revolution about to overtake England. Living at the cusp of the medieval world turning towards the Renaissance, they helped usher in the intellectual, cultural and sociological changes that define the modern era. Jacquetta of Luxembourg's marriage to Sir Richard Wydeville and Edward IV's decision to marry Elizabeth helped revolutionise the concept of marriage, by placing emotional wellbeing above financial gain, political expediency and social rank. The institution of marriage began to change from a business liaison into a personal engagement. They were not the first to follow their hearts, but they were in the vanguard of a movement that allowed love to become a factor in marriage.

Elizabeth Wydeville's family in general challenged medieval traditions. Their rise through the ranks of English nobility – achieved through merit and service, rather than through birthright and inheritance – set the pattern that would become commonplace in later centuries. In the generation of Elizabeth's grandfather, Thomas Wydeville, fee-holder and country gentleman, served as justice of the peace and sheriff, while his younger brother, Richard, entered military service and became a trusted lieutenant to the Duke of Bedford. In the next generation, the son of Richard Wydeville, Esquire, was knighted by Henry VI and earned renown through his prowess as a chevalier. Sir Richard Wydeville married Jacquetta, the daughter of European nobility and the widow of a duke, and earned his baronage through military service as Seneschal of Aquitaine and Lieutenant of Calais. Among the cultured and literate children of Lord Rivers and the Duchess of Bedford, Elizabeth became Queen Consort to Edward IV and Anthony translated the first book published in England by Caxton.

As the Queen's talented Wydeville family displaced established nobility, their upward mobility provoked resentment and antagonism. That deadliest of sins − envy − slandered their achievements, mocked their erudition, and murdered when it could. But the sociological revolution they heralded was profound and irreversible. They helped to inaugurate the Renaissance, where men of intelligence and dedication gradually replaced the old nobility who relied on birthright and heritage to secure position and wealth. Under the Tudors, men of talent and ambition seized the day and dominated court circles. The world has never looked back.

The medieval Wydevilles, however, paid the ultimate price for their precedency. The entrenched nobility whom they threatened − Warwick, Clarence, Richard *et al.* − responded in the only way they knew how. Ironically, the slander and murder perpetrated by those of the 'blood royal' ultimately proved self-destructive. Not only were their own families and fortunes annihilated, but the vacuum of leadership they created opened paths for more new men to ascend, a stunning example of the law of unintended consequences at work. Birth and rank would no longer remain unchallenged by ability and dedication.

The children of Elizabeth Wydeville experienced both success and failure in their disparate lives. In her lifetime, she gave birth to twelve children − two by Sir John Grey and ten by Edward IV. One son, Sir Richard Grey, was murdered on orders of Richard III. Two sons, Edward V and Prince Richard, disappeared while in the custody of Richard III, their Protector. Of the remaining children, two − Margaret and George − died as infants. Another daughter, Mary, died at the age of fifteen. Her surviving daughters lived lives of mixed blessings. Cecily, Anne and Katharine certainly never enjoyed the splendid royal marriages planned by their father.

The marriage of her eldest daughter, Elizabeth, however, determined much of modern history. *The Great Chronicle* refers to this Queen with warmth and pleasure:

Elizabeth the first child of King Edward... was married unto that noble Prince Henry the Seventh, and demeaned her so virtuously that she was named the Gracious Queen.[2]

'The Gracious Queen' reminds us of the lifestyle of the Wydevilles, and the home in which Elizabeth of York grew up. Like her mother, Elizabeth of York fulfilled her role as consort faithfully and gave birth to eight children in her thirty-seven years of life. Arthur, Margaret, Henry and Mary survived infancy and changed the world.

Arthur, the eldest, born on 20 September 1486, exhibited the spirit and good looks of his maternal grandparents, Edward IV and Elizabeth Wydeville. Destined to become King, he was betrothed to Catherine of Aragon in 1489, a liaison that must have pleased Elizabeth Wydeville, given her brother Edward's reports of Spanish culture and wealth. The marriage of Arthur and Catherine took place on 14 November 1501, following which the couple spent the winter together at Ludlow. Suddenly becoming ill – perhaps with the sweating sickness – Arthur died there on 2 April 1502. The progress of the English Reformation would hinge on whether Arthur, aged fifteen, and Catherine, aged sixteen, had consummated their marriage during their five months at Ludlow Castle.

Margaret, the eldest daughter, married James IV, King of Scotland, and became the grandmother of Mary, Queen of Scots, and great-grandmother of James VI of Scotland/James I of England.

Henry was betrothed to his brother's widow in June 1503, after a papal dispensation based on the claim that Arthur's marriage with Catherine had never been consummated. The marriage itself was delayed by politics while Henry VII supported the Hapsburgs against Ferdinand of Spain, but when Henry VII died, his son immediately married Catherine, on 11 June 1509. Twenty years later, Henry VIII claimed that his marriage was invalid because he was incestuously cohabiting with his brother's wife. Henry VIII proved God's displeasure by citing his failure to produce a male heir. Refused an annulment by the Pope, who depended on Catherine's nephew, Charles V, for military and financial support, Henry VIII declared himself Supreme Head of the Church of England. That act institutionalised the English Reformation and permitted Henry's serial marriages – his second, to Anne Boleyn, producing the great monarch Elizabeth I, who carried the name of her great-grandmother Elizabeth Wydeville.

Mary, youngest daughter of Henry VII and Elizabeth of York, married Louis XII of France in October 1514, but was left a widow by December. She subsequently married Charles Brandon, Duke of Suffolk. Their granddaughter, Lady Jane Grey, was declared Queen for nine days between the death of Edward VI and the accession of Mary Tudor.

Elizabeth Wydeville's younger daughters fared less well. The beautiful Cecily, once betrothed to the heir of James III of Scotland, married considerably beneath that rank to John, Viscount Wells, sometime before Christmas 1487. Whether Queen Dowager Elizabeth attended the wedding is unknown. Viscount Wells, twenty years older than Cecily and half-brother of Margaret Beaufort, possessed none of the status or wealth of the Beaufort family. Cecily, second daughter of Edward IV and next heiress after Elizabeth of York, had lived under the supervision of Margaret Beaufort from September 1485 on and was perhaps encouraged by the Countess to marry the Viscount.[3]

Cecily did not attend her mother's funeral, where she was represented by Viscount Wells. Both of her children and her husband died before Cecily was thirty years old. Margaret Beaufort helped the widow retain property rights to some of her husband's estates when he died in 1499, and gave Cecily a special dispensation to worship regularly in the household of the Countess.[4] Cecily may have returned to her sister's court, for she carried the bride's train at the wedding of Prince Arthur to Catherine of Aragon in 1501. She angered Henry VII, however, when she remarried without his permission and denied the King the opportunity of selecting a husband of his choosing. Cecily apparently married the second time for love; her new husband, a squire, is recorded in history merely as 'Thomas Kyme of Lincolnshire'.

For a while, Margaret Beaufort allowed the disgraced couple to stay at her palace at Collyweston, four miles south of Stamford,[5] but ultimately this most beautiful of Elizabeth's daughters retreated to the Isle of Wight, where she lived in obscurity and relative poverty, gave birth to two children never recognised by her royal relatives, and died in 1507 at the age of thirty-eight. Margaret Beaufort paid some of the funeral expenses.[6] Cecily was buried at the Abbey of Quarre on the Isle of Wight, but any memorial that might have existed was annihilated when her nephew Henry VIII destroyed the monasteries of England.

Princess Anne, once betrothed to Philip, son of Maximilian of Austria, was aged seventeen at her mother's death. She married Thomas, Lord

Howard, son of the Earl of Surrey, in 1495. Three of their children died in infancy, and a fourth, Thomas, at the age of twelve. Anne died sometime after 22 November 1511, at the age of thirty-seven or thirty-eight. When Henry VIII destroyed her burial site at the priory at Thetford, her effigy was transferred to the church at Framlingham.

Princess Katherine, whom her father hoped would marry the Infant of Spain, was aged thirteen at her mother's death. She married Lord William Courtenay, heir to the Earl of Devon, sometime before October 1495. Her early years of marriage were spent on her husband's rich Devonshire estates, from which they participated in splendid events at court, including the marriage of Prince Arthur to Catherine of Aragon and the betrothal of Princess Margaret to James IV of Scotland. When Lord Courtenay fell under suspicion of treason, was attainted, and sent to the Tower, Katherine and her three children were forced to depend on the beneficence of her sister, the Queen.

Katherine lived in obscurity until the death of Henry VII, when her husband was released from prison. Henry VIII and Catherine of Aragon selected Katherine to act as sole godmother to their firstborn son, Henry Tudor, in January 1511, but the child's death just six weeks later ended early hopes of a Tudor dynasty. When Lord Courtenay died, Katherine took a vow of chastity and returned to her Devonshire estates, where she died in 1527 at the age of forty-nine. Her family, too, experienced more tragedy than triumph. Her daughter, Lady Margaret Courtenay, died during her mother's lifetime, and both of her sons were executed as Papist traitors by Henry VIII. Her grandson died childless in Padua, Italy, after banishment by Queen Mary Tudor.

Elizabeth's youngest daughter, Bridget, entered England's only community of Dominican nuns, at Dartford in Kent, at the age of ten, leading to speculation that she may have suffered from a mental or physical disability. Bridget left the convent only once, at the age of twelve, to attend her mother's funeral, accompanied by the Marchioness of Dorset. Dartford Priory, founded by Edward III in 1346, was one of the largest and wealthiest in medieval England and provided quiet, reclusive quarters for this princess. Queen Elizabeth sent money to this convent, as did Bridget's eldest sister, Elizabeth of York, when she became Queen Consort.[7] When Bridget's grandmother, Cecily Neville, died in 1495, she willed three books to the fifteen-year-old girl: the *Legenda Aurea*, in vellum, a book of the life of St Catherine of Siena, and a 'Book of Saint Matilde'.[8] Bridget took the veil, but never achieved higher status than an ordinary nun.[9] She died sometime between 1513 and 1517, the date obscured by Henry VIII's destruction of the priory church where she was buried.

Elizabeth Wydeville's eldest son by her first marriage thrived under Henry VII, once he was cleared of suspicion concerning the Lambert Simnel rebellion. On 4 June 1492, just four days before his mother's death, Thomas Grey, Marquis of Dorset, was pardoned 'of all offences committed before May 1 last'.[10] As male head of the family, he rendered the offering at his mother's funeral Mass and paid the costs of the service. Under Henry VII, Dorset commanded troops in support of Emperor Maximilian against the French, and fought in the battle of Blackheath in 1497. He became an early patron of Wolsey and sent three of his sons to study under Wolsey at Magdalene College, Oxford.

Dorset's second marriage to Cicely, heiress of William Bonville, Lord Harington, produced seven sons and eight daughters. He extended the family fortunes and began building a magnificent manor house at Bradgate Park, on the ancestral lands of the Greys of Groby. This project was completed by his son Thomas, 2nd Marquis of Dorset, after his father's death on 20 September 1501. Dorset's grandson, Henry Grey, married Frances Brandon, daughter of Mary Tudor and granddaughter of Henry VII and Elizabeth of York (Dorset's half-sister). That union produced Lady Jane Grey, who made her Bradgate birthplace famous.

Lady Jane Grey thus inherited Elizabeth Wydeville's blood through both sides of her family. When her father and father-in-law tried to usurp the throne from Queen Mary I, Lady Jane Grey became another unfortunate child sacrificed to the ambition of powerful men seeking yet more power. Declared Queen of England for nine sad days, she lost her life in the new wars of the Tudor cousins.

Elizabeth Wydeville's blood flowed in the veins of every Tudor and Stuart monarch from Henry VIII's ascension to the throne in 1509 until Queen Anne's death in 1714. The Hanoverians, too, inherited her blood via Sophia, daughter of Frederick, Elector Palatine, and his wife Elizabeth, a sixth-generation descendant of her namesake Elizabeth Wydeville.

Despite this legacy, Elizabeth Wydeville has not fared well in history. In part, her reputation suffered because no one survived to tell her story. Only a bell at Grafton – 'Tenor... to the Bells then there' – rang from its lonely perch as 'a Remembrance of the last of the blood'.[11] Henry VII was intent on creating his own Tudor legacy, to which his Queen Consort's heritage was irrelevant. Thus the Wydevilles took with them to their graves their courtly reputations and their contributions to education, philosophy and religion. The stories preserved by Mancini, More and other contemporary chroniclers focused on the fate of the two princes, the accession of Richard III, and the ascendant Tudors. With no one to refute slanders against the family name, the lies of the Wydevilles' worst enemies – Warwick, Clarence, and Richard III – turned into 'facts', propaganda into 'history'. Elizabeth Wydeville's life of charitable, pious acts and her never-flagging devotion to family, King and country were forgotten, an omission that has skewed the perception of the era. The time is long overdue to retrieve Elizabeth Wydeville from obscurity and to correct the misinformation that has slandered her reputation.

Genealogical Tables

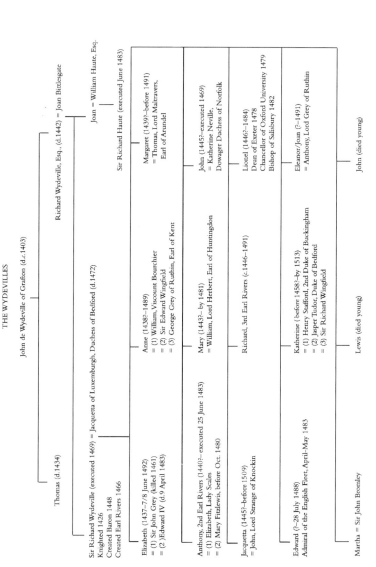

THE WYDEVILLES

John de Wydeville of Grafton (d.c.1403)

Richard Wydeville, Esq., (d.1442) = Joan Bittlesgate

Thomas (d.1434)

Joan = William Haute, Esq.

Sir Richard Haute (executed June 1483)

Sir Richard Wydeville (executed 1469) = Jacquetta of Luxemburgh, Duchess of Bedford (d.1472)
Knighted 1426
Created Baron 1448
Created Earl Rivers 1466

Elizabeth (1437–7/8 June 1492)
= (1) Sir John Grey (killed 1461)
= (2) Edward IV (d.9 April 1483)

Anne (1438?–1489)
= (1) William, Viscount Bourchier
= (2) Sir Edward Wingfield
= (3) George Grey of Ruthin, Earl of Kent

Margaret (1439?–before 1491)
= Thomas, Lord Maltravers,
Earl of Arundel

Anthony, 2nd Earl Rivers (1440?–executed 25 June 1483)
= (1) Elizabeth, Lady Scales
= (2) Mary Fitzlewis, before Oct. 1480

Mary (1443?– by 1481)
= William, Lord Herbert, Earl of Huntingdon

John (1445?–executed 1469)
= Katherine Neville,
Dowager Duchess of Norfolk

Jacquetta (1445?–before 1509)
= John, Lord Strange of Knockin

Richard, 3rd Earl Rivers (c.1446–1491)

Lionel (1446?–1484)
Dean of Exeter 1478
Chancellor of Oxford University 1479
Bishop of Salisbury 1482

Edward (?–28 July 1488)
Admiral of the English Fleet, April–May 1483

Katherine (before 1458?–by 1513)
= (1) Henry Stafford, 2nd Duke of Buckingham
= (2) Jasper Tudor, Duke of Bedford
= (3) Sir Richard Wingfield

Eleanor/Joan (?–1491)
= Anthony, Lord Grey of Ruthin

Martha = Sir John Bromley

Lewis (died young)

John (died young)

THE HOUSE OF YORK

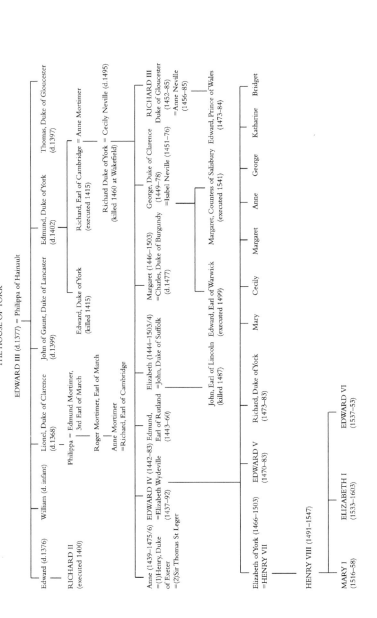

EDWARD III (d.1377) = Philippa of Hainault

Edward (d.1376)

RICHARD II
(executed 1400)

William (d. infant)

Lionel, Duke of Clarence
(d.1368)

Philippa = Edmund Mortimer,
3rd Earl of March

Roger Mortimer, Earl of March

Anne Mortimer
=Richard, Earl of Cambridge

John of Gaunt, Duke of Lancaster
(d.1399)

Edmund, Duke of York
(d.1402)

Edward, Duke of York
(killed 1415)

Richard, Earl of Cambridge = Anne Mortimer
(executed 1415)

Richard Duke of York = Cecily Neville (d.1495)
(killed 1460 at Wakefield)

Thomas, Duke of Gloucester
(d.1397)

Anne (1439–1475/6) EDWARD IV (1442–83) Edmund,
=(1)Henry, Duke   =Elizabeth Wydeville   Earl of Rutland
of Exeter   (1437–92)   (1443–60)
=(2)Sir Thomas St Leger

Elizabeth (1444–1503/4)
=John, Duke of Suffolk

Margaret (1446–1503)
=Charles, Duke of Burgundy
(d.1477)

George, Duke of Clarence
(1449–78)
=Isabel Neville (1451–76)

RICHARD III
Duke of Gloucester
(1452–85)
=Anne Neville
(1456–85)

John, Earl of Lincoln
(killed 1487)

Edward, Earl of Warwick
(executed 1499)

Margaret, Countess of Salisbury
(executed 1541)

Edward, Prince of Wales
(1473–84)

Elizabeth of York (1466–1503)
=HENRY VII

EDWARD V
(1470–83)

Richard, Duke of York
(1473–83)

Mary   Cecily   Margaret   Anne   George   Katharine   Bridget

EDWARD VI
(1537–53)

HENRY VIII (1491–1547)

MARY I
(1516–58)

ELIZABETH I
(1533–1603)

LANCASTER, YORK AND TUDOR CONNECTIONS

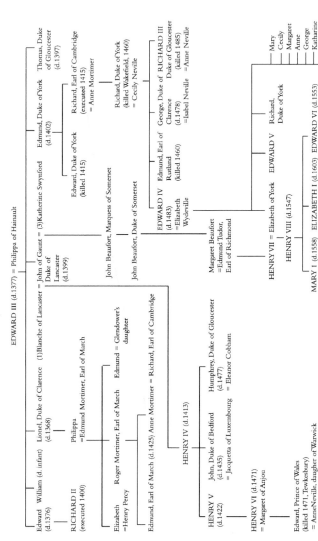

EDWARD III (d.1377) = Philippa of Hainault

Edward (d.1376) | William (d. infant) | Lionel, Duke of Clarence (d.1368) | (1)Blanche of Lancaster = John of Gaunt = (3)Katherine Swynford Duke of Lancaster (d.1399) | Edmund, Duke of York (d.1402) | Thomas, Duke of Gloucester (d.1397)

RICHARD II (executed 1400)

Philippa = Edmund Mortimer, Earl of March

Edmund = Glendower's daughter

John Beaufort, Marques of Somerset

Edward, Duke of York (killed 1415)

Richard, Earl of Cambridge (executed 1415) = Anne Mortimer

Elizabeth = Henry Percy

Roger Mortimer, Earl of March

John Beaufort, Duke of Somerset

Richard, Duke of York (killed Wakefield, 1460) = Cecily Neville

Edmund, Earl of March (d.1425) Anne Mortimer = Richard, Earl of Cambridge

HENRY IV (d.1413)

Margaret Beaufort = Edmund Tudor, Earl of Richmond

EDWARD IV (d.1483) = Elizabeth Wydeville

Edmund, Earl of Rutland (killed 1460)

George, Duke of Clarence (d.1478) = Isabel Neville

RICHARD III Duke of Gloucester (killed 1485) = Anne Neville

HENRY V (d.1422)

John, Duke of Bedford (d.1435) = Jacquetta of Luxembourg

Humphrey, Duke of Gloucester (d.1477) = Eleanor Cobham

HENRY VII = Elizabeth of York

EDWARD V

Richard, Duke of York

Mary
Cecily
Margaret
Anne
George
Katharine
Bridget

HENRY VIII (d.1547)

HENRY VI (d.1471) = Margaret of Anjou

MARY I (d.1558)   ELIZABETH I (d.1603) EDWARD VI (d.1553)

Edward, Prince of Wales (killed 1471, Tewkesbury) = Anne Neville, daughter of Warwick

LANCASTER   TUDOR   YORK

THE YORK-NEVILLE CONNECTION

EDWARD III = Philippa of Hainault

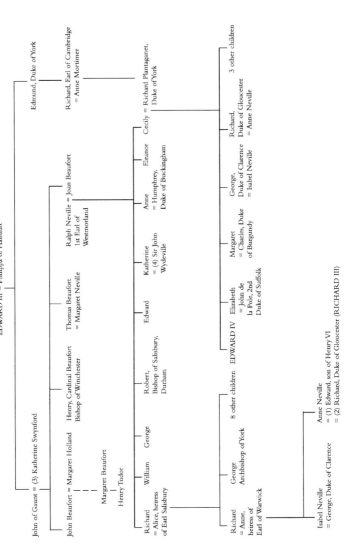

THE LANCASTER, BEAUFORT, TUDOR CONNECTIONS

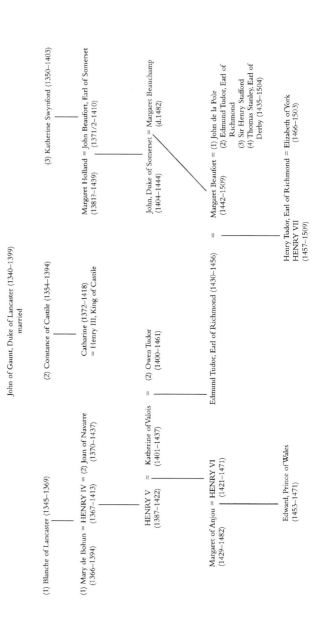

ELIZABETH WYDEVILLE DESCENDANTS

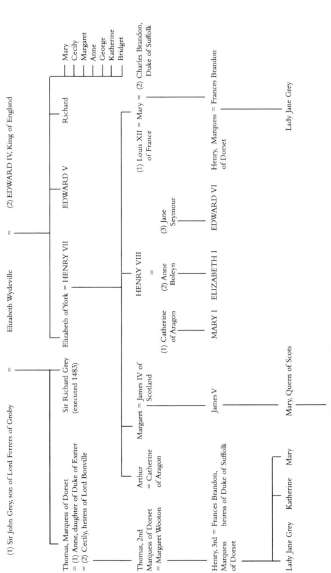

Charts

Timeline: Edward IV and the Wydevilles

1460	January	Lord Rivers, Jacquetta, and Anthony, Lord Scales captured at Sandwich and transported to Calais, where Salisbury, Warwick and Edward, Earl of March taunt their titles.
	30 December	Richard, Duke of York killed at Wakefield. His son Edward, Earl of March becomes head of the Yorkist cause.
1461	2 February	Edward, Earl of March defeats Lancastrian forces at Mortimer's Cross.
	17 February	Sir John Grey, husband of Elizabeth Wydeville, killed at second battle of St Albans. Lancaster wins, but fails to take London.
	4 March	Edward, Earl of March marches into London and is proclaimed King Edward IV.
	29 March	Yorkist victory at Towton. Lord Rivers accompanies King Henry VI, Margaret and Prince Edward in retreat to Newcastle. Anthony, Lord Scales reported dead.
	5 April	Edward IV leaves Towton for Sheen (in Richmond).
	14 May	Edward IV confiscates all possessions of Richard Wydeville, knight.
	1 June	Edward IV arrives at Sheen after two-day stopover at Stony Stratford.
	12 June	Edward IV pardons Richard Wydeville, knight, Lord Rivers of all offences and trespasses.
	12 July	Patent Rolls record pardon of Lord Rivers and restore his 'possessions and offices'.
	23 July	Anthony, Lord Scales is pardoned and his property restored.
	31 July	Lord Rivers and Lord Scales are reported in a letter to the Duke of Milan to be Warwick's prisoners in the Tower.
	10 December	Jacquetta's dowry as Duchess of Bedford is restored.
	12 December	Lord Rivers is reappointed Chief Rider of the King's forest of Saucy (rights initially granted by Henry VI).
1463	26 May	Property dispute of Lady Elizabeth Grey, *née* Wydeville, is settled in her favour.

1464　　　1 May　　Edward IV secretly marries Lady Elizabeth Grey. He is aged twenty-two; she is twenty-seven.

The Wydeville Family

Sir Richard Wydeville (1405?–12 August 1469). Beheaded.
> Knighted Palm Sunday, 19 May 1426.
> Married Jacquetta, Duchess of Bedford between 6 February 1436 and 23 March 1437.
> Created Baron and Lord de Rivers, 9 May 1448.
> Created Earl Rivers, 24 May 1466.

Jacquetta, Duchess of Bedford (1416?–30 May 1472).
> Daughter of Pierre, Count of Luxembourg and St Pol, and Marguerite del Balzo (whose father, Francesco del Balzo, was Duke of Andrea in Apulia, a dukedom in the kingdom of Naples).
> Married (1) John of Lancaster, Duke of Bedford (1389–1435) in May 1433. Lady of the Garter 1435.
> Married (2) Sir Richard Wydeville, between 6 February 1436 and 23 March 1437.

Children

Elizabeth (1437–7 or 8 June 1492).
> Married (1) Sir John Grey of Groby (1432?–killed 1461), *c.*1452.
> Married (2) Edward IV, King of England, 1 May 1464.
> Crowned Queen of England, 26 May 1465.

Anne (1438?–1489).
> Married (1) William, Viscount Bourchier, eldest son of the Earl of Essex (killed 1471).
> Married (2) Sir Edward Wingfield.
> Married (3) George Grey, second son of Lord Grey of Ruthin, Earl of Kent (died 1503).

Margaret (1439?–before 1491).
> Married Thomas, Lord Maltravers, Earl of Arundel (1450?–1524).

Anthony (1440?–25 June 1483). Executed.
> Knighted by January 1460.
> Married (1) Elizabeth, heir and daughter of Lord Scales (1436?–1473). At his marriage, sometime before July 1461 (possibly before March 1461), Anthony became Lord Scales in right of his wife.
> 2nd Earl Rivers, 1469.
> Married (2) Mary, daughter of Sir Henry FitzLewis, before October 1480.

Mary (1443?– by 1481).

> Married William, Lord Herbert, Earl of Pembroke, later Earl of Huntingdon (died 1491).

John (1445?–12 August 1469). Beheaded.

> Married Katherine Neville, Dowager Duchess of Norfolk (1407?–after 1483).

Jacquetta (1445?–before 1509).

> Married John, Lord Strange of Knockin (died 1479). Their daughter Joan married George, Lord Stanley's eldest son, who was held hostage by Richard III at Bosworth.

Richard (before 1446–6 March 1491).

> 3rd Earl Rivers, 1485.

Lionel (1446?–1484).

> Dean of Exeter, 1478.
>
> Chancellor of Oxford University, 1479.
>
> Bishop of Salisbury, 1482.

Edward (died 28 July 1488).

> Admiral of the English Fleet, April–May 1483.
>
> Died fighting for the Bretons in the battle of St Aubin du Cormier, 28 July 1488.

Katherine (before 1458–by 1513).

> Married (1) Henry Stafford, 2nd Duke of Buckingham (1454–2 November 1483), 1466.
>
> Married (2) Jasper Tudor, Duke of Bedford (*c*.1431–1495), before 7 November 1485.
>
> Married (3) Sir Richard Wingfield (1468–1525), after 21 December 1495.

Eleanor, sometimes called Joan (died 1491).

> Married Sir Anthony Grey de Ruthin, son and heir of Lord Grey of Ruthin, Earl of Kent (died 1480).

Martha.

> Married Sir John Bromley of Bartomley and Hextall. Almost nothing is known of their life.

Lewis, died young.

John, died young.

Birth years are uncertain, but all children were born between 1437 and the coronation of Elizabeth in 1464.

Wydeville Marriages

Elizabeth, married (1) Sir John Grey, son of Lord Ferrers of Groby. Date of marriage unknown.

(2) Edward IV, King of England, 1 May 1464.

Anne, married (1) William, Lord Bourchier, heir to the Earl of Essex, before 15 August 1467.

(2) Sir Edward Wingfield

(3) George Grey, Earl of Kent, Lord Grey of Ruthin (brother of Eleanor's husband), after 12 February 1483.

Margaret, married Thomas, Lord Maltravers, heir of the Earl of Arundel, October 1464.

Anthony, married (1) Elizabeth, daughter and heir of Thomas, Lord Scales, before July 1461 (possibly before March 1461).

(2) Mary, daughter of Sir Henry FitzLewis, before October 1480.

Mary, married William, Lord Herbert, 2nd Earl of Pembroke and later Earl of Huntington, September 1466.

John, aged twenty, married Katherine Neville, Duchess of Norfolk, aged over sixty, in January 1465.

Jacquetta, married John, Lord Strange of Knockyn.

Richard, 3rd and last Earl Rivers, died with no heirs, ending the Wydeville male lineage.

Lionel, never married. Entered the Church and became Chancellor of Oxford University and Bishop of Salisbury.

Edward, a naval officer, was killed at St Aubin du Dormier, 28 July 1488. He died with no heirs.

Katherine, aged ten?, married (1) Henry Stafford, Duke of Buckingham, Edward's first cousin and ward, aged nine, in 1466.

(2) Jasper Tudor, Duke of Bedford, between 2 November 1483 and 7 November 1485.

(3) Sir Richard Wingfield.

Eleanor (also known as Joan), married Anthony, Lord Grey of Ruthin, eldest son and heir of the Earl of Kent.

Martha, married Sir John Bromley of Bartomley and Hextall, Shropshire, about whom nothing is known.

Two brothers, Lewis and John, died young.

The Cousins' Wars: Battles and Events

22 May 1455	First battle of St Albans. Yorkist victory over Lancastrian troops, with Richard, Duke of York appointed Protector of the Realm, Lord Salisbury the Chancellor, and Warwick Captain of Calais. From 1450–1460 Richard, Duke of York dominated the baronial faction including the Nevilles, Mowbrays and Bourchiers – all kinsmen – with Richard Neville, Earl Warwick, his

	principal lieutenant. After Prince Edward of Lancaster was born in October 1453, Queen Margaret begins to take an active interest in politics and will ultimately lead King Henry VI's party.
23 September 1459	Yorkist forces, even though outnumbered two to one, defeat 3,000 Lancastrian troops at Blore Heath.
12 October 1459	York prepares to attack Queen Margaret's army at Ludford Bridge, near Ludlow, but he is deserted by his followers and no battle is fought. York flees to Ireland. Salisbury, Warwick and Edward, Earl of March (York's son) flee to Calais.
14 January 1460	Lancastrians Sir Richard Wydeville, Lord Rivers and his son Sir Anthony Wydeville, Lord Scales are captured in a surprise attack at Sandwich. Transported to Calais, they are imprisoned by Warwick.
June 1460	Warwick returns from France.
10 July 1460	Warwick crushes the Lancastrian army at Northampton and captures King Henry VI. Queen Margaret and Prince Edward take refuge at Durham. Richard, Duke of York returns from Ireland.
31 October 1460	Parliament at Westminster decides that Henry will retain his crown for life, but York and his heirs will succeed to the throne at Henry VI's death. Edward, Prince of Wales, is disinherited, strengthening Margaret's resolve to fight.
30 December 1460	Lancastrian troops surprise York's men at Wakefield. Richard, Duke of York and his son, the Earl of Rutland, are slain in a Lancastrian victory.
2 February 1461	Edward, Earl of March defeats Lancastrian forces at Mortimer's Cross.
17 February 1461	Second battle of St Albans. Lancastrian troops defeat Warwick. Sir John Grey, husband of Elizabeth Wydeville, dies leading the Lancastrian cavalry into battle. King Henry VI is reunited with Margaret.
4 March 1461	Edward, Earl of March enters London and is declared King Edward IV.
29 March 1461	Battle of Towton. Edward IV, who has pursued the Lancastrians northwards, destroys their troops in the bloodiest battle ever fought on English soil. Henry VI and family flee to Scotland.
25 April 1464	Yorkist victory in a minor skirmish with Lancastrians at Hedgeley Moor.
15 May 1464	Battle of Hexham destroys remnants of Lancastrian troops.
23 June 1464	Alnwick Castle captured after a long siege. Sir Anthony Wydeville fights with Edward IV and the Yorkist troops.
13 July 1465	Henry VI captured and imprisoned in Tower of London.

1467	Edward IV splits with Warwick. Edward IV dismisses George Neville as Chancellor and rejects a treaty with Louis XI of France negotiated by Warwick. Edward IV allies England with Burgundy.
April 1469	Warwick provokes armed protest in Yorkshire, led by 'Robin of Redesdale'. Warwick marries his daughter Isabel to George, Duke of Clarence and invades Kent.
26 July 1469	Warwick defeats Edward's army at Edgecote and takes the King prisoner. Edward is imprisoned at Coventry, 2 August, moved to Warwick Castle, 8–12 August, then to Middleham Castle, 25 August.
12 August 1469	Sir Richard Wydeville, Earl Rivers (the Queen's father) and Sir John Wydeville (her brother) are beheaded by Warwick's men without trial.
April 1470	Warwick, lacking support from the people, returns to Calais with Clarence. He allies himself with Margaret, Lancastrian Queen-in-exile.
September 1470	Warwick invades England.
1 October 1470	Queen Elizabeth enters sanctuary at Westminster Abbey.
3 October 1470	Edward IV flees to Holland. Henry VI restored to the throne. Warwick rules as Henry VI's lieutenant for six months, with little trust from the Lancastrians who fear his previous Yorkist ties.
2 November 1470	Edward, V is born to Queen Elizabeth in sanctuary.
14 March 1471	Ravenspur. Edward IV lands, claiming his ancestral rights as Duke of York.
12 April 1471	Edward IV enters London and is reunited with Queen Elizabeth.
14 April 1471	Edward IV's army fight the Lancastrian troops at Barnet and kill Warwick on Easter Sunday. Queen Margaret and her son Edward land at Weymouth and gather Lancastrian support in the west.
4 May 1471	Margaret's army is crushed at Tewkesbury and her son, Edward, Prince of Wales, is slain. Edward IV begins twelve years of uninterrupted rule.
21–22 May 1471	Henry VI dies in the Tower of London. Richard, Duke of Gloucester is named as the assassin by historians André, Rous, Polydore Vergil and Pietro Carmeliano.
18 February 1478	George, Duke of Clarence is executed in the Tower of London.
9 April 1483	Edward IV dies. Edward V becomes King.
April/May 1483	Richard, Duke of Gloucester is recognised as Protector of Edward V, aged twelve.

30 April 1483	Edward V is seized at Stony Stratford by Gloucester and Buckingham. Anthony Wydeville, Earl Rivers; Sir Richard Grey; and Sir Thomas Vaughan, the King's chamberlain, are arrested and sent north to prison.
1 May 1483	Queen Elizabeth, Prince Richard, and her daughters enter sanctuary at Westminster.
13 June 1483	William, Lord Hastings, is executed at the Tower.
16 June 1483	Prince Richard, Duke of York leaves Westminster Sanctuary.
25 June 1483	Anthony Wydeville, Earl Rivers; Sir Richard Grey; and Sir Thomas Vaughan are executed.
Late summer 1483	Last sighting of Edward V and Prince Richard at the Tower. Reports of their deaths circulate through London.
2 November 1483	Buckingham, after rebelling against Richard III, is executed at Salisbury.
Months following	Marriage between Henry Tudor, Earl of Richmond and Princess Elizabeth is negotiated by Queen Elizabeth and Margaret Beaufort, Countess of Richmond.
25 December 1483	Richmond takes formal oath of betrothal to Elizabeth of York at Rennes Cathedral.
January 1484	Parliament declares the nineteen-year marriage of Edward IV and Elizabeth to be invalid and their children illegitimate because of a prior marriage contract between Edward IV and Lady Eleanor Butler.
*c.*9 April 1484	Richard III's only son, Edward, dies.
7 August 1485	Richmond invades England, landing at Milford Haven. Joined by Welsh troops, he marches through Shrewsbury to meet Richard III's army.
22 August 1485	Richard III is killed at Bosworth Field. Henry VII declared King.

Children of Elizabeth Wydeville (1437–8 June 1492)

Married (1) Sir John Grey, 2nd Baron Ferrers of Groby. Before 1453.

1. Thomas Grey, 1st Marquis of Dorset. Unknown date of birth–30 September 1501. Great-grandfather of Lady Jane Grey.
2. Richard Grey. Born 1453?–25 June 1483.

Married (2) Edward IV, King of England, on 1 May 1464.

(Edward IV born at Rouen, France, on 28 April 1442. Died at Westminster 9 April 1483.)

3. Elizabeth, born at Westminster, 11 February 1466. Died 11 February 1503.

Married Henry VII, 18 January 1486. Children:

    Arthur, 20 September 1486–2 April 1502.

    Margaret, 29 November 1489–18 October 1541.

        Married (1) James IV of Scotland.

            Great-grandmother of James I of England (VI of Scotland).

        Married (2) Archibald Douglas, Earl of Angus.

        Married (3) Henry Stewart, Lord Methven.

    Henry VIII, 28 June 1491–28 January 1547.

        Married (1) Catherine of Aragon, mother of Mary Tudor.

        Married (2) Anne Boleyn, mother of Elizabeth I.

        Married (3) Jane Seymour, mother of Edward VI.

        Married (4) Anne of Cleves.

        Married (5) Catherine Howard.

        Married (6) Catherine Parr.

    Elizabeth, 2 July 1492–14 September 1495.

    Mary, 18 May 1496–26 June 1533.

        Married (1) Louis XII of France.

        Married (2) Charles Brandon.

            Grandmother of Lady Jane Grey.

    Edmund, 20 February 1499–19 June 1500.

    Edward, unknown date of birth and death.

    Katherine, 2 February 1503–20 February 1503.

4. Mary, born at Westminster, 12 August 1467. Died 23 May 1482.

5. Cecily, born at Westminster, 20 March 1469. Died 24 August 1507.

    Married (1) John Viscount Welles before December 1487.

    Married (2) Thomas Kyme of Boston, Lincolnshire, between 8 February 1499 and January 1503.

6. Edward V, born at Westminster Sanctuary, 2 November 1470. Died after July 1483.

7. Margaret, born at Windsor, 19 April 1472. Died 11 December 1472.

8. Richard, born at the Dominican Friary, Shrewsbury, 17 August 1473. Died after July 1483.

9. Anne, born at Westminster, 2 November 1475. Died after 22 November 1511. Married Thomas Howard, Duke of Norfolk and Earl of Surrey, 4 February 1495.

10. George, born at Windsor before 12 April 1477. Died March 1479.

11. Katharine, born at Eltham, August 1479. Died 15 November 1527. Married William Courtenay, Earl of Devon, before October 1495.

12. Bridget, born at Eltham, 10 November 1480. Died in Dominican convent at Dartford, 1517?

Abbreviations

Arrival	*Historie of the Arrivall of Edward IV, in England, and the Finall Recouerye of His Kingdomes from Henry VI. A.D. 1471.*
Bluemantle	'The Record of Bluemantle Pursuivant,' in Kingsford.
CCR	*Calendar of the Close Rolls.*
CFR	*Calendar of the Fine Rolls.*
CP	*Complete Peerage.*
CPR	*Calendar of Patent Rolls.*
CL	*Chronicles of London.*
Croyland	*Ingulph's Chronicle of the Abbey of Croyland.*
CWR	*The Chronicles of the White Rose of York.*
DNB	*Dictionary of National Biography.*
GC	*The Great Chronicle of London.*
Letters	*Letters of the Kings of England.*
Mancini	Mancinus, Dominicus. *The Usurpation of Richard the Third.*
Milan	*Calendar of State Papers and Manuscripts, existing in the Archives Collections of Milan.*
Paston	*The Paston Letters.*
Rozmital	*The Travels of Leo of Rozmital.*
Stonor	*Kingsford's Stonor Letters and Papers.*
Wills	*A Collection of all the Wills, now known to be extant, of the Kings and Queen of England…*
Wills… Doctors	*Wills from Doctors' Commons*

Other references will be found in the bibliography, under the last name of the author or first word of the title.

Notes and Citations

The first reference to a source gives full citation; subsequent references cite the last name of the author or first word of the title.

Chapter 1. The Widow and the King

1   *Calendar of Patent Rolls: Edward IV 1461–1467* (London: Her Majesty's Stationery Office, 1897), 35.
2   *The Complete Peerage of England Scotland Ireland Great Britain and the United Kingdom*, ed. George Edward Cokayne (New York: St. Martin's Press, 1984), XI:20.
3   Mary Clive, *This Sun of York: A Biography of Edward IV* (New York: Alfred A. Knopf, 1974), 14.
4   Thomas More, *The History of Richard III*, ed. Richard S. Sylvester (New Haven: Yale University Press, 1963), II: 61-62.
5   More, II: 62.
6   I wish to thank my friend and colleague Sebastian Cassarino for his translation.
7   Dominicus Mancinus, *The Usurpation of Richard the Third*, trans. C.A.J. Armstrong, 2nd ed. (Oxford: Clarendon Press, 1969), 61.
8   'Hearne's Fragment of an Old Chronicle, from 1460–1470', *The Chronicles of the White Rose of York* (London: James Bohn, 1845), 15-16.
9   More, II: 61.
10 Alison Weir, *The Wars of the Roses* (New York: Ballantine, 1995), 323.
11 Anne Crawford, 'Elizabeth Woodville, Wife of Edward IV', *Letters of the Queens of England 1100–1547* (Dover, N.H.: Alan Sutton, 1994), 130.
12 Charles Derek Ross, *The Wars of the Roses* (New York: Thames and Hudson, 1976), 72 and 94.
13 Michael Stroud, 'Chivalric Terminology in Late Medieval Literature', *Journal of the History of Ideas* 37 (1976): 324.
14 Weir, *Wars*, 18.
15 Agnes Strickland, *Lives of the Queens of England*, (Chicago: Belford, Clarke and Co., 1843), I: 385-6.
16 C.L. Grace, *The Book of Shadows*, (New York: St Martin's Press, 1996), 196.
17 Grace, 28-9.
18 Bertram Fields, *Royal Blood: Richard III and the Mystery of the Princes*, (New York: HarperCollins, 1998), 34.
19 Fields, 35.
20 Fields, 72.

21 *Calendar of State Papers and Manuscripts, existing in the Archives and Collections of Milan*, ed. Allen B. Hinds (London: His Majesty's Stationery Office, 1912), I: 131.

Chapter 2. Edward's Decision to Marry Lady Elizabeth

1   Edward Hall, *Hall's Chronicle; Containing the History of England, during the Reign of Henry the Fourth, and the Succeeding Monarchs, to the End of the Reign of Henry the Eighth*, 1548. (Reprint, New York: AMS Press, 1965), 264.

2   Strickland, 613-4.

3   *The Paston Letters A.D. 1422–1509*, ed. James Gairdner (London: Chatto & Windus, 1904), III: 267.

4   Milan, 65, 66, 68, 72, 77.

5   Milan, 68, 73.

6   *CPR, Edward IV, 1461–68*, I: 35.

7   *Paston*, III: 223.

8   Robert Fabyan, *The New Chronicles of England and France*, ed. Henry Ellis (London: Rivington, *et al*, 1811), 635.

9   'Gregory's Chronicle', *The Historical Collections of a Citizen of London*, ed. James Gairdner (Camden Society. Westminster: Nichols and Sons, 1876), 206.

10 *Paston*, III: 203-4.

11 John Rous, *The Rous Roll*, ed. Charles Ross (Gloucester: Alan Sutton, 1980), 56.

12 Milan, 100.

13 *CPR, Edward IV, 1461-68*, I: 97.

14 *CPR, Edward IV, 1461-68*, I: 97.

15 *CPR, Edward IV, 1461-68*, I: 169-70.

16 *CPR, Edward IV, 1461-68*, I: 81.

17 *CPR, Edward IV, 1461-68*, I: 188.

18 *Hearne's Fragment*, 10.

19 *Calendar of the Close Rolls: Edward IV 1461–68* (London: His Majesty's Stationery Office, 1949), I: 179.

20 Livia Visser-Fuchs, 'English Events in Caspar Weinreich's Danzig Chronicle, 1461-1495', *The Ricardian* 7 (1986): 313.

21 More, II: 61-2.

22 More, II: 63.

23 More, II: 63-4.

24 More, II: 64.

25 More, II: 64-5.

26 Henry Ellis, *Original Letters, Illustrative of English History*. Second Series (New York: AMS Press, 1970), 4:152.

27 Fabyan, 654.

28 Ellis, *Original Letters*, Vol. 1 (New York: AMS Press, 1970), I: 10.

29 Bodleian MS 264, quoted from *The Romance of Alexander*, ed. M.R. James, (Oxford: Oxford University Press, 1933), 5. I wish to thank my friend and colleague Danielle Trudeau for assistance with the translation.

30   *Excerpta Historica, or Illustrations of English History* (London: Samuel Bentley, 1831), 178.

31   Hall, 264.

32   Hall, 264

Chapter 3. The Truth about the Wydevilles

1   David Baldwin, *Elizabeth Woodville: Mother of the Princes in the Tower* (Gloucestershire: Sutton Publishing, 2002), 1; David MacGibbon, *Elizabeth Woodville (1437–1492): Her Life and Times* (London: Arthur Baker, 1938), 45, 225.

2   *The Great Chronicle of London*, ed. A.H. Thomas and I.D. Thornley (London: George Jones, 1938), 421n.

3   Marina Belozerskaya, *Rethinking the Renaissance: Burgundian Arts Across Europe.* (Cambridge University Press, 2002).

4   *The Coventry Leet Book: or Mayor's Register*, ed. Mary Dormer Harris (London: Early English Text Society, 1907–13), 152.

5   *CPR, Henry VI, 1429–1436*: 516.

6   *CPR, Henry VI, 1436–1441*: 53.

7   *CPR, Henry VI, 1436–1441*: 53. *Rotuli Parliamentorum*, ed. John Strachey, *et al.* 6 Vols. (London: 1767–77), IV: 498.

8   *CPR, Henry VI, 1436–144*: 311; *Henry VI, 1441–46*: 46-7.

9   *Foedera*, ed. Thomas Rymer (London: J. Tonson, 1728–35), X: 677.

10 *Calendar of the Fine Rolls, Henry VI, 1437–1445* (His Majesty's Stationery Office, 1937), 90-91, 315; *Henry VI, 1445–1452*: 76, 198. See also *CCR, Henry VI 1435–41*: 91, 141-2, 395, 400-1, 405, 407 and *Henry VI 1441–47*: 414-5.

11 *CPR Henry VI 1422–29*: 13; *CCR Henry VI 1435–41*: 314.

12 *CPR Henry VI 1422–29*: 353.

13 Fabyan, 596.

14 *CCR Henry VI 1441–47*: 340.

15 *Excerpta*, 249-50.

16 *CPR Henry VI 1429–36*: 593.

17 *CCR Henry VI 1422–29*: 99, 102, 472; *Henry VI 1429–35*: 6.

18 George Baker, *The History and Antiquities of the County of Northampton* (London: J.B. Nichols and Son, 1841), II: 162.

19 Baker, 162.

20 *CP* XI: 19.

21 *Chronicles of London*, ed. Charles Lethbridge Kingsford (Oxford: Clarendon Press, 1905), 138.

22 *CPR Henry VI 1436–1441*: 41.

23 *CPR Henry VI 1436–1441*: 72.

24 *CPR Henry VI 1436–1441*: 146, 369.

25 *CPR Henry VI 1436–1441*: 537.

26 *CL*, 146.

27 *CPR Henry VI 1436–1441*: 426.

28 *CCR Henry VI 1435–41*: 397.

29 *CL*, 148.
30 *CPR Henry VI 1441–46*: 453.
31 Paston II: 150.
32 *CPR Henry VI 1446–52*: 385.
33 *CCR Henry VI 1447–54*: 219, 221.
34 *CPR Henry VI 1446–52*: 414, 438, 444, 456, 462, 472, 476, 478.
35 Baldwin, 8.
36 *CPR 1452–61*: 394.
37 *Coventry Leet*, 300.
38 A.R. Myers, *Crown, Household and Parliament in Fifteenth Century England* (London: Hambledon Press, 1985), 212.
39 Myers, *Crown*, 184.
40 Myers, *Crown*, 217-8.
41 *Proceedings and Ordinances of the Privy Council of England*, ed. Harris Nicolas London: Commissoners on the Public Records, 1837), 276-7; *Rotuli* V: 297, 341.
42 James H. Ramsay, *Lancaster and York: A Century of English History* (Oxford: Clarendon, 1892) II: 210.
43 *CPR Henry VI 1452–1461*: 443.
44 *CPR Henry VI 1452–1461*: 555.
45 *GC*, 190.
46 Myers, *Crown*, 182.
47 *CP* , V, 361.
48 Baldwin, 5.
49 Beryl Richardson, 'The Old Hall, Groby', *The Groby Book*, ed. Allison Coates (Groby Village Society, 2000).
50 *The Coronation of Elizabeth Wydeville: Queen Consort of Edward IV on May 26th, 1465*, ed. George Smith (London: 1935. Reprint Gloucester, 1975), 29ff.
51 *CCR Edward IV 1461–68*: 179.

Chapter 4. The Cousins' Wars

1 Hall, 208.
2 Hall, 208.
3 *Henry VI*, Act 2, Scene 4.
4 James H. Ramsay, *Lancaster and York: A Century of English History*. 2 Vols. (Oxford: Clarendon Press, 1892), II:216.
5 *CL*, 173.
6 *GC*, 194.
7 Milan, 49-50.

Chapter 5. Consternation and Coronation

1 Milan, 69.
2 Milan, 102.

3   *Coronation*, 31-2.

4   Quoted from MacGibbon, 38.

5   *The Travels of Leo of Rozmital through Germany, Flanders, England, France, Spain, Portugal and Italy 1465–1467*, ed. Malcolm Letts (Cambridge: Cambridge University Press, 1957), 56

6   *Coronation*, 61-5.

7   Glynne Wickham, *Early English Stages, 1300–1660* (London: Routledge and Kegan Paul, 1959), 324-31.

8   *Coronation*, 8.

Chapter 6. Setting Up Housekeeping

1   John Stow, *A Survey of London Written in the Year 1598*, ed. Antonia Fraser. (Gloucestershire: Sutton, 1994), 246.

2   *CPR Edward IV 1461–1467*: 433; *CPR Edward IV 1467–77*: 64.

3   *CPR Edward IV 1461–1467*: 525.

4   C.M. Woolgar, *The Great Household in Late Medieval England* (New Haven: Yale University Press, 1999), 9.

5   *The Chronicles of the White Rose of York* (London: James Bohn, 1845), lxiii; Fabyan, 207.

6   Woolgar, *Great Household*, 12.

7   *The Household of Edward IV: The Black Book and the Ordinance of 1478* ed. A.R. Myers, (Manchester: University Press, 1959), 9.

8   *Household... Black Book,* 76ff.

9   *Letters of the Kings of England*, ed. James Orchard Halliwell (London: Henry Colburn, 1846), 101.

10 Myers, *Crown*, 254.

11 *CPR Edward IV 1461–1467*: 430.

12 Myers, *Crown*, 280.

13 Davies, 81.

14 Myers, *Crown*, 147.

15 Myers, *Crown*, 252.

16 Myers, *Crown*, 154.

17 Myers, *Crown*, 146.

18 Myers, *Crown*, 252.

19 Myers, *Crown*, 144.

20 Myers, *Crown*, 288.

21 Myers, *Crown*, 287.

22 Myers, *Crown*, 300-14.

23 *CPR Edward IV 1461–1467*: 463, 464.

24 W. G. Searle, *The History of the Queens' College of St. Margaret and St. Bernard in the University of Cambridge, 1446–1560* (Cambridge: Cambridge University Press, 1867), 15.

25 *CPR Henry VI 1446–1452*: 144.

26 Searle, 69.

27   *CPR Edward IV 1461–1467*: 495.
28   Charles Henry Cooper, *Memorials of Cambridge* (Cambridge: William Metcalfe, 1860), I: 289.
29   Searle, 71.
30   *CPR Edward IV, Edward V, Richard III 1476–1485*: 34.
31   *CPR Edward IV 1461–1467*: 196.
32   *CPR Edward IV 1461–1467*: 446.
33   Maxwell Lyte, *History of Eton College* (Macmillan, 1910), 69.
34   Lyte, 80; Lipscomb, *History and Antiquities of Buckinghamshire* (London: J. and . Robins, 1867), 4: 485.
35   Lyte, 70.
36   Lyte, 70.
37   *CPR Edward IV 1461–67*: 516.

Chapter 7. Marriages Made in Court

1   *CCR Edward IV 1461–68*: 162.
2   J.R. Lander, 'Marriage and Politics in the Fifteenth Century: The Nevilles and the Wydevilles', *Bulletin of the Institute of Historical Research* 36 (November 1963), 119-52.
3   Lander, 121.
4   *CPR Edward IV 1461–67*: 462.
5   *CPR Edward IV 1461–67*: 421, 444, 483, *ad infinitum*.

Chapter 8. The Queen's Churching

1   Fabyan, 655.
2   David Cressy, 'Purification, Thanksgiving and the Churching of Women in Post-Reformation England', *Past & Present*, 141 (Nov. 1993), 112.
3   *The Travels of Leo of Rozmital through Germany, Flanders, England, France, Spain, Portugal and Italy 1465–1467*, ed. Malcolm Letts (Cambridge: Cambridge University Press, 1957), 45.
4   Rozmital, 45-6.
5   Rozmital, 46-7.
6   Rozmital, 47-8.
7   Rozmital, 47n.
8   Milan, 19.
9   Cora L. Scofield, *The Life and Reign of Edward the Fourth* (London: Longmans, Green and Co., 1923), I: 399.
10   Myers, *Crown*, 143.
11   Myers, *Crown*, 143.

Chapter 9. Fun, Games and Politics at Court

1   Richard Vaughan, *Philip the Good: The Apogee of Burgundy* (New York: Barnes and Noble, 1970), 134.

2 Christine Weightman, *Margaret of York, Duchess of Burgundy, 1446–1503* (New York: St Martin's Press, 1989), 79.
3 *Excerpta*, 197.
4 *Excerpta*, 204.
5 Stow, 353.
6 *GC*, 203.
7 *Excerpta*, 204.
8 *Excerpta*, 206.
9 *Excerpta*, 208.
10 *Excerpta*, 209.
11 Fabyan, 656.
12 *Excerpta*, 212.
13 MacGibbon, 65.
14 J.R. Lander, 'Council, Administration and Councillors, 1461–85', *Bulletin of the Institute of Historical Research*, 32 (1959), 138.
15 Weightman, 37.

Chapter 10. Enemies Within

1 *CPR Edward IV 1467–77*: 110.
2 *Coventry Leet*, 336ff.
3 *CPR Edward IV 1467–77*: 25.
4 *CPR Edward IV 1467–77*: 39.
5 *CPR Edward IV 1467–77*: 41.
6 *Ingulph's Chronicle of the Abbey of Croyland with the Continuations by Peter of Blois and Anonymous Writers*, trans. Henry T. Riley (London: Henry G. Bohn, 1854). <http://www.r3.org/bookcase/croyland/croy5.html>
7 *Excerpta*, 228.
8 *Excerpta*, 228.
9 *Excerpta*, 239.
10 *GC*, 206.
11 Charles Derek Ross, *Edward IV* (Berkeley: University of California Press, 1974), 100.
12 *GC*, 206.
13 *GC*, 207.
14 Myers, *Crown*, 142.
15 Retha M. Warnicke, *The Rise and Fall of Anne Boleyn: Family politics at the court of Henry VIII* (Cambridge: Cambridge University Press, 1989), 133.
16 *GC*, 208.
17 *GC*, 213.
18 *GC*, 214.
19 *GC*, 207.
20 MacGibbon, 42-3, emphasis mine.
21 Goddard H. Orpen, 'Statute Rolls of the Parliament of Ireland, 1-12 Edward IV', *English Historical Review* 30 (1915): 342-3.

22 *GC*, 208.
23 Milan, 131.
24 Milan, 131.

Chapter 11. War Within the Family

1 *Paston*, V: 34.
2 Henry Harrod, 'Queen Elizabeth Woodville's Visit to Norwich in 1469', *Norfolk Archaeology* 5 (1859): 34.
3 Ross, *Edward IV*, 132.
4 *GC*, 310; *Coventry Leet*, 346.
5 John Warkworth, *A Chronicle of the First Thirteen Years of the Reign of King Edward the Fourth*, ed. James Orchard Halliwell (London: Camden Society, 1839), 46.
6 Warkworth, 47.
7 Warkworth, 47, emphasis mine.
8 Warkworth, 49-50,.
9 Milan, 132.
10 *CPR Edward IV 1467–77:* 190
11 *Three Fifteenth-Century Chronicles*, ed. James Gairdner (Camden Society, 1880), 63.
12 Ralph A. Griffiths, *King and Country: England and Wales in the Fifteenth Century* (London: Hambledon Press, 1991), 252; *CL,* 149.
13 *CPR Edward IV 1467–77:* 190.
14 Hearne's Fragment, 28.
15 Milan, 139-40.
16 Quoted from M.A. Hicks, *False, Fleeting, Perjur'd Clarence* (Gloucester, Alan Sutton, 1980), 81.
17 Searle, 78.

Chapter 12. Elizabeth in Sanctuary

1 *CL*, 182; *GC*, 211.
2 Paston, V: 85.
3 Stow, 410.
4 Gervase Rosser, *Medieval Westminster 1200–1540* (Oxford: Clarendon Press, 1989), 69.
5 Rosser, 68.
6 Rosser, 86-7.
7 Baldwin, 47.
8 *CPR Edward IV 1467–77*: 154 and 547.
9 Weightman, 93.
10 Weightman, 210.
11 *Historie of the Arrivall of Edward IV, in England and the Finall Recouerye of His Kingdomes from Henry VI. A.D. M.CCCC.LXXI*, ed. John Bruce (London: Camden Society, 1838). <http://www.r3.org/bookcase/arrival2.html>; *CWR*, 38; *GC* 432n.

12   *Arrival*, <http://www.r3.org/boookcase/arrival2.html>; *CWR*, 51.
13   *Arrival*, <http://www.r3.org/bookcase/arrival3.html>; *CWR,* 57.
14   Philippe de. Commynes, *Memoirs: The Reign of Louis XI 1461–83*, trans. Michael Jones (Penguin, 1972). <http://www.r3.org/bookcase/de_commynes/decom_5.html>
15   Fabyan, 660.
16   Ross, *Edward IV*, 166.
17   *Arrival*, <http://www.r3.org/bookcase/arrival3.html>; *CWR*, 60.
18   *Arrival*, <http://www.r3.org/bookcase/arrival3.html>; *CWR*, 60-61.

Chapter 13. York Restored

1   *Arrival*, <http://www.r3.org/bookcase/arrival5.html>; *CWR,* 82.
2   *Arrival*, <http://www.r3.org/bookcase/arrival5.html>; *CWR*, 87.
3   *Arrival*, <http://www.r3.org/bookcase/arrival5.html>; *CWR*, 91.
4   Croyland, <http://www.r3.org/bookcase/croyland/croy6.html>
5   Thomas Wright, ed., *Political Poems and Song relating to English History, composed during the Period from the Accession of Edward III to that of Richard III*, (London: Longman, Green, Longman, and Roberts: 1861), II: 278.
6   Davies, 133.
7   *CPR Edward IV 1467–77*: 547 and 336.
8   Wright, 281-2.
9   Charles Lethbridge Kingsford, *English Historical Literature in the Fifteenth Century* (NY: Burt Franklin, 1963, Reprint Oxford, 1913), 379.
10   Strickland, I: 603.
11   Paston, V: 130-31.
12   Francis Leary, *The Golden Longing* (London: John Murray, 1959), 341.
13   *CWR*, 128n.
14   Hicks, *Clarence*, 112.
15   John Cherry, *The Middleham Jewel and Ring* (York: Yorkshire Museum, 1994), 9.
16   Ellis, Third Series I: ix-x.
17   *CPR Edward IV 1467–77*: 455; emphasis mine.
18   *CPR Edward IV 1467–77*: 455.
19   *CPR Edward IV 1467–77*: 457.
20   Kingsford, 386.
21   Kingsford, 387-8.
22   Kingsford, 382.
23   Kingsford, 382.
24   Kingsford, 383.

Chapter 14. Problems in Paradise

1   More, II: 11.
2   More, II: 55.
3   *The Hastings Papers* o.s. Box 14. The Huntington Library.

4   *CPR Edward IV 1467–1477*: 456.

5   Baldwin, 63 and 206n.

6   Anne Sutton and Livia Visser-Fuchs, 'The Royal Burials of the House of York at Windsor: II. Princess Mary, May 1482, and Queen Elizabeth Woodville, June 1492', *The Ricardian* 11 (1999), 456.

7   More, II: 56.

8   Mancini, 138; Paston, VI: 81.

9   *Kingsford's Stonor Letters and Papers 1290–1483*, ed. Christine Carpenter (Cambridge: Cambridge University Press, 1996), 123.

10   *Kingsford's Stonor Letters*, 123.

11   *Kingsford's Stonor Letters*, 383-4, 406.

12   Coronation, 40.

13   Paston, V: 106.

14   Ross, 206.

15   Paston, V: 157.

16   Anthony Wydeville, Earl Rivers, *The Dictes or Sayengis of the Philosophres* (Westminster, 1477, reprint: Amsterdam: Walter J. Johnson, Inc., 1979), 1.

17   Ross, 96.

18   Lander, 'Marriage', 142.

19   Lander, 'Marriage', 122.

20   *Letters of the Kings of England*, ed. James Orchard Halliwell (London: Henry Colburn, 1846), 137.

21   *Letters*, 137.

22   *Letters*, 138.

23   *Letters*, 140.

24   *CPR Edward IV 1467–1477*: 417.

25   Fields, 64.

26   Paston, V: 179.

Chapter 15. Life at Ludlow

1   H.T. Evans, *Wales and the Wars of the Roses* (Gloucestershire: Alan Sutton, 1915, reprint 1998), 116.

2   Evans, 117

3   *CPR Edward IV 1467–77*: 429.

4   Evans, 117.

5   *CPR Edward IV 1467–77*: 574.

6   David Lloyd, *The Concise History of Ludlow* (Ludlow: Merlin Unwin Books, 1999), 32.

7   Lloyd, *Concise History*, 20.

8   *Letters*, 140.

9   *Letters*, 142.

10   *Letters*, 144.

11   R.B. Pugh, ed., 'House of Dominican Friars', *The Victoria History of the Counties of England* (London: Oxford University Press, 1973), II: 92.

12   Dorothy Cromarty, *Everyday Life in Medieval Shrewsbury* (Shrewsbury: Shropshire Books, 1991, reprint 1995), 104.
13   Lansdowne MS. 285, f. 57, quoted from *Excerpta*, 242-43.
14   *Coventry Leet*, 391-4.
15   *Coventry Leet*, 407.
16   *Coventry Leet*, 407.
17   *Coventry Leet*, 405-6.
18   *CPR Edward IV 1467–77*: 394.
19   Cooper, *Memorials*, I: 289.
20   *CPR Edward IV 1467–77*: 394.

Chapter 16. War and Peace

1   Ross, 214.
2   John Twigg, *A History of Queens' College, Cambridge 1448–1986* (Bury St Edmunds: Boydell, 1987), 9.
3   *A Miscellany containing the host foundation of the college, the names of the first Benefactors… Misc. A.* (Queens' College, University of Cambridge, QCV 76); Searle, 45, 72.
4   *Excerpta, 369.*
5   *Excerpta, 369.*
6   *Excerpta, 378.*
7   Commynes, Book 4, Ch. 9.
8   Ross, 233; Commynes, Book 6, Ch. 11.
9   Commynes, Book 4, Ch. 10.
10   James Gairdner, *History of the Life and Reign of Richard the Third* (Cambridge: Cambridge University Press, 1898; Kraus Reprint, New York: 1968), 27-28.
11   Milan, 198.
12   *CPR Edward IV 1467–77*: 571.
13   Anne Sutton and Livia Visser-Fuchs, *The Reburial of Richard Duke of York 21-30 July 1476* (London: The Richard III Society, 1996).
14   Sutton and Visser-Fuchs, *Reburial*, 33.
15   Sutton and Visser-Fuchs, *Reburial*, 19.
16   Sutton and Visser-Fuchs, *Reburial*, 19.
17   Sutton and Visser-Fuchs, *Reburial*, 37.

Chapter 17. George, Duke of Clarence: Perpetual Malcontent

1   Croyland, <http://www.r3.org/bookcase/croyland/croy7.html>
2   Commynes, Book 6, Ch. 1.
3   J.R. Lander, *Crown and Nobility 1450–1509* (Montreal: McGill-Queen's University Press, 1976), 248.
4   *CPR Edward IV. Edward V. Richard III. 1476–1485*: 72, emphasis mine.
5   *CPR Edward IV. Edward V. Richard III. 1476–1485*: 73.
6   *CPR Edward IV. Edward V. Richard III. 1476–1485*: 73.

7   Lander, *Crown*, 248.

8   Hicks, *Clarence*, 135.

9   Hicks, *Clarence*, 136.

10   Croyland, <http://www.r3.org/bookcase/croyland/croy7.html>

11   Croyland, <http://www.r3.org/bookcase/croyland/croy7.html>

12   Mancini, 63.

13   Mancini, 63.

14   Mancini, 63.

15   Hicks, *Clarence*, 143.

16   *Illustrations of ancient state and chivalry from manuscripts preserved in the Ashmolean museum*, ed. William Henry (London: W. Nicol, 1840), 29.

17   *Illustrations*, 30.

18   *Illustrations*, 32-3.

19   *Illustrations*, 40.

20   Hicks, *Clarence*, 152-3, emphasis mine.

21   Hicks, *Clarence*, 154.

22   Hicks, *Clarence*, 158.

23   *CPR Edward IV. Edward V. Richard III. 1476–1485*: 115, emphasis mine.

24   Hicks, *Clarence*, 142.

25   *CPR Edward IV. Edward V. Richard III. 1476–1485*: 212.

26   *CPR Edward IV. Edward V. Richard III. 1476–1485*: 139.

Chapter 18. Anthony Wydeville, Courtier *Par Excellence*

1   Mancini, 61.

2   Mancini, 63.

3   Mancini, 69.

4   *Excerpta*, 240.

5   *Foedera* XI: 630.

6   Warkworth, 9.

7   David Grummitt, 'William, Lord Hastings, the Calais Garrison and the Politics of Yorkist England', *The Ricardian* 12 (June 2001), 269.

8   *CPR Edward IV 1467–1477*: 450.

9   D.E. Lowe, 'Patronage and Politics: Edward IV, the Wydevills, and the Council of the Prince of Wales, 1471–83', *Bulletin of the Board of Celtic Studies* 29 (1981), 561.

10   Milan, 196.

11   Milan, 222.

12   Paston, V: 258 (21 March, 1476).

13   *Dictionary of National Biography* (London: Oxford University Press, 1959–60), XXI: 883.

14   Milan, 228.

15   Anthony Wydeville, Earl Rivers, *Cordiale siue de quatuor nouissimis* (Westminster: W. Caxton, 1479), 150.

16   Wydeville, *Dictes*, 2.

17   Wydeville, *Dictes*, 4-5.

18 Wydeville, *Dictes*, 11.

19 Wydeville, *Dictes*, 14.

20 Wydeville, *Dictes*, 22, *passim*.

21 Curt Bühler, 'The Dictes and Sayings of the Philosophers', *The Library* 15 (1934), 316.

22 Wydeville, *Dictes*, 146.

23 *The Dictes or Sayengis of the Philosophres*, MS 265, Lambeth Palace Library.

24 Sutton and Visser-Fuchs, 'Richard III's Books: Mistaken Attributions', *The Ricardian* (1992), 309, n17.

25 Carol Meale, 'Manuscripts, Readers and Patrons in Fifteenth-Century England: Sir Thomas Malory and Arthurian Romance', *Arthurian Literature* IV, ed. Richard Barber (Totowa, NJ: Barnes and Noble, 1985), 118.

26 Lambeth MS 265.

27 Montague Rhodes James, *A Descriptive Catalogue of the Manuscripts in the Library of Lambeth Palace* (Cambridge, 1930), I: 414.

28 Anthony Wydeville, Earl Rivers, *The Morale Prouerbes of Christyne* (Westminster, 1478; Reprint: Da Capo Press, Amsterdam, 1970).

29 Anthony Wydeville, Earl Rivers, *Cordiale siue de quatuor nouissimis* (Westminster: W. Caxton, 1479).

30 Wydeville, *Cordiale*, 150.

31 Wydeville, *Cordiale*, 151.

32 Lotte Hellinga, *Caxton in Focus* (London: British Library, 1982), 89.

33 Hellinga, 90.

34 Anthony Wydeville, Earl Rivers, 'Balet', published in Joseph Ritson, *Ancient Songs and Ballads,* ed. Joseph Ritson, Rev. W. Carew Hazlitt (London, 1877), 150–51.

35 M.A. Hicks, 'The Changing Role of the Wydevilles in Yorkist Politics to 1483', *Patronage, Pedigree, and Power in Later Medieval England*, ed. Charles Ross (Gloucester: Alan Sutton, 1979), 74.

36 *Materials for a History of the Reign of Henry VII*, ed. William Campbell (London: Longman & Co., 1873), II: 562.

Chapter 19. The Queen's Happy Years, 1475–1482

1 Meale, 93-4.

2 British Library MS Harleian 4431.

3 Myers, *Crown*, 318.

4 British Library, Royal MS 14E.iii.

5 Huntington Library, MS R.B. 62222.

6 Sutton and Visser-Fuchs, 'A "Most Benevolent Queen": Queen Elizabeth Woodville's Reputation, her Piety and her Books', *The Ricardian* 10 (June 1995): 230.

7 Sutton and Visser-Fuchs, 'The Cult of Angels in Late Fifteenth-Century England: An Hours of the Guyardian Angel presented to Queen Elizabeth Woodville', *Women and the Book: Assessing the Visual Evidence*, ed. Lesley Smith and Jane Taylor (Toronto: University of Toronto Press, 1997), 234.

8   N.F. Blake, *Caxton's Own Prose* (London: André Deutsch, 1973), 104.

9   *CPR Edward IV 1467–77*: 592.

10   John Anstis, ed., *The Register of the Most Noble Order of the Garter, from its Cover in Black Velvet Usually Called the Black Book* (London: John Barber, 1724), 197.

11   *Illustrations*, 30.

12   Herbert Francis Westlake, *Westminster Abbey the Church, Convent, Cathedral and College of St. Peter, Westminster* (London: Philip Allan & Co., 1923), 153; *CPR Edward IV Edward IV. Edward V. Richard III. 1476–85:* 133.

13   *CPR Edward IV Edward IV. Edward V. Richard III. 1476–85*: 133.

14   *Liber Niger Cartulary* (Westminster Abbey), folio 93.

15   *Acts of Court of the Mercers' Company, 1453–1527*, ed. Laetitia Lyell and F.D. Watney (Cambridge: Cambridge University Press, 1936), 123.

16   *Acts of Court,* 125.

17   *Acts of Court,* 128.

18   Davies, 177; Weightman, 134.

19   Weightman, 134-5.

20   *The Gentleman's Magazine* (January 1831), 25.

21   Paul Lee, *Nunneries, Learning and Spirituality in Late Medieval English Society: The Dominican Priory of Dartford* (Suffolk: York Medieval Press, 2001), 30.

22   MacGibbon, 132.

23   Sutton and Visser-Fuchs, 'Royal Burials', 446-51.

24   *Coventry Leet*, 505.

25   Ross, *Edward IV*, 292.

26   Croyland, <http://www.r3.org/bookcase/croyland/croy7.html>

Chapter 20. 1483 Begins

1   Scofield, II: 359.

2   E.W. Ives, 'Andrew Dymmock and the Papers of Antony, Earl Rivers, 1482-3', *BIHR* 41 (1968), 223.

3   Ives, 229.

4   Croyland, <http://www.r3.org/bookcase/croyland/croy7.html>

5   Mancini, 81.

6   Commynes, Book 6, Ch.1.

7   Ross, 280.

8   More, II: 13.

9   More, II: 13.

10   More, II: 11

11   Croyland, <http://www.r3.org/bookcase/croyland/croy7.html>

12   More, II: 176, n 14/2.

13   Croyland, <http://www.r3.org/bookcase/croyland/croy7.html>

14   More, II: 17.

15   C.E. Moreton, 'A Local Dispute and the Politics of 1483: Roger Townshend, Earl Rivers and the Duke of Gloucester', *The Ricardian* 107 (1989), 305-6.

16   More, II: 17.

17   More, II: 19.
18   Mancini, 77-79.
19   *Letters*, 144.
20   More, II: 184, n 20/13-14.
21   More, II: 20-21.
22   More, II: 21-22.
23   *Registrum Thome Bourgchier, Cantuariensis Archiepiscopi, AD 1454–1486*, ed. F.R.H. DuBoulay (Canterbury and York Soc., Liv, 1957), 52; I wish to thank my friend and colleague Marianina Olcott for the translation.
24   *Excerpta*, 379.
25   Mancini, 59-61.
26   Croyland, <http://www.r3.org/bookcase/croyland/croy7.html>
27   Alison Weir, *The Princes in the Tower* (New York: Ballantine, 1992), 63.
28   *Excerpta*, 378.
29   *Excerpta*, 13.
30   Mancini, 85.
31   Mancini, 122.
32   *Excerpta*, 16.
33   *Letters*, 150.
34   More, II: 47.
35   More, II: 48.
36   More, II: 48.
37   *GC*, 231.
38   Mancini, 91.

Chapter 21. The Mother *v*. The Protector

1   More, II: 33.
2   More, II: 39.
3   More, II: 40.
4   More, II: 41.
5   More, II: 42.
6   *CL*, 190.
7   More, II: 66-68.
8   Michael K. Jones, *Bosworth, 1485: The Psychology of a Battle* (Stroud, Gloucestershire: Tempus Publishing, 2002), 65-71.
9   *Rotuli*, VI: 194.
10   *Wills from Doctors' Commons*, ed. John Gough Nichols and John Bruce (London: Camden Society, 1863), 1, emphasis mine.
11   More, II: 68.
12   More, II: 59; *GC*, 435n.
13   More, II: 72.
14   More, II: 73.
15   *GC*, 668.
16   *Excerpta*, 246.

17   *Excerpta*, 248.
18   *CWR*, 209.
19   Mancini, 101.
20   *Excerpta*, 382.
21   More, II: 82.
22   More, II: 85.
23   *Excerpta*, 16-17.
24   Croyland, <http://www.r3.org/bookcase/croyland/croy7.html>
25   Mancini, 93.
26   Mancini, 93.
27   Croyland, <http://www.r3.org/bookcase/croyland/croy7.html>
28   Livia Visser-Fuchs, 'English Events in Caspar Weinreich's Danzig Chronicle, 1461–1495', *The Ricardian* 7 (1986), 316.
29   Weightman, 145.
30   Croyland, <http://www.r3.org/bookcase/croyland/croy8.html>
31   *CL*, 191.
32   *GC*, 236.
33   Commynes, Book I, Ch. 7.
34   Croyland, <http://www.r3.org/bookcase/croyland/croy8.html>
35   Mancini, 91, 126.
36   Croyland, <http://www.r3.org/bookcase/croyland/croy8.html>
37   Polydore Vergil, *Three Books of Polydore Vergil's English History, comprising the Reigns of Henry VI., Edward IV., and Richard III*, ed. Henry Ellis (London: John Bowyer Nichols, 1844), 37.

Chapter 22. A Woman Alone

1   *Calendar of Papal Letters* (London: Her Majesty's Stationery Office, 1960), XIV: 20.
2   Michael K. Jones, *The King's Mother: Lady Margaret Beaufort, Countess of Richmond and Derby* (Cambridge: Cambridge University Press, 1992), 60.
3   Vergil, *Three Books*, 195; Jones, *King's Mother*, 63.
4   Vergil, *Three Books*, 195.
5   Vergil, *Three Books*, 196.
6   *GC*, 670.
7   Vergil, *Three Books*, 200.
8   J.A.F. Thomson, 'Bishop Lionel Woodville and Richard III', *BIHR* 59 (1986): 132.
9   Fabyan, 670; *GC*, 235, 436.
10   *CPR Edward IV. Edward V. Richard III. 1476–1485*: 371; Proclamation of Richard III at Leicester, October 23, 1483.
11   Thomson, 134.
12   Thomson, 134; *CPR Edward IV. Edward V. Richard III. 1476–1485*: 387.
13   *DNB*, XXI: 885.
14   *Excerpta*, 16.
15   <http://www.r3.org/bookcase/texts/tit_reg.html>

16 <http://www.r3.org/bookcase/texts/tit_reg.html>
17 *Arrival*, 4.
18 *Excerpta*, 354.
19 John Ashdown-Hill, 'Edward IV's Uncrowned Queen: The Lady Eleanor Talbot, Lady Butler', *The Ricardian* 11 (1997), 188 n.33; W.E. Hampton, 'A Further Account of Robert Stillington', *The Ricardian* (1976), 27.
20 Croyland, <http://www.r3.org/bookcase/croyland/croy8.html>
21 Ellis, *Letters*, Second Series, 4: 149-50.
22 Croyland, <http://www.r3.org/bookcase/croyland/croy8.html>
23 Croyland, <http://www.r3.org/bookcase/croyland/croy8.html>
24 Croyland, <http://www.r3.org/bookcase/croyland/croy8.html>
25 Croyland, <http://www.r3.org/bookcase/croyland/croy8.html>
26 George Buck, *The History of King Richard the Third (1619)*, ed. Arthur Kincad (Gloucester: Alan Sutton, 1979), 191.
27 Polydore Vergil, *The Anglica Historia of Polydore Vergil A.D. 1485–1537*, ed. Denys Hay (London: Royal Historical Society, 1950), 3.
28 Gairdner, *History of the Life and Reign of Richard the Third*, 202.
29 *GC*, 236.
30 *GC*, 237.
31 Croyland, <http://www.r3.org/bookcase/croyland/croy9.html>

Chapter 23. Queen Dowager Elizabeth

1 *Materials*, I: 121.
2 *Materials*, I: 122.
3 *Materials*, I: 123.
4 *Materials*, I: 338, 347-50; *CPR Henry VII 1485–1494*: 75.
5 *Lease Book Number 1, 1486-1505* (Westminster Abbey), folio 9.
6 Vergil, *Anglica*, 18-19.
7 Vergil, *Anglica*, 19.
8 Sutton, *et al.*, 'The Retirement of Elizabeth Woodville, and her Sons', *The Ricardian* 11 (1999), 563.
9 *Materials*, II, 142.
10 *Materials*, II, 148.
11 *Materials*, II, 221.
12 Anne Crawford, 'The Queen's Council in the Middle Ages', *English Historical Review* 116 (2001): 1193-1212.
13 Crawford, *Letters*, 135-6.
14 Fields, 203.
15 *Materials*, II, 225.
16 *Materials*, II, 273.
17 *Materials*, II, 319-20.
18 *Materials*, II, 322.
19 *Materials*, II, 555; *CCR Henry VII. Vol. I. 1485-1500*: 122; *CPR Henry VII 1485–1494*: 302.

20   *Materials*, II, 337.

21   *CPR Edward IV 1467–1477*: 115.

22   *CPR Edward IV 1467–1477*: 360.

23   *CPR Edward IV 1467–1477*: 414.

24   *CPR Edward IV 1467–1477*: 547.

25   *CPR Edward IV. Edward V. Richard III. 1476–1485*: 156.

26   Ann Sutton and Livia Visser-Fuchs, 'The Device of Queen Elizabeth Woodville: A Gillyflower or Pink', *The Ricardian* 11 (1997), 17-24.

27   *Calendar of Papal Letters*, XI: 90.

28   Edward T. Clarke, *Bermondsey: Its Historic Memories and Associations* (London: Elliot Stock, 1902), 125.

29   *Foedera* XII: 328-9.

30   Vergil, *Anglica*, 33.

31   *CPR Henry VII 1485–1494*: 112, 117.

32   *CPR Henry VII 1485–1494*: 154.

33   Roger B. Merriman, 'Edward Woodville – Knight Errant', *American Antiquarian Society* (October) 1903, 135.

34   Merriman, 135-6.

35   Merriman, 136.

36   Merriman, 138.

37   Merriman, 144.

38   Davies, 217.

39   *Materials*, II, 103.

40   *CPR Henry VII 1485–1494*: 106, 279.

41   Baker, II: 165-66.

42   *Wills*, 350-51.

43   MS BL Arundel 26, ff 29v-30. Quoted from Sutton and Visser-Fuchs, 'Royal Burials'. I have modernised spelling and punctuation of their exact transcription.

Chapter 24. Legacy

1   *CPR Henry VII 1485–1494*: 308.

2   *GC*, 203.

3   Jones, *King's Mother*, 126.

4   Jones, *King's Mother*, 134, 162.

5   Jones, *King's Mother*, 134.

6   Jones, *King's Mother*, 162.

7   C.F.R. Palmer, 'History of the Priory of Dartford, in Kent', *Archaeological Journal* XXXVI (1879), 261.

8   *Wills… Doctor's*, 2-3.

9   Palmer, 262.

10   *CPR Henry VII 1485–1494*: 388.

11   Baker II: 166.

Bibliography

Biographies of Elizabeth Wydeville (Woodville)

Baldwin, David. *Elizabeth Woodville: Mother of the Princes in the Tower*. Gloucestershire: Sutton Publishing, 2002.

Davies, Katharine. *The First Queen Elizabeth*. London: Lovat Dickson Limited, 1937.

MacGibbon, David. *Elizabeth Woodville (1437–1492): Her Life and Times*. London: Arthur Baker, 1938.

Strickland, Agnes. *Lives of the Queens of England*. Vol. I. Chicago: Belford, Clarke and Co., 1843.

Contemporary Documents

Acts of Court of the Mercers' Company, 1453–1527. Ed. Laetitia Lyell and F.D. Watney. Cambridge: Cambridge University Press, 1936.

Baker MS 42 (Mm.1.53). University of Cambridge.

Calendar of the Close Rolls.
   Henry VI. Vol. 1. 1422–29. London: His Majesty's Stationery Office, 1933.
   Henry VI. Vol. II. 1429–35. London: His Majesty's Stationery Office, 1933.
   Henry VI. Vol. III. 1435–41. London: His Majesty's Stationery Office, 1937.
   Henry VI. Vol. IV. 1441–47. London: His Majesty's Stationery Office, 1937.
   Henry VI. Vol. V. 1447–54. London: His Majesty's Stationery Office, 1947.
   Henry VI. Vol. VI. 1454–61. London: His Majesty's Stationery Office, 1947.
   Edward IV. Vol. I. 1461–68. London: His Majesty's Stationery Office, 1949.
   Edward IV. Vol. II. 1468–76. London: His Majesty's Stationery Office, 1953.
   Edward IV, Edward V, Richard III. 1476–85. London: Her Majesty's Stationery Office, 1954.
   Henry VII. Vol. I. 1485–1500. London: Her Majesty's Stationery Office, 1955.

Calendar of Entries in the Papal Registers relating to Great Britain and Ireland: Papal Letters 1471–1485. Vol. XIII, Part I. London: Her Majesty's Stationery Office, 1955.

Calendar of the Fine Rolls.
   Henry VI. 1430–1437. London: His Majesty's Stationery Office, 1936.
   Henry VI. 1437–1445. London: His Majesty's Stationery Office, 1937.
   Henry VI. 1445–1452. London: His Majesty's Stationery Office, 1939.
   Henry VI. 1452–1461. London: His Majesty's Stationery Office, 1939.
   Edward IV, Henry VI. 1467–1471. London: Her Majesty's Stationery Office, 1949.
   Edward IV, Edward V, Richard III. Vol. XXI. 1471–85. London: Her Majesty's Stationery Office, 1961.

Henry VII. Vol. XXII. 1485–1509. London: Her Majesty's Stationery Office, 1962.

Calendar of Papal Letters. Vols XI and XIV. London: Her Majesty's Stationery Office, 1960.

Calendar of Patent Rolls.

    Henry VI. 1422–1429. London: His Majesty's Stationery Office, 1901.

    Henry VI. 1429–1436. London: His Majesty's Stationery Office, 1907.

    Henry VI. 1436–1441. London: His Majesty's Stationery Office, 1907.

    Henry VI. 1441–46. Reprint Kraus-Thomson, Nendeln/Liechtenstein, 1971.

    Henry VI. 1446–1452. Reprint Kraus-Thomson, Nendeln/Liechtenstein, 1971.

    Henry VI. 1452–1461. London: His Majesty's Stationery Office, 1910.

    Edward IV. 1461–1467. London: Her Majesty's Stationery Office, 1897.

    Edward IV, Henry VI. 1467–1477. London: Her Majesty's Stationery Office, 1900.

    Edward IV, Edward V, Richard III. 1476–1485. London: Her Majesty's Stationery Office, 1901.

    Henry VII. 1485–1494. London: His Majesty's Stationery Office, 1914.

Calendar of State Papers and Manuscripts, existing in the Archives and Collections of Milan. Vol. 1. Ed. Allen B. Hinds. London: His Majesty's Stationery Office, 1912.

Caxton, William. *Recuyell of the Histories of Troy.* Huntington Library R.B. 62222.

Chronicles of London. Ed. Charles Lethbridge Kingsford. Oxford: Clarendon Press, 1905.

The Chronicles of the White Rose of York: A Series of Historical Fragments, Proclamations, Letters, and Other Contemporary Documents Relating to the Reign of King Edward the Fourth. London: James Bohn, 1845.

A Collection of all the Wills, now known to be extant, of the Kings and Queens of England, Princes and Princesses of Wales, and every branch of the Blood Royal, from the reign of William the Conqueror, to that of Henry the Seventh, exclusive. London: J. Nichols, 1780.

Commynes, Philippe de. *Memoirs: The Reign of Louis XI 1461–83.* Trans. Michael Jones. Penguin, 1972. <http//www.r3.org/bookcase/de_commynes/decom_1.html>

The Coronation of Elizabeth Wydeville: Queen Consort of Edward IV on May 26th, 1465. Ed. George Smith. London: 1935. Reprint Gloucester: 1975.

Cornazzano, Antonio. 'La Regina d'ingliterra' quoted in Conor Fahy's 'The Marriage of Edward IV and Elizabeth Woodville: A New Italian source', *English Historical Review* 76 (1961), 660-72. Poem translated by Sebastian Cassarino.

The Coventry Leet Book: or Mayor's Register. Ed. Mary Dormer Harris. London: Early English Text Society, 1907–13.

Ellis, Henry. *Original Letters, Illustrative of English History.* New York: AMS Press, 1970. *Second Series.* New York: AMS Press, 1970. *Third Series.* New York: AMS Press, 1970.

Excerpta Historica, or Illustrations of English History. London: Samuel Bentley, 1831.

Fabyan, Robert. *The New Chronicles of England and France.* Ed. Henry Ellis. London: Rivington, *et al.*, 1811.

Foedera. Vols 10 and 11. Ed. Thomas Rymer. London: J. Tonson, 1728–35.

The Great Chronicle of London. Ed. A.H. Thomas and I.D. Thornley. London:

George Jones, 1938.

Gregory. 'Gregory's Chronicle', *The Historical Collections of a Citizen of London*. Ed. James Gairdner, Camden Society. Westminster: Nichols and Sons, 1876.

Hall, Edward. *Hall's Chronicle; Containing the History of England, during the Reign of Henry the Fourth, and the Succeeding Monarchs, to the End of the Reign of Henry the Eighth. 1548.* Reprint, New York: AMS Press, 1965.

The Hastings Papers. Huntington Library MS CD1043.L52.

'Hearne's Fragment of an Old Chronicle, from 1460–1470', *The Chronicles of the White Rose of York*. London: James Bohn, 1845.

Historie of the Arrivall of Edward IV, in England and the Finall Recouerye of His Kingdomes from Henry VI. A.D. M.CCCC.LXXI. Ed. John Bruce. London: Camden Society, 1838. <http://www.r3.org/bookcase/arrival.html>. Also in *CWR*, 31-96.

The Household of Edward IV: The Black Book and the Ordinance of 1478, ed. A.R. Myers. Manchester: Manchester University Press, 1959.

Illustrations of ancient state and chivalry from manuscripts preserved in the Ashmolean museum. Ed. William Henry. London: W. Nicol, 1840.

Ingulph's Chronicle of the Abbey of Croyland with the Continuations by Peter of Blois and Anonymous Writers. Trans. Henry T. Riley. London: Henry G. Bohn, 1854. <http://www.r3.org/bookcase/croyland>. Judie Gall, Richard III Society.

Kingsford's Stonor Letters and Papers 1290–1483. Ed. Christine Carpenter. Cambridge: Cambridge University Press, 1996.

'The Last Ten Years of the Reign of King Edward the Fourth, extracted from originall Letters and Documents', in *Chronicles of the White Rose of York*.

Lease Book Number 1. 1486–1505. Folio 9. Westminster Abbey.

Letters of the Kings of England. Ed. James Orchard Halliwell. London: Henry Colburn, 1846.

Liber Niger cartulary. Folio 93. Westminster Abbey.

Mancinus, Dominicus. *The Usurpation of Richard the Third.* Trans. C.A.J. Armstrong. 2nd ed. Oxford: Clarendon Press, 1969.

Materials for a History of the Reign of Henry VII. Ed. William Campbell. 2 Vols. London: Longman & Co., 1873.

A Miscellany containing the host foundation of the college, the names of the first Benefactors… Misc. A. Queens' College, University of Cambridge. QCV 76.

More, Thomas. *The History of Richard III. Vol. 2.* Ed. Richard S. Sylvester. New Haven: Yale University Press, 1963.

Oeuores poètiques de Christine de Pison. MS Harleian 4431. British Library.

The Paston Letters 1422–1509. Ed. James Gairdner. London: Chatto & Windus, 1904.

Proceedings and Ordinances of the Privy Council of England. Ed. Harris Nicolas. London: Commissoners on the Public Records, 1837.

Registrum Thome Bourgchier, Cantuariensis Archiepiscopi, 1454–1486. Ed. F.R.H. DuBoulay. Canterbury and York Soc., Liv, 1957.

Rotuli Parliamentorum. Ed. John Strachey, *et al.* 6 Vols. London: 1767–77.

Rous, John. *Antiquarii Warwicensis: Historia Regum Angliae.* Ed. Thomas Hearns.

Oxford: E Theatro Sheldoniano, 1745.

—*The Rous Roll*. Ed. Charles Ross. Gloucester: Alan Sutton, 1980.

Sacrist's roll for 1486–7. Folio 9. Westminster Abbey.

Statuta Collegii Reginalis Anno 1529. Queens' College, University of Cambridge. QCV 60 and 65.

Three Fifteenth-Century Chronicles. Ed. James Gairdner. Camden Society, 1880.

Titulus Regius. <http://www.r3.org/bookcase/texts/tit_reg.html>

The Travels of Leo of Rozmital through Germany, Flanders, England, France, Spain, Portugal and Italy 1465–1467. Ed. Malcolm Letts. Cambridge: Cambridge University Press, 1957.

Vergil, Polydore. *Three Books of Polydore Vergil's English History, comprising the Reigns of Henry VI, Edward IV, and Richard III*. Ed. Henry Ellis. London: John Bowyer Nichols, 1844.

—*The Anglica Historia of Polydore Vergil A.D. 1485–1537*. Ed. Denys Hay. London: Royal Historical Society, 1950.

Warkworth, John. *A Chronicle of the First Thirteen Years of the Reign of King Edward the Fourth*. Ed. James Orchard Halliwell. London: Camden Society, 1839.

Wills from Doctors' Commons: A Selection from the Wills of Eminent Persons proved in the Prerogative Court of Canterbury, 1495–1695. Ed. John Nichols and John Bruce. Westminster: Camden Society o.s., 1863.

Worcestre, William. *Itineraries*. Ed. John H. Harvey. Oxford: Clarendon Press, 1969. Reprint J. Nasmith. Cambridge, 1778.

Wydeville, Anthony, Earl Rivers. 'Balet'. Published in Joseph Ritson and W. Carew Hazlitt (eds), *Ancient Songs and Ballads*. London: 1877.

—*Cordiale siue de quatuor nouissimis*. Westminster: W. Caxton, 1479.

—*The Dictes or Sayengis of the Philosophres*. MS 265. Lambeth Palace Library.

—*The Dictes or Sayengis of the Philosophres*. Westminster, 1477. Reprint: Walter J. Johnson, Inc. Amsterdam: 1979

—*The Morale Prouerbes of Christyne*. Westminster, 1478. Reprint: Da Capo Press. Amsterdam, 1970.

Secondary Sources

Anderson, Judith H. *Biographical Truth: The Representation of Historical Persons in Tudor Stuart Writing*. (New Haven: Yale University Press, 1984).

Anstis, John (ed.). *The Register of the Most Noble Order of the Garter, from its Cover in Black Velvet Usually Called the Black Book*. 2 Vols. London: John Barber, 1724.

Ashdown-Hill, John. 'Edward IV's Uncrowned Queen: The Lady Eleanor Talbot, Lady Butler', *The Ricardian* 11 (1997), 166–90.

Bacon, Francis. *The History of the Reign of King Henry the Seventh*. Ed. F.J. Levy. New York: Bobbs-Merrill, 1972.

Baker, George. *The History and Antiquities of the County of Northampton*. Vol. II. London: J.B. Nichols and Son, 1841.

Bayley, A.R. 'Edward IV and Lady Elizabeth Butler', *Notes and Queries* 151 (1926), 408–9.

Bellamy, J.G. *The Law of Treason in England in the Later Middle Ages*. Cambridge: Cambridge University Press, 1970.

Belozerskaya, Marina. *Rethinking the Renaissance: Burgundian Arts Across Europe*. Cambridge: Cambridge University Press, 2002.

Berry, Henry F. (ed.). 'Statute Rolls of the Parliament of Ireland, 1-12 Edward IV', *The English Historical Review* 30 (1915), 341-43.

Blake, N.F. *Caxton's Own Prose*. London: André Deutsch, 1973.

Brett, Martin. 'The annals of Bermondsey, Southwark and Merton', *Church and City 1000–1500*, ed. David Abulafia *et al.* Cambridge: Cambridge University Press, 1992, pp. 279-311.

Brooke-Little, John and Motto, John. *Knights of the Middle Ages: Their Armour and Coats of Arms*. London: Hugh Evelyn Limited, 1966.

Buck, George. *The History of King Richard the Third* (1619). Ed. Arthur Kincad. Gloucester: Alan Sutton, 1979.

Bühler, Curt. F. 'The Dictes and Sayings of the Philosophers', *The Library* 15 (1934), 316-29.

Cherry, John. *The Middleham Jewel and Ring*. York: Yorkshire Museum, 1994.

'The Children of King Edward IV', *The Gentleman's Magazine*, Jan 1831, 23-26.

Chrimes, S.B. *Henry VII*. Berkeley: University of California Press, 1972.

Clarke, Edward T. *Bermondsey: Its Historic Memories and Associations*. London: Elliot Stock, 1902.

Clive, Mary. *This Sun of York: A Biography of Edward IV*. New York: Alfred A. Knopf, 1974.

The Complete Peerage of England, Scotland, Ireland, Great Britain and the United Kingdom. Ed. George Edward Cokayne. New York: St Martin's Press, 1984.

Cooper, Charles Henry. *Annals of Cambridge. Vol. 1*. Cambridge: Warwick and Co., 1842.

—*Memorials of Cambridge, Vol. 1*. Cambridge: William Metcalfe, 1860.

Crawford, Anne. 'Elizabeth Woodville, Wife of Edward IV', *Letters of the Queens of England 1100–1547*. Dover, N.H.: Alan Sutton, 1994.

—'The Queen's Council in the Middle Ages', *English Historical Review* 116 (2001) 1469, pp. 1193-1212.

Cressy, David. 'Purification, Thanksgiving and the Churching of Women in Post-Reformation England.' *Past & Present* 141 (Nov. 1993), 106-46.

Cromarty, Dorothy. *Everyday Life in Medieval Shrewsbury*. Shrewsbury: Shropshire Books, 1991, reprint 1995.

Davis, Norman (ed.). *Paston Letters and Papers of the Fifteenth Century*. Oxford: Clarendon Press, 1971.

A Descriptive and Historical Guide to Ashby-de-la-Zouch. Ashby-de-la-Zouch: T. Wayne, 1831.

Dictionary of National Biography. Ed. Leslie Stephen and Sidney Lee. 22 Vols. London: Oxford University Press, 1959–60.

Drummond-Murray, James *et al.* 'Recent Archaeological Work in the Bermondsey District of Southwark', *The London Archaeologist* 7 (1994), 251-57.

Erler, Mary and Kowaleski,, Maryanne (eds). *Women and Power in the Middle Ages*. Athens: University of Georgia Press, 1988.

Evans, H.T. *Wales and the Wars of the Roses*. Gloucestershire: Alan Sutton, 1915, reprint 1998.

Fahy, Conor. 'The Marriage of Edward IV and Elizabeth Woodville: A New Italian Source', *English Historical Review* 76 (1961), 660-72.

Fields, Bertram. *Royal Blood: Richard III and the Mystery of the Princes*. New York: HarperCollins, 1998.

FitzRoy, Charles and Harry, Keith. *Grafton Regis: The History of a Northamptonshire Village*. Cardiff: Merton Priory Press, 2000.

Fox, Alistair. *Thomas More: History and Providence*. New Haven: Yale, 1982.

Gairdner, James. *History of the Life and Reign of Richard the Third*. Cambridge: Cambridge University Press, 1898. Kraus Reprint, New York: 1968.

The Gentleman's Magazine. January 1831, 23-25.

Gray, H.L. 'Incomes from land in England in 1436', *English Historical Review* XLIX (1934), 607-39.

Gies, Frances and Joseph. *A Medieval Family: the Pastons of Fifteenth-Century England*. New York: HarperCollins, 1998.

Gill, Louise. 'William Caxton and the Rebellion of 1483', *The English Historical Review* 112 (Feb. 1997), 105-19.

Grace, C.L. *The Book of Shadows*. New York: St Martin's Press, 1996.

Green, Richard Firth. 'Historical Notes of a London Citizen, 1483–1488', *English Historical Review* 96 (1981), 585-90.

Griffiths, Ralph A. *King and Country: England and Wales in the Fifteenth Century*. London: Hambledon Press, 1991.

—*Patronage, The Crown, and the Provinces*. Gloucester: Alan Sutton, 1981.

Grummitt, David. 'William, Lord Hastings, the Calais Garrison and the Politics of Yorkist England', *The Ricardian* 12 (June 2001), 262-74.

Hammond, P.E. *The Battles of Barnet and Tewkesbury*. New York: St Martin's Press, 1990.

Hampton, W.E. 'A Further Account of Robert Stillington', *The Ricardian* (1976), 24-7.

Hansen, Charles M. and Thompson, Neil D. 'The Wydevills' Quartering for Beauchamp', *The Coat of Arms* 9 (1992), 178-87.

Hardy, Thomas. *Syllabus of the Documents relating to England and Other Kingdoms contained in the Collection known as 'Rymer's Foedera'. Vols II and III*. London: Longman & Co., 1873.

Harriss, G.L. 'The Struggle for Calais: An Aspect of the Rivalry between Lancaster and York', *English Historical Review* 75 (1960), 30-53

Harrod, Henry, 'Queen Elizabeth Woodville's Visit to Norwich in 1469,' *Norfolk Archaeology* 5 (1859) 32-7.

Harvey, Nancy Lenz. *Elizabeth of York: The Mother of Henry VIII*. New York: Macmillan, 1973.

—*The Rose and the Thorn: The Lives of Mary and Margaret Tudor*. New York: Macmillan, 1975.

Hastings, Peter. *The Hastings of Ashby-de-la-Zouch*. 1994.

Hellinga, Lotte. *Caxton in Focus*. London: British Library, 1982.

Hellinga, Lotte and Trapp, J.B. *The Cambridge History of the Book in Britain. Vol. III 1400–1557*. Cambridge: Cambridge University Press, 1999.

Henisch, Bridget Ann. *The Medieval Calendar Year*. University Park, PA: Pennsylvania State University Press, 1999.

Hepburn, Frederick. *Portraits of the Later Plantagenets*. Suffolk: Boydell Press, 1986.

Hicks, M.A. *False, Fleeting, Perjur'd Clarence*. Gloucester: Alan Sutton, 1980. *Warwick the Kingmaker*. Oxford: Blackwell, 1998

Hillier, Kenneth. *The Book of Ashby-de-la-Zouch*. Buckingham: Barracuda Books, 1984.

The History and Description of Ashby-de-la-Zouch. London: Hall & Co. 1852.

Hodges, Geoffrey. *Ludford Bridge & Mortimer's Cross*. Herefordshire: Logaston Press, 2001.

Hoskins, W.G. and McKinley, R.A. *The Victoria History of the County of Leicester*. Vol. II. London: University of London Institute of Historical Research, 1969.

Hunt, S.J. *A History of Fotheringhay*. Peterborough: M.G. Hillson, 1999.

The Huntingdon Papers (The Archives of the Noble Family of Hastings). Part I. London: Maggs Bros., 1926.

Hyde, F.E. and Markham, S.F. *A History of Stony Stratford and the Immediate Vicinity*. London: McCorquodale, 1948.

Ives, E.W. 'Andrew Dymmock and the Papers of Antony, Earl Rivers, 1482–3', *BIHR* 41 (1968), 216-29.

Ives, Eric. 'Marrying for Love: The Experience of Edward IV and Henry VIII', *History Today* 50 (2000), i12, 48ff.

James, Montague Rhodes. *A Descriptive Catalogue of the Manuscripts in the Library of Lambeth Palace. Part I*. Cambridge, 1930.

James, M.R. (ed.). *The Romance of Alexander*. Oxford: Oxford University Press, 1933.

Jones, Michael K. '1477 – The Expedition that Never Was: Chivalric Expectation in Late Yorkist England', *The Ricardian* 12 (June 2001), 275-92.

—*Bosworth, 1485: The Psychology of a Battle*. Stroud, Gloucestershire: Tempus Publishing, 2002.

—*The King's Mother: Lady Margaret Beaufort, Countess of Richmond and Derby*. Cambridge: Cambridge University Press, 1992

Kehler, Dorothea. 'Shakespeare's Richard III', *The Explicator* 56 (1998), 118-21.

Kendall, Paul Murray. *The Yorkist Age: Daily Life during the Wars of the Roses*. New York: W.W. Norton, 1962.

Kekewich, Margaret. 'Edward IV, William Caxton and Literary Patronage in Yorkist England', *Modern Language Review*, 66 (1971), 481-7.

Kelly, H.A. 'The Case Against Edward IV's Marriage and Offspring: Secrecy; Witchcraft; Secrecy; Precontract', *The Ricardian* 11 (1998), 326-35.

Khanna, Lee Cullen. 'No Less Real Than Ideal: Images of Women in More's Work', *Moreana* 55 (1977), 35-51.

Kingsford, Charles Lethbridge. *English Historical Literature in the Fifteenth Century*. NY: Burt Franklin, 1963. Reprint Oxford, 1913.

Kuskin, William. 'Caxton's Worthies Series: The Production of Literary Culture', *ELH* 66 (1999), 511-551.

Lander, J.R. 'Council, Administration and Councillors, 1461–85', *Bulletin of the Institute of Historical Research. Vol. XXXII* (1959), 138-80.

—*Crown and Nobility 1450–1509.* Montreal: McGill-Queen's University Press, 1976.

—'Marriage and Politics in the Fifteenth Century: The Nevilles and the Wydevilles', *Bulletin of the Institute of Historical Research* 36 (November 1963), 119-52.

Leary, Francis. *The Golden Longing.* London: John Murray, 1959.

Lee, Paul. *Nunneries, Learning and Spirituality in Late Medieval English Society: The Dominican Priory of Dartford.* Suffolk: York Medieval Press, 2001.

Leyser, Henrietta. *Medieval Women: A Social History of Women in England, 450–1500.* London: Weidenfeld and Nicolson, 1995.

Lipscomb. *History and Antiquities of Buckinghamshire. Vol. 4.* London: J. and W. Robins, 1867.

Lloyd, David. *The Concise History of Ludlow.* Ludlow: Merlin Unwin Books, 1999.

—*Ludlow Castle: A History and A Guide.* Welshpool.

Loach, Jennifer. 'The Function of Ceremonial in the Reign of Henry VIII', *Past & Present* (February 1994), 43-69.

Lowe, D.E. 'Patronage and Politics: Edward IV, the Wydevills, and the Council of the Prince of Wales, 1471–83', *Bulletin of the Board of Celtic Studies* 29 (1981), 545-73.

Lyte, Maxwell. *History of Eton College.* Macmillan, 1910.

Markham, Frank. *A History of Milton Keynes and District. Vol. I.* Luton: White Crescent Press, 1973.

Marius, Richard. *Thomas More: A Biography.* New York: Knopf, 1984.

McFarlane, K.B. 'The Education of the Nobility in Later Medieval England', in *The Nobility of Later Medieval England.* Oxford: Clarendon Press, 1973.

Meale, Carol. 'Manuscripts, Readers and Patrons in Fifteenth-Century England: Sir Thomas Malory and Arthurian Romance', *Arthurian Literature IV*, ed. Richard Barber. Totown, NJ: Barnes and Noble, 1985.

Merriman, Roger B. 'Edward Woodville – Knight Errant', *American Antiquarian Society* (October) 1903, 127-44.

Moreton, C.E., 'A Local Dispute and the Politics of 1483: Roger Townshend, Earl Rivers and the Duke of Gloucester', *The Ricardian* 107 (1989), 305-7.

Mowat, A.J. 'Robert Stillington', *The Ricardian* (1976), 23-8.

Myers, A.R. *Crown, Household and Parliament in Fifteenth Century England.* London: Hambledon Press, 1985.

—*England in the Late Middle Ages.* Baltimore: Penguin, 1963.

—*The Household of Edward IV: The Black Book and the Ordinance of 1478.* Manchester: University Press, 1959.

Nichols, John. *The History and Antiquities of the County of Leicester. 'Ashby de la Zouch'. Vol. 3, Part II.* Wakefield: S.R. Publishers Limited, reprint 1971, of John Nichols and Son, London, 1804.

— 'Groby', Vol. 14, Part II. Wakefield: S.R. Publishers Limited, reprint 1971, of John Nichols and Son, London, 1811.

Orme, Nicholas. *From Childhood to Chivalry: The Education of the English Kings and Aristocracy 1066–1530*. London: Mathuen, 1984

Orpen, Goddard H. 'Statute Rolls of the Parliament of Ireland, 1-12 Edward IV'. *English Historical Review* 30 (1915), pp. 341-43.

Palmer, C.F.R. 'The Friar-Preachers, or Blackfriars, of Shrewsbury', *Transactions of the Shropshire Archaelogical and Natural History Society*, IX (1886), 251-66.

— 'History of the Priory of Dartford, in Kent', *Archaeological Journal XXXVI* (1879), 241-71.

Pannett, Mandy. 'Fleshing Out the Bones: the Brief Lives of Edward V and Richard, Duke of York', *Contemporary Review* (March 1996) 268: 151-6.

Pollard, A.J. 'Dominic Mancini's Narrative of the Events of 1483', *Nottingham Medieval Studies XXXVIII* (1994), 152-63

— *Richard III and the Princes in the Tower*. New York: St Martin's Press, 1991.

— *The Wars of the Roses*. New York: St Martin's Press, 1995.

Pugh, R.B. (ed.). 'House of Dominican Friars', *The Victoria History of the Counties of England*. London: Oxford University Press, 1973. Vol. II: 91-3.

Ramsay, James H. *Lancaster and York: A Century of English History*. 2 Vols. Oxford: Clarendon Press, 1892.

Report of the Manuscripts of the Late Reginald Rawdon Hastings, Esq. of the Manor House, Ashbby de la Zouche. Vol. I. London: His Majesty's Stationery Office, 1928.

Richardson, Beryl. 'The Old Hall, Groby', *The Groby Book*, ed. Allison Coates. Groby Village Society, 2000.

Richardson, Geoffrey. *The Popinjays: A History of the Woodville Family and an account of their involvement in English History during the Late Medieval Age*. Shipley: Baildon Books, 2000.

Richmond, Colin. 'Propaganda in the Wars of the Roses', *History Today* 42 (July 1992), 12-19.

Rosenthal, Joel. *Medieval Women and the Sources of Medieval History*. Athens: University of Georgia Press, 1990.

Ross, Charles Derek. *Edward IV*. Berkeley: University of California Press, 1974.

— *The Wars of the Roses*. New York: Thames and Hudson, 1976.

— *Patronage, Pedigree, and Power in Later Medieval England*. Gloucester: Alan Sutton, 1979.

Rosser, Gervase. *Medieval Westminster 1200–1540*. Oxford: Clarendon Press, 1989.

Ryan, Francis X. 'Sir Thomas More's Use of Chaucer', *Studies in English Literature 1500–1900* 35 (1995), 1-17.

Scofield, Cora L. 'The Capture of Lord Rivers and Sir Anthony Woodville, 19 January 1460', *The English Historical Review* 37 (1922), 253-5.

— 'Elizabeth Wydevile in the Sanctuary at Westminster, 1470', *The English Historical Review* 24 (1909), 90-1.

— *The Life and Reign of Edward the Fourth*. 2 Vols. London: Longmans, Green & Co., 1923.

Scott, W. *The Story of Ashby-de-la-Zouch*. Ashby-de-la-Zouch: George Brown, 1907.

Searle, W.G. *The History of the Queens' College of St. Margaret and St. Bernard in the University of Cambridge. 1446–1560.* Cambridge: Cambridge University Press, 1867.

Seymour, William. *Battles in Britain and their Political Background 1066–1746.* Ware: Wordsworth, 1997.

Shepard, Alan Clarke. '"Female Perversity", Male Entitlement: The Agency of Gender in More's *The History of Richard III*', *Sixteenth Century Journal* 26 (1995), 311-28.

Smith, Lesley and Taylor, Jane H.M. *Women and the Book: Assessing the Visual Evidence.* Toronto: University of Toronto Press, 1997.

Steele, Alison. 'Beneath the Trocette: Evidence for Roman and Medieval Bermondsey', *London Archaeologist* 8 (1998), 265-270.

Stow, John. *A Survey of London Written in the Year 1598*, ed. Antonia Fraser. Gloucestershire: Sutton, 1994.

Stroud, Michael. 'Chivalric Terminology in Late Medieval Literature', *Journal of the History of Ideas* 37, No. 2 (1976), 323-34.

Sutton, Anne F. 'Sir Thomas Cook and his "troubles": an Investigation', *Guildhall Studies in London History* 3 (1978), 85-108.

Sutton, Anne, *et al.* 'The "Retirement" of Elizabeth Woodville, and her Sons', *The Ricardian* 11 (1999), 558-64.

Sutton, Anne and Visser-Fuchs, Livia, 'A "Most Benevolent Queen" Queen Elizabeth Woodville's Reputation, her Piety and her Books', *The Ricardian* 10 (June 1995): 214-45.

—'The Cult of Angels in Late Fifteenth-Century England: An Hours of the Guyardian Angel presented to Queen Elizabeth Woodville', *Women and the Book: Assessing the Visual Evidence.* Ed. Smith, Lesley and Taylor, Jane. Toronto: University of Toronto Press, 1997.

—'The Device of Queen Elizabeth Woodville: A Gillyflower or Pink', *The Ricardian* 11 (1997), 17-24.

—*The Reburial of Richard Duke of York 21-30 July 1476.* London: The Richard III Society, 1996.

—'Richard III's Books: Mistaken Attributions', *The Ricardian* (1992), 303-10.

—'The Royal Burials of the House of York at Windsor: II. Princess Mary, May 1482, and Queen Elizabeth Woodville, June 1492', *The Ricardian* 11 (1999), 446-62.

Tanner, Lawrence and Lord Mottistone. *The Abbot's House and Deanery of Westminster Abbey.* Reprint from The Transactions of the Ancient Monuments Society. New Series, Vol. II, 1955.

Tanner, Lawrence and Wright, William, 'Recent Investigations Regarding the Fate of the Princes in the Tower', *Archaeologia* 84 (1935), 1-25.

Thomas, Keith. *Religion and the Decline of Magic.* New York: Charles Scribner's Sons, 1971.

Thomson, J.A.F. 'Bishop Lionel Woodville and Richard III', *BIHR* 59 (1986), 130-5.

Twigg, John. *A History of Queens' College, Cambridge 1448–1986.* Bury St Edmunds: Boydell, 1987.

Vaughan, Richard. *Charles the Bold: the Last Valois Duke of Burgundy.* New York:

Barnes and Noble, 1974

—*Philip the Good: The Apogee of Burgundy*. New York: Barnes and Noble, 1970.

—*Valois Burgundy*. London: Penguin Books, 1975.

Visser-Fuchs, Livia, 'English Events in Caspar Weinreich's Danzig Chronicle, 1461–1495', *The Ricardian* 7 (1986), 310-20.

Waldron, W.J. *The Greys of Groby*. Leicester: Wilford, 1919.

Warnicke, Retha M. *The Rise and Fall of Anne Boleyn: Family politics at the court of Henry VIII*. Cambridge: Cambridge University Press, 1989.

Warner, George F. and Gilson, Julius P. *Catalogue of Western Manuscripts in the Old Royal and King's Collections. Vol. I*. London: British Museum, 1921.

Weightman, Christine. *Margaret of York, Duchess of Burgundy, 1446–1503*. New York: St Martin's Press, 1989.

Weir, Alison. *The Princes in the Tower*. New York: Ballantine, 1992. .

—*The Wars of the Roses*. New York: Ballantine, 1995.

—*Britain's Royal Families: The Complete Genealogy*. London: Pimlico, 2002.

Westlake, Herbert Francis. *Westminster Abbey the Church, Convent, Cathedral and College of St Peter, Westminster*. London: Philip Allan and Company, 1923.

Wheeler, Jeff. *The Westminster Contradiction: Sanctuary Privileges during the Ricardian Usurpation*. Thesis, San José State University. August 1997.

Wickham, Glynne. *Early English Stages, 1300–1660*. London: Routledge and Kegan Paul, 1959.

Williamson, David. *Kings and Queens of Britain*. Great Britain: Webb and Bower, 1991.

Wolffe, B.P. 'The Management of English Royal Estates Under the Yorkist Kings', *English Historical Review*, 71 (1956), 1-27.

Woolgar. C.M. *The Great Household in Late Medieval England*. New Haven: Yale University Press, 1999.

—*Household Accounts in Medieval England*. Oxford: Oxford University Press, 1992.

Wright, Thomas (ed.). *Political Poems and Song relating to English History, composed during the Period from the Accession of Edward III to that of Richard III. Vol. II*. London: Longman, Green, Longman, and Roberts, 1861.

List of Illustrations

Maps

Index

TEMPUS – REVEALING HISTORY

Quacks Fakers and Charlatans in Medicine
ROY PORTER

'A delightful book' *The Daily Telegraph*
'Hugely entertaining' *BBC History Magazine*

£12.99   0 7524 2590 0

The Tudors
RICHARD REX

'Up-to-date, readable and reliable. The best introduction to England's most important dynasty' *David Starkey*
'Vivid, entertaining... quite simply the best short introduction' *Eamon Duffy*
'Told with enviable narrative skill... a delight for any reader' *THES*

£9.99   0 7524 3333 4

The Kings & Queens of England
MARK ORMROD

'Of the numerous books on the kings and queens of England, this is the best'
Alison Weir

£9.99   0 7524 2598 6

The Covent Garden Ladies
Pimp General Jack & the Extraordinary Story of Harris's List
HALLIE RUBENHOLD

'Sex toys, porn... forget Ann Summers, Miss Love was at it 250 years ago' *The Times*
'Compelling' *The Independent on Sunday*
'Marvellous' *Leonie Frieda*
'Filthy' *The Guardian*

£9.99   0 7524 3739 9

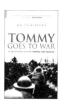

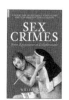

Okinawa 1945
GEORGE FEIFER

'A great book... Feifer's account of the three sides and their experiences far surpasses most books about war'
Stephen Ambrose

£17.99   0 7524 3324 5

Tommy Goes To War
MALCOLM BROWN

'A remarkably vivid and frank account of the British soldier in the trenches'
Max Arthur
'The fury, fear, mud, blood, boredom and bravery that made up life on the Western Front are vividly presented and illustrated'
The Sunday Telegraph

£12.99   0 7524 2980 4

Ace of Spies The True Story of Sidney Reilly
ANDREW COOK

'The most definitive biography of the spying ace yet written... both a compelling narrative and a myth-shattering *tour de force*'
Simon Sebag Montefiore
'The absolute last word on the subject' *Nigel West*
'Makes poor 007 look like a bit of a wuss'
The Mail on Sunday

£12.99   0 7524 2959 0

Sex Crimes
From Renaissance to Enlightenment
W.M. NAPHY

'Wonderfully scandalous'
Diarmaid MacCulloch

£10.99   0 7524 2977 9

If you are interested in purchasing other books published by Tempus, or in case you have difficulty finding any Tempus books in your local bookshop, you can also place orders directly through our website

www.tempus-publishing.com